Mark Alan Stewart
Frederick J. O'Toole

ARCO Teach Yourself the GMAT* CAT in 24 Hours

2000 Edition

Macmillan • USA

*GMAT is a registered trademark of the Graduate Management Admission Council, which does not endorse this book.

2000 Edition

Macmillan Reference USA
A Pearson Education Macmillan Company
1633 Broadway
New York, NY 10019-6785

Macmillan Publishing books may be purchased for business or sales promotional use. For information please write: Special Markets Department, Macmillan Publishing USA, 1633 Broadway, New York, NY 10019.

An ARCO book

International Standard Serial number information available upon request.

ISBN: 0-02-863335-0 (book only)
ISBN: 0-02-863461-6 (book with CD-ROM)

Manufactured in the United States of America

10–9–8–7–6–5–4–3–2–1

About This Book

Congratulations! You have in your hands the best fast-track GMAT self-study course available today! *ARCO Teach Yourself the GMAT CAT in 24 Hours* gives you a structured, step-by-step tutorial program that can help you master all the basics—no matter how limited your study time. In just 24 hour-long lessons, it cuts straight to the essentials, covering all the key points and giving you the practice you need to make each minute count. Even if the test is just days away, this *ARCO Teach Yourself* course will help you learn everything it takes to get the high GMAT score you want.

In your very first hour-long lesson, you'll get an overview of everything that's on the test and how it's scored. Then you'll examine every test subject and question type, and in practically no time, you'll be sailing through confidence-building workshops, quizzes, and full-length sample exams, sharpening your skills and building your confidence so that when test day comes, you'll be ready!

Who Should Use This Book

ARCO Teach Yourself the GMAT CAT in 24 Hours is written for students who want to prepare for the GMAT the smartest way—but whose study time is limited. This book is for you if:

- You know that you'll get the most out of a structured, step-by-step tutorial program that takes the guesswork out of test prep
- You want to prepare on your own time, at your own pace—but you don't have time for a preparation program that takes weeks to complete
- You want a guide that covers all the key points—but doesn't waste time on topics you don't absolutely have to know for the test
- You want to avoid taking risks with this all-important test by relying on those "beat the system" guides that are long on promises—but short on substance

Overview

Contents

About the Authors

Mark Alan Stewart is an attorney (J.D., University of California at Los Angeles) and private test preparation consultant based in Southern California. He is one of today's leading authorities in the field of standardized exam preparation, bringing to this publication more than a decade of experience in coaching college students as they prepare for the GMAT. His other Macmillan (ARCO) publications for graduate-level admissions include:

GMAT CAT: Answers to the Real Essay Questions

30 Days to the GMAT CAT

Teach Yourself the GRE in 24 Hours

30 Days to the LSAT

Perfect Personal Statements—Law, Business, Medical, Graduate School

Words for Smart Test-Takers

Math for Smart Test-Takers

GRE-LSAT Logic Workbook

GRE-LSAT-GMAT-MCAT Reading Comprehension Workbook

Frederick J. O'Toole (Ph.D. Philosophy, University of California) is a Professor of Philosophy at California Polytechnic State University, San Luis Obispo. His areas of specialization include Critical Thinking, Symbolic Logic, and History and Philosophy of Science. He brings to this publication over two decades of experience teaching students critical thinking concepts and skills. His other Macmillan (ARCO) publications for graduate-level admissions include:

GMAT CAT: Answers to the Real Essay Questions

30 Days to the GMAT CAT

Teach Yourself the GRE in 24 Hours

30 Days to the LSAT

Authors' Acknowledgments

The authors wish to thank Linda Bernbach and Cindy Kitchel at ARCO for their assistance. Mark Stewart also wishes to thank Kirk Taylor, Eva Anda, Judy Flynn, and Patrick Cunningham for their contributions; and Annette, Cinder, and Little Boo for their moral support. Fred O'Toole would like to thank his beautiful ladies, Joyce Connelly and Oona O'Toole, for their patience and support. Thanks also to Pearl, Tina, and Boo Bear.

Credits

"The Artful Encounter," by Richard Wendorf, *Humanities*, July/August 1993, pp. 9–12. Published by The National Endowment for the Humanities.

"Large Format Expands *Little Buddha*," by Bob Fisher, *American Cinematographer*, Vol. 75, No. 5 (May 1994), p. 41. Reprinted by permission of *American Cinematographer.*

"The American Renaissance," by James S. Turner, *Humanities*, March/April 1992. Published by The National Endowment for the Humanities.

"Images of Dorothea Lange," by Therese Thau Heyman, *Humanities,* Vol. 14, No. 5 (September/October 1993), pp. 6, 8–10. Published by The National Endowment for the Humanities.

"The Great War and the Shaping of the Twentieth Century," Blaine Baggett, Jay M. Winter, and Joseph Angier, *Humanities*, November/December 1996. Published by The National Endowment for the Humanities.

"Confronting Science: The Dilemma of Genetic Testing," *Humanities*, March/April 1997. Published by The National Endowment for the Humanities.

"Economic Analysis of Research Spillovers: Implications for the Advanced Technology Program," by Adam B. Jaffe, Brandeis University and the National Bureau of Economic Research. Prepared for the Advanced Technology Program, December 1996.

"Affirmative Action," ACLU Briefing Paper, American Civil Liberties Union, Copyright 1998. Reprinted by permission of the American Civil Liberties Union.

"Free Radical Activity: A Matter of Living or Dying Young," Bill Misner, Ph.D., Copyright 1998, The Internet Medical Journal. Adaption used with permission.

"The Rallying Cry," Eric Foner, *Humanities*, March/April 1998. Published by The National Endowment for the Humanities.

Introduction

Welcome to *ARCO Teach Yourself the GMAT CAT in 24 Hours*. By working your way through these pages, you'll get a fast-paced cram course on all the key points you need to know to raise your GMAT score. In just 24 one-hour lessons, you'll review all of the topics and concepts that are tested on the GMAT, and you will learn powerful strategies for answering every question type.

How to Use This Book

This book has been designed as a 24-hour teach-yourself training course complete with examples, workshops, quizzes, and full-length sample test sections. It is expected that you can complete each lesson in about an hour. However, you should work at your own rate. If you think you can complete more than one lesson in an hour, go for it! Also, if you think that you should spend more than one hour on a certain topic, spend as much time as you need.

How This Book Is Organized

Part I, "Start with the Basics," gives you a quick overview of important facts you need to know about the GMAT. You'll learn how to register for the test, how the test is structured, how it's scored—and some general test-taking tips that will help you score higher on test day.

Part II, "Learn to Answer GMAT Quantitative Questions," starts in Hours 2 and 3 with an overview of the math areas covered on the GMAT CAT and an in-depth look at each quantitative question type. Then, in Hours 4–9 you'll teach yourself the arithmetic, algebra and geometry concepts you'll need to score high on the GMAT. At the end of each hour, you'll practice applying the concepts you learned by taking a GMAT-style quiz.

Part III, "Learn to Answer GMAT Verbal Questions," focuses on the concepts and strategies you'll need to know for the GMAT Verbal section. In Hours 10–12, you'll learn to recognize and fix the errors of grammar and expression that appear most often in GMAT Sentence Correction questions. In Hours 13–15, you'll concentrate on building essential Critical Reasoning skills; and in Hour 16, you'll zero in on the Reading Comprehension skills you'll need for GMAT success. Once again, you'll sharpen your skills with numerous quizzes.

Part IV, "Learn to Answer GMAT Analytical Writing Questions," provides everything you need to know about the two required GMAT essays. In just two hours, you'll learn valuable strategies for writing high scoring essays using the CAT word processor.

Part V, "Practice with Sample Exams," contains two full-length practice GMAT CATs that are as close as you can get to the real thing. Take them under timed conditions, and you'll experience just how it feels to take the actual exam. Once you've finished each one, check your answers against the Answer Key and read the explanation (see Appendix A) for each question you missed. Once you've finished, you will have completed this entire intensive, superconcentrated preparation program—and you'll be ready to get your best score on the real GMAT.

Special Features of This Book

This book contains the following special features to help highlight important concepts and information.

NOTE

A Note presents interesting pieces of information related to the surrounding discussion.

TIP

A Tip offers advice or teaches you an easier way to do something.

TIME SAVER

A Time Saver tells you about a faster way to answer a question or solve a problem.

CAUTION

A Caution advises you about potential problems and helps you steer clear of disaster.

ONLINE

An Online tells you where you can go online to find more information on a particular test subject or additonal test questions for practice.

ACTION PLAN

The Action Plan icon identifies the steps to follow in answering each type of test question.

Part I

Start with the Basics

Hour 1

Get to Know the GMAT

To start your preparation for the GMAT, you'll spend this first hour familiarizing yourself with the format of the test and with the computerized testing environment. You'll also learn some basic test-taking strategies that you can use for all sections of the GMAT. Here are your goals for this hour:

- Become familiar with the format of the GMAT
- Learn how the GMAT is scored and evaluated, and learn how your scores are reported to the business schools
- Familiarize yourself with the computerized aspects of the test
- Learn general strategies for performing your best on the exam

Five Acronyms You Should Know for this Hour

GMAT (*Graduate Management Admission Test*): The standardized test that provides graduate business schools (as well as vocational counselors and prospective applicants) with predictors of academic performance in MBA programs. Approximately 850 graduate business schools worldwide *require* GMAT scores for admission. Another 450 graduate business schools use—but don't require—GMAT scores to assess applicants' qualifications.

GMAC (*Graduate Management Admission Council*): The organization that develops guidelines, policies, and procedures for the graduate business school admission process and provides information about the admission process to the schools and to prospective applicants. The GMAC consists of representatives from more than 100 graduate business schools.

ETS (*Educational Testing Service*): This organization develops and administers the GMAT in consultation with the GMAC. ETS also conducts ongoing research projects aimed at improving the test.

CAT (*Computer-Adaptive Test*): Except for some locations outside of North America, the GMAT is offered only by computer now. CAT refers to the computerized version of the GMAT.

AWA (*Analytical Writing Assessment*): This is the name that applies to both of the two essay sections of the GMAT.

The GMAT at a Glance

Section	*No. of Questions*	*Time Allowed*
Computer Tutorial	Not applicable	Not applicable
Analysis of an Issue	1 essay	30 minutes
Analysis of an Argument	1 essay	30 minutes
Break (optional)	Not applicable	5 minutes
Quantitative Section	37 (28 scored, 9 unscored)	75 minutes (2 minutes per question, on average)
• Problem Solving	23-24	
• Data Sufficiency	13-14	
Break (optional)	Not applicable	5 minutes
Verbal Section	41 (30 scored, 11 unscored)	75 minutes (1¾ minutes per question, on average)
• Critical Reasoning	14-15	
• Sentence Correction	14-15	
• Reading Comprehension	12-13 (four sets)	
(Total testing time, excluding breaks)		3½ hours

NOTE

Unscored questions are mixed in with scored questions, and you won't be able to distinguish them. So don't waste your time trying. The test-makers include unscored ("pretest") questions in order to assess their integrity, fairness, and difficulty. Some of these questions may show up on the GMAT in the future as scored questions.

Sequence of Exam Sections

The two AWA sections always appear first (in either order), *before* the Quantitative and Verbal sections.

The Quantitative and Verbal sections can appear in either order.

The Two 30-Minute AWA Sections

Each of the two Analytical Writing Assessment (AWA) sections involves a 30-minute writing task. You record your essay response using the word processor built into the GMAT CAT. Handwritten responses are not permitted.

ANALYSIS OF AN ISSUE: This section tests your ability to present a position on an issue effectively and persuasively. Your task is to compose an essay in which you respond to a brief (1–2 sentence) opinion about an issue. You should consider various perspectives, take a position on the issue and argue for that position. You will not be able to choose among topics.

NOTE

In the Analysis-of-an-Issue section, there is no "correct" answer. In other words, what's important is how effectively you present and support your position, not what your position is.

ANALYSIS OF AN ARGUMENT: This section is designed to test your critical reasoning and analytic (as well as writing) skills. Your task is to compose an essay in which you critique the stated argument and indicate how it could be improved, but not to present your own views on the argument's topic. You will not be able to choose among questions.

NOTE

To see some simulated AWA questions, take a peek at one of the Analytical Writing sample tests toward the back of this book (Hours 19 and 22). Also, ETS has published its official test bank of 230 AWA questions. See *Appendix C* in the back of this book for instructions about obtaining the test bank.

The 75-Minute Quantitative Section

The Quantitative section measures your basic mathematical skills, your understanding of basic math concepts, and your ability to reason quantitatively, solve quantitative problems, and interpret graphical data. The Quantitative section covers the following areas:

- Arithmetical operations
- Integers, factors, and multiples
- The number line and ordering
- Decimals, percentages, ratios, and proportion
- Exponents and square roots
- Statistics (mean, median, mode, range, probability, standard deviation)
- Operations with variables
- Algebraic equations and inequalities
- Geometry, including coordinate geometry

Algebraic concepts on the GMAT are those normally covered in a first-year high school algebra course. The GMAT does not cover more advanced areas such as trigonometry and calculus.

Each Quantitative question conforms to one of two formats:

- Problem Solving (23–24 multiple-choice questions)
- Data Sufficiency (13–14 multiple-choice questions)

PROBLEM SOLVING questions require you to solve a mathematical problem and then select the correct answer from among five answer choices.

DATA SUFFICIENCY problems each consist of a question followed by two statements—labeled (1) and (2). Your task is to analyze each of the two statements to determine whether it provides sufficient data to answer the question.

Any of the math areas listed above is fair game for either question format.

NOTE

> To see examples of each format, take a peek at one of the Quantitative sample tests toward the back of this book (Hours 20 and 23).

The 75-Minute Verbal Section

The Verbal section covers three different areas:

- Critical Reasoning (14–15 multiple-choice questions)
- Sentence Correction (14–15 multiple-choice questions)
- Reading Comprehension (12–13 multiple-choice questions, grouped in four sets)

CRITICAL REASONING questions measure your ability to understand, criticize, and draw reasonable conclusions from arguments. Each argument consists of a brief one-paragraph passage.

SENTENCE CORRECTION questions measure your command of the English language and of the conventions of Standard Written English. Areas tested include grammar, diction, usage, and effective expression (but not punctuation). In each question, part (or all) of a sentence is underlined. Your task is to determine which is correct— the original underlined part or one of four alternatives.

READING COMPREHENSION questions measure your ability to read carefully and accurately, to determine the relationships among the various parts of the passage, and to draw reasonable inferences from the material in the passage. You'll encounter four sets of three questions. All three questions in a set pertain to the same passage. The passages are drawn from for a variety of subjects, including the humanities, the social sciences, the physical sciences, ethics, philosophy, and law.

NOTE

To see examples of each question type, take a peek at one of the Verbal sample tests toward the back of this book (Hours 21 and 24).

The Two Optional 5-Minute Breaks

You can pause for a brief break (up to 5 minutes) immediately after the second AWA section as well as after the first of the two multiple-choice sections. The breaks are optional; if you wish, you can take shorter breaks or proceed immediately to the next section.

CAUTION

The CAT system's clock continues to run during these breaks. After 5 minutes, the next exam section starts—with or without you! Also, if you wait too long to begin answering questions once the next section has begun, the exam session automatically terminates and no responses or scores are tabulated or reported.

How the Computer-Adaptive GMAT Works

For each test-taker, the CAT system builds a customized test, by drawing on questions from a large pool. The AWA pool includes 115 Analysis-of-an-Issue questions, and 115 Analysis-of-an-Argument questions. The sizes of the Quantitative and Verbal pools are undisclosed.

During the two multiple-choice sections, the CAT continually tailors its difficulty level to your level of ability. The initial few questions are average in difficulty level. As you respond *correctly* to questions, the CAT steps you up to more difficult questions. Conversely, as you respond *incorrectly* to questions, the CAT steps you down to easier ones.

We've experimented during the CAT by intentionally responding incorrectly, as well as correctly, to consecutive questions. Here's what we've observed: Early in the exam section the CAT can shift from the easiest level to a very challenging level (or vice versa) in as few as 3 or 4 successive questions. But later in the section, when your ability level is well established, the difficulty level will not vary as widely.

What You Should Know About the CAT System

The CAT does not let you skip questions. Given the interactive design of the test, this makes sense. The computer-adaptive algorithm cannot determine the appropriate difficulty level for the next question without a response (correct or incorrect) to each question presented in sequence.

The CAT does not let you return to any question already presented (and answered). Why? The computer-adaptive algorithm that determines the difficulty of subsequent questions depends on the correctness of prior responses. For example, suppose that you answer question 5 incorrectly. The CAT responds by posing slightly easier questions. Were the CAT to let you return to question 5 and change your response to the correct one, the questions following question 5 would be easier than they should have been, given your amended response. In other words, the process by which the CAT builds your score would be undermined.

The CAT does not require you to finish each section. The CAT gives you the *opportunity* to respond to a total of 78 multiple-choice questions (37 Quantitative and 41 Verbal). But the CAT does *not* require you to finish either section. The CAT will calculate a score based on the questions you've answered.

The CAT requires you to do some work on every section. In order to generate a score report, the CAT requires a minimum number of responses during each multiple-choice section. (ETS has not disclosed this minimum number, but it's probably *very* low—perhaps just 1.) Also, during each AWA section you must record something on the editing screen—anything. Otherwise, the CAT will not permit you to continue the test.

Fast, accurate typists have a clear advantage in the AWA section—no doubt about it. But fast-fingered test-takers enjoy no advantage for the multiple-choice sections, because test-takers use only the mouse (not the keyboard) during these sections. And if you're unaccustomed to using a computer, you won't be disadvantaged as a result, because all computerized aspects of the GMAT you will learn and can easily master during the pre-test tutorial.

During each section, the CAT provides a 5-minute warning. When 5 minutes remain during each timed section, the on-screen clock (in the upper left corner of the screen) will blink silently several times to warn you. This 5-minute warning will be your only reminder.

NOTE

Beepers and alarms aren't allowed in the testing room, although silent timing devices are permitted.

The GMAT CAT Interface

The screen shot on page 10 shows the GMAT CAT interface (and a typical Reading Comprehension passage and question). Let's examine the features of the interface that are common to all exam sections.

The CAT Title Bar

A dark title bar will appear across the top of the computer screen at all times during all test sections. You can't hide this title bar, which displays three items:

left corner: time remaining for the current section (hours and minutes)

middle: the name of the test

right corner: the current question number and total number of questions in the current section

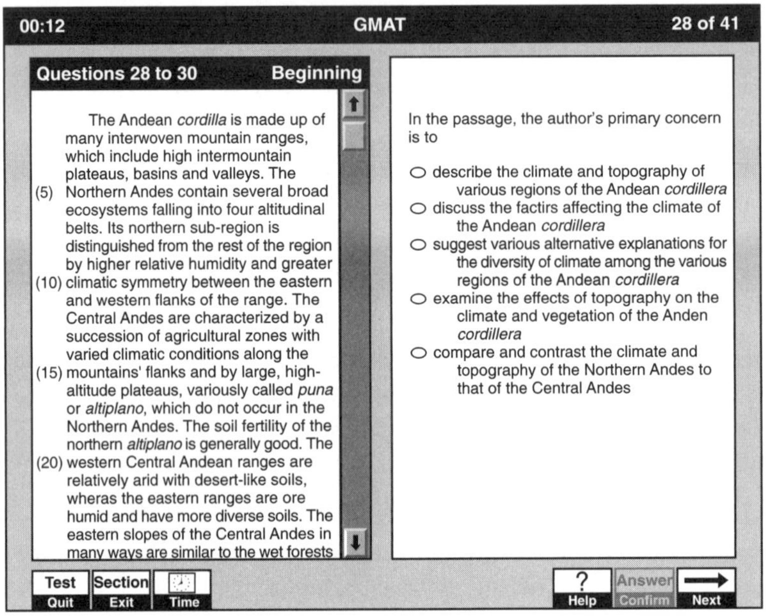

The CAT Toolbar

A series of six buttons appear in a "toolbar" across the bottom of the computer screen at all times (you cannot hide the toolbar) during all test sections.

QUIT TEST

Click on this button to stop the test and cancel your scores for the entire test. If you click here, a dialog box will appear on the screen, asking you to confirm this operation.

EXIT SECTION

Click on this button if you finish the section before the allotted time expires and wish to proceed immediately to the next section. A dialog box will appear on the screen, asking you to confirm this operation.

TIME

Click on this button to display the time remaining to the nearest *second*. By default, the time remaining is displayed (in the upper left corner) in hours and minutes, but not to the nearest second.

HELP

Click on this button to access the directions for the current question type, as well as the general test directions and the instructions for using the toolbar items.

NEXT and CONFIRM ANSWER

Click on the NEXT button when you're finished with the current question. When you do so, the current question will remain on the screen until you click on CONFIRM ANSWER. Until you confirm, you can change your answer as often as you wish. But once you confirm, the question disappears forever and the next one appears in its place.

NOTE

Whenever the NEXT button is enabled (appearing dark gray), the CONFIRM ANSWER button is disabled (appearing light gray), and vice versa.

CAUTION

Stay away from the QUIT TEST button, unless you're absolutely sure you wish your GMAT score for the day to "vaporize" and you're willing to throw away your exam registration fee. Also stay away from the EXIT SECTION button, unless you've already answered every question in the current section and don't feel you need a breather before starting the next one!

The Quantitative and Verbal Screens

To respond to multiple-choice questions, just click your mouse on one of the ovals next to the answer choices. You can't use the keyboard to select answers. When you point and click on an oval, it will turn black; if you then click on a different oval, that one will turn black instead.

NOTE

On the CAT, the answer choices are *not* lettered (you'll click on blank ovals). But on the paper-based GMAT, and in the sample questions throughout this book, the answer choices are lettered.

SPLIT SCREENS. For some multiple-choice questions, the screen splits either horizontally or vertically.

Reading Comprehension: The screen splits vertically. The left side displays the passage; the right side displays the question and answer choices.

Quantitative questions that include figures: The screen splits horizontally. The figure appears at the top; the question and answer choices appear at the bottom.

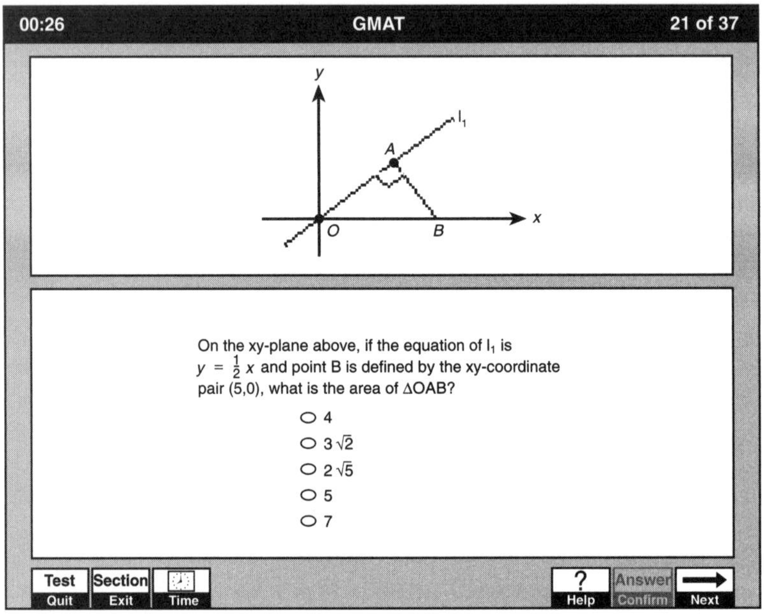

VERTICAL SCROLLING. For some multiple-choice questions, you'll have to scroll up and down (using the vertical scroll bar) to view all the material that pertains to the current question.

Reading Comprehension: Passages are too long for you to see on the screen in their entirety; you'll have to scroll.

Quantitative questions that include figures: Some figures—especially charts and graphs—won't fit on the screen in their entirety; you'll have to scroll.

CAUTION

In Quantitative questions that include charts or graphs, be sure to scroll up and down to view not only the entire chart or graph, but also the information above and below it. Important numbers or other information you should know can sometimes hide just below the horizontal split!

The AWA Screen

As illustrated in the screen on the next page, the AWA topic and question appear at the top of your screen. As you key in your essay response it will appear on screen below the topic and question. (The screen in the figure includes the first few lines of a response.) Notice that you

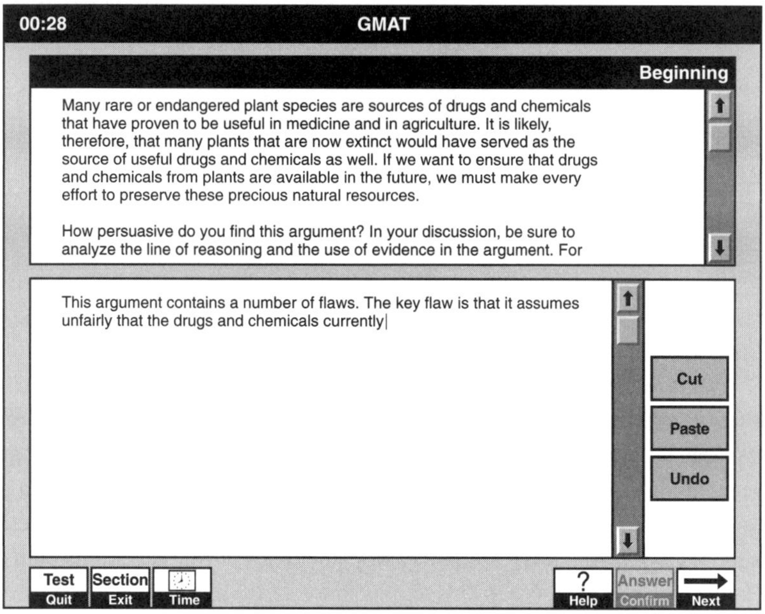

have to scroll down to read the entire topic and question. You compose your essays using the CAT word processor. You'll look closely at its features and limitations during Hour 18.

DO's and DON'Ts During the Exam

Do	**Don't**

DON'T resort to random guesses. Instead, always try to eliminate at least one answer choice before you confirm your response.

DO find your optimal pace and stay on it.

DON'T be a perfectionist.

DO maintain an active mind set.

DO use your pencil and scratch paper.

DO move the keyboard away to the side for the multiple choice sections.

Do **Don't**

DON'T waste time reading directions while the clock is running; make sure you already know them inside and out.

DO step through the computer tutorial as quickly as possible.

DO take advantage of the two 5-minute breaks, but don't exceed the time limit.

DO read each question in its entirety, and read every answer choice.

DO take your time with the first few Quantitative and Verbal questions.

DON'T resort to random guesses. Instead, always try to eliminate at least one answer choice before you confirm your response. If you must guess, always try to eliminate obvious wrong-answer choices first, then go with your hunch. Eliminating even one choice improves your odds. If you're out of time on a section, there's no advantage to guessing randomly on the remaining questions. Why? You might luck out and guess correctly. But incorrect responses move you down the ladder of difficulty to easier questions, and correct responses to easier questions aren't worth as much as correct response to more difficult ones. So on balance, there's no net advantage or disadvantage to guessing randomly.

DO find your optimal pace and stay on it. Time is definitely a factor on every section of the GMAT. On the multiple-choice sections, expect to work at a quicker pace than is comfortable for you. Similarly, the 30-minute time limit for each AWA response requires a lively writing pace, allowing little time for editing, revising, and fine-tuning.

During the multiple-choice sections, check your pace after every 10 questions or so (three times during a section), and adjust it accordingly so that you have time to at least consider every question in the section. During the AWA sections, be sure to leave yourself enough time to cover all your main points and to wrap up your essay with a brief concuding paragraph.

TIP

The best way to avoid the time squeeze is to practice under timed conditions, so that you get a sense for your optimal pace.

DON'T be a perfectionist. You might find yourself reluctant to leave a question until you're sure your answer is correct. The design of the CAT contributes to this mind set, because your reward for correct responses to difficult questions is greater than your reward for easier questions. But a stubborn attitude will only defeat you, because it reduces the number of questions that you attempt, which in turn can lower your score. As you take the quizzes and sample tests in this book, get comfortable with a quick pace by adhering strictly to the time limits imposed. Set aside your perfectionist tendencies, and remember: You can miss quite a few questions and still score high. Develop a sense of your optimal pace—one that results in the greatest number of correct responses.

DO maintain an active mind set. During the GMAT it's remarkably easy to fall into a passive mode—one in which you let your eyes simply pass over the words while you hope that the correct response jumps out at you as you scan the answer choices. Fight this tendency by interacting with the test as you read it. Keep in mind that each question on the GMAT is designed to measure a specific ability or skill. So try to adopt an active, investigative approach to each question, in which you ask yourself:

- What skill is the question measuring?
- What is the most direct thought process for determining the correct response?
- How might a careless test-taker be tripped up on this type of question?

NOTE

Answering these three questions is in large part what the rest of this book is all about.

DO use your pencil and scratch paper (both are provided). Doing so helps keep you in an active mode. Making brief notes or drawing diagrams and flow charts will help keep your thought process clear and straight.

DO move the keyboard away to the side for the multiple-choice sections. You won't use the keyboard at all for these sections. So put your scratch paper right in front of you, and get the keyboard out of the way.

DON'T waste time reading directions while the clock is running; make sure you already know them inside and out. At the start of each new section, as well as just before each particular type of question (e.g., Data Sufficiency or Reading Comprehension) appears for the first time, the CAT will display the directions for that section or question type. The clock will be running! So dismiss the direction as quickly as you can by clicking on the DISMISS DIRECTIONS button—without taking any time to read them. (This advice presupposes that you already know the directions—which of course you will.)

DO step through the computer tutorial as quickly as possible. Although the tutorial is not timed, the longer you spend on it, the more fatigued you'll be for the actual exam. The tutorial isn't worth more attention or eye strain than absolutely necessary. So get past it as quickly as possible.

DO take advantage of the two 5-minute breaks, but don't exceed the time limit. Remember: The GMAT CAT clock is always running, even during the two scheduled 5-minute breaks. By all means, take advantage of these breaks to leave the room, perhaps grab a quick snack from your locker, and do some stretching or relaxing. But don't get too relaxed! Five minutes goes by very quickly, and the test will begin after that time has elapsed—with or without you!

DO read each question in its entirety, and read every answer choice. You'll discover during the hours ahead that the test-makers love to bait you with tempting wrong answer choices. This applies to every type of multiple-choice question on the exam. So unless you're quickly running out of time, never hasten to select and confirm an answer until you've read all the choices! This blunder is one of the leading causes of incorrect responses on the GMAT.

DO take your time with the first few Quantitative and Verbal questions. The CAT uses your responses to the first few questions to move you either up or down the ladder of difficulty. Of course, you want to move up the ladder, not down, because your reward is greater for correct responses to tougher questions. So take great care with the initial questions—perhaps moving at a somewhat slower pace initially. Otherwise, you'll have to answer several questions just to reverse the trend by proving to the CAT that you're smarter than it thinks you are.

The CAT Test-Taking Experience

When you take a test as important as the GMAT, it's a good idea to minimize test anxiety by knowing exactly what to expect on exam day. So lets walk through the pre-test and post-test procedures for the CAT. You'll also learn about the CAT testing environment.

When You Arrive at the Test Center

Here's what you can expect when you arrive at the test center:

- The supervisor will show you a roster, which includes the names of test-takers scheduled for that day, and will ask you to initial the roster next to your name, and indicate on the roster your arrival time.
- The supervisor will ask you to read a two-page list of testing procedures and rules. (We'll cover all these rules in the pages immediately ahead.)
- The supervisor will give you a "Nondisclosure Statement." You're to read the printed statement, then *write* the statement (in the space provided on the form) and sign it. In the statement, you agree to the testing policies and rules, and you agree not to repro-

duce or disclose any of the actual test questions. The supervisor will not permit you to enter the exam room until you've written and signed the statement.

- You'll probably have to sit in a waiting room for a while—until the supervisor calls your name. A 5–10 minute wait beyond your scheduled testing time is not uncommon. (Taking the GMAT CAT is a lot like going to the dentist—in several respects!)
- The supervisor will check your photo identification. (You won't be permitted to take the test unless you have one acceptable form of photo identification with you.)
- The test center will provide a secure locker (free of charge) for stowing your personal belongings during the test.
- To help ensure that nobody else takes any part of the exam in your place, the supervisor will take a photograph of you.
- The supervisor might give you some rudimentary tips about managing your time during the exam. Just ignore the supervisor's tips, because they might not be good advice for you!
- Before you enter the testing room, you must remove everything from your pockets—except your photo I.D and locker key.
- The supervisor will provide you with exactly six pieces of scratch paper (stapled together), along with two pencils. These are the only items you'll have in hand as you enter the testing room.

Testing Procedures and Rules

- If you want to exit the testing room for any reason, you must raise your hand and wait for the supervisor to come in and escort you from the room. (You won't be able to pause the testing clock for any reason.)
- No guests are allowed in the waiting room during your test.
- No food or drink is allowed in the testing room.
- No hats are allowed.
- You must sign out whenever you exit the testing room.
- You must sign in whenever you re-enter the testing room (the supervisor will ask to see your photo I.D. each time).
- If you need more scratch paper during the exam, just raise your hand and ask for it. The supervisor will happily replace your six-piece bundle with a new batch.
- The supervisor will replace your tired pencils with fresh, sharp ones upon your request anytime during the exam (just raise your hand).

What You Should Know About the CAT Testing Environment

- Individual testing stations are like library carrels; they're separated by half-walls.
- The height of you chair's seat will be adjustable, and the chair will swivel. Chairs at most testing centers have arms.
- Computer monitors are of the 14-inch variety. You can adjust contrast. If you notice any flickering, ask the supervisor to move you to another station. (You won't be able to tell if you monitor has color capability, because the GMAT is strictly a black-and-white affair.)

NOTE

> You can't change the size of the font on the screen, unless you specifically request before the exam begins that a special ZOOMTEXT function be made available to you.

- If your mouse has two buttons, you can use either button to click your way through the exam (both buttons serve the same function). Don't expect that nifty wheel between buttons for easy scrolling, because you're not going to get it. For all you gamers and laptop users, trackballs are available, but only if you request one before you begin the test.
- Testing rooms are not soundproof. During your test, expect to hear talking and other noise from outside the room.
- Expect the supervisor to escort other test-takers in and out of the room during your test—and to converse with them while doing so. This can be distracting!
- If the testing room is busy, expect to hear lots of mouse-clicking during your test. Because the room is otherwise fairly quiet, the incessant mouse-clicking can become annoying!
- Earplugs are available upon request.
- Expect anything in terms of room temperature, so dress in layers.
- You'll be under continual audio and video surveillance. To guard against cheating, and to record any irregularities or problems in the testing room as they occur, the room is continually audio-taped and videotaped. (Look for the cameras or two-way mirrors, then smile and wave!)

Before You Begin the Test—The Computer Tutorial

Okay, the supervisor has just escorted you into the inner sanctum and to your station, and has wished you luck. (My supervisor also encouraged me to "have fun!") Before you begin the test, the CAT System will lead you through a tutorial which includes five sections (each section steps you through a series of "screens"):

1. How to use the mouse (6 screens)
2. How to select and change an answer (6 screens)
3. How to scroll the screen display up and down (6 screens)
4. How to use the toolbars (21 screens); here you'll learn how to
    - Quit the test
    - Exit the current section
    - Access the directions
    - Confirm your response and move to the next question
5. How to use the AWA word processor features (14 screens)

NOTE

> If you want to see what some of the tutorial screens look like, ETS provides a variety of samples in its official GMAT *Bulletin*.

Here's what you need to know about the CAT tutorial:

- You won't be able to skip any section or any screen during the tutorial.
- As you progress, the system requires that you demonstrate competency in using the mouse, selecting and confirming answer choices, and accessing the directions. So you can't begin taking the actual test unless you've shown that you know how to use the system. (Don't worry: no test-taker has ever flunked the CAT system competency test.)

- At the end of each tutorial section (series of screens), you can repeat that section, at your option. But once you leave a section you can't return to it.

CAUTION

Don't choose to repeat any tutorial section. Why not? If you do, you'll be forced to step through the entire sequence of screens in that section again (an aggravating time-waster, especially for the 21-screen section!)

- You won't see any *true* GMAT-style questions during the tutorial. Instead, again and again you'll encounter the same insipid sample question: "What is the capital of the United States of America?" Oddly, this sample question includes only four answer choices (a bit misleading, since every multiple choice question on the actual GMAT includes five choices).
- The AWA section of the tutorial allows you to practice using the word processor.
- If you carefully read all the information presented to you, expect to spend about 20 minutes on the tutorial.

TIME SAVER

On test day, you'll already know how the CAT system works. So step through the tutorial as quickly as you can, reading as little as possible. You can easily dispense with the tutorial in 5–10 minutes this way. Remember: The less time you spend with the tutorial, the less fatigued you'll be during the exam itself.

Post-Test CAT Procedures

Okay, it's been about 4 hours since you first entered the testing center, and you've just completed the second of two multiple-choice GMAT sections. You may think you've finished the CAT, but the CAT has not quite finished with you yet! There are yet more hoops to jump through before you're done.

1. **Respond to a brief questionnaire.** The CAT will impose on you a brief questionnaire (a series of screens) about your test-taking experience (believe it or not, these questions are multiple-choice, just like the exam itself). The questionnaire will ask you, for example:

    - whether your supervisor was knowledgeable and helpful
    - whether the testing environment was comfortable

- how long you waited after you arrived at the testing site to begin the test
- whether you were distracted by noise during your exam

2. **Cancel your test, at your option.** The most important question you'll answer while seated at your testing station is this next one. The CAT will ask you to choose whether to:

    - cancel your scores (no scores are recorded; partial cancellation is not provided for) *or*
    - see your scores immediately

    Once you elect to see your scores, you can no longer cancel them—ever! So you should take a few minutes to think it over. The CAT gives you 5 minutes to choose. If you haven't decided within 5 minutes, the CAT will automatically show you your scores (and you forfeit your option to cancel).

NOTE

> If you click on the CANCEL SCORES button, the CAT will then give you yet another 5 minutes to think over your decision. So you really have 10 minutes altogether to make up you mind.

3. **View and record your scores.** If you elect to see your scores, you should write them down on your scratch paper. When you leave the testing room, the supervisor will allow you to transcribe them onto another sheet of paper (one that you can take home with you), so that you don't have to memorize them.
4. **Direct your scores to the schools of your choice.** Once you've elected to see your scores, the CAT will ask you to select the schools you wish to receive your score report (the CAT provides a complete list of schools).

TIP

> You can select as many as five schools at this time—without incurring an additional fee. This is your last chance for a freebie, so you should take full advantage of it. So compile your list of schools—before exam day.

Before You Leave the Testing Center

Upon your exiting the testing room for the final time:

- The supervisor will collect your pencils and scratch paper, and will count the number of sheets of paper to make sure you aren't trying to sneak out with any. (Then, if you're lucky you'll be allowed to watch while the supervisor ceremoniously rips up your scratch paper and drops it in the trash basket!)
- The supervisor will remind you to collect your belongings from your locker (if you used one), and turn in your locker key.
- The supervisor will provide you with an ETS pamphlet that explains how to interpret your test scores (you can take this home with you).
- The supervisor will provide you with a postcard-sized invitation to"blow the whistle" on anybody you suspect of cheating on the exam (the invitation ends with the assurance: "Confidentiality guaranteed").

Scoring, Evaluation, and Reporting

Within one week after the test, your two AWA essays will be read and graded, and your scores for all sections will be sent to the schools to which you have directed your score reports. In the pages ahead, we'll explain how all of this works.

Your Four GMAT Scores

You'll receive four scores for the GMAT:

1. A scaled *Quantitative* score, on a 0–60 scale
2. A scaled *Verbal* score, on a 0–60 scale
3. A *total* score, on a 200–800 scale, based on both your Quantitative and Verbal scores
4. An *AWA* score, on a 0–6 scale, which averages (to the nearest one-half point) the ratings of your responses to the two AWA topics

How the Quantitative and Verbal Sections Are Scored

Because of the interactive nature of the CAT, the scoring system for the Quantitative and Verbal sections is a bit tricky. Your score for each of these two sections is based on two factors:

- how many questions you answer correctly
- the difficulty level of the questions you've answered

So even if you don't answer all 37 Quantitative (or 41 Verbal) questions, you can still achieve a high score for the section if a high percentage of your responses are correct. (Remember: As you respond correctly to questions, subsequent questions become more difficult).

NOTE

The CAT system's algorithms for moving you from one level of difficulty to another and for calculating your scores are well-guarded ETS secrets. But knowing exactly how the system works wouldn't affect your exam preparation or test-taking strategy, anyway.

How Your Two AWA Essays Are Scored

Two readers will read and score your Analysis-of-an-Issue essay, and two *other* readers will read and score your Analysis-of-an-Argument essay. Each reader evaluates your writing independently of the other readers, and no reader is informed of the others' scores. Each reader will employ a "holistic" grading method in which he or she will assign a single score from 0 to 6 (0, 1, 2, 3, 4, 5 or 6) based on the overall quality of your writing.

NOTE

During Hour 17, you'll learn more about the AWA scoring criteria.

Your final AWA score is the average of the four readers' grades (in half-point intervals). Average scores falling midway between half-point intervals are rounded *up*.

NOTE

According to ETS, all GMAT essay readers are college or university faculty members, drawn from various academic areas, including management education. But our inside sources tell us that some graders are unemployed Ph.D.'s or Ph.D. candidates.

Interpreting Your GMAT Scores

For each of your four GMAT scores, you'll receive a percentile rank (0–99%). A percentile rank of 60%, for example, indicates that you scored higher than 60% of all other test-takers (and lower than 40% of all other test-takers). Percentile ranks reflect your performance relative to the entire GMAT test-taking population during the most recent three-year period.

NOTE

For a sample score-conversion table, see Appendix B.

Reporting Scores to Test-Takers and to the Schools

Within two weeks after testing, ETS will mail to you an official score report for all four sections. At the same time, ETS will mail a score report to each school that you have designated to receive your score report. (You can send reports to as many as five schools without charge.)

At this time, score reports don't include the AWA essays themselves, although the GMAC is working on it. Eventually, the CAT system will provide for disclosure of each test-taker's complete exam (including the questions). But ETS and GMAC admit that implementation is years away.

NOTE

Absences from and cancellations of the GMAT also appear on your official report, but they will not adversely affect your chances of admission.

How the Schools Evaluate GMAT Scores

Each business school develops and implements its own policies for evaluating GMAT scores. Some schools place equal weight on GMAT scores and GPA, others weigh GMAT scores more heavily, whereas others weigh GPA more heavily. ETS reports your three most recent GMAT scores to each business school receiving your scores and transcripts. Most schools *average* reported scores; a minority of schools consider only your *highest* reported score. A few schools have adopted a *hybrid* approach by which they average reported scores unless there is a sufficiently large discrepancy between scores, in which case the school considers only your highest score.

Any business school will gladly tell you which method it uses among the three mentioned above. But don't expect any school to tell you exactly how much weight it places on each exam section or on different admission criteria (such as GMAT scores, GPA, work experience, and personal statements).

NOTE

To learn more about admission criteria, read our in-depth interviews with admission officials at several top-ranked B-schools in the following ARCO book: *Perfect Personal Statements—Law, Business, Medical, Graduate School.* For more information, point your Web browser to *www.west.net/~stewart/ps*

DO's and DON'Ts for GMAT Preparation

Do | **Don't**

DO take the GMAT early to allow yourself the option of retaking it (you can take the GMAT only once during each calendar month).

DON'T be too confident about your test-taking prowess; overconfidence is the leading cause of careless mistakes and therefore lower-than-optimal GMAT scores.

DON'T obsess about scores.

DON'T cram for the GMAT, but don't overprepare either.

DO be realistic in your expectations; given your own raw potential, there's only so much you can do to score your personal best.

DO practice taking GMAT essays using a word processor.

DO take at least one of the sample tests in this book as you would the real exam—with only a few short breaks between sections.

DO take the real GMAT once just for practice—as a dress rehearsal—if you have the time and can afford it.

Registering to Take the GMAT

For detailed information about GMAT registration procedures, consult the official GMAT website (*http://www.gmat.org*) or refer to the printed *GMAT Information Bulletin*, published annually by the GMAC. This free bulletin is available directly from ETS and GMAC as well as through career-planning offices at most four-year colleges and universities.

To obtain the *Bulletin* or other information about the GMAT, you can contact ETS by any of these methods:

Telephone:	1-609-771-7330 (general inquiries and publications) 1-800-462-8669 (CAT registration only)
E-mail:	gmat@ets.org
World Wide Web:	http://www.gmat.org http://www.ets.org (the ETS home page)
Mail:	GMAT Educational Testing Service P.O. Box 6103

TIP

> The GMAT Bulletin is published only once a year, so for the most up-to-date official information you should check the ETS Web site.

Part II

Learn to Answer GMAT Quantitative Questions

Hour

Hour 2

Teach Yourself Quantitative Skills I

This hour you'll take a close-up look at the Quantitative section, and you'll learn some basic strategies for handling questions in the Problem Solving format. Here are your goals for this hour:

- Familiarize yourself with the directions and ground rules for the Quantitative section
- Learn what areas of math are covered on the GMAT
- Learn what Problem Solving questions look like and how to answer them
- Learn some DO's and DON'Ts for handling Problem Solving questions
- Apply what you learn to some GMAT-style Quantitative questions

The Quantitative Section—at a Glance

TIME LIMIT:

75 minutes

NUMBER OF QUESTIONS:

- 37 total
- 28 questions are scored, 9 are unscored

AVERAGE TIME PER QUESTION: 2 minutes

BASIC FORMAT:

- All 37 questions are multiple-choice (you choose among five answer choices)
- About half the questions are word problems (in a "real world" setting)
- 23–24 questions are *Problem Solving* questions
- 13–14 are *Data Sufficiency* questions
- Data Sufficiency questions are interspersed with Problem Solving questions

GROUND RULES:

- Calculators are prohibited
- Scratch paper is allowed and provided

ABILITIES TESTED:

- proficiency in arithmetical operations
- proficiency at solving algebraic equations
- ability to convert verbal information to mathematical terms
- ability to visualize geometric shapes and numerical relationships
- ability to devise intuitive and unconventional solutions to conventional mathematical problems

AREAS COVERED: The following section shows a breakdown of the areas covered on the Quantitative section, along with their frequency of appearance:

Properties of Numbers and Arithmetical Operations (13–17 Questions)

- linear ordering (positive and negative numbers, absolute value)
- properties of integers (factors, multiples, prime numbers)
- arithmetical operations
- laws of arithmetic
- fractions, decimals and percentages
- ratio and proportion
- exponents (powers) and roots
- average (arithmetic mean), median, mode, range, standard deviation
- basic probability

Algebraic Equations and Inequalities (11–15 Questions)

- simplifying linear and quadratic algebraic expressions
- solving equations with one variable (unknown)
- solving equations with two variables (unknowns)
- solving factorable quadratic equations
- inequalities

Geometry, Including Coordinate Geometry (5–8 Questions)

- intersecting lines and angles
- perpendicular and parallel lines
- triangles
- quadrilaterals (4-sided polygons)
- circles
- rectangular solids (three-dimensional figures)
- cylinders
- pyramids
- coordinate geometry

Interpreting Statistical Charts, Graphs, and Tables (2–4 Questions)

- pie charts
- tables
- bar graphs
- line charts

AREAS NOT COVERED:

- complex calculations involving large and/or unwieldy numbers
- advanced algebra concepts
- formal geometry proofs
- trigonometry
- calculus

WHAT YOU CAN ASSUME: The following assumptions apply to all Quantitative questions:

- All numbers used are real numbers.
- All figures lie in a plane unless otherwise indicated.
- All lines shown as straight are straight. Lines that appear "jagged" can be assumed to be straight (lines can look somewhat jagged on the computer screen).

NOTE

Additional assumptions about figures (diagrams and graphics) are different for Problem Solving questions than for Data Sufficiency questions. (You'll look at these assumptions when you examine each of the two formats.)

TERMINOLOGY YOU SHOULD KNOW: Although the GMAT is not designed as a vocabulary test, you'll need to know certain basic math terms. Don't worry: The list of "Areas Covered" (above) includes most of the vocabulary you'll need to know, and we'll define all of these and any other terms you should know during the hours ahead.

The Problem Solving Format

Problem Solving questions require you to work to a solution (a numerical value or other expression), then find that solution among the five answer choices.

HOW MANY: 23–24 questions (out of 37 Quantitative questions altogether)

WHERE: Interspersed with Data Sufficiency questions

WHAT'S COVERED: Any of the Quantitative areas listed on pages 31 and 32 is fair game for a Problem Solving question.

DIRECTIONS: Whenever you encounter a Problem Solving question, you'll access the following directions by clicking on the HELP button:

Solve this problem and indicate the best of the answer choices given.

Numbers: All numbers used are real numbers.

Figures: A figure accompanying a problem solving question is intended to provide information useful in solving the problem. Figures are drawn as accurately as possible EXCEPT when it is stated in a specific problem that its figure is not drawn to scale. Straight lines may sometimes appear jagged. All figures lie on a plane unless otherwise indicated.

To review these directions for subsequent questions of this type, click on HELP.

What Problem Solving Questions Look Like

Let's look at two typical Problem Solving questions. Take a minute or two to attempt each one. We'll analyze them a few pages ahead. Question 1 is a word problem involving the concept of *percent decrease*. (Word problems account for about half of the Quantitative questions.) Question 2 involves the concept of *arithmetic mean* (simple average).

QUESTION 1. If Susan drinks 10% of the juice from a 16-ounce bottle immediately before lunch and 20% of the remaining amount with lunch, approximately how many ounces of juice are left to drink after lunch?

(A) 4.8

(B) 5.5

(C) 11.2

(D) 11.5

(E) 13.0

QUESTION 2. The average of six numbers is 19. When one of those numbers is taken away, the average of the remaining five numbers is 21. What number was taken away?

(A) 2

(B) 8

(C) 9

(D) 11

(E) 20

What You Should Know About the Problem Solving Format

Numerical answer choices are listed in order—from smallest in value to greatest in value. Notice in both sample questions that the numerical values in the answer choices got *larger* as you read down from (A) to (E). That's the way it is with every Problem Solving question whose answer choices are all numbers.

NOTE There is one exception to this pattern. If a question asks you which answer choice is greatest (or smallest) in value, the answer choices will not necessarily be listed in ascending order of value—for obvious reasons.

Expect word problems to account for about half of your Problem Solving questions. This will be true regardless of the overall difficulty level of your particular CAT, since word problems are not necessarily more difficult than other Problem Solving questions.

Some Problem Solving questions will include figures (geometry figures, graphs, and charts). Most of the 5–8 geometry questions will be accompanied by some type of figure.

Also, each Data Interpretation question will be accompanied by a chart or graph (expect to see 2-4 questions of this type).

Figures are drawn accurately unless the problem indicates otherwise. Accompanying figures are intended to provide information useful in solving the problems. They're intended to help you, not to mislead or trick you by their visual appearance. If a figure is not drawn to scale, you'll see this warning near the figure: "*Note:* Figure not drawn to scale."

CAUTION

It's a whole different ball game when you come to Data Sufficiency questions, in which you assume that figures are *not* necessarily drawn to scale. (You'll look at the Data Sufficiency format next hour.)

How to Approach a Problem Solving Question

Here's a 5-step approach that will help you to handle any Problem Solving question.

ACTION PLAN

1. **Size up the question.**
2. **Size up the answer choices.**
3. **Look for a shortcut to the answer.**
4. **Set up the problem and solve it.**
5. **Verify your response before moving on.**

Let's Apply the 5-Step Action Plan

It's time to go back to the two sample questions you looked at on page 34. Let's walk through them—one at a time—using the five-step approach you just learned.

QUESTION 1. If Susan drinks 10% of the juice from a 16-ounce bottle immediately before lunch and 20% of the remaining amount with lunch, approximately how many ounces of juice are left to drink after lunch?

(A) 4.8

(B) 5.5

(C) 11.2

(D) 11.5

(E) 13.0

ANALYSIS The correct answer is **(D)**. This is a relatively easy question. Approximately 80% of test-takers respond correctly to questions like this one. Here's how to solve the problem with the 5-step approach:

1. This problem involves the concept of *percent*—more specifically, *percentage decrease.* The question is asking you to perform two computations—in sequence. (The result of the first computation is used to perform the second one.) Percent questions tend to be relatively simple. All that is involved here is a two-step computation.

2. The five answer choices in this question provide two useful clues:

   - Notice that they range in value from 4.8 to 13.0. That's a wide spectrum, isn't it? But what general size should we be looking for in a correct answer to this question? Without crunching any numbers, it's clear that most of the juice will still remain in the bottle, even after lunch. So you're looking for a value much closer to 13 than to 4. Eliminate (A) and (B).
   - Notice that each answer choice is carried to exactly one decimal place, and that the question asks for an *approximate* value. These two features are clues that you can probably round off your calculations to the nearest "tenth" as you go.

3. You already eliminated (A) and (B) in step 1. But if you're on your toes, you can eliminate all but the correct answer without resort to precise calculations. Look at the question from a broader perspective. If you subtract 10% from a number, then 20% from the result, that adds up to *a bit less* than a 30% decrease from the original number. 30% of 16 ounces is 4.8 ounces. So the solution must be a number that is a bit larger than 11.2 (16 – 4.8). Answer choice (D), 11.5, is the only choice that fits the bill!

TIP

> The GMAT Problem Solving questions are designed to reward you for recognizing easier, more intuitive ways of narrowing down the choices to the correct answer. Don't skip over step 3. It's well worth your time to look for a more intuitive solution to any problem.

4. If your intuition fails you, go ahead and crunch the numbers. First, determine 10% of 16, then subtract that number from 16:

   $16 \times .1 = 1.6$
   $16 - 1.6 = 14.4$

Susan now has 14.4 ounces of juice. Now perform the second step. Determine 20% of 14.4, then subtract that number from 14.4:

$14.4 \times .2 = 2.88$
Round off 2.88 to the nearest tenth: 2.9
$14.4 - 2.9 = 11.5$

5. 11.5 is indeed among the answer choices. Before moving on, however, ask yourself whether your solution makes sense—in this case, whether the size of our number (11.5) "fits" what the question asks for. If you performed step 2, you should already realize that 11.5 is in the right ballpark. If you're confident that your calculations were careful and accurate, confirm your response and move on to the next question.

QUESTION 2. The average of six numbers is 19. When one of those numbers is taken away, the average of the remaining five numbers is 21. What number was taken away?

(A) 2
(B) 8
(C) 9
(D) 11
(E) 20

ANALYSIS The correct answer is **(C)**. This question is average in difficulty level. Approximately 60% of test-takers respond correctly to questions like this one. Here's how to solve the problem with the 5-step approach:

1. This problem involves the concept of *arithmetic mean* (simple average). To handle this question, you need to be familiar with the formula for calculating the average of a series of numbers. Notice that the question does not ask for the average, but rather for one of the numbers in the series. This curve-ball makes the question a bit tougher than most arithmetic mean problems.

2. Take a quick look at the answer choices for clues. Notice that the middle three are clustered closely together in value. Take a closer look at the two aberrations: (A) and (E). Choice (A) would be the correct answer to the question: "What is the difference between 19 and 21?" But this question is asking something entirely different, so you can probably rule out (A) as a "sucker bait" answer choice. (E) might also be a "sucker bait" choice, since 20 is simply 19 + 21 divided by 2. If this solution strikes you as too simple, you've got good instincts! The correct answer is probably either (B), (C), or (D). If you're pressed for time, guess one of these, and move on to the next question. Otherwise, go to step 3.

TIP

In complex questions, don't look for easy solutions. Problems involving algebraic formulas generally aren't solved simply by adding (or subtracting) a few numbers. Your instinct should tell you to reject easy answers to these kind of problems.

3. If you're on your "intuitive toes," you might recognize a shortcut to the answer here. You can solve this problem quickly by simply comparing the two *sums*. Before the sixth number is taken away, the sum of the numbers is 114 (6×19). After taking away the sixth number, the sum of the remaining numbers is 105 (5×21). The difference between the two sums is 9, which must be the value of the number taken away.

4. Lacking a burst of intuition (step 3), you can solve this problem in a conventional (and slower) manner. The formula for the arithmetic mean can be expressed this way:

$$AM = \frac{a + b + \ldots}{N}$$

In this formula, each term in the numerator is a different number in the series, and N is the number of terms altogether. In the question, we started with six terms, so let f equal the number that is taken away:

$$19 = \frac{a + b + c + d + e + f}{6}$$
$$114 = a + b + c + d + e + f$$
$$f = 114 - (a + b + c + d + e)$$

Here's the arithmetic mean formula for the remaining five numbers:

$$21 = \frac{a + b + c + d + e}{5}$$
$$105 = a + b + c + d + e$$

Substitute 105 for $(a + b + c + d + e)$ in the first equation:

$$f = 114 - 105$$
$$f = 9$$

5. If you have time, check to make sure you got the formula right and check your calculations. Also make sure you didn't inadvertently switch the numbers 19 and 21 in your equations. (It's remarkably easy to commit this careless error under time pressure!) If

you're satisfied that your analysis is accurate, confirm your answer and move on to the next question.

CAUTION

Take heed: On the GMAT, careless errors—such as switching two numbers in a problem—are far and away the leading cause of incorrect responses.

DO's and DON'Ts for Problem Solving

Here's a useful list of DO's and DON'Ts for Problem Solving questions. Some of these tips we've already touched on during our sample question walk-through. Others are mentioned here for the first time.

Do **Don't**

DO use your pencil and scratch paper.

DO look for simple solutions to simple problems, but complex solutions to complex problems.

DON'T split hairs with word problems; instead, accept the premise at face value.

DON'T rely on accompanying diagrams to solve the problem (except for data interpretation questions).

DON'T do more work than needed to get to the answer.

DO narrow down answer choices by sizing up the question.

DO check the answer choices for clues.

DO start with what you know, and ask yourself what else you know.

DO use trial-and-error if you're stuck (plug in numbers in place of variables).

DO answer the precise question being asked.

DON'T be fooled by "sucker bait" answer choices.

NOTE

You'll learn how to apply these DO's and DON'Ts in this hour's Workshop.

Workshop

For this hour's Workshop, we've hand-picked 10 Problem Solving questions which illustrate the DO's and DON'Ts you just learned. (The problems get tougher as you go along.) For each question, you'll see one or two hints to help you focus on those DO's and DON'Ts. Don't worry if you come across some mathematical concepts you don't understand. You'll learn them during the next several hours. Right now, focus on the *art* of the GMAT.

ONLINE

Additional Quantitative questions are available online at the authors' Web site: *http://www.west.net/~stewart/gmat*

Quiz

(Answers and explanations begin on page 43.)

DIRECTIONS: Attempt the following 10 questions. Try to limit your time to 15 minutes. Be sure to read the explanations that follow. They're just as important as the questions themselves, because they explain how the DO's and DON'Ts come into play.

1. Which of the following fractions is equal to $\frac{1}{4}\%$?

   (A) $\frac{1}{400}$

   (B) $\frac{1}{40}$

   (C) $\frac{1}{25}$

   (D) $\frac{4}{25}$

   (E) $\frac{1}{4}$

   (Hint: Look for simple solutions to simple problems.)

   (Hint: Look out for "sucker-bait" answer choices.)

2. Jill is now 20 years old and her brother Gary is now 14 years old. How many years ago was Jill three times as old as Gary was at that time?

   (A) 3
   (B) 8
   (C) 9
   (D) 11
   (E) 13

   (Hint: Use the trial-and-error method if you're stuck.)

   (Hint: Be sure to answer the precise question that's asked.)

3. Which of the following is nearest in value to $\sqrt{664} + \sqrt{414}$?

   (A) 16
   (B) 33
   (C) 46
   (D) 68
   (E) 126

   (Hint: Don't do more work than needed to get to the answer.)

   (Hint: Look out for "sucker-bait" answer choices.)

4. At ABC Corporation, five executives earn \$150,000 each per year, three executives earn \$170,000 each per year, and one executive earns \$180,000 per year. What is the average salary of these executives?

   (A) \$156,250
   (B) \$160,000
   (C) \$164,480
   (D) \$166,670
   (E) \$170,000

   (Hint: Complex questions call for complex solutions.)

   (Hint: Narrow down the answer choices by making a common-sense estimate.)

5. If $2x + 1$ is a multiple of 5, and if $2x + 1 < 100$, how many possible values for x are prime numbers?

   (A) 5
   (B) 6
   (C) 7
   (D) 8
   (E) 9

   (Hint: Don't do more work than needed to get to the answer.)

   (Hint: Use your pencil and scratch paper to plug in numbers.)

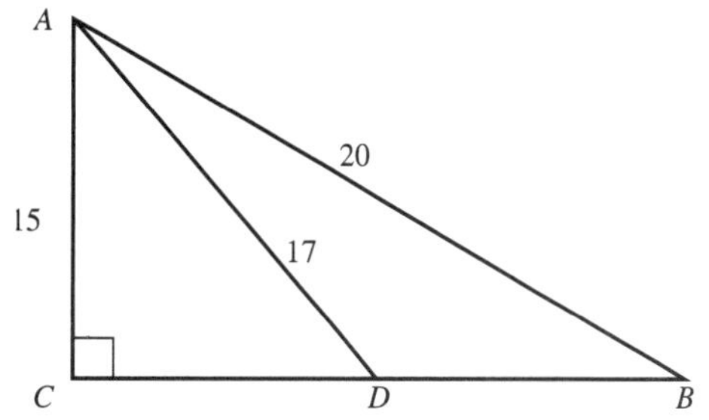

Note: Figure not drawn to scale.

6. In the figure above, what is the length of DB?

   (A) $5\sqrt{21} - 8$
   (B) 12
   (C) $8\sqrt{3}$
   (D) $5\sqrt{7} - 8$
   (E) $18 - 2\sqrt{6}$

   (Hint: Check the answer choices for clues.)

   (Hint: Don't rely on a figure's visual proportions to solve the problem.)

2

7. If a train travels $r + 2$ miles in h hours, which of the following represents the number of miles the train travels in one hour and 30 minutes?

(A) $\frac{3r + 6}{2h}$

(B) $\frac{3r}{h + 2}$

(C) $\frac{r + 2}{h + 3}$

(D) $\frac{r}{h + 6}$

(E) $\frac{3}{2}(r + 2)$

(Hint: Check the answer choices for clues.)

(Hint: Look out for "sucker bait" answer choices.)

8. A container holds 10 liters of a solution which is 20% acid. If 6 liters of pure acid are added to the container, what percent of the resulting mixture is acid?

(A) 10
(B) 20
(C) $33\frac{1}{3}$
(D) 40
(E) 50

(Hint: Estimate the size of the answer you're looking for in order to narrow down the answer choices and to check your work.)

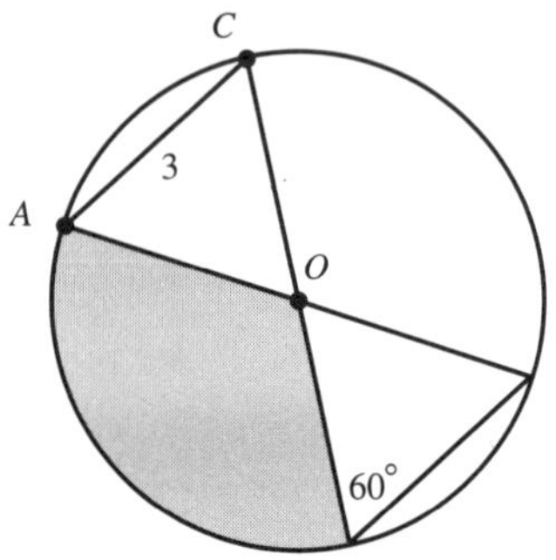

Note: Figure not drawn to scale.

9. If O is the center of the circle in the figure above,what is the area of the shaded region?

(A) $\frac{3}{2}\pi$
(B) 2π
(C) $\frac{5}{2}\pi$
(D) 3π
(E) $\frac{10}{3}\pi$

(Hint: In dealing with complex problems, start with what you know, and ask yourself what else you know.)

10. Two water hoses feed a 40-gallon tank. If one of the hoses dispenses water at the rate of 2 gallons per minute, and the other hose dispenses water at the rate of 5 gallons per minute, how many minutes does it take to fill the 40-gallon tank, if the tank is empty initially?

(A) $2\frac{5}{8}$
(B) $5\frac{5}{7}$
(C) 7
(D) 12
(E) 28

(Hint: Narrow down answer choices by sizing up the question.)

(Hint: Look out for "sucker-bait" answer choices.)

Answers and Explanations

1. **(A)** This is a relatively simple *percent-fraction conversion* problem (one of the topics for Hour 4). To solve the problem, divide the fraction by 100, dropping the percent sign:

   $$\frac{1}{4}\% = \frac{\frac{1}{4}}{100} = \left(\frac{1}{4}\right)\left(\frac{1}{100}\right) = \frac{1}{400}$$

   Remember: Don't assume a question is more complex than it appears to be. This sort of thinking can waste time and can lead you down the wrong path.

   Notice the "sucker bait" answer choices here. Here's the common mistake:

   $$\frac{1}{4} = 25\%$$

   So maybe the correct answer will include some form of the number 25.

   So the correct answer is probably either (C) or (D).

   Wrong!

2. **(D)** This problem involves setting up and solving a *linear equation*. (You'll learn all the skills you need to handle problems like this one during Hours 6 and 7). There are two ways to solve this problem: (1) the conventional way, and (2) by trial-and-error.

   The conventional way:

   Set up and solve an equation. Jill's age x years ago can be expressed as $20 - x$. At that time, Gary's age was $14 - x$. The following equation emerges:

   $$\begin{aligned} 20 - x &= 3(14 - x) \\ 20 - x &= 42 - 3x \\ 2x &= 22 \\ x &= 11 \end{aligned}$$

   Jill was three times as old as Gary 11 years ago. (Jill was 9 and Gary was 3.)

   By trial-and-error:

   Try each answer choice, one at a time. Start with (A):

   $$20 - 3 = 17$$
   $$14 - 3 = 11$$

   Is 17 three times greater than 11? No.

   Go on to answer choice (B).

   Eventually, you'll get to the correct answer (D):

   $$20 - 11 = 9$$
   $$14 - 11 = 3$$

Is 9 three times greater than 3? Yes!

Notice the "sucker bait" answer choice here. 11 years ago, Jill was 9 years old. A test-taker who forgets exactly what the question asks for might look for *Jill's age* among the answer choices and choose (C).

3. **(C)** This problem involves the *square root* concept (one of the topics for Hour 5). There's no need to calculate either root since the question asks for an approximation. 664 is slightly greater than 625, which is 25^2. 414 is slightly greater than 400, which is 20^2. Thus the sum of the terms is just over 45 (approximately 46).

   Notice the "sucker-bait" answer choice here. Here's the common mistake:

   $$664 + 414 = 1078$$
   $$\sqrt{1078} \approx 33$$

   The correct answer must be (B).

   Wrong!

4. **(B)** This question covers the concept of *weighted average* (one of the topics for Hour 7). The salaries range from \$150,000 to \$180,000. Since 5 of the 8 executives earn the lowest salary in the range, common sense should tell you that the average salary is *not* midway between these figures (the midway point is near \$166,000), but rather closer to \$150,000. The problem is too complex to solve by simply calculating a simple average of three numbers. So you can eliminate (D) and (E). Now here's how to solve the problem. Assign a "weight" to each of the three salary figures, then determine the weighted average of the nine salaries:

   $$5(150{,}000) = 750{,}000$$
   $$3(170{,}000) = 510{,}000$$
   $$1(180{,}000) = 180{,}000$$
   $$750{,}000 + 510{,}000 + 180{,}000 = 1{,}440{,}000$$
   $$1{,}440{,}000 \div 9 = 160{,}000$$

5. **(A)** This problem involves integers, factors, and prime numbers. (You'll explore these concepts during Hour 5.) Don't waste time trying to reason through this problem in a purely abstract manner. Instead, start plugging in numbers for x, and keep going until you see a pattern that allows you to get to the answer as quickly as possible. And use your pencil! Here's how to do it. A prime number is a positive integer that is not divisible by any integer other than itself and 1. The smallest prime number is 2. Since the question asks for prime numbers, x must be positive. To check for a pattern (read: shortcut), start scratching out some equations, working your way up from the lowest possible value for x:

   $$2(2) + 1 = 5$$
   $$2(4.5) + 1 = 10$$
   $$2(7) + 1 = 15$$
   $$2(9.5) + 1 = 20$$
   $$2(12) + 1 = 25$$

Notice that as the sum increases in multiples of 5, the value of x in *every other equation* is an integer that also increases in multiples of 5 and ends with either 2 or 7. This makes the rest of your job much easier. No integer ending in 2 (other the integer 2) is a prime number. So you know that, in addition to the integer 2, you need only consider values for x ending in 7 that are less than 49 (because $2x + 1 < 100$):

$\{2, 7, 17, 27, 37, 47\}$

Five of these integers—2, 7, 17, 37, and 47—are prime numbers.

6. **(D)** This problem involves the Pythagorean Theorem, which applies to all right triangles—triangles with one 90° angle. (You'll learn all about the Theorem during Hour 8.) Notice that all but one of the answer choices include a square root, and that three of them indicate a difference (one term is subtracted from another). These features provide a clue that you need to find the difference between two lengths ($CB - CD$), and that you'll probably use the Pythagorean Theorem to do it.

   To find DB, you subtract CD from CB. Thus, you need to find those two lengths first. ΔACD is a right triangle with sides 8, 15, and 17 (one of the Pythagorean triplets you'll learn about during Hour 8). Thus, $CD = 8$. CB is one of the legs of ΔABC. Determine CB by applying the Theorem:

$$
\begin{aligned}
15^2 + (CB)^2 &= 20^2 \\
225 + (CB)^2 &= 400 \\
(CB)^2 &= 175 \\
CB &= \sqrt{25 \cdot 7} = 5\sqrt{7}
\end{aligned}
$$

   Accordingly, $DB = 5\sqrt{7} - 8$

   If you had tried to answer the question *visually* by comparing the length of DB to the other lengths in the figure, then estimating the numerical values of the answer choices, you no doubt would have chosen the wrong answer. DB appears to be about 8 or 9 units in length, yet its actual length (based on the numbers provided) is just over 5!

7. **(A)** This is an algebraic word problem involving the concept of rate. (You'll explore more problems like this one during Hour 7). Notice that all of the answer choices contain fractions. This is a clue that you should try to create a fraction as you solve the problem. Here's how to do it. Given that the train travels $r + 2$ miles in h hours, you can express its rate in miles per hour as $\frac{r+2}{h}$. In $\frac{3}{2}$ hours, the train would travel $\frac{3}{2}$ this distance:

$$\frac{3}{2}\left(\frac{r+2}{h}\right) = \frac{3r+6}{2h}$$

   Look out for answer choice (E). It has all the elements of a correct answer, except that it omits h! Common sense should tell you that the correct answer must include both r and h.

8. **(E)** This is an algebraic word problem involving the concept of mixture. (You'll explore more problems like this one during Hour 7). Your common sense should tell you that when you add more acid to the solution, the percent of the solution that is acid will increase. So you're looking for an answer that's greater than 20—either (C), (D), or (E). If you need to guess at this point, your odds are 1 in 3. Here's how to solve the problem. The original amount of acid is (10)(20%) = 2 liters. After adding 6 liters of pure acid, the amount of acid increases to 8 liters, while the amount of total solution increases from 10 to 16 liters. The new solution is $\frac{8}{16}$ (or 50%) acid.

9. **(D)** To analyze this question, you need to understand equilateral triangles as well as how to compute the area of a circle. (You'll explore these two topics during Hours 8 and 9, respectively.) The starting point in analyzing this question is the 60° angle in the figure. Given this angle, all three interior angles of both triangles must measure 60°, and therefore all sides of both triangles are the same length: 3 (as provided in the figure). Notice that this length (3) is also the circle's radius (the distance from the circle's center to its circumference).

   Next, determine the area of the circle. The area of any circle is πr^2, where r is the circle's radius. Thus, the area of the circle in the figure is 9π.

   Finally, you need to determine what portion of the circle's area is shaded. The four angles formed at the circle's center (O) total 360°. We know that two of these angles account for 120 (or $\frac{1}{3}$) of those 360°. Your intuition should tell you that each of the two larger angles also account for 120° ($\frac{1}{3}$ of 360°), and accordingly that the shaded region accounts for $\frac{1}{3}$ the area of the circle, or 3π.

10. **(B)** In order to solve this problem, you need to know the algebraic formula for combining rates of work. (You'll learn algebraic formulas during Hour 7.) Letting A equal the aggregate (combined) time, you can express the portion of the job that each hose performs per minute as $\frac{A}{20}$ and $\frac{A}{8}$. The sum of the two portions is 1 (the entire job):

$$\frac{A}{20} + \frac{A}{8} = 1$$

$$\frac{2A + 5A}{40} = 1$$

$$\frac{7A}{40} = 1$$

$$7A = 40$$

$$A = \frac{40}{7}, \text{ or } 5\frac{5}{7}$$

   Looking for a shortcut or a quick way of checking your work? You can probably narrow down the answer choices by estimating the *size* of the number you're looking for. Use common sense. The *second* hose alone would obviously take 8 minutes to fill the tank (a 40 gallon tank is filled at the rate of 5 gallons per minute). The *first* hose speeds up the process, but just a little. So you're looking for an answer that's a bit less that 8. (B) and (C) are the only viable answer choices. The number 7—choice (C)— is simply the sum of the two rates. So (C) should strike you as far too easy a solution to this complex problem. That leaves (B), which happens to be the correct answer!

Notice the "sucker-bait" answer choices in this question. Here are two common mistakes:

The first hose alone can fill the tank in 20 minutes.

The second hose alone can fill the tank in 8 minutes.

Subtract: 20 – 8 = 12.

Thus the correct answer choice is (D).

Wrong!

The first hose alone can fill the tank in 20 minutes.

The second hose alone can fill the tank in 8 minutes.

Add: 20 + 8 = 28.

Thus the correct answer choice is (E).

Wrong!

Hour 3

Teach Yourself Quantitative Skills II

This hour you'll continue to take a close-up look at the Quantitative section. Specifically, you'll learn some basic strategies for handling the Data Sufficiency format and for tackling Data Interpretation (charts and graphs) questions. Here are your goals for this hour:

- Learn what Data Sufficiency questions look like and how to answer them
- Learn some DO's and DON'Ts for handling Data Sufficiency questions
- Learn what Data Interpretation questions look like and how to approach them
- Learn some DO's and DON'Ts for handling Data Interpretation questions
- Apply what you learn to some GMAT-style Quantitative questions

The Data Sufficiency Format

The other type of Quantitative question format is called *Data Sufficiency.* This format is unique to the GMAT; you won't find it on any other standardized test! Each Data Sufficiency question includes a question followed by two statements (labeled 1 and 2). Your job is to analyze each of the two statements to determine whether it provides sufficient data to answer the question.

HOW MANY:

13–14 questions (out of a total of 37 Quantitative questions)

WHERE:

Interspersed with Problem Solving questions

WHAT'S COVERED:

Data Sufficiency questions cover the same mix of arithmetic, algebra, and geometry as Problem Solving questions.

NOTE

Remember: The difficulty level of your GMAT CAT questions is determined by the accuracy of your responses to prior questions. So if you respond incorrectly to toughies, you'll see fewer of them later in your Quantitative section.

DIRECTIONS: Here are the directions for Data Sufficiency questions. (You access these directions when you click on the HELP button.) Notice that some of the directions are new. In other words, they don't apply to Problem Solving questions.

This data sufficiency problem consists of a question and two statements, labeled (1) and (2), in which certain data are given. You have to decide whether the data given in the statements are sufficient for answering the question. Using the data given in the statements plus your knowledge of mathematics and everyday facts (such as the number of days in July or the meaning of *counterclockwise*), you must indicate whether:

(A) statement (1) ALONE is sufficient, but statement 2 alone is not sufficient to answer the question asked;

(B) statement (2) ALONE is sufficient, but statement 1 alone is not sufficient to answer the question asked;

(C) BOTH statements (1) and (2) TOGETHER are sufficient to answer the question asked; but NEITHER statement ALONE is sufficient;

(D) EACH statement ALONE is sufficient to answer the question asked;

(E) statements (1) and (2) TOGETHER are NOT sufficient to answer the question asked, and additional data specific to the problem are needed.

Numbers: All numbers used are real numbers.

Figures: A figure accompanying a data sufficiency problem will conform to the information given in the question, but will not necessarily conform to the additional information in statements (1) and (2).

Lines shown as straight can be assumed to be straight and lines that appear jagged can also be assumed to be straight.

You may assume that positions of points, angles, regions, etc., exist in the order shown and that angle measures are greater than zero.

All figures lie in a plane unless otherwise indicated.

Note: In data sufficiency problems that ask you for the value of a quantity the data given in the statements are sufficient only when it is possible to determine exactly one numerical value for the quantity.

To review these directions for subsequent questions of this type, click on HELP.

What Data Sufficiency Questions Look Like

Let's take a look at three typical Data Sufficiency questions. At the risk of giving away the answers up front, the correct answer is different for each question. Take a minute or two to attempt each one. (We'll analyze all three questions a few pages ahead.)

NOTE

We've labeled the answer choices here (A) through (E). Remember, however, that on the actual GMAT CAT screen, you'll select your choice by clicking on one of five *blank ovals* (instead of *lettered* answer choices). But the answer choices themselves will always be exactly the same (and in the same order) as (A) through (E) here.

QUESTION 1. If ■ represents a digit in the 5-digit number 62,■79, what is the value of ■?

(1) 62,■79 is a multiple of 3.

(2) The sum of the digits of 62,■79 is divisible by 4.

(A) Statement 1 ALONE is sufficient, but statement 2 alone is NOT sufficient to answer the question asked.

(B) Statement 2 ALONE is sufficient, but statement 1 alone is NOT sufficient to answer the question.

(C) BOTH statements (1) and (2) TOGETHER are sufficient to answer the question asked, but NEITHER statement ALONE is sufficient.

(D) EACH statement ALONE is sufficient to answer the question asked.

(E) Statements (1) and (2) TOGETHER are NOT sufficient to answer the question asked, and additional data specific to the problem are needed.

QUESTION 2. If $xy \neq 0$, is $x > y$?

(1) $|x| > |y|$

(2) $x = 2y$

(A) Statement (1) ALONE is sufficient, but statement 2 alone is NOT sufficient to answer the question asked.

(B) Statement (2) ALONE is sufficient, but statement 1 alone is NOT sufficient to answer the question.

(C) BOTH statements (1) and (2) TOGETHER are sufficient to answer the question asked, but NEITHER statement ALONE is sufficient.

(D) EACH statement ALONE is sufficient to answer the question asked.

(E) Statements (1) and (2) TOGETHER are NOT sufficient to answer the question asked, and additional data specific to the problem are needed.

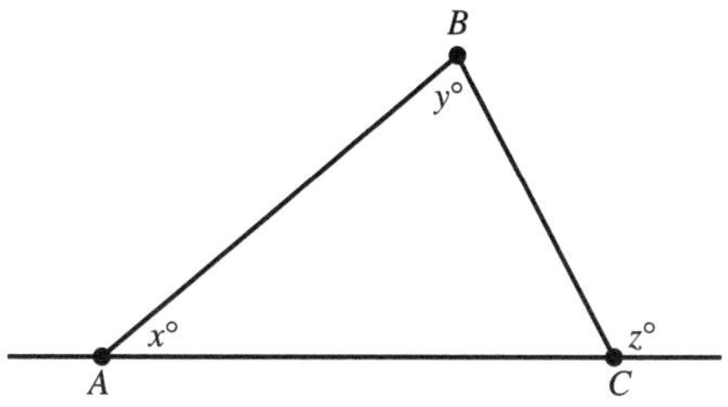

QUESTION 3. In the figure above, is *AB* equal in length to *AC*?

(1) $x + y = z$

(2) $y = 180 - z$

(A) Statement (1) ALONE is sufficient, but statement 2 alone is NOT sufficient to answer the question asked.

(B) Statement (2) ALONE is sufficient, but statement 1 alone is NOT sufficient to answer the question.

(C) BOTH statements (1) and (2) TOGETHER are sufficient to answer the question asked, but NEITHER statement ALONE is sufficient.

(D) EACH statement ALONE is sufficient to answer the question asked.

(E) Statements (1) and (2) TOGETHER are NOT sufficient to answer the question asked, and additional data specific to the problem are needed.

NOTE Some Data Sufficiency questions will include diagrams (geometry figures, graphs, and charts), but most won't.

What You Should Know About the Data Sufficiency Format

Before you learn how to approach Data Sufficiency questions, let's look closer at how Data Sufficiency questions are designed.

The answer choices are the same for all Data Sufficiency questions. One feature that makes Data Sufficiency questions unique among other types of GMAT questions is that the answer choices are exactly the same for all Data Sufficiency questions.

Data Sufficiency questions can vary widely in difficulty level. Assuming you're familiar with their unique format, these questions are not inherently easier or tougher than Problem Solving questions. The level of difficulty and complexity can vary widely (depending on the correctness of your responses to earlier questions).

A Data Sufficiency question that asks for a specific numerical value is answerable only if *one and only one value* results. Some, but not all, Data Sufficiency questions will ask for a particular *numerical value,* for example:

- What is the area of the circle?
- What is the value of x?
- What is the area of triangle ABC?
- How much did Judith pay for the ring?

CAUTION

> You must keep in mind that in any Data Sufficiency question, if the question asks for a numerical value (no variables), then the question is answerable only if *one and only one value* results—not a range of numbers, not a positive or negative number, not an expression that includes a variable.

The two statements (1) and (2) will not conflict with each other. Perhaps you're wondering which response you should choose—(D) or (E)—if you can answer the question with either statement alone but where you get two conflicting answers. Don't worry; this won't happen. If you can answer the question given either statement alone, *the answer will be the same in both cases.* In other words, statements 1 and 2 will *never* conflict with each other. Why? The test-makers design Data Sufficiency questions this way, in order to avoid the "D vs. E" conundrum.

Expect word problems (math problems in a "real world" setting) to account for at least half of your Data Sufficiency questions. This will be true regardless of the overall difficulty level of your particular GMAT CAT, since word problems are not necessarily more difficult than other questions.

Figures are not necessarily drawn to scale, unless noted. Any figure accompanying a Data Sufficiency question will conform to the information in the question itself, but it will not necessarily conform to either statement 1 or 2. So although the figures are not designed to mislead you, they are not necessarily drawn to scale.

CAUTION

> Never try to answer a Data Sufficiency question by visual estimation or measurement of a figure. Rely on the information in the question and statements, not on a figure's appearance.

Calculating is not what Data Sufficiency is primarily about. Expect to do far less number crunching and equation solving for Data Sufficiency questions than for Problem Solving questions. What's being tested here is your ability to recognize and understand *principles,* not to work step-by-step toward a solution. (That's what Problem Solving is about.)

How to Approach a Data Sufficiency Question

Here's a 5-step approach that you should follow for every Data Sufficiency question.

ACTION PLAN

1. **Size up the question first.**
2. **Size up the two statements, and look for a shortcut to the correct answer.**
3. **Consider statement (1) alone.**
4. **Consider statement (2) alone.**
5. **If neither statement alone suffices to answer the question, consider both statements together.**

Let's Apply the 5-Step Action Plan

Now let's revisit Examples 1–3. We'll walk you through each question, using the 5-step approach you just learned.

NOTE

By now you're probably familiar enough with the five answer choices, so we won't bother including them with the questions from now on.

QUESTION

1. If ■ represents a digit in the 5-digit number 62,■79, what is the value of ■?

(1) 62,■79 is a multiple of 3.

(2) The sum of the digits of 62,■79 is divisible by 4.

ANALYSIS

The correct answer is **(C)**. This question is average in difficulty level. Approximately 65% of test-takers respond correctly to questions like this one. Here are the steps:

1. This question is testing on *factors* and *divisibility.* The peculiar use of a "placeholder" is a typical GMAT technique for testing your understanding of integers and digits. Questions such as these are usually straightforward once you know the basic rules as well as a few shortcuts for divisibility.

2. Both statements appear to add different information to the question. So there's no obvious shortcut here. (Go on to step 3.)

3. Consider statement (1) alone. If the sum of the digits of a number is divisible by 3, the number is also divisible by 3. Excluding the digit represented by ■, the sum of the digits in the number 62,■79 is 24. Thus, if the number is a multiple of (divisible by) 3, the missing digit must be either 0, 3, 6, or 9. Thus, statement (1) alone is insufficient to answer the question. Eliminate (A) and (D).

4. Consider statement (2) alone. The number represented by ■ can equal either 0, 4, or 8. Thus, statement (2) alone is insufficient to answer the question. Eliminate (B).

5. Consider statements (1) and (2) together. The two statements together establish that the missing digit is 0, because 0 is the only number common to both lists of possible values for ■. Thus, statements (1) and (2) together are sufficient to answer the question, and the correct answer choice is (C).

QUESTION 2. If $xy \neq 0$, is $x > y$?

(1) $|x| > |y|$

(2) $x = 2y$

ANALYSIS The correct answer is **(E)**. This is a moderately difficult question. Approximately 45% of test-takers respond correctly to questions like this one. Here are the steps:

1. This is a typical *absolute value* question. Whenever you see inequalities and variables but no numbers, that's a clue that you'll need to consider different types of numbers—such as negative numbers, positive numbers, fractions, and perhaps the numbers 0 and 1—to determine the correct answer choice. Getting to the answer might entail performing some simple calculations, and perhaps a bit of trial and error (plugging in possible values).

2. Both statements appear to add different information to the question, so there's no obvious shortcut here. A good reasoned guess at this point would be that the correct answer choice is (E). Why? Because the question doesn't restrict the value of either x or y (except that neither can equal 0). So if you're pressed for time, guess (E) and move on to the next question. Otherwise, go on to step 3.

3. You must consider both positive and negative values for x and y. Given $|x| > |y|$, an x-value of either 4 or –4 and a y-value of 2, for example, satisfies the inequality but results in two different answers to the question. Thus statement (1) alone is insufficient to answer the question. Eliminate (A) and (D).

4. Similarly, given $x = 2y$, if you use negative values for both x and y (for example, $x = -4$ and $y = -2$), the answer to the question is *no*; but if you use positive values (for example, $x = 4$ and $y = 2$), the answer to the question is *yes*. Thus, statement (2) alone is insufficient. Eliminate (B).

5. Statements (1) and (2) together are still insufficient. For example, if $x = -4$ and $y = -2$, both statements (1) and (2) are satisfied, $x < y$, and the answer to the question is *no*. However, if $x = 4$ and $y = 2$, both statements (1) and (2) are satisfied, but $x > y$, and the answer to the question is *yes*. Eliminate (C). The correct answer choice must be (E).

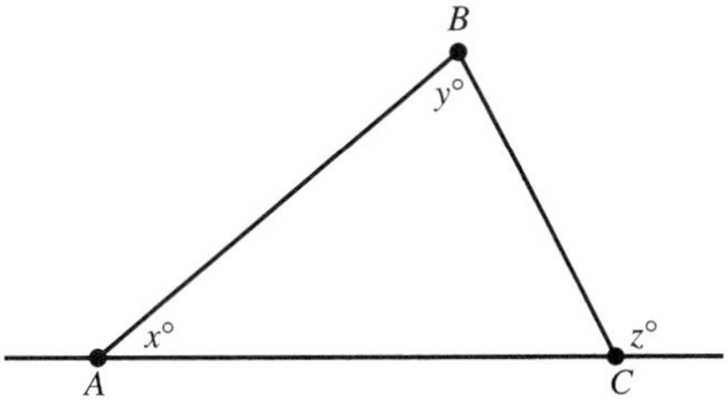

3

QUESTION 3. In the figure above, is *AB* equal in length to *AC*?

(1) $x + y = z$

(2) $y = 180 - z$

ANALYSIS The correct answer is **(B)**. This is a relatively difficult question. Approximately 25% of test-takers respond correctly to questions like this one. Here are the steps:

1. This question is a *geometry* problem involving the *isosceles triangle*. (You'll see anywhere from 5 to 8 geometry questions on your GMAT CAT.) This question involves three distinct rules of geometry. Two of these rules (A and C below) apply specifically to triangles:

   Rule A: If two angles of a triangle are equal in size, then the two sides opposite those angles are equal in length.

   Rule B: If angles formed from the same vertex form a straight line, their degree measures total 180 (and they are known as "supplementary" angles).

   Rule C: In any triangle, the sum of the degree measures of the three interior angles is 180.

   If you're unfamiliar with any of the three rules stated in step 1, you won't get very far with this question! So if you're pressed for time, and if you're particularly weak in this area of geometry (you won't be after Hours 8 and 9), consider taking a guess and moving on.

2. Intuition alone probably won't get you very far on this question. If you're really on your toes, you'll notice that statement (1) merely restates Rule C (see step 1) in a different form. (You'll learn why in step 3.) Also, because statement (2) includes a number, this statement is probably more likely than statement (1) to suffice in answering the question. (This amounts to little more than a guess, however.) So let's move on to step 3.

CAUTION

Don't shortcut the analysis by simply measuring the lengths of *AB* and *AC* with your eye. Take heed: Data Sufficiency figures are not necessarily drawn to scale. So analyze these problems using you knowledge of mathematics, not your eye!

3. Consider statement (1) alone. Given Rule A (see step 1), to answer the question you need to know whether angle y is equal in size to the triangle's unidentified angle—the interior angle at point *C*. Let's call this angle a. If $a = y$, then the answer to the question is *yes*. Otherwise, the answer is *no*. In either case, we need to know whether $a = y$ in order to answer the question.

   Angles a and y together form a straight line—the line passing through points *A* and *C*:

   $$a + y = 180$$
   $$a = 180 - z$$

   The sum of x, y, and a is 180 (Rule C). You can substitute $(180 - z)$ for a in this equation, and manipulate the result so that it is identical to the equation in statement 1:

$x + y + a = 180$	Rule C (sum of angle measures 180)
$x + y + (180 - z) = 180$	substituting $(180 - z)$ for a
$x + y - z = 0$	subtract 180 from each side
$x + y = z$	add z to each side

   Statement (1) essentially restates a rule that is true for any triangle, so it is insufficient alone to answer the question. Eliminate (A) and (D) as viable answer choices.

TIP

You could have shortcut this entire analysis had you already been aware of the rule that an exterior angle of a triangle is always equal in size to the sum of the two remote interior angles. You'll revisit this geometry shortcut and learn many others during Hours 8 and 9.

4. Now consider statement (2) alone. (Disregard statement (1) for now.) The expression $(180 - z)$ equals our third unidentified angle, which we called a in step 3. Given that $(180 - z)$ also equals y, the two angles a and y are equal. The two sides opposite a and y must also be equal (Rule A). Thus, statement (2) alone suffices to answer our question.

5. Because statement (1) alone is insufficient to answer the question while statement (2) alone is sufficient, the correct response is (B). There's no need to consider the two statements together. Based on statement (2), the answer to the question itself is *yes*, but you don't need to go this far. Had neither (1) nor (2) alone been sufficient to answer the question, you would have then considered both statements together to determine whether the correct response is (C) or (E).

DO's and DON'Ts for Handling Data Sufficiency Questions

Here's a useful list of DO's and DON'Ts for Data Sufficiency questions. Some of these tips we've already touched on during our sample question walk-through. Others are mentioned here for the first time.

NOTE You'll learn how to apply these DO's and DON'Ts in this hour's Workshop.

Do **Don't**

DO memorize the answer choices (they're the same for every Data Sufficiency question).

DO accept word problems at face value; make reasonable real-world assumptions.

DO be sure to consider each statement alone.

DON'T do more work than necessary; remember, you don't need to answer the question itself.

DO look for a quicker, more intuitive route to the correct answer.

DON'T perform endless calculations; if you find yourself doing a lot of pencil work, you're probably off track.

DON'T rely solely on a diagram (figure) to analyze a Data Sufficiency question; remember, Data Sufficiency figures are not necessarily drawn to scale.

DO consider all the possibilities when it comes to unknowns (variables).

Do **Don't**

DON'T try to do all the work in your head.

DO make educated guesses—if you're running out of time—by eliminating answer choices.

DO look for two statements that say essentially the same thing; if they do, then the correct answer is either (D) or (E).

DO check each statement to see if it provides numbers needed to answer the question; if it doesn't, it can't suffice alone to answer the question.

Data Interpretation (Statistical Graphs, Charts, and Tables)

Data Interpretation questions require you to analyze information presented graphically in statistical charts, graphs, and tables.

HOW MANY: 2–4 questions (typically in sets of two questions)

WHERE: Interspersed with other Quantitative questions (look for the first and second sets to appear, respectively, about one-third and two-thirds of the way through the section)

FORMAT:

- Data Interpretation questions usually appear in the Problem Solving format.
- Each question in a set pertains to the same graphical data.
- Each question (and each set) involves either *one or two* distinct graphs, charts, or tables.

NOTE

The size of the computer screen, along with the limited quality of the graphical display, does not allow for more than two graphs, charts, or tables at a time.

WHAT'S COVERED: Four types of graphical displays appear most frequently:

1. pie charts
2. tables
3. bar graphs
4. line graphs

NOTE

> You're more likely to encounter tables and pie charts than the other two display types. Why? On the computer screen, it's difficult to make visual measurements required for interpreting bar and line graphs, but visual measurements aren't required for pies charts and tables. Nevertheless, all four types are fair game, so be ready for them all!

SKILLS TESTED: Your ability to calculate percentages, ratios, and fractions based on the numbers you glean from graphical data.

What Data Interpretation Questions Look Like

Let's take a look at a Data Interpretation question. This one involves two related *pie charts.*

INCOME AND EXPENSES—DIVISIONS A, B, C, AND D OF XYZ COMPANY (YEAR X)

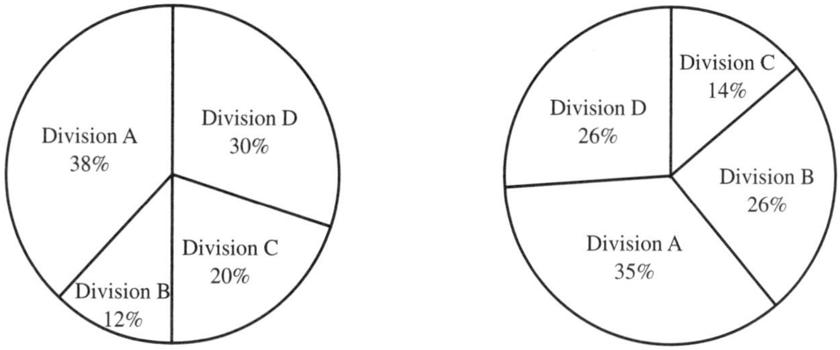

INCOME
(Total Income = $1,560,000)

EXPENSES
(Total Expenses = $495,000)

QUESTION 1. By approximately what amount did Division C's income exceed Division B's expenses?

(A) $125,000 (B) $127,000 (C) $140,000

(D) $180,000 (E) $312,000

QUESTION 2. With respect to the division whose income exceeded its expenses by the greatest percent among the four divisions, by approximately what amount did the division's income exceed its own expenses?

(A) $69,000 (B) $90,000 (C) $150,000

(D) $185,000 (E) $235,000

What You Should Know About Data Interpretation

Most Data Interpretation questions are long and wordy. Data Interpretation questions are notoriously difficult to understand. Get used to it; that's the way the test-makers design them. You'll probably find that you have more trouble interpreting the questions than the figures.

You'll probably have to scroll (vertically) to see the entire display. Graphical displays usually appear at the top of the screen (above the question), rather than to one side of the question. Some vertical scrolling may be necessary to view the entire display, including the information above and below the chart, graph, or table.

Bar graphs and line charts are drawn to scale. Remember: All figures on the Quantitative section are drawn as accurately as possible EXCEPT where the problem indicates that its figure is not drawn to scale. So you can rely on the visual appearance of a bar graph or line chart. Keep in mind:

- Bar graphs will be drawn to scale.
- Line charts will be drawn to scale.
- Pie charts are not necessarily drawn to scale (you'll see a note letting you know that it's not).
- Visual scale is irrelevant with tables.

(You'll see a line chart and a bar chart during this hour's Quiz.)

Important assumptions will be provided. Any additional information that you might need to know to interpret the figures will be indicated above and below the figures. (Be sure to read this information.)

Nearly all questions ask for an approximation. You'll see some form of the word *approximate* in nearly all Data Interpretation questions. This is because the test-makers are trying to gauge your ability to interpret graphical date, not your ability to crunch numbers to the "n-th" decimal place. (Notice the word *approximately* in both sample questions on page 61.)

Many of the numbers used are *almost* round. This feature relates to the previous one. The GMAT rewards test-takers who recognize that rounding off numbers (to an appropriate extent) will suffice to get to the right answer, so they pack Data Interpretation figures with numbers that are close to "easy" ones. (The numbers accompanying the pie charts on page 61 serve as good examples. $1,560,000 is close to $1,500,000 million and $495,000 is close to $500,000.)

Figures are not drawn to deceive you or to test your eyesight. In bar graphs and line charts, you won't be asked to split hairs to determine values. These figures are designed with a comfortable margin for error in visual acuity. Just don't round up or down too far. (You'll see a line chart and a bar chart during this hour's Quiz.)

How to Approach Data Interpretation Questions

Follow these 5 steps to handle any Data Interpretation question.

ACTION PLAN

1. **Look at the "big picture" first.**
2. **Read the entire Data Interpretation question very carefully.**
3. **Perform the steps needed to get to the answer.**
4. **Check choices (A) through (E) for your answer.**
5. **Check your calculations, and make sure the size and form (number, percentage, total, etc.) of your solution conforms with what the question asks.**

Let's Apply the 5-Step Action Plan

Now let's apply this 5-step approach to the sample question on page 61. We'll walk through the question in detail for you.

1. Size up the two charts, and read the information above and below them. Notice that we're only dealing with one company during one year here. Notice also that dollar totals are provided, but that the pie segments are all expressed only as percentages. That's a clue that your main task will be to calculate dollar amounts for various pie segments. Now read the question.

QUESTION

1. By approximately what amount did Division C's income exceed Division B's expenses?

(A) $125,000

(B) $127,000

(C) $140,000

(D) $180,000

(E) $312,000

ANALYSIS The correct answer is **(D)**. This is a relatively easy question; approximately 65% of test-takers respond correctly to questions like this one. Here's how to solve the problem using the 5-Step approach:

1. You already performed step 1.
2. This question involves three tasks: (1) calculate Division C's income, (2) calculate Division B's expenses, and (3) compute their difference. There's no shortcut to these three tasks, so go on to step 3.
3. Division B's expenses accounted for 26% of XYZ's total expenses, given as \$495,000. Rounding off these figures to 25% and \$500,000, Division B's expenses totaled approximately \$125,000. Income from Division C sales was 20% of total XYZ income, given as \$1,560,000. Rounding this total down to \$1,500,000, income from Division C sales was approximately \$300,000. Income from Division C sales exceeded Division B's expenses by approximately \$175,000.
4. The only answer choice close to this solution is (D). If you have extra time, go to step 5.
5. Make sure you started with the right numbers. Did you compare Division C's income with B's expenses (and not some other combination)? If you're satisfied that the numbers you used were the right ones and that your calculations are okay, move on to the next question.

QUESTION 2. With respect to the division whose income exceeded its expenses by the greatest percent among the four divisions, by approximately what amount did the division's income exceed its own expenses?

(A) \$69,000 (B) \$90,000 (C) \$150,000 (D) \$185,000 (E) \$235,000

ANALYSIS The correct answer is **(E)**. This is a very difficult question; approximately 20% of test-takers respond correctly to questions like this one. Here's how to solve the problem, using the 5-step approach:

1. You already performed step 1.
2. This is a very complex question. First you need to compare profitability—in dollar amount—among the four divisions. You can rule out Division B, since its expenses exceeded its income. That leaves Divisions A, C, and D. Be careful: Question 2 does not ask you to simply compare the percentages appearing in the two charts, but rather to calculate dollar amounts, then compute percent profit based on those amounts.
3. For Divisions A, C, and D, compare two dollar figures in terms of percent:

   Division A: 38% of total income and 35% of total expenses

   Division C: 20% of total income and 14% of total expenses

   Division D: 30% of total income and 25% of total expenses

Division C's income was a bit more than $300,000 (20% of $1,500,000). Division C's expenses were approximately $75,000 (15% of $500,000). Perform similar calculations for Divisions A and D, and you'll discover that Division C was the most profitable one in percentage terms. Division C's income exceeded its expenses by a bit more than $225,000.

4. Answer choice (E), $235,000, is the only one close to our approximation.
5. If you have time, rethink step 3. Make sure you're convinced that Division C's percentage profit was greater than either A's or D's. Also, ask yourself if $235,000 is in the right ballpark? If you're confident in your analysis, move on to the next question.

DO's and DON'Ts for Data Interpretation Questions

Do | **Don't**

DON'T confuse percentages with raw numbers.

DON'T go to the wrong part of a chart for your numbers.

DO save time and avoid computation errors by rounding off.

DON'T distort numbers by rounding off inappropriately.

DO handle lengthy, confusing questions one part at a time.

DON'T split hairs in reading line charts and bar graphs.

DO formulate a clear idea as to the overall size of number the question is calling for.

DO scroll vertically to see the entire display.

Workshop

For this hour's Workshop, we've hand-picked 6 Data Sufficiency questions and 4 Data Interpretation questions which illustrate the DO's and DON'Ts you just learned. For each question, you'll see one or two hints to help you focus on those DO's and DON'Ts. Don't worry if you come across some mathematical concepts you don't understand. You'll learn them during the next several hours. Right now, focus on the *art* of the GMAT.

ONLINE

Additional Quantitative questions are available online at the authors' Web site: *http://www.west.net/~stewart/gmat*

Quiz

(Answers and explanations begin on page 69.)

Directions: Attempt the following 10 questions. Try to limit your time to 20 minutes. Be sure to read the explanations that follow. They're just as important as the questions themselves, because they explain how the DO's and DON'Ts come into play.

1. What is the value of $a - b$?

   (1) $b = 3a$

   (2) $ab = 27$

   (Hint: If you're stuck, try manipulating one or both of the equations.)

2. In the figure below, is l_1 parallel to l_2?

   (1) $x + 90 = 280 - y$

   (2) $w + y = x + z$

   (Hint: Rely on the numbers and the text information, not on the visual proportions of the figure.)

   (Hint: Look for statements that add no useful information to the question.)

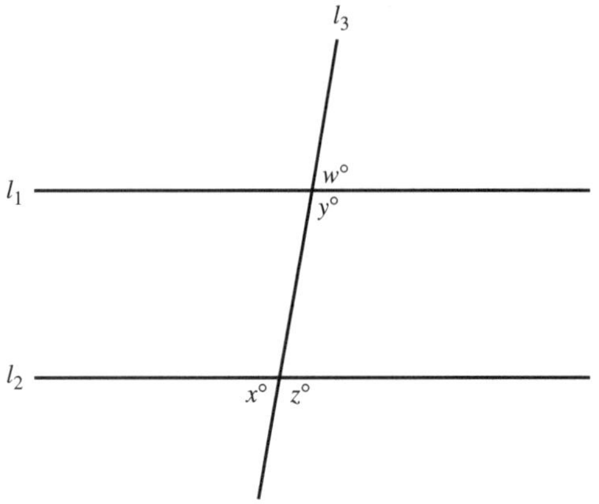

3. Is $xyz < 0$?

   (1) $x^3y^2z < 0$

   (2) $z^3yx < 0$

   (Hint: Consider all the possibilities when it comes to unknowns.)

4. How long would it take five typists to type 30 pages if all five typists type at the same speed?

   (1) One typist can type four pages in 30 minutes.

   (2) Three typists can type eight pages in 20 minutes.

   (Hint: Check the two statements to see if they are essentially the same.)

   (Hint: Often there's an intuitive alternative to number crunching.)

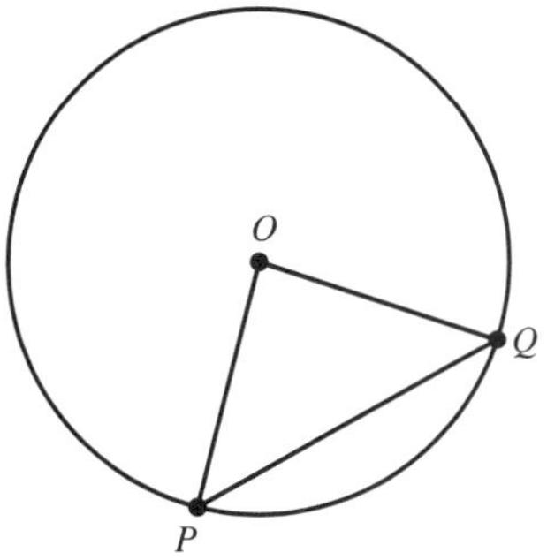

5. In the figure above, if point O lies at the center of the circle, what is the area of triangle OPQ?
   (1) The radius of the circle is 3.
   (2) PO is equal in length to PQ.

   (Hint: If numbers are needed to answer the question, check each statement to see if it provides the numbers.)

6. A certain granola recipe calls for a simple mixture of raisins costing \$3.50 per pound with oats. At a cost of \$2.00 per pound for the granola mixture, how many pounds of oats must be added to 10 pounds of raisins?
   (1) Oats cost \$1.00 per pound.
   (2) The granola mixture is packaged in one-pound bags.

   (Hint: Narrow down answer choices by asking yourself whether each statement provides useful and relevant information.)

   (Hint: Ask yourself what additional information you need to answer the question.)

Questions 7 and 8 refer to the following chart.

PRICE OF COMMON STOCK OF XYZ CORP. AND ABC CORP. (YEAR X)

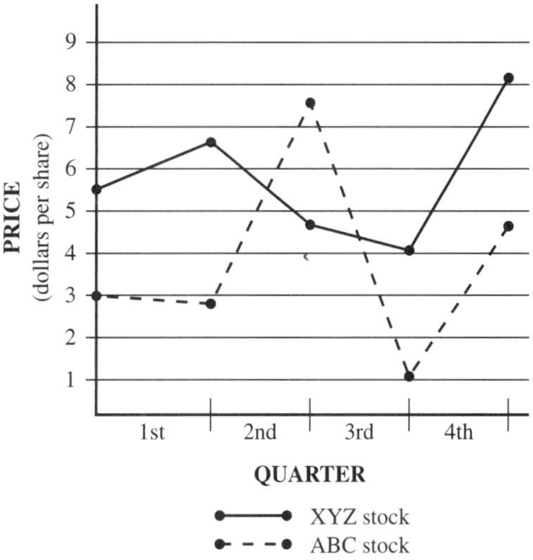

7. At the time during year X when the difference between the price of ABC common stock and the price of XYZ common stock was at its greatest, the price of ABC common stock was approximately what percent of the price of XYZ common stock and ABC common stock combined?
   (A) 16%
   (B) 31%
   (C) 36%
   (D) 42%
   (E) 103%

   (Hint: It's okay to approximate, but don't distort numbers by rounding off inappropriately.)

3

8. At the time during year *X* when the aggregate price of ABC and XYZ stock was the greatest, the price of XYZ stock was approximately what percent of the price of ABC stock?

   (A) 25%
   (B) 60%
   (C) 70%
   (D) 140%
   (E) 170%

   (Hint: A quick visual inspection can help narrow down your choices.)

   (Hint: Be sure not to get percentages backwards.)

WORLDWIDE SALES OF THREE XYZ MOTOR COMPANY MODELS, 1996-1997 MODEL YEAR

Purchaser Category	Automobile Model: Basic	Standard	Deluxe
U.S. institutions	3.6	8.5	1.9
U.S. consumers	7.5	11.4	2.0
Foreign institutions	1.7	4.9	2.2
Foreign consumers	1.0	5.1	0.8

Note: All numbers are in thousands

9. According to the table above, of the total number of automobiles sold to the institutions during the 1996-1997 model year, which of the following most closely approximates the percentage that were NOT standard models?

   (A) 24%
   (B) 36%
   (C) 41%
   (D) 59%
   (E) 68%

   (Hint: It's okay to approximate, but don't distort numbers by rounding off inappropriately.)

10. Among the years shown in the graph below, during the year in which the total amount of non-minority and minority funds awarded was the greatest, the difference between the two amounts was approximately

    (A) $130,000
    (B) $160,000
    (C) $220,000
    (D) $270,000
    (E) $400,000

    (Hint: A quick visual inspection can help narrow down your choices.)

STATE SCHOLARSHIP FUNDS AWARDED (1980-95)

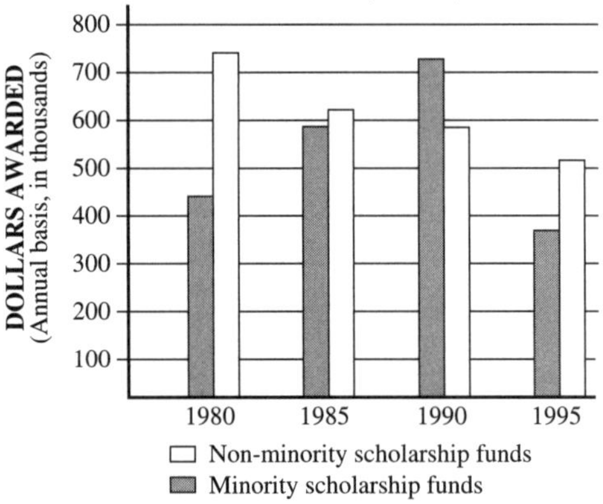

Answers and Explanations

1. **(E)** It should be obvious that neither statement alone suffices to answer the question, because each equation contains two variables. An unwary test-taker might assume (prematurely) that the two statements together do suffice to answer the question—since they appear at first glance to establish a system of two linear equations in two variables. But, the system is not linear. If you're not certain about this, try substituting $3a$ for b in the second equation:

$$a(3a) = 27$$
$$3a^2 = 27$$
$$a^2 = 9$$
$$a = \pm 3$$

You obtain two possible solutions, or "roots," for a (b has two roots as well). If you're not certain about this, try substituting $\frac{27}{b}$ for a in the first equation:

$$b = 3\left(\frac{27}{b}\right)$$
$$b^2 = 81$$
$$b = \pm 9$$

Again, there are two possible values for b. You've done enough work to prove that the correct response to this question is (E).

2. **(A)** You can express the equation in statement 1 as $x + y = 190$; thus, x and y are not supplementary angles (they don't add up to 180). This information suffices to establish that the angles created by the intersection of l_1 and l_3 are different from those created by the intersection of l_2 and l_3. Accordingly, l_1 cannot be parallel to l_2, and statement (1) alone suffices to answer the question. Statement (2) adds nothing to the question. It merely states that w and y add up to 180 and that x and z add up to 180. In other words, statement (2) merely reiterates what is already assumed in any GMAT figure: that all lines are straight. Thus, statement (2) alone is insufficient to answer the question.

3. **(B)** Given that $x^3y^2z < 0$, neither x, y, nor z can equal zero, and either all three terms (x^3, y^2, and z) are negative or exactly one of the three terms is negative [(-)(-)(-) < 0, (-)(+)(+) < 0]. However, whether y is negative or positive, y^2 is positive; thus either x or z (but not both) must be negative. Accordingly, xyz could be either positive or negative, depending on the value of y. Statement (1) alone is insufficient to answer the question. Given $z^3yx < 0$, either z, y, and x are all negative or exactly one of the three variables is negative. In either case, $xyz < 0$. Thus, statement (2) alone is sufficient to answer the question.

4. **(D)** You don't have do any pencil work here. Notice that the two statements provide essentially the same information—the rate at which a typist types. The test-makers are simply hiding the ball from you by expressing this rate a bit differently in each statement. Once you recognize this, you can eliminate (A), (B), and (C). Next, ask yourself if this rate would

3

be sufficient information to answer the question. Since it is, the correct answer must be (D).

If you fail to recognize this shortcut, you can determine the speed (or rate) at which a typist types, in terms of pages per unit of time. You can set up a general equation to express the time required by a typist to type one page:

$$\frac{(\#\text{ of typists})(\text{time})}{\#\text{ of pages}} = \text{time per page}$$

Based on the values provided in either statement (1) or (2), the typing rate of a single typist is 7½ minutes per page:

$$\frac{(1\text{ typist})(30\text{ minutes})}{4\text{ pages}} = 7\frac{1}{2} = \frac{(3\text{ typists})(20\text{ minutes})}{8\text{ pages}}$$

Once you know the typing rate, you can apply that rate to the numbers given in the question; so the correct answer is (D). You don't need to actually answer the question. Just for the record, five typists could type 30 pages in 45 minutes:

$$\frac{(5\text{ typists})(45\text{ minutes})}{30\text{ pages}} = 7\frac{1}{2}$$

5. **(C)** To answer the question, ask yourself what additional data you need. To determine the triangle's area, you need to know a lot more information. Neither statement alone provides all the missing pieces:

- Statement (1) provides no information about the area of triangle *OPQ* relative to the area of the circle.
- Statement (2) establishes that triangle *OPQ* is an equilateral triangle (all three sides are equal in length, and all three angles are 60°). But statement (2) provides no specific values to help determine the area.

Considering both statements together allows you to compute the area of the equilateral triangle. So the correct answer must be (C). There's no need to calculate the triangle's area. For the record, though, the area of any equilateral triangle is $\frac{s^2}{4}\sqrt{3}$, where s equals the length of each side. In this problem, then, the area of ΔOPQ is $\frac{9}{4}\sqrt{3}$.

6. **(A)** The question itself provides two of the three facts you need to answer it: the cost per pound of raisins and the cost per pound of the mixture. Statement (1) provides the third needed fact: the cost per pounds of oats. Although you don't need to do the math, here's how you would answer the question. Think of the quantities as costs per pound, and multiply the cost by the weight. The total mixture will consist of 10 pounds of raisins at $3.50 per pound, or ($3.50)(10), plus "x" pounds of oats at $1.00 per pound, or ($1.00)(x). The mixture costs $2.00 per pound, and it will be $(10 + x)$ pounds:

$$(\$3.50)(10) + (\$1.00)(x) = (\$2.00)(10 + x)$$
$$x = 15$$

15 pounds of oats are needed. Statement (2) alone provides no useful information for answering the question.

7. **(B)** The price difference was at its maximum at the end of the 1st quarter, when the price of ABC stock was about \$2.80 and the price of XYZ stock was about \$6.60. The total price of both was about \$9.40. \$2.80 is 28/94 of \$9.40. To estimate the percentage, round 28 *up* to 30 and round 94 *up* to 100: 30/100 = 30%. (Be sure to round off a numerator and denominator in the same direction!) Since you estimated prices by eye and rounded the numbers, look for an answer choice in the right ballpark. Answer choice (B) fits the bill.

8. **(E)** First, narrow down the viable data points by looking for pairs that are high up on the chart. The only two viable points in time are the end of the second quarter and the end of the fourth quarter. Compare these two pairs. Remember: Your task is to find that pair whose aggregate (combined) price is greater. It's a close call, but the total for the final pair (end of fourth quarter) is a bit larger than the total for the other pair:

   End of 2nd quarter: XYZ (\$4.60) + ABC (\$7.60) = \$12.10

   End of 4th quarter: XYZ (\$8.25) + ABC (\$4.75) = \$13.10

   Now go on to the second step. At the end of the fourth quarter, the price of XYZ stock was approximately \$8.25, and the price of ABC stock was approximately \$4.75. Be careful here: The question asks for the XYZ price as a percentage of the ABC price—*not* the other way around, and *not* how much greater one price is than the other! So, the percentage the question asks for is:

   $$100\% + \frac{8.25 - 4.75}{4.75} = 100\% + \frac{3.50}{4.75}$$

   Round 4.75 up to 5.00, then determine a percentage:

   $$100\% + \frac{3.50}{5.00} = 100\% + \frac{7}{10} = 170\%$$

9. **(C)** Answering this question requires two steps. First, the total number of product units sold to institutions = (3.6 + 8.5 + 1.9) + (1.7 + 4.9 + 2.2) = 22.8. The number of these units that were not standard models = (3.6 + 1.9) + (1.7 + 2.2) = 9.4. Now go on to the second step. Ask yourself: "9.4 is approximately what percent of 22.8?" This question is the same as asking the percent equivalent of $\frac{9.4}{22.8}$. Here's a quick way to approximate the percentage. Round down *both* the numerator and denominator to give you the fraction 8/20. It is clear now that you're looking for an answer choice that's around 40% (8/20 = 40/100). Only (C) fits the bill.

10. **(A)** A quick visual inspection should reveal that the aggregate amount awarded in 1990 exceeded that of any of the other 3 years shown. During that year, minority awards totaled approximately \$730,000 and non-minority awards totaled approximately \$600,000. The difference between the two amounts is \$130,000.

3

Hour 4

Teach Yourself Arithmetic I

This hour you'll begin to teach yourself the arithmetic you'll need for the GMAT. You'll focus on four of the test-makers' favorite topics: simple average, fractions, percents, and ratios/proportion. In this hour you will learn:

- The formula for arithmetic mean (average), and how to apply it to GMAT questions
- How to handle fractions effectively on the GMAT
- How to deal with GMAT problems involving percent
- The concepts of ratio and proportion, and how these concepts are covered on the GMAT
- How to apply the concepts you learn this hour to a GMAT-style Quiz

Problems Involving Descriptive Statistics

First up this hour is what the test-makers call *descriptive statistics.* This area includes many concepts, but here are the only five you need to know for the GMAT (in order by frequency of appearance on the exam):

arithmetic mean (average): In a set of n measurements, the sum of the measurements divided by n

median: The middle measurement after the measurements are ordered by size (or the average of the two middle measurements if the number of measurements is even)

mode: the measurement that appears most frequently in a set

range: the difference between the greatest measurement and the smallest measurement

standard deviation: a measure of dispersion among members of a set

We'll focus here on *mean* and *median* because these two concepts are covered on the GMAT far more frequently than the others. But first, here's a simple example that illustrates each of the five concepts:

Example: Given a set of six measurements, {8,–4,8,3,2,7}:

mean = 4	$(8 - 4 + 8 + 3 + 2 + 7) \div 6 = 24 \div 6 = 4$
median = 5	The average of 3 and 7—the two middle measurements in the set ordered in this way: {–4,2,3,7,8,8}
mode = 8	8 appears twice (more frequently than any other measurement)
range = 12	The difference between –4 and 8
standard deviation	(see below)

On the GMAT, you probably won't need to calculate standard deviation (it's a complex process). More likely, you'll be asked to *compare* standard deviations. And you'll probably be able to do this informally by simply remembering the general rule that *the greater the data are spread away from the mean, the greater the standard deviation.* Consider these two distributions:

Distribution A: {1, 2.5, 4, 5.5, 7}
Distribution B: {1, 3, 4, 5, 7}

In both sets, the mean and median is 4, and the range is 6. But the standard deviation of A is greater than that of B, because 2.5 and 5.5 are further away than 3 and 5 from the mean.

Arithmetic Mean (Simple Average)

Calculating a simple average of a series of numbers is pretty easy, and the test-makers know it. So GMAT simple-average questions are always a bit more complex than the simple calculation in our example on page 74.

QUESTION Dan scored an average of 72 on his first four math tests. After taking the next test, his average dropped by 2. Which of the following is his most recent test score?

(A) 60

(B) 62

(C) 64

(D) 66

(E) 68

ANALYSIS The correct answer is **(B)**. Dan's average after the fifth test was 72 – 2, or 70. Set up the formula for arithmetic mean, plugging in the information you already know (let *x* equal Dan's most recent test score):

$$A = \frac{(\text{score 1} + \text{score 2} + \text{score 3} + \text{score 4}) + \text{score 5}}{5}$$

$$70 = \frac{4(72) + x}{5}$$

$$70 = \frac{288 + x}{5}$$

$$350 = 288 + x$$

$$62 = x$$

TIP When you're facing any arithmetic mean problem, just plug the information that the question provides into the formula, and you'll be able to handle the problem with no sweat.

Median

In a set of numbers arranged from lowest to highest in value, the *median* is:

- the middle value, if the set includes an *odd* number of terms
- the average of the two middle values, if the set includes an *even* number of terms

QUESTION What is the difference in value between the median and the mean (average) of the numbers in the set {8,4,–3,6,–7,5}?

(A) –9

(B) 0

(C) $2\frac{1}{3}$

(D) 4

(E) $11\frac{1}{2}$

ANALYSIS The correct answer is **(C)**. To calculate the median, rearrange the terms in order of value: {–7,–3,4,5,6,8}. Since the set includes 6 terms (an even number), the median is the average of the two middle terms: $\frac{4+5}{2}$, or $\frac{9}{2}$. To calculate the mean, add the digits, then divide by 6: $\frac{8+4-3+6-7+5}{6} = \frac{13}{6}$. Finally, calculate the difference between the median and mean: $\frac{9}{2} - \frac{13}{6} = \frac{27}{6} - \frac{13}{6} = \frac{14}{6}$, or $2\frac{1}{3}$.

CAUTION

For the same set of values, the mean (simple average) and the median can be, but are not necessarily, the same. For example:

The set {3,4,5,6,7} has both a mean and median of 5.
The set {–2,0,5,8,9} has a mean of 4 but a median of 5.

Percent, Fraction, and Decimal Conversions

Many GMAT questions will require you to convert percents, fractions, and decimals back and forth from one form to another. You should know how to make any conversion quickly—without stopping to think how to do it.

> **NOTE**
>
> Percents are usually less than 100, but they can be 100 or greater as well. Percents greater than one hundred convert to numbers greater than 1:
>
> $140\% = 1.40 = 1\frac{4}{10}$ or $1\frac{2}{5}$
> $5893\% = 58.93 = 58\frac{93}{100}$

QUESTION How many fifths are in 280%

(A) 1.4
(B) 2.8
(C) 14
(D) 28
(E) 56

ANALYSIS The correct answer is **(C)**. Convert 280% to a fraction, then reduce to lowest terms: $280\% = \frac{280}{100} = \frac{28}{10} = \frac{14}{5}$.

4

Problems Involving Fractions

You'll find 4 basic types of fraction problems on the GMAT:

1. Adding or subtracting fractions
2. Multiplying fractions
3. Dividing fractions
4. Comparing fractions

1. **Adding or subtracting fractions.** To add (or subtract) fractions having different denominators, you'll first need to find a common denominator, then alter numerators accordingly. Try to find the lowest common denominator, by focusing on the largest of the denominators given. Here's an example:

$$\frac{1}{6}+\frac{1}{3}-\frac{2}{5}$$

Of the three denominators, 6 is the largest. Considering successive multiples of 6 (12...18...24...30), not until you get to 30 do you find a number that is also a multiple of both 5 and 3. So 30 is your lowest common denominator. Next, alter numerators accordingly, then combine:

$$\frac{1(5)}{6(5)} + \frac{1(10)}{3(10)} - \frac{2(6)}{5(6)} = \frac{5}{30} + \frac{10}{30} - \frac{12}{30} = \frac{3}{30}, \text{ or } \frac{1}{10}.$$

2. **Multiplying fractions.** To multiply fractions, multiply the numerators and multiply the denominators (the denominators need not be the same). To simplify the multiplication, always cancel factors where possible before you combine fractions. It's okay to cancel across fractions:

$$\frac{18}{11} \cdot \frac{22}{9} = \frac{{}^{2}\cancel{18}}{{}_{1}\cancel{11}} \cdot \frac{\cancel{22}^{2}}{\cancel{9}_{1}} = \frac{2}{1} \cdot \frac{2}{1} = \frac{4}{1}, \text{ or } 4$$

3. **Dividing fractions.** To divide fractions, multiply the numerator fraction by the reciprocal of the denominator fraction. (To obtain a reciprocal of a fraction, just switch numerator and denominator.)

$$\frac{\frac{2}{3}}{\frac{11}{6}} = \frac{2}{3} \cdot \frac{6}{11} = \frac{2}{{}_{1}\cancel{3}} \cdot \frac{\cancel{6}^{2}}{11} = \frac{4}{11}, \text{ or } 4$$

TIME SAVER

Whenever you perform either multiplication or division with fractions, first combine and factor terms within each fraction, where possible.

QUESTION $\dfrac{4\frac{1}{2}}{1\frac{1}{8}} - 3\dfrac{2}{3} =$

(A) $-\frac{1}{8}$ (B) $\frac{1}{12}$ (C) $\frac{5}{24}$ (D) $\frac{1}{3}$ (E) $\frac{2}{5}$

ANALYSIS The correct answer is **(D)**. First, convert all mixed numbers into fractions:

$$\frac{\frac{9}{2}}{\frac{9}{8}} - \frac{11}{3}$$

Next, eliminate the complex fraction. Multiply $\frac{9}{2}$ by $\frac{8}{9}$ (the reciprocal of $\frac{9}{8}$):

$$\frac{9}{2} \cdot \frac{8}{9} - \frac{11}{3} = \frac{8}{2} - \frac{11}{3}$$

Finally, express each fraction with the common denominator 6, then combine:

$$\frac{8}{2} - \frac{11}{3} = \frac{24}{6} - \frac{22}{6} = \frac{2}{6}, \text{ or } \frac{1}{3}$$

4. **Comparing fractions.** One way to compare the size of two fractions having different denominators is to find a common denominator, then compare numerators. A quicker way is with the cross-product method, in which you multiply the numerator of each fraction by the other's denominator, then compare the two products. The fraction whose numerator contributes to the larger product is the greater of the two fractions.

QUESTION Which of the following fractions is greatest in value?

(A) $\frac{3}{5}$ (B) $\frac{12}{32}$ (C) $\frac{11}{16}$ (D) $\frac{5}{8}$ (E) $\frac{7}{11}$

ANALYSIS The correct answer is **(C)**. To compare (B), (C), and (D), you can use a common denominator of 32:

(B) $\frac{21}{32}$ (C) $\frac{11}{16} = \frac{22}{32}$ (D) $\frac{5}{8} = \frac{20}{32}$

The largest of these is $\frac{11}{16}$. Compare $\frac{11}{16}$ to $\frac{7}{11}$ (answer choice E) using the cross-product method. $11 \cdot 11 > 16 \cdot 7$. Therefore, $\frac{11}{16} > \frac{7}{11}$. Finally, compare $\frac{11}{16}$ to $\frac{3}{5}$ (answer choice A) using the cross-product method. $11 \cdot 5 > 16 \cdot 3$. Thus, $\frac{11}{16} > \frac{3}{5}$.

4

NOTE In this particular type of problem, the answer choices won't necessarily be listed in ascending value, since doing so would give the answer away.

Operations with Decimal Points

GMAT problems involving decimal numbers sometimes require you to combine these numbers by either multiplying or dividing.

Multiplying decimal numbers. The number of decimal places (digits to the right of the decimal point) in a product should be the same as the total number of decimal places in the numbers you multiply. So to multiply decimal numbers quickly:

1. Multiply, but ignore the decimal points.
2. Count the total number of decimal places among the numbers you multiplied.
3. Include that number of decimal places in your product.

Here are two simple examples:

(23.6)(.07)	3 decimal places altogether
(236)(7) = 1652	Decimals temporarily ignored
(23.6)(.07) = 1.652	Decimal point inserted

(.01)(.02)(.03)	6 decimal places altogether
(1)(2)(3) = 6	Decimals temporarily ignored
(.01)(.02)(.03) = .000006	Decimal point inserted

Dividing decimal numbers. When you divide (or compute a fraction), you can move the decimal point in both numbers by the same number of places either to the left or right without altering the quotient (value of the fraction). Here are three related examples:

$$11.4 \div .3 \text{ (or } \frac{11.4}{.3}) = \frac{114}{3} = 38$$

$$1.14 \div 3 \text{ (or } \frac{1.14}{3}) = \frac{114}{300} = .38$$

$$114 \div .03 \text{ (or } \frac{114}{.03}) = \frac{11400}{3} = 3800$$

TIP

Removing decimal points from a fraction helps you to see the general size (value) of the fraction you're dealing with.

Problems Involving Percent

On the GMAT, you might find any one of four types of "pure" percent problems:

1. Finding a % of a number
2. Finding a number when a % is given
3. Finding what % one number is of another
4. Finding percent increase or decrease

The last type is by far the most likely of the four to appear on the GMAT.

QUESTION A clerk's salary is \$320.00 after a 25% raise. Before the clerk's raise, the supervisor's salary was 50% greater than the clerk's salary. If the supervisor also receives a raise in the same amount as the clerk's raise, what is the supervisor's salary after the raise?

(A) \$370

(B) \$424

(C) \$448

(D) \$480

(E) \$576

ANALYSIS The correct answer is **(C)**. \$320 is 125% of the clerk's former salary. Expressed algebraically:

$$320 = 1.25x$$
$$32000 = 125x$$
$$\$256 = x \text{ (clerk's salary before the raise)}$$

Thus, the clerk received a raise of \$64 (\$320 – \$256). The supervisor's salary before the raise was:

$$\$256 + 50\% \text{ of } \$256$$
$$= \$256 + \$128$$
$$= \$384$$

The supervisor received a \$64 raise. Thus, the supervisor's salary after the raise is \$448 (\$384 + \$64).

CAUTION

Semantics is important in problems of percent. Be sure you understand the distinction between these two statements:

6 is 100% greater than 3.
6 is 200% of 3.

If you confuse their meaning, you're asking for trouble on the GMAT!

Problems Involving Ratios and Proportion

GMAT ratio problems sometimes involve a whole divided into two or more *parts*, where your task is to determine either (1) the size of one of the parts or (2) the size of the whole. You can solve these problems by setting up algebraic equations. But, there's another approach that is usually quicker and more intuitive.

Think about a ratio as a whole made up of different parts—like a whole pie divided into pieces. For example, in a class of 12 males and 16 females, the ratio of males to females is 12:16 (or 3:4), and the "whole pie" consists of 28 equal slices—the total number of students; the whole equals the sum of its slices:

16 slices (females) + 12 slices (males) = the whole pie (28 students)
$\frac{16}{28} + \frac{12}{28} = \frac{28}{28}$ (the whole pie)

QUESTION Three lottery winners—*X*, *Y*, and *Z*—are sharing a lottery jackpot. *X*'s share is $\frac{1}{5}$ of *Y*'s share and $\frac{1}{7}$ of *Z*'s share. If the total jackpot is $195,000, what is the dollar amount of Z's share?

(A) $15,000

(B) $35,000

(C) $75,000

(D) $105,000

(E) $115,000

ANALYSIS The correct answer is **(D)**. Think about these shares as slices of a whole pie—the whole jackpot. First, express the winners' proportionate shares as ratios. The ratio of X's share to Y's share is 1 to 5. Similarly, the ratio of X's share to Z's share is 1 to 7. The jackpot share ratio is as follows:

$$X : Y : Z = 1 : 5 : 7$$

X's winnings account for 1 of 13 equal parts (1 + 5 + 7) of the total jackpot. $\frac{1}{13}$ of $195,000 is $15,000. Accordingly, *Z*'s share is 7 times that amount, or $105,000.

Setting Up Proportions (Equal Ratios)

A proportion is simply a statement that two ratios are equal. Since you can express ratios as fractions, you can express a proportion as an equation—for example, $\frac{16}{28} = \frac{4}{7}$. If one of the four terms is missing from the proportion, you can solve for the missing term using algebra.

QUESTION At *c* cents per pound, what is the cost of *a* ounces of candy?

(A) $\frac{c}{a}$

(B) $\frac{a}{c}$

(C) ac

(D) $\frac{ac}{16}$

(E) $\frac{16c}{a}$

ANALYSIS The correct answer is **(D)**. This question is asking: "*c* cents is to one pound as *how many cents* is to *a* ounces?" Set up a proportion, letting *x* equal the cost of *a* ounces. Because the question asks for ounces, convert 1 pound to 16 ounces. Use the cross-product method to solve quickly:

$$\frac{c}{16} = \frac{x}{a}$$

$$16x = ca$$

$$x = \frac{ca}{16}, \text{ or } \frac{ac}{16}$$

NOTE On the GMAT, you'll also see more complex word problems involving proportion (for example, problems involving motion and mixtures). These problems involve specific formulas, which you'll learn during Hour 7.

Altering a Ratio

A GMAT question might ask you to alter a ratio by adding or subtracting from one (or both) terms in the ratio. The number added or subtracted might be either known or unknown.

QUESTION Among registered voters in a certain district, the ratio of men to women is 3:5. If the district currently includes 24,000 registered voters, how many additional men must register to make the ratio 4:5?

(A) 2,000

(B) 3,000

(C) 4,000

(D) 5,000

(E) 6,000

ANALYSIS The correct answer is **(B)**. This question involves three steps. First, set up a proportion to determine the current number of registered male voters and female voters:

$$\frac{3}{8} = \frac{x}{24{,}000}$$
$$8x = 72{,}000$$
$$x = 9{,}000$$

$\therefore$ Of the 24,000 voters, 9,000 are men, and 15,000 are women.

Next, determine the number of male voters needed altogether for a 4:5 men/women ratio, given that the number of female voters remains unchanged (15,000):

$$\frac{4}{5} = \frac{x}{15{,}000}$$
$$5x = 60{,}000$$
$$x = 12{,}000$$

Since the district currently includes 9,000 male voters, 3,000 more are needed to make the ratio 4:5.

TIME SAVER

In the question above, the numbers are simple enough that you can probably use intuition instead of resorting to algebra. In the first step, it should be clear enough to you that $\frac{3}{8} = \frac{9}{24}$. In the second step, it should be equally clear that $\frac{4}{5} = \frac{12}{15}$.

Workshop

In this Workshop, you'll tackle a 10-question GMAT-style quiz, designed for you to review and apply the concepts and question types you learned about this hour.

ONLINE

Additional Quantitative questions are available online, at the authors' Web site: *http://www.west.net/~stewart/gmat*

Quiz

(Answers and explanations begin on page 87.)

DIRECTIONS: Attempt the following 10 GMAT-style questions. Try to limit your time to 15 minutes. For each question, you'll see one or two hints to help you if you're having trouble.

1. A number p equals $\frac{3}{2}$ the average of three terms—10,12, and q. In terms of p, what is the value of q?

   (A) $\frac{2}{3}p - 22$

   (B) $\frac{4}{3}p - 22$

   (C) $2p - 22$

   (D) $\frac{1}{2}p - 22$

   (E) $\frac{9}{2}p - 22$

   (Hint: Plug the information you know into the formula for arithmetic mean.)

2. If $a \neq 0$ or 1, $\dfrac{\frac{1}{a}}{2 - \frac{2}{a}} =$

   (A) $\frac{1}{2a - 2}$

   (B) $\frac{2}{a - 2}$

   (C) $\frac{1}{a - 2}$

   (D) $\frac{1}{a}$

   (E) $\frac{2}{2a - 1}$

   (Hint: You can divide by multiplying instead.)

3. The temperature at 12:00 noon is 66 degrees. If the temperature increases by 25% during the afternoon, then decreases by 25% during the evening, what is the temperature, in degrees, at the end of the evening?

   (A) $61\frac{7}{8}$
   (B) $62\frac{1}{4}$
   (C) $62\frac{3}{8}$
   (D) 63
   (E) 66

   (Hint: Compute percent change with the number before the change.)

   (Hint: Convert decimal numbers to fractions.)

4. Diane receives a base weekly salary of \$800 plus a 5% commission on sales. In a week in which her sales totaled \$8000, the ratio of her total weekly earnings to her commission was

   (A) 1:3
   (B) 5:8
   (C) 2:1
   (D) 5:2
   (E) 3:1

   (Hint: Be sure not to confuse total earnings with commission, and be sure not to reverse the ratio.)

5. Machine *X*, Machine *Y* and Machine *Z* each produce widgets. Machine *Y*'s rate of production is one third that of Machine *X*, and Machine *Z*'s production rate is twice that of Machine *Y*. If Machine *Y* can produce 35 widgets per day, how many widgets can the three machines produce per day working simultaneously?

   (A) 105
   (B) 164
   (C) 180
   (D) 210
   (E) 224

   (Hint: Convert ratios to fractional parts that add up to 1.)

6. There is enough food at a picnic to feed either 20 adults or 32 children. All adults eat the same amount, and all children eat the same amount. If 15 adults are fed, how many children can still be fed?

   (A) 4
   (B) 6
   (C) 8
   (D) 12
   (E) 24

   (Hint: Set up a proportion, or approach the question intuitively.

7. What number must be subtracted from the denominator of the fraction $\frac{7}{16}$ to change the value of the fraction to $\frac{4}{9}$?

   (A) $\frac{1}{16}$
   (B) $\frac{1}{4}$
   (C) $\frac{7}{9}$
   (D) $\frac{3}{2}$
   (E) $\frac{5}{3}$

   (Hint: Set up a proportion, then solve for the number.)

Questions 8–10 are Data Sufficiency problems.

8. What is the numerical ratio of $x:y:z$?
   (1) The ratio of $x:y$ is 1:2.
   (2) $z = 5$

   (Hint: Relative values and actual values are two different things.)

9. Three salespeople—*A, B,* and *C*—sold a total of 500 products among them during a particular month. During the month, did *A* sell more products than *B* sold as well as more products than *C* sold?
   (1) *A* sold 166 products during the month.
   (2) *C* sold 249 products during the month.

   (Hint: Examine individual sales figures as fractional parts of the total sales.)

10. At the beginning of a five-day trading week, the price of a certain stock was $10 per share. During the week, four of the five closing prices of the stock exceeded $10. Did the average closing price of the stock during the week exceed its price at the beginning of the week?
    (1) The stock's closing price on Tuesday was the same as its closing price on Thursday.
    (2) The sum of the stock's highest and lowest closing prices during the week was 20.

    (Hint: The question asks merely for a comparison, not for an average or other value.)

4

Answers and Explanations

1. **(C)** Apply the arithmetic mean formula, solving for q:

$$p = \frac{3}{2}\left(\frac{10 + 12 + q}{3}\right)$$
$$p = \frac{10 + 12 + q}{2}$$
$$2p = 22 + q$$
$$2p - 22 = q$$

2. **(A)** Combine terms in the denominator, then multiply the numerator fraction by the reciprocal of the denominator fraction:

$$\frac{\frac{1}{a}}{\frac{2a-2}{a}} = \frac{1}{a} \cdot \frac{a}{2a - 2} = \frac{1}{2a - 2}$$

3. **(A)** 25% of 66 is 16.5. Thus, the temperature increased to 82.5 degrees during the afternoon. 25% of 82.5 ($\frac{1}{4}$ of 82.5) is 20.625, or $20\frac{5}{8}$. Thus, the temperature decreased to $61\frac{7}{8}$ degrees during the evening.

4. **(E)** Diane's commission can be expressed as: (.05)(8,000) = \$400. Adding her commission to her base salary: \$800 + \$400 = \$1,200 (total earnings). The ratio of \$1,200 to \$400 is 3:1.

5. **(D)** The ratio of *X*'s rate to *Y*'s rate is 3 to 1, and the ratio of *Y*'s rate to *Z*'s rate is 1 to 2. You can express the ratio among all three as 3:1:2 (*X*:*Y*:*Z*). Accordingly, *Y*'s production accounts for $\frac{1}{6}$ of the total widgets that all three machines can produce per day. Given that *Y* can produce 35 widgets per day, all three machines can produce (35)(6) = 210 widgets per day.

6. **(C)** You can set up the proportion $\frac{15}{20} = \frac{x}{32}$, where x equals the number of children that can be fed instead of 15 adults. Solve for x:

$$\frac{15}{20} = \frac{x}{32}$$
$$\frac{3}{4} = \frac{x}{32}$$
$$4x = 96$$
$$x = 24$$

32 – 24, or 8 children can still be fed. You can also approach this question intuitively. $\frac{15}{20}$, or $\frac{3}{4}$, of the food is gone. The $\frac{1}{4}$ of the food that remains will feed $\frac{1}{4}$ of the 32 children—8 children.

7. **(B)** Set up a proportion, then solve for x by cross-multiplying:

$$\frac{7}{16 - x} = \frac{4}{9}$$
$$4(16 - x) = (7)(9)$$
$$64 - 4x = 63$$
$$-4x = -1$$
$$x = \frac{1}{4}$$

8. **(E)** Statement (1) alone provides no information about z. Statement (2) provides a value for z, but provides no information about either x or y. Together, the two statements are still insufficient to answer the question. The value of x and y relative to z is still unknown.

9. **(A)** Given that a total of 500 products were sold, statement (1) alone is sufficient to answer the question. If *A* sold 166 products, *A* sold just less than $\frac{1}{3}$ of the total number. Either *B* or *C* must sell more than $\frac{1}{3}$, and the answer to the question is *no*. Statement (2) alone is insufficient to answer the question. If *C* sold 249 products, *A* could have sold anywhere from 0 to 251 products; if *A* sold either 250 or 251 products, *A* would have sold more products than either *B* or *C*. However, if A sold 0–249 products, *A* would not have sold more products than *C*.

10. **(B)** Statement (1) provides no information about any of the closing prices relative to the stock's initial price of $10. Thus, statement (1) alone is insufficient to answer the question. Statement (2) establishes that the average of the highest and lowest closing prices during the week was $10. In other words, the lowest closing price was less than the stock's initial price by the same amount as the amount by which the highest closing price exceeded the stock's initial price. Given that the three remaining closing prices were all greater than $10, the average of all five closing prices must be greater than $10. Thus, statement (2) alone suffices to answer the question.

Hour 5

Teach Yourself Arithmetic II

This hour you'll broaden your arithmetical horizon by dealing with numbers in more abstract, theoretical settings. You'll examine a variety of relationships and patterns among numbers—just the sort of stuff the test-makers love to cover on the GMAT! Here are your goals for this hour:

- Understand the concept of absolute value
- Determine factors and multiples of numbers
- Recognize prime numbers
- Know the impact of exponents and radicals on the size and sign of numbers
- Learn how to combine base numbers, exponents, and radicals
- Learn to recognize numerical progressions, to compare large sets of numbers, and to deal with simple probability questions
- Review the concepts you learn by applying them to a GMAT-style quiz

Absolute Value

The absolute value of a real number refers to the number's distance from zero (the origin) on the number line. The symbol for absolute value is a pair of vertical lines—for example, the absolute value of x is $|x|$. Although any negative number is less than any positive number, the absolute value of a negative number can be less than, equal to, or greater than a positive number. Here's one instance of each:

$$|-7| = 7 < |8| \qquad |-7| = 7 = |7| \qquad |-7| = 7 > |6|$$

Try this Data Sufficiency question. (See pages 50–51 for directions.)

QUESTION If a is a non-negative number, is $a > b$?

(1) $|b| > |a|$

(2) $ab > 0$

ANALYSIS The correct answer is **(C)**. Statement (1) alone is insufficient because b could be either a positive or negative number. Statement (2) alone tells you only that a and b are both positive—not enough information to answer the question. Together, however, the statements tell you that both are positive and that $b > a$. (The answer to the question posed is *no*.)

Shortcuts for Finding Factors

Determining all the factors of large integers can be tricky; it's easy to overlook some factors. Keep in mind the following rules to help you determine quickly whether one integer is a multiple of (is divisible by) another integer:

1. Any integer is a factor of itself.
2. 1 an −1 are factors of all integers (except 0).
3. The integer zero has no factors and is not a factor of any integer.
4. A positive integer's largest factor (other than itself) will never be greater than one half the value of the integer.

Here are some shortcuts to determining divisibility by common numbers:

If the integer has this feature:	*Then it is divisible by:*
It ends in 0, 2, 4, 6 or 8	2
The sum of the digits is divisible by 3	3
The number formed by the last 2 digits is divisible by 4	4
The number ends in 5 or 0	5
The number meets the tests for divisibility by 2 and 3	6
The number formed by the last 3 digits is divisible by 8	8
The sum of the digits is divisible by 9	9

TIP

Memorize these shortcuts for the GMAT; you'll be glad you did. A great way to learn them is to apply them to the numbers between 0 and 100 that are *not* included in the list of prime numbers on page 94.

QUESTION By what amount is the sum of all positive factors of 48 greater than the sum of all positive factors of 36?

(A) 12

(B) 20

(C) 27

(D) 33

(E) 42

ANALYSIS The correct answer is **(D)**. The positive factors of 48 are: {1,2,3,4,6,8,12,16,24,48}. The positive factors of 36 are: {1,2,3,4,6,9,12,18,36}. The two sets have in common the terms 1,2,3,4,6, and 12. Thus, you need only compare these two sums:

$$8 + 16 + 24 + 48 = 96$$
$$9 + 18 + 36 = 63$$

Prime Numbers

A *prime number* is a positive integer having only two positive factors: 1 and the number itself. In other words, a prime number is not divisible by (a multiple of) any positive integer other than itself and 1.

NOTE

Zero and 1 are not considered prime numbers. 2 is the first prime number.

Recognizing prime numbers is important when simplifying numbers on the GMAT. For example, if you know that 59 is a prime number, then you won't waste any time trying to reduce $\frac{9}{59}$ to a simpler fraction (a fraction with smaller numbers). Learn to recognize all the prime numbers between 0 and 100, without having to think about it. Here they are:

Prime numbers between zero (0) and 100:

2	11	23	31	41	53	61	71	83	97
3	13	29	37	43	59	67	73	89	
5	17			47			79		
7	19								

Try this Data Sufficiency question. (See page 50–51 for directions.)

QUESTION What is the value of x?

(1) x is a prime number containing two digits.

(2) The sum of the digits in x is 5.

ANALYSIS The correct answer is **(E)**. There are two double-digit prime numbers that satisfy both statements: 23 and 41. Thus, even considering statements (1) and (2) together, you cannot answer the question.

Patterns to Look for When Combining Integers

What happens to integers when you combine them by adding, subtracting, multiplying, or dividing? Here are some useful observations:

Addition and subtraction:

integer ± integer = integer

even integer ± even integer = even integer (or zero, if the two integers are the same)

even integer ± odd integer = odd integer

odd integer ± odd integer = even integer (or zero, if the two integers are the same)

Multiplication and division:

integer – integer = integer

integer ÷ non-zero integer = integer, but only if the numerator is divisible by the denominator (if the result is a quotient with no remainder)

odd integer × odd integer = odd integer

even integer × non-zero integer = even integer

even integer ÷ 2 = integer

odd integer ÷ 2 = non-integer

QUESTION If $\frac{x}{y}$ is a negative integer, which of the following terms must also be a negative integer?

(A) $\frac{x^2}{y}$

(B) $-\frac{x^2}{y^2}$

(C) $\frac{x}{y^2}$

(D) $x + y$

(E) xy

ANALYSIS The correct answer is **(B)**. Of the five expressions, only (B) must be a negative integer, even if x and y are not themselves integers. Because the overall fraction is an integer, $\frac{x^2}{y^2}$ must be an integer. Any number squared is positive, so $\frac{x^2}{y^2}$ must be positive. Accordingly, $-\frac{x^2}{y^2}$ must be negative.

(A) can be either a positive or negative integer, depending on whether y is positive or negative.

(C) can be a non-integer, since the denominator of the original expression is squared. Also, (C) can be either positive or negative, depending on the sign of x.

(D) must be an integer, but can be either positive or negative, depending on whether x is negative or y is negative.

(E) must be negative, but it is not necessarily an integer—for example:

$$\frac{-\frac{2}{3}}{\frac{2}{3}} = -1, \text{ but } -\frac{2}{3} \cdot \frac{2}{3} = -\frac{4}{9} \text{ (a non-integer)}$$

Exponents (Powers) and Roots (Radicals)

On the GMAT, questions that focus on the concept of exponents come in two basic types (we'll look at both types just ahead):

- questions about the effect of exponents on the *size* and *sign* of a number (or other term)
- questions about *combining* terms that contain exponents

Exponents and the Real Number Line

Raising numbers to powers can have surprising effects on the size and/or sign (negative vs. positive) of the base number. This is one of the test-makers' favorite areas! The impact of raising a number to an exponent (power) depends on the region on the number line where the number and exponent fall. Here are the four regions you need to consider:

1. less than –1 (to the left of –1 on the number line)
2. between –1 and 0
3. between 0 and 1
4. greater than 1 (to the right of 1 on the number line)

QUESTION If $-1 < x < 0$, which of the following expressions is smallest in value?

(A) x^2

(B) x^3

(C) x^0

(D) $-x$

(E) $\frac{1}{x^3}$

ANALYSIS The correct answer is **(E)**. From largest to smallest, the order is: (C), (D), (A), (B), (E). (C) equals 1 (any non-zero term raised to the power of zero equals 1). (D) is a positive number between 0 and 1. (A) is a positive number between 0 and $|x|$, which is the value of (D). (B) is a negative number between 0 and x, which is the value of (A). (E) is a negative number less than (to the left of) –1.

Combining Base Numbers and Exponents

When you add or subtract terms, you cannot combine base numbers or exponents. It's as simple as that. Let's express this prohibition in terms of those intrepid variables *a*, *b*, and *x*:

$$a^x + b^x \neq (a + b)^x$$

It's a whole different story for multiplication and division. First, remember these two simple rules:

1. You can combine base numbers first, but only if the exponents are the same.
2. You can combine exponents first, but only if the base numbers are the same.

Let's assume first that exponents are the same:

General rule:	*Examples:*
$a^x \cdot b^x = (ab)^x$	$2^3 \times 3^3 = (2 \times 3)^3 = 6^3 = 216$
	$2^3 \times 3^3 = (8)(27) = 216$
$\frac{a^x}{b^x} = \left(\frac{a}{b}\right)^x$	$\frac{2^3}{3^3} = \frac{8}{27}$
	$\left(\frac{2}{3}\right)^3 = \frac{2}{3} \cdot \frac{2}{3} \cdot \frac{2}{3} = \frac{8}{27}$

Now let's assume that base numbers are the same. When multiplying these terms, add the exponents. When dividing them, subtract the denominator exponent from the numerator exponent:

General rule:	*Examples:*
$a^x \cdot a^y = a^{x+y}$	$2^3 \cdot 2^2 = 2^{(3+2)} = 2^5 = 32$
	$2^3 \cdot 2^2 = 8 \cdot 4 = 32$
$\frac{a^x}{a^y} = a^{x-y}$	$\frac{2^5}{2^2} = 2^{(5-2)} = 2^3 = 8$
	$\frac{2^5}{2^2} = \frac{32}{4} = 8$

QUESTION $\dfrac{9^{11} \cdot 11^9}{11^{11} \cdot 9^9} =$

(A) $\dfrac{1}{9}$

(B) $\dfrac{81}{121}$

(C) $\dfrac{9}{11}$

(D) 1

(E) 9

ANALYSIS The correct answer is **(B)**. The key to this question is to recognize that since the base numbers 9 and 11 appear in both the numerator and denominator, you can factor out 9^9 and 11^9:

$$\frac{9^{11} \cdot 11^9}{11^{11} \cdot 9^9} = \frac{(9^9 \cdot 9^2) \cdot 11^9}{(11^9 \cdot 11^2) \cdot 9^9} = \frac{9^2}{11^2} = \frac{81}{121}$$

CAUTION

Remember: You can't combine base numbers or exponents of two terms unless you're multiplying or dividing the terms *and* either the base numbers are the same or the exponents are the same.

Additional Exponent Rules

The only kind of exponents you're likely to see on the GMAT are positive integers. Keep in mind, though, that exponents can also be *negative*, and they can also be *non-integers*. So remember these two rules—one for negative exponents and the other for fractional exponents—just in case:

1. Raising a number to a negative power is the same as "1 over" the same number but with a positive exponent.

$$n^{-2} = \frac{1}{n^2} \qquad 3^{-2} = \frac{1}{3^2} = \frac{1}{9}$$

2. The numerator of a fractional exponent becomes the number's exponent. The denominator becomes the root.

$$n^{1/2} = \sqrt{n} \qquad 9^{1/2} = \sqrt{9} = 3$$

$$n^{2/3} = \sqrt[3]{n^2} \qquad 8^{2/3} = \sqrt[3]{8^2} = \sqrt[3]{64} = 4$$

$$n^{3/2} = \sqrt{n^3} \qquad 4^{3/2} = \sqrt{4^3} = \sqrt{64} = 8$$

To cover all your bases, also keep in mind these two additional rules for exponents:

3. When raising an exponent to a power, multiply the exponents.

$$(a^x)^y = a^{xy} \qquad (2^2)^4 = 2^8 = 256$$

4. Any non-zero number raised to the zero (0) power equals 1.

$$a^0 = 1 \ (a \neq 0) \qquad 34^0 = 1$$

For the GMAT, memorize the exponential values in the following table. You'll be glad you did, since these are the ones that you're most likely to see on the exam.

Base	*Power and Corresponding Value*						
	2	3	4	5	6	7	8
2	4	8	16	32	64	128	256
3	9	27	81	243			
4	16	64	256				
5	25	125	625				
6	36	216					

5

Roots and the Real Number Line

As with exponents, the root of a number can bear a surprising relationship to the size and/or sign (negative vs. positive) of the number (another favorite area for the test-makers). Here are four observations you should remember:

1. If $n > 1$, then $1 < \sqrt[3]{n} < \sqrt{n} < n$ (the higher the root, the lower the value). However, if n lies between 0 and 1, then $n < \sqrt{n} < \sqrt[3]{n} < 1$ (the higher the root, the higher the value).

2. The square root of any negative number is an imaginary number, not a real number. Remember: you won't encounter imaginary numbers on the GMAT.
3. Every negative number has exactly one cube root, and that root is a negative number. The same holds true for all other odd-numbered roots of negative numbers.
4. Every positive number has two square roots: a negative number and a positive number (with the same absolute value). The same holds true for all other even-numbered roots of positive numbers.

CAUTION Don't take this fourth observation too far! Every positive number has only one *cube* root, and that root is always a positive number. The same holds true for all other odd-numbered roots of positive numbers.

QUESTION If $x < -1$, which of the following is largest in value?

(A) $\sqrt{-(x^3)}$

(B) $-\sqrt[3]{x}$

(C) $\sqrt[3]{x}$

(D) $\frac{1}{\sqrt[3]{x}}$

(E) x^3

ANALYSIS The correct answer is **(B)**. From largest to smallest (left to right on the number line), the order is: (B), (A), (D), (C), (E). Here's the analysis of each answer choice:

(B) must be a positive number greater than 1

(A) must be a positive non-integer between zero and 1.

(D) must be a negative non-integer between zero and −1

(C) must be greater than (to the right of) x, between x and −1 on the number line

(E) must be smaller than x (to the left of x on the number line)

If you wish to confirm this analysis, let $x = -2$ in each of the five expressions.

Combining Radicals

The rules for combining terms that include roots are quite similar to those for exponents. One rule applies to addition and subtraction, while another rule applies to multiplication and division.

Addition and subtraction: If a term under a radical is being added to or subtracted from a term under a different radical, you cannot combine the two terms under the same radical.

General rule:	*Examples:*
$\sqrt{x} + \sqrt{y} \neq \sqrt{x + y}$	$\sqrt{4} + \sqrt{16} = 2 + 4 = 6$, but $\sqrt{4 + 16} = \sqrt{20} \approx 4.4$
$\sqrt{x} - \sqrt{y} \neq \sqrt{x - y}$	$\sqrt{25} - \sqrt{9} = 5 - 3 = 2$, but $\sqrt{25 - 9} = \sqrt{16} = 4$
$\sqrt{x} + \sqrt{x} = 2\sqrt{x}$ (not $\sqrt{2x}$)	$\sqrt{36} + \sqrt{36} = 2\sqrt{36} = 2(6) = 12$, but $\sqrt{2 \cdot 36} = \sqrt{72} \approx 8.5$

Multiplication and Division: Terms under different radicals can be combined under a common radical if one term is multiplied or divided by the other, but only if the root is the same. Here are three different cases:

General rule:	*Examples:*
$\sqrt{x}\sqrt{x} = x$	$\sqrt{33.9}\sqrt{33.9} = 33.9$
$\sqrt{x}\sqrt{y} = \sqrt{xy}$	$\sqrt{9}\sqrt{4} = \sqrt{9 \cdot 4} = \sqrt{36} = 6$
$\frac{\sqrt{x}}{\sqrt{y}} = \sqrt{\frac{x}{y}}$	$\frac{\sqrt[3]{125}}{\sqrt[3]{8}} = \sqrt[3]{\frac{125}{8}} = \frac{5}{2}$

Simplifying Radicals

On the GMAT, always look for the possibility of simplifying radicals by moving part of what's inside the radical to the outside. Check inside your square-root radicals for factors that are squares of nice tidy numbers (especially integers).

5

QUESTION $\sqrt{\dfrac{x^2}{36} + \dfrac{x^2}{25}} =$

(A) $\dfrac{x^2}{11}$

(B) $\dfrac{x}{30}\sqrt{61}$

(C) $\dfrac{11x}{30}$

(D) $\dfrac{x^2}{15}\sqrt{\dfrac{x}{2}}$

(E) $\dfrac{x}{30}$

ANALYSIS The correct answer is **(B)**. You cannot move either term out of the radical without first combining them, using a common denominator:

$$\sqrt{\frac{x^2}{36} + \frac{x^2}{25}} = \sqrt{\frac{25x^2 + 36x^2}{(36)(25)}} = \sqrt{\frac{61x^2}{(36)(25)}} = \frac{x}{6 \cdot 5}\sqrt{\frac{61}{1}} = \frac{x}{30}\sqrt{61}$$

TIP

> On the GMAT, if you can reduce an expression under a radical sign by removing terms or factors, do it! Also, eliminate radicals from denominators. More than likely, these steps will be necessary to solve the problem at hand.

For the GMAT, memorize the roots in the following table. You'll be glad you did, since these are the ones that you're most likely to see on the exam.

Common square roots:	*Common cube roots:*
$\sqrt{121} = 11$	$\sqrt[3]{8} = 2$
$\sqrt{144} = 12$	$\sqrt[3]{27} = 3$
$\sqrt{169} = 13$	$\sqrt[3]{64} = 4$
$\sqrt{196} = 14$	$\sqrt[3]{125} = 5$
$\sqrt{225} = 15$	$\sqrt[3]{216} = 6$
$\sqrt{625} = 25$	$\sqrt[3]{343} = 7$
	$\sqrt[3]{512} = 8$
	$\sqrt[3]{729} = 9$
	$\sqrt[3]{1000} = 10$

Problems Involving Sets

A *set* is simply a group of two or more numbers or other terms. GMAT problems involving sets come in four different varieties:

- *descriptive statistics* (mean, median, mode, range, standard deviation)
- *progressions* (recognizing a pattern among a series of terms)
- *comparisons* (finding sums of and differences between different sets of numbers)
- *probability* (determining possible combinations of terms within sets as well as between sets)

The first variety you examined last hour along with other pure number-crunching concepts. Now you'll explore the other three types.

Progressions

You might encounter a GMAT question involving a series of numbers (or other terms) in which the terms *progress* according to some pattern. Your task is to recognize the pattern and to identify unknown terms based on it.

QUESTION In the series $\{N_1, N_2, N_3, \ldots\}$, where $N_x = x^2 - 2x$, what is the value of $(N_{50} - N_{49}) - (N_{48} - N_{47})$?

(A) –16

(B) 4

(C) 9

(D) 22

(E) 49

ANALYSIS The correct answer is **(B)**. Don't try to solve this problem by crunching large numbers. Instead, look for a pattern. Apply the formula for N_x to the first several terms of the series: $N_1 = -1$, $N_2 = 0$, $N_3 = 3$, $N_4 = 8$, $N_5 = 15$, $N_6 = 24$. Notice the linear progression in which the difference between each successive term and the preceeding one increases by 2. As a result, given four successive terms, the difference between the third and fourth terms will always be greater than the difference between the second and third terms by 2. It follows that the difference between the third and fourth terms will always be greater than the difference between the first and second terms by 4. Accordingly, $(N_{50} - N_{49}) - (N_{48} - N_{47}) = 4$. If you failed to see this pattern, you could have used some "test" numbers to discover it:

$$N_4 - N_3 - N_2 - N_1 = (8 - 30) - [0 - (-1)] = 4$$
$$N_5 - N_4 - N_3 - N_2 = (15 - 8) - (3 - 0) = 4$$
$$N_6 - N_5 - N_4 - N_3 = (24 - 15) - (8 - 3) = 4$$

Comparisons

The test-makers might also ask you to compare two sets of numbers. Some pattern among the numbers might provide a shortcut to determining their sum.

QUESTION What is the difference between the sum of all positive even integers less than 102 and the sum of all positive odd integers less than 102?

(A) 0

(B) 1

(C) 50

(D) 51

(E) 101

ANALYSIS The corrrect answer is **(D)**. To see the pattern, compare the initial terms of each sequence:

even integers: {2,4,6, . . . 100}
odd integers: {1,3,5, . . . 99, 101}

Notice that, for each successive term, the odd integer is *one less* than the corresponding even integer. There are a total of 50 corresponding integers, so the difference between the sums of all these corresponding integers is 50. But the odd-integer sequence includes one additional integer: 101. So the difference is (–50 + 101), or 51.

TIME SAVER

Whenever you're about to tally up a long string of numbers, stop! Look for a pattern to shortcut the process. Your knack at recognizing these patterns is just what the test-makers are trying to gauge!

Probability

A GMAT question might ask for the number of possible combinations in a set or the probability of selecting any one term or combination of terms from a set. By definition, the probability of an event occurring ranges from 0 to 1.

QUESTION Inside a hat are four tickets: *a*, *b*, *c*, and *d*. If two of the tickets are drawn randomly from the hat, what is the probability that tickets *b* and *c* have been drawn?

(A) $\frac{1}{9}$

(B) $\frac{1}{8}$

(C) $\frac{1}{6}$

(D) $\frac{1}{4}$

(E) $\frac{1}{3}$

ANALYSIS The correct answer is **(C)**. You can approach questions such as this one intuitively, without resorting to formal mathematics. Ask yourself: How many possible combinations of two tickets are there? Tally up the possibilities methodically, working from left to right alphabetically:

Combinations with *a*: $\{ab\}$ $\{ac\}$ $\{ad\}$
Combinations with *b* (not already accounted for): $\{bc\}$ $\{bd\}$
Combinations with *c* (not already accounted for): $\{cd\}$
Combinations with *d* have all been accounted for

As you can see, there are six distinct two-ticket combinations. Accordingly, the probability of selecting any one combination is 1 in 6, or $\frac{1}{6}$.

Workshop

In this hour's Workshop, you'll tackle a 10-question GMAT-style quiz, designed for you to review and apply the concepts and question types you learned about this hour.

ONLINE Additional Quantitative questions are available online, at the authors' Web site: *http://www.west.net/~stewart/gmat*

Quiz

(Answers and explanations begin on page 108.)

DIRECTIONS: Attempt the following 10 GMAT-style questions. Try to limit your time to 15 minutes. For each question, you'll see one or two hints to help you if you're having trouble.

1. On the real number line, if the distance between x and y is 16.5, which of the following could be the values of x and y?

   (A) −11.5 and 5.5
   (B) 8.25 and −8.75
   (C) 14.5 and 30.5
   (D) −11 and 5.5
   (E) −16.5 and 16.5

(Hint: Visualize the real number line and think absolute value.)

2. If n is the first of two consecutive odd integers, and if the difference of their squares is 120, which of the following equations can be used to find their values?
   (A) $(n + 1)^2 - n^2 = 120$
   (B) $n^2 - (n + 2)^2 = 120$
   (C) $[(n + 2) - n]^2 = 120$
   (D) $(n + 2)^2 - n^2 = 120$
   (E) $n^2 - (n + 1)^2 = 120$

   (Hint: The difference between n and n + 2 must be positive.)

3. $\dfrac{\frac{3a^2c^4}{4b^2}}{6ac^2} =$
   (A) $\dfrac{ac^2}{8b^2}$
   (B) $\dfrac{ac^2}{4b^2}$
   (C) $\dfrac{4b^2}{ac^2}$
   (D) $\dfrac{8b^2}{ac^2}$
   (E) $\dfrac{ac^2}{6b^2}$

   (Hint: You can divide by multiplying instead.)

   (Hint: Look for common factors.)

4. What is the difference between the sum of the integers 15 through 33, inclusive, and the sum of the integers 11 through 31, inclusive?
   (A) 11
   (B) 15
   (C) 26
   (D) 32
   (E) 41

   (Hint: When comparing sets, sometimes you can cancel common terms.)

5. A sock drawer contains five pairs of socks: two black, two blue, and one white pair. If two pairs are randomly selected from the drawer, what is the probability that the white pair and a black pair have been selected?
   (A) $\frac{1}{3}$
   (B) $\frac{1}{4}$
   (C) $\frac{1}{5}$
   (D) $\frac{1}{6}$
   (E) $\frac{1}{8}$

   (Hint: Count each pair of the same color as a distinct term in the set.)

6. $42\sqrt{40x^3y^6} \div 3\sqrt{5xy^2} =$
   (A) $14y\sqrt{3xy}$
   (B) $12xy\sqrt{3xy}$
   (C) $16x^2y^2$
   (D) $28xy^2\sqrt{2}$
   (E) $36xy^2\sqrt{3xy}$

   (Hint: Look for squares that you can remove from inside the radical.)

5

7. If x is the sum of all prime factors of 38, and if y is the sum of all prime factors of 84, then $x - y =$

   (A) 5
   (B) 9
   (C) 13
   (D) 17
   (E) 18

   (Hint: On the GMAT, it helps to know your prime numbers like the back of your hand.)

Questions 8–10 are Data Sufficiency questions.

8. If x, y, and z are non-negative integers, is $5(x + y) + z$ divisible by 5?

   (1) $(x + y)$ is a multiple of 5.
   (2) z is divisible by 5.

   (Hint: Any multiple of 5 is divisible by 5.)

9. Is $xyz > 0$?

   (1) $\frac{xy}{z} > 0$
   (2) $xy^2z > 0$

   (Hint: The product of two negative numbers is always positive.)

10. If $xy \neq 0$, does $x = y$?

   (1) $|x| = |y|$
   (2) $y^3 = x^2$

   (Hint: Consider all the possibilities for x and y.)

Answers and Explanations

1. **(D)** Distance on the number line is always positive, so add 11 to 5.5. The difference between –11 and 5.5 is 16.5.

2. **(D)** The other integer is $n + 2$. Since the difference between n and $(n + 2)$ is positive, the term $(n + 2)$ must appear first in the equation.

3. **(A)** You can simplify by multiplying the numerator fraction by the reciprocal of the denominator:

$$\frac{3a^2c^4}{4b^2} \cdot \frac{1}{6ac^2}$$

Factor out 3, a, and c^2 from both the numerator and the denominator:

$$\frac{ac^2}{4b^2} \cdot \frac{1}{2} = \frac{ac^2}{8b^2}$$

4. **(B)** You need not add all the terms of each sequence. Instead, notice that the two sequences have in common integers 15 through 31, inclusive. Thus, those terms cancel out, leaving $32 + 33 = 65$ in the first sequence and $11 + 12 + 13 + 14 = 50$ in the second sequence. The difference is 15.

5. **(C)** There are ten possible two-pair combinations. Label the pairs Black A, Black B, Blue A, Blue B, and White. Two of these ten combinations (or 1 in 5) include a black pair and the white pair:

   Black A, Black B
   Black A, Blue A
   Black A, Blue B
   Black A, White
   Black B, Blue A
   Black B, Blue B
   Black B, White
   Blue A, Blue B
   Blue A, White
   Blue B, White

6. **(D)**

$$\frac{42\sqrt{40x^3y^6}}{3\sqrt{5xy^2}} = \frac{42}{3}\sqrt{\frac{40x^3y^6}{5xy^2}}$$
$$= 14\sqrt{8x^2y^4} = 28xy^2\sqrt{2}$$

7. **(B)** The prime factors of 38 include: {2, 19}. The sum of these numbers is 21. The prime factors of 84 include: {2, 3, 7}. The sum of these numbers is 12. 21 – 12 = 9. Thus, $x - y = 9$.

8. **(B)** By definition, $5(x + y)$ is divisible by 5 (assuming x and y do not both equal 0); but you also need to know whether z is divisible by 5. Statement (1) provides no additional information. However, statement (2) alone is sufficient to answer the question. A quantity that is divisible by 5, $5(x + y)$, added to another quantity, z, that is also divisible by 5 results in a sum that is divisible by 5. (If x and y both equal 0, then $5(x + y) + z = z$.)

9. **(A)** Considering statement (1) alone, either x, y, and z are all positive, or any two of them are negative. In either case, $xyz > 0$. However, statement (2) alone is insufficient to answer the question. Given that $xy^2z > 0$, x and z must both be either negative or positive, but y can be either negative or positive. Accordingly, xyz could be either negative or positive, depending on y's value.

10. **(C)** Statement (1) alone is insufficient to answer the question because x and y could each be either positive or negative. Statement (2) alone is insuffucient; x and y could both equal 1, or x could equal 8 while y equals 4. (Other value pairs are possible as well.) Statements (1) and (2) together establish that x and y must both equal 1.

Hour 6

Teach Yourself Basic Algebra

This hour you'll continue to prepare for the Quantitative section by forging ahead to algebra. In this hour you will learn:

- How to solve a linear equation with one variable
- How to solve a system of two equations with two variables
- How to factor quadratic expressions and to find the roots of quadratic equations
- How to recognize unsolvable equations when you see them
- How to handle algebraic inequalities on the GMAT

Linear Equations with One Variable

Algebraic expressions are usually used to form equations, which set two expressions equal to each other. Most equations you'll see on the GMAT are *linear* equations, in which the variables don't come with exponents. To solve any linear equation containing one variable, your goal is always the same: isolate the unknown (variable) on one side of the equation. To accomplish this, you may need to perform one or more of the following operations on both sides, depending on the equation:

1. Add or subtract the same term from both sides
2. Multiply or divide the same term from both sides
3. Clear fractions by cross-multiplication
4. Clear radicals by raising both sides to the same power (exponent)

Performing any of these operations on *both* sides does not change the equality; it merely restates the equation in a different form.

TIP

> If you don't remember anything else this hour, remember this key to solving any equation: Whatever operation you perform on one side of an equation you must also perform on the other side; otherwise, the two sides won't be equal!

You're no doubt familiar with the first two operations listed above, so let's take a look at each of the last two operations.

Where the original equation equates two fractions, use cross-multiplication to eliminate the fractions. Multiply the numerator from one side of the equation by the denominator from the other side. Set the product equal to the product of the other numerator and denominator. (In effect, cross-multiplication is a shortcut method of multiplying both sides of the equation by both denominators.)

QUESTION If $\frac{7a}{8} = \frac{a+1}{3}$, then $a =$

(A) $\frac{8}{13}$

(B) $\frac{7}{8}$

(C) 2

(D) $\frac{7}{3}$

(E) 15

ANALYSIS The correct answer is **(A)**. First, cross-multiply as we've described:

$$(3)(7a) = (8)(a + 1)$$

Next, combine terms (distribute 8 to both a and 1):

$$21a = 8a + 8$$

Next, isolate a-terms on one side by subtracting $8a$ from both sides; then combine the a-terms:

$$21a - 8a = 8a + 8 - 8a$$
$$13a = 8$$

Finally, isolate a by dividing both sides by its coefficient 13:

$$\frac{13a}{13} = \frac{8}{13}$$
$$a = \frac{8}{13}$$

Where the variable is under a square-root radical sign, remove the radical sign by squaring both sides of the equation. (Use a similar technique for cube roots and other roots.)

QUESTION If $3\sqrt{2x} = 2$, then $x =$

(A) $\frac{1}{18}$

(B) $\frac{2}{9}$

(C) $\frac{1}{3}$

(D) $\frac{5}{4}$

(E) 3

ANALYSIS The correct answer is **(B)**. First, clear the radical sign by squaring all terms:

$$(3)^2\left(\sqrt{2x}\right)^2 = 2^2$$
$$(9)(2x) = 4$$
$$18x = 4$$

Next, isolate x by dividing both sides by 18:

$$x = \frac{4}{18}, \text{ or } \frac{2}{9}$$

CAUTION

Look out when you square both sides of an equation! In some instances, doing so will reveal that you're really dealing with a quadratic equation—perhaps with more than one solution. Don't panic; you'll learn all about quadratic equations a bit later this hour.

Linear Equations with Two Variables

What we've covered up to this point is pretty basic stuff. If you haven't quite caught on, you should probably stop here and consult a basic algebra workbook for more practice. On the other hand, if you're with us so far, let's forge ahead and add another variable. Here's a simple example:

$$x + 3 = y + 1$$

Quick . . . what's the value of x? It depends on the value of y, doesn't it? Similarly, the value of y depends on the value of x. Without more information about either x or y, you're stuck; well, not completely. You can express x in terms of y, and you can express y in terms of x:

$$x = y - 2$$
$$y = x + 2$$

Let's look at one more: $4x - 9 = \frac{3}{2}y$

Solve for x in terms of y:

$$4x = \frac{3}{2}y + 9$$
$$x = \frac{3}{8}y + \frac{9}{4}$$

Solve for y in terms of x:

$$\frac{4x - 9}{\frac{3}{2}} = y$$
$$\frac{2}{3}(4x - 9) = y$$
$$\frac{8}{3}x - 6 = y$$

To determine numerical values of x and y, you need a system of two linear equations with the same two variables. Given this system, there are two different methods for finding the values of the two variables:

1. the *substitution* method
2. the *addition-subtraction* method

Next we'll apply each method to determine the values of two variables in a two-equation system.

6

NOTE

You can't solve one equation if it contains two unknowns (variables). You either need to know the value of one of the variables, or you need a second equation.

The Substitution Method

To solve a system of two equations using the substitution method, follow these steps (we'll use x and y here):

1. In *either* equation isolate one variable (x) on one side
2. Substitute the expression that equals x in place of x in the other equation.
3. Solve that equation for y.
4. Now that you know the value of y, plug it into either equation to find the value of x.

QUESTION If $\frac{2}{5}p + q = 3q - 10$, and if $q = 10 - p$, then $\frac{p}{q} =$

(A) $\frac{5}{7}$

(B) $\frac{3}{2}$

(C) $\frac{5}{3}$

(D) $\frac{25}{6}$

(E) $\frac{35}{6}$

ANALYSIS The correct answer is **(A)**. Don't let the fact that the question asks for $\frac{p}{q}$ (rather than simply p or q) throw you. Because you're given two linear equations with two unknowns, you know that you can first solve for p and q, then divide p by q. First thing's first: Combine the q-terms in the first equation:

$$\frac{2}{5}p = 2q - 10$$

Next, substitute $(10 - p)$ for q (from the second equation) in the first equation:

$$\frac{2}{5}p = 2(10 - p) - 10$$

$$\frac{2}{5}p = 20 - 2p - 10$$

$$\frac{2}{5}p = 10 - 2p$$

Move the p-terms to the same side, then isolate p:

$$\frac{2}{5}p + 2p = 10$$
$$\frac{12}{5}p = 10$$
$$p = \left(\frac{5}{12}\right)(10)$$
$$p = \frac{50}{12}, \text{ or } \frac{25}{6}$$

Substitute $\frac{25}{6}$ for p in either equation to find q (we'll use the second equation):

$$q = 10 - \frac{25}{6}$$
$$q = \frac{60}{6} - \frac{25}{6}$$
$$q = \frac{35}{6}$$

The question asks for $\frac{p}{q}$, so do the division:

$$\frac{p}{q} = \frac{\frac{25}{6}}{\frac{35}{6}} = \frac{25}{35}, \text{ or } \frac{5}{7}$$

The Addition-Subtraction Method

Another way to solve for two unknowns in a system of two equations is with the addition–subtraction method. Here are the steps:

1. Make the coefficient of either variable the same in both equations (you can disregard the sign)
2. Make sure the equations list the same variables in the same order
3. Place one equation above the other
4. Add the two equations (work down to a sum for each term), or subtract one equation from the other, to eliminate one variable
5. You can repeat steps 1–3 to solve for the other variable.

QUESTION If $3x + 4y = -8$, and if $x - 2y = \frac{1}{2}$, then $x =$

(A) -12

(B) $-\frac{7}{5}$

(C) $\frac{1}{3}$

(D) $\frac{14}{5}$

(E) 9

ANALYSIS The correct answer is **(B)**. To solve for *x*, you want to eliminate *y*. You can multiply each term in the second equation by 2, then add the equations:

$$\begin{array}{r} 3x + 4y = -8 \\ \underline{2x - 4y = 1} \\ 5x + 0y = -7 \\ x = -\frac{7}{5} \end{array}$$

Since the question asked only for the value of *x*, stop here. If the question had asked for both *x* and *y* (or for *y* only), you could have multiplied both sides of the second equation by 3, then subtracted the second equation from the first:

$$\begin{array}{r} 3x + 4y = -8 \\ \underline{3x - 6y = \frac{3}{2}} \\ 0x + 10y = -9\frac{1}{2} \\ 10y = -\frac{19}{2} \\ y = -\frac{19}{20} \end{array}$$

NOTE

> If a question requires you to find values of both unknowns, you can combine the two methods. For example, after using addition-subtraction to solve for *x* in the last question, you can then substitute $-\frac{7}{5}$, the value of *x*, into either equation to find *y*.

Factorable Quadratic Equations

Up to this point in our quest for the value of x, we've been avoiding those pesky exponents. But on the GMAT, you'll be asked to solve not only linear equations but also quadratic equations, which include a "squared" variable, such as x^2. An equation is quadratic if you can express it in this general form:

$$ax^2 + bx + c = 0$$

Keep in mind that in this general form:

x is the variable

a, b, and c are constants (numbers)

$a \neq 0$

b can equal 0

c can equal 0

Let's look at four examples of a quadratic equation. Notice that the b-term and c-term are not essential; in other words, either b or c (or both) can equal zero:

Quadratic equation	*Same equation, but in the form: $ax^2 + bx + c = 0$*
$2w^2 = 16$	$2w^2 - 16 = 0$ (no b-term)
$x^2 = 3x$	$x^2 - 3x = 0$ (no c-term)
$3y = 4 - y^2$	$y^2 + 3y - 4 = 0$
$7z = 2z^2 - 15$	$2z^2 - 7z - 15 = 0$

Every quadratic equation has exactly two solutions, called roots. On the GMAT, all quadratic equations can be solved by *factoring*.

6

To solve any factorable quadratic equation, follow these three steps:

1. Put the equation into the standard form: $ax^2 + bx + c = 0$.
2. Factor the terms on the left side of the equation into two linear expressions (with no exponents).
3. Set each linear expression (root) equal to zero and solve for the variable in each one.

Some quadratic expressions are easier to factor than others. If either of the two constants b or c is zero, the expression will be easier to factor. Otherwise, factoring is a bit trickier.

Let's walk through the last two of the four equations from the previous page to see how you factor and solve them.

Example: $3y = 4 - y^2$

First, put the equation into quadratic form:

$y^2 + 3y - 4 = 0$

There are no factors common to all three terms. So you need to factor the quadratic expression into two binomials, using the FOIL (First-Outer-Inner-Last) method. Under the FOIL method, the sum of the following four terms is equivalent to the original (non-factored) quadratic expression:

(F) the product of the first terms of the two binomials

(O) the product of the outer terms of the two binomials

(I) the product of the inner terms of the two binomials

(L) the product of the last (second) terms of the two binomials

Note the following relationships:

(F) is the first term (ax^2) of the quadratic expression

(O + I) is the second term (bx) of the quadratic expression

(L) is the third term (c) of the quadratic expression

To apply the FOIL method to the equation, first set up the following shell:

$(y \quad)(y \quad) = 0$

To determine the missing values of the two second terms, find two numbers the product of which is c (in this case, –4) and the sum of which is b (in this case, 3). Those two numbers are 4 and –1:

$(y + 4)(y - 1) = 0$

Now set each binomial factor equal to zero, and solve for y:

$y + 4 = 0, y - 1 = 0$

$y = -4, 1$

To check your work, reverse the process, using the FOIL method to multiply the two binomials together:

y^2 (first) $- y$ (outer) $- 4y$ (inner) $- 4$ (last) $= 0$

$y^2 + 3y - 4 = 0$

Example: $7z = 2z^2 - 15$

First, put the equation into quadratic form:

$$2z^2 - 7z - 15 = 0$$

Notice that z^2 has a coefficient of 2. This complicates the process of factoring into two binomials. A bit of trial and error may be required to determine all coefficients in both binomials. Set up two binomial shells:

$$(2z \quad)(z \quad) = 0$$

One of the two missing constants must be negative, since their product (the "L" term under the FOIL method) is –15. The possible integral pairs for these constants are:

(1,–15) (–1,15) (3,–5) (–3,5)

Substituting each value pair for the two missing terms in the shell equation reveals that 3 and –5 are the missing constants (remember to take into account that the first *x*-term includes a coefficient of 2):

$$(2z + 3)(z - 5) = 0$$

You can check your work by reversing the process:

$$2z^2 - 10z + 3z - 15 = 0$$
$$2z^2 - 7z - 15 = 0$$

Now, solve for z:

$$(2z^2 + 3)(z - 5) = 0$$
$$2z + 3 = 0, z - 5 = 0$$
$$z = -\frac{3}{2}, 5$$

TIP

When dealing with a quadratic equation, your first step is usually to put it into the general form $ax^2 + bx + c = 0$. But keep in mind: The only essential term is ax^2.

6

Non-Linear Equations with Two Variables

In the "real" math world, solving non-linear equations with two or more variables can be very complicated, even for bona-fide, card-carrying mathematicians. But on the GMAT, all you need to remember are these three general forms:

Sum of two variables, squared: $(x + y)^2 = x^2 + 2xy + y^2$

Difference of two variables, squared: $(x - y)^2 = x^2 - 2xy + y^2$

Difference of two squares: $x^2 - y^2 = (x + y)(x - y)$

Let's verify these equations using the FOIL method:

$(x + y)^2$	$(x - y)^2$	$(x + y)(x - y)$
$= (x + y)(x + y)$	$= (x - y)(x - y)$	$= x^2 + xy - xy - y^2$
$= x^2 + xy + xy + y^2$	$= x^2 - xy - xy + y^2$	$= x^2 - y^2$
$= x^2 + 2xy + y^2$	$= x^2 - 2xy + y^2$	

QUESTION If $x^2 - y^2 = 100$, and if $x + y = 2$, then $x - y =$

(A) -2

(B) 10

(C) 20

(D) 50

(E) 200

ANALYSIS The correct answer is **(D)**. If you're on the lookout for the difference of two squares, you can handle this question with no sweat. Use the third equation you just learned:

$$x^2 - y^2 = (x + y)(x - y)$$
$$100 = (x + y)(x - y)$$
$$100 = 2(x - y)$$
$$50 = x - y$$

TIP

For the GMAT, memorize the three special equations listed above. When you see one form on the exam, it's a sure bet that your task is to convert it to its other form.

Equations that Can't be Solved

Never assume that one equation with one variable is solvable. Similarly, never assume that a system of two equations with two variables is solvable. The test-makers love to use the Data Sufficiency format to find out if you know an unsolvable equation when you see one. You need to be on the lookout for three different types:

1. Identities
2. Quadratic equations in disguise
3. Equivalent equations

Identities

Be on the lookout for equations that you can reduce to $0 = 0$. You cannot solve any such equation.

QUESTION If $3x - 3 - 4x = x - 7 - 2x + 4$, what is the value of x?

(1) $x > -1$

(2) $x < 1$

ANALYSIS The correct answer is **(E)**. All terms on both sides cancel out:

$$\begin{aligned} 3x - 3 - 4x &= x - 7 - 2x + 4 \\ -x - 3 &= -x - 3 \\ 0 &= 0 \end{aligned}$$

Thus, even considering both statements together, x could equal any real number between -1 and 1 (not just the integer 0).

Quadratic Equations in Disguise

Some equations that appear linear (variables include no exponents) may actually be quadratic. For the GMAT, here are the two situations you need to be on the lookout for:

1. The same variable inside a radical also appears outside:

$$\begin{aligned} \sqrt{x} &= 5x \\ \left(\sqrt{x}\right)^2 &= (5x)^2 \\ x &= 25x^2 \\ 25x^2 - x &= 0 \end{aligned}$$

2. The same variable that appears in the denominator of a fraction also appears elsewhere in the equation:

$$\begin{aligned} \frac{2}{x} &= 3 - x \\ 2 &= x(3 - x) \\ 2 &= 3x - x^2 \\ x^2 - 3x + 2 &= 0 \end{aligned}$$

You can see that in both scenarios you're dealing with a quadratic (non-linear) equation!

6

QUESTION What is the value of x?

(1) $6x = \sqrt{3x}$

(2) $x > 0$

ANALYSIS The correct answer is **(C)**. An unwary test-taker might assume that the equation in statement (1) is linear—because x is not squared. Not so! Clear the radical by squaring both sides of the equation, then isolate the x-terms on one side of the equation, and you'll see that the equation is quite quadratic indeed:

$$36x^2 = 3x$$

$$36x^2 - 3x = 0$$

To ferret out the two roots, factor out x, then solve for each root:

$$x(36x - 3) = 0$$

$$x = 0, \ 36x - 3 = 0$$

$$x = 0, \ \frac{1}{12}$$

Because there is more than one possible value for x, statement (1) alone is insufficient to answer the question. Statement (2) alone is obviously insufficient. But the two together eliminate the root value 0, leaving $\frac{1}{12}$ as the only possible value for x.

Equivalent Equations

In some cases, what appears to be a system of two equations with two variables is actually one equation expressed in two different ways.

QUESTION Does $a = b$?

(1) $a + b = 30$

(2) $2b = 60 - 2a$

ANALYSIS The correct answer is **(E)**. An unwary test-taker might assume that the values of both a and b can be determined with both equations together, because they appear at first glance to provide a system of two linear equations with two unknowns. Not so! You can easily manipulate the second equation so that it is identical to the first:

$$2b = 60 - 2a$$
$$2b = 2(30 - a)$$
$$b = 30 - a$$
$$a + b = 30$$

So you're really dealing with one equation, even considering both statements together. You can't solve one equation in two unknowns, so the correct answer must be (E).

TIME SAVER

When you encounter any Data Sufficiency question that calls for solving one or more equations, stop in your tracks before taking pencil to paper. Size up the equation to see whether it's one of the three unsolvable animals you learned about here. If so, then unless you're given more information, the correct answer must be (E).

Solving Algebraic Inequalities

You can solve algebraic inequalities in the same manner as equations. Isolate the variable on one side of the equation, factoring and canceling wherever possible. However, one important rule distinguishes inequalities from equations: Whenever you multiply or divide by a negative number, you must reverse the inequality symbol. Simply put: If $a > b$, then $-a < -b$. Here's an example:

$12 - 4x < 8$	original inequality
$-4x < -4$	12 subtracted from each side; inequality unchanged
$x > 1$	both sides divided by –4; inequality reversed

Here's a sample question in the Data Sufficiency format.

6

QUESTION If $ab \neq 0$, is $\frac{c}{a} > \frac{c}{b}$?

(1) $c \neq 0$

(2) $a > b$

ANALYSIS The correct answer is **(E)**. Statement (1) alone is obviously insufficient to answer the question, since it provides no information about *a* or *b*. Most test-takers would conclude incorrectly that Statement (2) alone is sufficient to answer the question. (About half of these test-takers would assert that the answer to the question is *no*, while the other half would claim that the answer to the question is *yes*.) Both groups would be wrong, of course. If $c < 0$, then dividing c by unequal quantities does not change the inequality. But if $c > 0$, dividing c by unequal quantities reverses the inequality. If you're the least bit unsure about this, it's a good idea to plug in a few simple numbers. For example, let $a = 2$ and $b = 1$. If $c = 1$ (a positive value), then $\frac{c}{a} < \frac{c}{b}$ ($\frac{1}{2} < \frac{1}{1}$). But if $c = -1$ (a negative number), then $\frac{c}{a} > \frac{c}{b}$ ($-\frac{1}{2} > -\frac{1}{1}$).

TIP

When handling inequality problems, its always a good idea to "plug in" some simple numbers, even if you think you've got the answer right. Also, as with any problem involving a range of possible values, be sure to consider all possibilities that aren't explicitly ruled out by the question: negative numbers, positive numbers, fractions between −1 and 0, fractions between 0 and 1, and the special numbers 0 and 1.

Workshop

In this hour's Workshop, you'll tackle a 10-question GMAT-style quiz, designed for you to review and apply the concepts and question types you learned about this hour.

ONLINE

Additional Quantitative questions are available online, at the authors' Web site: *http://www.west.net/~stewart/gmat*

Quiz

(Answers and explanations begin on page 128.)

DIRECTIONS: Attempt the following 10 GMAT-style questions. Try to limit your time to 15 minutes. For each question, you'll see one or two hints to help you if you're having trouble.

1. If $\frac{2y}{9} = \frac{y-1}{3}$, then $y =$

   (A) $\frac{1}{3}$

   (B) $\frac{4}{9}$

   (C) $\frac{9}{15}$

   (D) $\frac{9}{4}$

   (E) 3

   (Hint: You can cross-multiply to solve for y quickly.)

2. If $ax - b = cx + d$, then in terms of a, b, c, and d, $x =$

   (A) $-\frac{bd}{ac}$
   (B) $a - c + b + d$
   (C) $\frac{a - c}{b + d}$
   (D) $\frac{b + d}{a - c}$
   (E) $\frac{a + d}{b - c}$

   (Hint: Isolate the x-terms on one side of the equation, then factor.)

3. If $3x + 2y = 5a + b$, and $4x - 3y = a + 7b$, then $x =$

   (A) $a + b$
   (B) $a - b$
   (C) $2a + b$
   (D) $4a - 6b$
   (E) $17a + 17b$

   (Hint: You can "line up" corresponding terms, then use addition-subtraction.)

4. If $x + y = 8$, $x + z = 7$, and $y + z = 6$, what is the value of x?

   (A) 3
   (B) 3.5
   (C) 4
   (D) 4.5
   (E) 5

   (Hint: Given three equations in three variables, you can solve for any variable.)

5. Which of the following is a factor of $x^2 - x - 20$?

   (A) $x - 10$
   (B) $x - 2$
   (C) $x - 4$
   (D) $x + 4$
   (E) $x + 5$

   (Hint: Use the FOIL method to factor the expression into two binomials.)

6. If $\frac{9b^3 - 15b^2 - 6b}{18b^2 + 6b} = 13b - 17$, then $b =$

   (A) $-\frac{14}{5}$
   (B) $\frac{5}{16}$
   (C) $\frac{32}{25}$
   (D) 3
   (E) $\frac{7}{2}$

   (Hint: Start by factoring out common terms in each expression.)

Questions 7–10 are Data Sufficiency questions.

7. If $|a| > |b|$ and if a and b are both integers, is $\sqrt{a^2 - b^2}$ an integer?

   (1) $a^2 + 1 = \frac{a^2}{b^2}$

   (2) $a - b$ is an odd integer.

   (Hint: Manipulate statement (1) to reveal the quantity asked for in the question.)

8. Is $x > y$?

   (1) $5x - 4y = 3$

   (2) $4y - 5x = 3$

   (Hint: Notice that in both statements the left-hand expression equals 3.)

9. What is the value of $p^2 - q^2$?

   (1) $p + q = -4$

   (2) $p - q = 4$

   (Hint: The algebraic expression given in the question should look familiar.)

10. If x is a non-zero integer, what is the value of x?

    (1) $-4x - 7 > x - 14$

    (2) $5x + 3 > -2(x + 1)$

    (Hint: Ask yourself what range of values for x are possible.)

Answers and Explanations

1. **(E)**

$$\begin{aligned} 9(y - 1) &= 2y(3) \\ 9y - 9 &= 6y \\ 3y &= 9 \\ y &= 3 \end{aligned}$$

2. **(D)** Isolate the x-terms, factor out x, then isolate x:

$$\begin{aligned} ax - b &= cx + d \\ ax - cx &= b + d \\ x(a - c) &= b + d \\ x &= \frac{b + d}{a - c} \end{aligned}$$

3. **(A)** Multiply the first equation by 3, the second by 2, then add:

$$\begin{aligned} 9x + 6y &= 15a + 3b \\ 8x - 6y &= 2a + 14b \\ \hline 17x + 0y &= 17a + 17b \\ x &= a + b \end{aligned}$$

4. **(D)** This problem involves a system of three equations with three variables. The following solution employs both the substitution and addition-subtraction methods.

   Express x in terms of y: $x = 8 - y$. Substitute this expression for x in the second equation: $(8 - y) + z = 7$ or $-y + z = -1$. Add this equation to the third equation in the system.

$$\begin{aligned} -y + z &= -1 \\ y + z &= 6 \\ \hline 2z &= 5 \\ z &= 2.5 \end{aligned}$$

   Substitute z's value for z in the second equation to find the value of x:

$$\begin{aligned} x + 2.5 &= 7 \\ x &= 4.5 \end{aligned}$$

5. **(D)**

$$\begin{aligned} & x^2 - x - 20 \\ &= x^2 - 5x + 4x - 20 \\ &= (x - 5)(x + 4) \end{aligned}$$

6. **(C)** Here are the steps required to solve for b:

$$\begin{aligned} \frac{3b(3b^2 - 5b - 2)}{6b(3b + 1)} &= 13b - 17 \\ \frac{3b(3b + 1)(b - 2)}{6b(3b + 1)} &= 13b - 17 \\ \frac{b - 2}{2} &= 13b - 17 \\ b - 2 &= 26b - 34 \\ 25b &= 32 \\ b &= \frac{32}{25} \end{aligned}$$

7. **(A)** Manipulate the equation in statement (1) to isolate a term that bears a clear relationship to $\sqrt{a^2 - b^2}$:

$$\begin{aligned} a^2 + 1 &= \frac{a^2}{b^2} \\ b^2(a^2 + 1) &= a^2 \\ b^2a^2 + b^2 &= a^2 \\ b^2a^2 &= a^2 - b^2 \\ ab &= \sqrt{a^2 - b^2} \end{aligned}$$

Given that a and b are both integers, ab must be an integer. Accordingly, $\sqrt{a^2 - b^2}$ must be an integer, and statement (1) suffices alone to answer the question. Turning to statement (2), given that $a - b$ is an odd integer, whether $\sqrt{a^2 - b^2}$ is also an odd integer depends on the values of a and b. For example; if $a = 5$ and $b = 4$, then $5 - 4 = 1$ (an odd integer), and $\sqrt{5^2 - 4^2} = \sqrt{9} = 3$ (an integer). However, if $a = 5$ and $b = 2$, then $5 - 2 = 3$ (an odd integer), but $\sqrt{5^2 - 2^2} = \sqrt{21}$ (not an integer). Thus, statement (2) alone is insufficient to answer the question.

8. **(E)** In each equation, the right side is the same—the number 3. Thus, $5x - 4y = 4y - 5x$. Solving for x in terms of y, you'll find that $x = \frac{8}{10}y$. Whether x is greater than y depends on whether x and y are positive or negative numbers.

9. **(C)** Before you evaluate either statement alone, recognize that:

$$p^2 - q^2 = (p + q)(p - q)$$

Although neither statement alone suffices to answer the question (because you're dealing with a quadratic rather than a linear equation, statements (1) and (2) together provide the two binomials, allowing you to answer the question. (To calculate the answer, you would simply multiply: $-4 \cdot 4 = -16$.)

6

10. **(C)** You can solve for x in statement (1):

$$-4x - 7 > x - 14$$
$$-5x - 7 > -14$$
$$-5x > -7$$
$$-x > -\frac{7}{5}$$
$$x < \frac{7}{5}$$

You can solve for x in statement (2):

$$5x + 3 > -2(x + 1)$$
$$5x + 3 > -2x - 2$$
$$7x > -5$$
$$x > -\frac{5}{7}$$

Neither statement (1) nor (2) alone suffices to determine the value of x. However, considering both statements together, $-\frac{5}{7} < x < \frac{7}{5}$. Only two integral x-values—0 and 1—fall within this range. Given that x is a non-zero integer, $x = 1$. Both statements (1) and (2) together suffice to determine the value of x, which is 1.

Hour 7

Teach Yourself Algebra Word Problems

This hour you'll look at the various types of GMAT word problems that involve setting up and solving algebraic equations. In this hour you'll learn to handle all the most common types of word problems including:

- Weighted average problems
- Currency (coin and bill) problems
- Motion problems
- Work problems
- Mixture problems
- Age problems
- Overlapping set problems
- Investment problems

NOTE

On the GMAT, most algebra word problems appear in the Problem Solving format. So we'll use this format for the samples you'll see this hour (although the Workshop includes some algebra problems in the Data Sufficiency format as well.)

Weighted Average Problems

During Hour 4, you examined the concept of simple average (arithmetic mean). Recall the formula for determining the average (A) of a series of terms (numbers), where n equals the number of terms (numbers) in the series:

$$A = \frac{a + b + c + \ldots}{n}$$

Thus, the arithmetic mean of –2, 7, 22, and 19 is 11.5:

$$A = \frac{-2 + 7 + 22 + 19}{4} = \frac{46}{4} = 11.5$$

When some numbers among the terms to be averaged are given greater "weight" than others, however, you have to make some adjustments to the basic formula to find the average. As a simple illustration, suppose that a student receives grades of 80 and 90 on two exams, but the former grade receives three times the weight of the latter exam. The student's weighted-average grade is not 85 but rather some number closer to 80 than 90. One way to approach this problem is to think of the first grade (80) as three scores of 80, which added to the score of 90 and divided by 4 (not 2) results in the weighted average:

$$WA = \frac{80 + 80 + 80 + 90}{4} = \frac{330}{4} = 82.5$$

You can also approach this problem more intuitively (less formally). You're looking for a number between 80 and 90 (a range of 10). The simple average would obviously lie midway between the two. Given that the score of 80 receives three times the weight of the score of 90, the weighted average is three times closer to 80 than to 90, or three-fourths of the way from 90 to 80. Dividing the range into four segments, it is clear that the weighted average is 82.5. Similarly, if 80 received twice the weight of 90, the weighted average is $83\frac{1}{3}$, and if 80 received four times the weight of 90, the weighted average is 82.

QUESTION Mike's average monthly salary for the first four months that he worked was \$3000. What must his average monthly salary be for each of the next eight months, so that his average monthly salary for the year is \$3,500?

(A) \$3600

(B) \$3750

(C) \$3800

(D) \$3850

(E) \$4000

ANALYSIS The correct answer is **(B)**. The \$3000 salary receives a weight of 4, while the unknown salary receives a weight of 8. You can approach this problem in strict algebraic fashion:

$$3500 = \frac{4(3000) + 8x}{12}$$

$$(12)(3500) = 12{,}000 + 8x$$

$$30{,}000 = 8x$$

$$x = 3750$$

Mike's salary for each of the next eight months must be \$3750 for Mike to earn an average of \$3500 a month during the entire 12 months.

You can also approach this problem more intuitively. One-third of the monthly salary payments are "underweighted" (less than the desired \$3500 average) by \$500. Thus, to achieve the desired average with 12 salary payments, you must overweight the remaining two-thirds of the payments (exceeding \$3500) by half that amount—that is, by \$250.

TIME SAVER

> Weighted average is a concept we can all relate to intuitively in our everyday lives. So use your common sense on GMAT problems to quickly rule out answer choices that strike you as too high or low.

Currency (Coin and Bill) Problems

Currency problems are really quasi-weighted-average problems, because each item (bill or coin) in a problem is weighted according to its monetary value. Unlike weighted average problems, however, the "average" value of all the bills or coins is not at issue. In solving currency problems, remember the following:

- You must formulate algebraic expressions involving both *number* of items (bills or coins) and *value* of items.
- You should convert the value of all moneys to a common unit (that is, cents or dollars) before formulating an equation. If converting to cents, for example, you must multiply the number of nickels by 5, dimes by 10, and so forth.

QUESTION Jim has $2.05 in dimes and quarters. If he has four fewer dimes than quarters, how much money does he have in dimes?

(A) 20 cents

(B) 30 cents

(C) 40 cents

(D) 50 cents

(E) 60 cents

ANALYSIS The correct answer is **(B)**. Letting x equal the number of dimes, $x + 4$ represents the number of quarters. The total value of the dimes (in cents) is $10x$, and the total value of the quarters (in cents) is $25(x + 4)$ or $25x + 100$. Given that Jim has $2.05, the following equation emerges:

$$\begin{aligned} 10x + 25x + 100 &= 205 \\ 35x &= 105 \\ x &= 3 \end{aligned}$$

Jim has three dimes, so he has 30 cents in dimes.

TIP

You can also solve most GMAT currency problems by trial-and-error. Plug each value into the problem to see if it works. Let's use trial-and-error for choices (A) and (B):

(A) 20 cents is 2 dimes, so Jim has 6 quarters. 20 cents plus $1.50 add up to $1.70. Wrong answer!

(B) 30 cents is 3 dimes, so Jim has 7 quarters. 30 cents plus $1.75 add up to $2.05. Correct answer!

Motion Problems

Motion problems involve the linear movement of persons or objects over time. Fundamental to all GMAT motion problems is the following simple and familiar formula:

$$\text{distance} = \text{rate} \times \text{time}$$
$$d = r \cdot t$$

CAUTION

Don't confuse *motion* problems with *work* problems. Although both involve rate, work problems do not involve movement over a distance but rather rate of work and results of production.

Nearly every GMAT motion problem falls into one of three categories:

- Two objects moving in opposite directions
- Two objects moving in the same direction
- One object making a round trip

NOTE

A fourth type of motion problem involves perpendicular (right-angle) motion—for example, where one object moves in a northerly direction while another moves in an easterly direction. However, this type is really just as much a geometry as an algebra problem, because you determine the distance between the two objects by applying the Pythagorean Theorem to determine the length of a triangle's hypotenuse. (The topic of triangles is one of the main courses on next hour's geometry menu.)

QUESTION Janice left her home at 11 a.m., traveling along Route 1 at 30 mph. At 1 p.m., her brother, Richard, left home and started after her on the same road at 45 mph. At what time did Richard catch up to Janice?

(A) 2:45 p.m.
(B) 3:00 p.m.
(C) 3:30 p.m.
(D) 4:15 p.m.
(E) 5:00 p.m.

ANALYSIS The correct answer is **(E)**. Notice that the distance that Janice covered is equal to the distance Richard covered—that is, distance is constant. Letting x equal Janice's time, you can express Richard's time as $x - 2$. Substitute these values for time and the values for rate given in the problem into the motion formula for Richard and Janice:

Formula: rate $\times$ time = distance

Janice: $(30)(x) = 30x$

Richard: $(45)(x - 2) = 45x - 90$

Because the distance is constant, you can equate Janice's distance to Richard's, then solve for x:

$$\begin{aligned} 30x &= 45x - 90 \\ 15x &= 90 \\ x &= 6 \end{aligned}$$

Janice had traveled six hours when Richard caught up with her. Because Janice left at 11:00 a.m., Richard caught up with her at 5:00 p.m.

QUESTION How far can Scott drive into the country if he drives out at 40 mph, returns over the same road at 30 mph, and spends eight hours away from home including a one-hour stop for lunch?

(A) 105

(B) 115

(C) 120

(D) 125

(E) 130

ANALYSIS The correct answer is **(C)**. Scott's actual driving time is 7 hours, which you must divide into two parts: his time spent driving into the country and his time spent returning. Letting the first part equal x, the return time is what remains of the seven hours, or $7 - x$. Substitute these expressions into the motion formula for each of the two parts of Scott's journey:

Formula: rate $\times$ time = distance

Going: $(40)(x) = 40x$

Returning: $(30)(7 - x) = 210 - 30x$

Because the journey is round trip, the distance going equals the distance returning. Simply equate the two algebraic expressions, then solve for x:

$$40x = 210 - 30x$$
$$70x = 210$$
$$x = 3$$

Scott traveled 40 mph for 3 hours, so he traveled 120 miles.

TIP

Regardless of which type of motion problem you're dealing with, you should always start with the same task: set up *two* distinct equations patterned after the simple motion formula ($r \cdot t = d$).

Work Problems

Work problems involve one or more "workers" (people or machines) accomplishing a task or job. In work problems, there's an inverse relationship between the number of workers and the time that it takes to complete the job—in other words, the more workers, the quicker the job gets done. A GMAT work problem might specify the rates at which certain workers work alone and ask you to determine the rate at which they work together, or vice versa. Here's the basic formula for solving a work problem:

$$\frac{A}{x} + \frac{A}{y} = 1$$

In this formula:

- x and y represent the time needed for each of two workers, x and y, to complete the job alone
- A represents the time it takes for both x and y to complete the job working in the *aggregate* (together).

So each fraction represents the portion of the job completed by a worker. The sum of the two fractions must be 1, if the job is completed. (If you don't understand this formula, don't worry about it. Just memorize it!)

NOTE

In the real world, teamwork often creates a synergy whereby the team is more efficient than the individuals working alone. But on the GMAT, you can assume that no additional efficiency is gained by two or more workers working together.

QUESTION One printing press can print a daily newspaper in 12 hours, while another press can print it in 18 hours. How long will the job take if both presses work simultaneously?

(A) 7 hours, 12 minutes

(B) 9 hours, 30 minutes

(C) 10 hours, 45 minutes

(D) 15 hours

(E) 30 hours

ANALYSIS The correct answer is **(A)**. Just plug the two numbers 12 and 18 into our work formula, then solve for *A*:

$$\frac{A}{12} + \frac{A}{18} = 1$$

$$\frac{3A}{36} + \frac{2A}{36} = 1$$

$$\frac{5A}{36} = 1$$

$$5A = 36$$

$$A = \frac{36}{5}, \text{ or } 7\frac{1}{5} \text{ hours, or 7 hours, 12 minutes}$$

TIP

Had you needed to guess the answer, you could have easily ruled out answer choices (D) and (E), which both nonsensically suggest that the aggregate time it takes both presses together to produce the newspaper is *longer* than the time it takes either press alone. Remember: In work problems, use your common sense to narrow down answer choices!

Now we're going to throw a "slowball" at you. Be ready for the GMAT work problem in which one worker operates counter-productively to the other. You handle this scenario simply by subtracting one fraction from the other, instead of adding them together.

QUESTION A certain tank holds a maximum of 450 cubic meters of water. If a hose can fill the tank at a rate of 5 cubic meters per minute, but the tank has a hole through which a constant .5 cubic meters of water escapes each minute, how long does it take to fill the tank to its maximum capacity?

(A) 81 minutes

(B) 90 minutes

(C) 100 minutes

(D) 112 minutes

(E) 125 minutes

ANALYSIS The correct answer is **(C)**. In this problem, the hole (which is the is the second "worker") is acting counter-productively, so you must subtract its rate from the hose's rate to determine the aggregate rate of the hose and the hole. The hose alone takes 90 minutes to fill the tank. The hole alone empties a full tank in 900 minutes. Plug these values into our slightly modified formula, then solve for *A*:

$$\frac{A}{90} - \frac{A}{900} = 1$$

$$\frac{10A}{900} - \frac{A}{900} = 1$$

$$\frac{10A - A}{900} = 1$$

$$\frac{9A}{900} = 1$$

$$9A = 900$$

$$A = 100$$

It takes 100 minutes to fill the tank to its maximum capacity.

Mixture Problems

In mixture problems, you combine substances with different characteristics, resulting in a particular mixture or proportion. Here are some typical scenarios:

- *Wet mixtures* involving liquids, gases, or granules, which are measured and mixed by volume or weight, not by number (quantity).
- *Dry mixtures* involving a number of discreet objects, such as coins, cookies, or marbles, that are measured and mixed by number (quantity) as well as by relative weight, size, value, and so on.

Wet mixture problems usually involve percentages, while dry mixture problems involve raw numbers (quantities). But whether the mixture is dry or wet, you should use the same basic approach.

QUESTION How many quarts of pure alcohol must you add to 15 quarts of a solution that is 40% alcohol to strengthen it to a solution that is 50% alcohol?

(A) 2.5

(B) 3.0

(C) 3.25

(D) 3.5

(E) 4.0

ANALYSIS The correct answer is **(B)**. The original amount of alcohol is 40% of 15. Letting x equal the number of quarts of alcohol that you must add to achieve a 50% alcohol solution, $.4(15) + x$ equals the amount of alcohol in the solution after adding more alcohol. You can express this amount as 50% of $(15 + x)$. Thus, you can express the mixture algebraically as follows:

$$\begin{aligned}(.4)(15) + x &= (.5)(15 + x)\\ 6 + x &= 7.5 + .5x\\ .5x &= 1.5\\ x &= 3\end{aligned}$$

You must add three quarts of alcohol to achieve a 50% alcohol solution.

If you have difficulty expressing mixture problems algebraically, use a table such as the following to indicate amounts and percentages, letting x equal the amount or percentage that you're asked to solve for:

	# of quarts	×	*% alcohol*	=	*amount of alcohol*
original	15		40%		6
added	x		100%		x
new	$15 + x$		50%		$.5(15 + x)$

QUESTION How many pounds of nuts selling for 70 cents per pound must you mix with 30 pounds of nuts selling at 90 cents per pound to make a mixture that sells for 85 cents per pound?

(A) 8

(B) 10

(C) 11

(D) 14

(E) 15

ANALYSIS The correct answer is **(B)**. The cost (in cents) of the nuts selling for 70 cents per pound can be expressed as $70x$, letting x equal the number that you're asked to determine. You then add this cost to the cost of the more expensive nuts ($30 \times 90 = 2{,}700$) to obtain the total cost of the mixture, which you can express as $85(x + 30)$. You can state this algebraically and solve for x as follows:

$$\begin{aligned} 70x + 2700 &= 85(x + 30) \\ 70x + 2700 &= 85x + 2550 \\ 150 &= 15x \\ x &= 10 \end{aligned}$$

You must add 10 pounds of 70-cent-per-pound nuts to make a mixture that sells for 85 cents per pound.

As with wet mixture problems, if you have trouble formulating an algebraic equation needed to solve the problem, indicate the quantities and values in a table such as the one shown in the figure below, letting x equal the value that you're asked to determine.

	# of pounds	×	*price per pound*	=	*total value*
less expensive	x		70		$70x$
more expensive	30		90		2,700
mixture	$x + 30$		85		$85(x + 30)$

CAUTION

Mixture problems often involve units of measurement—such as weight, price, and distance. This feature gives the test-makers a great opportunity to trap you by commingling ounces and pounds, cents and dollars, inches and feet, and so forth. Don't fall for this ploy! Once you set up your equation, always convert terms to the same unit of measurement. You'll be glad you did.

Age Problems

Age problems ask you to compare ages of two or more people at different points in time. In solving age problems, you might have to represent a person's age at the present time, several years from now, or several years ago. Any age problem allows you to set up an equation to relate the ages of two or more people, as in the following examples:

- If X is 10 years younger than Y at the present time, you can express the relationship between X's age and Y's age as $X = Y - 10$ (or $X + 10 = Y$).
- Five years ago, if A was twice as old as B, you can express the relationship between their ages as $2(B - 5) = A - 5$, where A and B are the present ages of A and B, respectively.

QUESTION Fred, Geri, and Holly were each born on May 15, but in different years. Fred is twice as old as Geri was 4 years ago, and Holly is five years older than Geri will be one year from now. If the ages of Fred, Geri, and Holly total 78, what is Fred's current age?

(A) 20

(B) 26

(C) 32

(D) 36

(E) 44

ANALYSIS The correct answer is **(C)**. Fred's age can be expressed in terms of Geri's, and Geri's age can be expressed in terms of Holly's:

$$F = 2(G - 4) = 2G - 8$$
$$H = G + 6$$

Given that the total age of F, G, and H is 78, substitute these two expressions for F and G in the equation $F + G + H = 78$, then solve for G:

$$\begin{aligned}(2G - 8) + G + (G + 6) &= 78\\ 4G - 2 &= 78\\ 4G &= 80\\ G &= 20\end{aligned}$$

To find F, substitute 20 for G in the equation $F = 2G - 8$:

$$F = 2(20) - 8$$
$$F = 32$$

Problems Involving Overlapping Sets

Overlapping set problems involve distinct sets that share some number of members. Don't confuse these problems with the statistics problems you examined during Hour 4. GMAT overlapping set problems come in one of two varieties:

1. Single overlap (easier)
2. Double overlap (tougher)

QUESTION Each of the 24 people auditioning for a community-theater production is either an actor, a musician, or both. If 10 of the people auditioning are actors and 19 of the people auditioning are musicians, how many of the people auditioning are musicians but not actors?

(A) 10

(B) 14

(C) 19

(D) 21

(E) 24

ANALYSIS The correct answer is **(B)**. You can approach this relatively simple problem somewhat informally: The number of actors plus the number of musicians equals 29 ($10 + 19 = 29$); however, only 24 people are auditioning; thus, 5 of the 24 are actor-musicians, so 14 of the 19 musicians must not be actors.

Here's a more formal way to approach this problem. It includes three mutually exclusive sets:

1. actors who are not musicians
2. musicians who are not actors
3. actors who are also musicians

The total number of people among these three sets is 24. You can represent this scenario with the following algebraic equation (n = number of actors-musicians), solving for $19 - n$ to respond to the question:

$$\begin{aligned}(10 - n) + n + (19 - n) &= 24\\ 29 - n &= 24\\ n &= 5\\ 19 - n &= 14\end{aligned}$$

7

There are 14 musicians auditioning who are not actors. To keep from getting confused when dealing with problems such as this one, try drawing a Venn diagram in which overlapping circles represent the set of musicians and the set of actors:

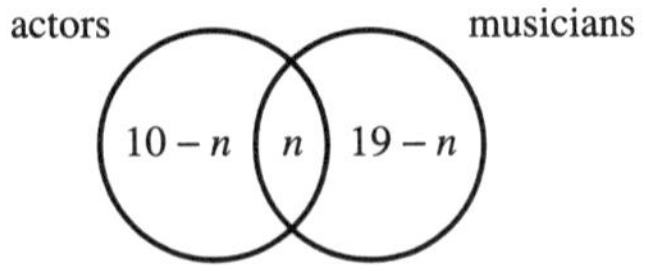

QUESTION The inventory at a certain men's clothing store includes 480 neckties, each of which is either 100% silk or 100% polyester. 40% of the ties are striped, and 130 of the ties are silk. 52 of the silk ties are striped. How many of the ties are polyester but are not striped?

(A) 180

(B) 210

(C) 240

(D) 350

(E) 400

ANALYSIS The correct answer is **(B)**. This double overlap problem involves four distinct sets: striped silk ties, striped polyester ties, non-striped silk ties, and non-striped polyester ties. Set up a table representing the four sets, filling in the information given in the problem as shown in the figure (the value required to answer the question is indicated by the question mark).

	silk	polyester	
striped	52		40%
non-striped		?	60%
	130	350	

Given that 130 ties are silk (see the left column), 350 ties must be polyester (see the right column). Also, given that 40% of the 480 ties (192 ties) are striped (see the top row), 140 of the polyester ties (192 – 52) must be be striped. Accordingly, 350 – 140, or 210, of the ties are polyester and non-striped.

Investment Problems

GMAT investment problems usually involve interest and require more than simply calculating interest earned on a given principal amount at a given rate. They usually call for you to set up and solve an algebraic equation, although sometimes you can solve these problems intuitively.

QUESTION Dr. Kramer plans to invest \$20,000 in an account paying 6% interest annually. How much more must she invest at the same time at 3% so that her total annual income during the first year is 4% of her total initial investment?

(A) \$32,000

(B) \$36,000

(C) \$40,000

(D) \$47,000

(E) \$49,000

ANALYSIS The correct answer is **(C)**. You can solve this problem intuitively—as a weighted average problem. Notice that 4% is exactly *one-third* of the way from 3% to 6%. So to reduce an overall 6% return to an overall 4% return, it makes sense that an additional investment earning 3% should be exactly twice the amount earning 6%, which is given as \$20,000 (in other words, the ratio of the amount earning 3% to the amount earning 6% must be 2:1). Lacking this intuition, you can solve the problem algebraically. Letting x equal the amount invested at 3%, you can express Dr. Kramer's total investment as $20{,}000 + x$. The interest on \$20,000 plus the interest on the additional investment equals the total interest from both investments. You can state this algebraically as follows:

$$.06(20{,}000) + .03x = .04(20{,}000 + x)$$

Multiply all terms by 100 to eliminate decimals, then solve for x:

$$\begin{aligned} 6(20{,}000) + 3x &= 4(20{,}000 + x) \\ 120{,}000 + 3x &= 80{,}000 + 4x \\ 40{,}000 &= x \end{aligned}$$

She must invest \$40,000 at 3% for her total annual income to be 4% of her total investment (\$60,000).

TIP

In solving GMAT investment problems, it's best to eliminate percentage signs (or multiply by 100 to eliminate decimals).

Workshop

In this hour's Workshop, you'll tackle a 10-question GMAT-style quiz, designed for you to review and apply the concepts and question types you learned about this hour.

ONLINE

Additional Quantitative questions are available online, at the authors' Web site: *http://www.west.net/~stewart/gmat*

Quiz

(Answers and explanations begin on page 148.)

DIRECTIONS: Attempt the following 10 GMAT-style questions. Try to limit your time to 15 minutes. For each question, you'll see one or two hints to help you if you're having trouble.

1. Sue and Nancy have $4.00 in quarters, dimes, and nickels between them. If they have 35 coins, and if the number of quarters is half the number of nickels, how many quarters do they have?

   (A) 5
   (B) 10
   (C) 20
   (D) 3
   (E) 6

   (Hint: Express all money values in cents, then add them together)

2. Gina leaves home on her bicycle, riding at a rate of 12 mph. Twenty minutes after she leaves, Jim leaves home by automobile along the same route at 36 mph. How many miles must Jim drive before he catches up with Gina?

   (A) 6
   (B) 7.5
   (C) 9
   (D) 10.5
   (E) 12

   (Hint: Use the motion formula ($r \times t = d$) to set up two motion equations, one for Gina and one for Jim)

3. Alfredo leaves his lodge at 11 a.m. and drives to the top of a mountain at an average rate of 24 miles per hour, arriving at the summit at 11:15 a.m. If he spends 50 minutes at the summit, then skies back to the lodge, arriving at 12:30 p.m., what is the average speed at which Alfredo skied?

   (A) 10.2 mph
   (B) 12.8 mph
   (C) 14.4 mph
   (D) 15.0 mph
   (E) 15.4 mph

   (Hint: First determine the distance from the lodge to the summit.)

4. Barbara has invested $2,400 in the National Bank at a 5% annual rate of return. How much additional money must she invest at an 8% annual rate of return so that the total annual income will be equal to 6% of her entire initial investment?

   (A) $1,000
   (B) $1,200
   (C) $2,400
   (D) $3,000
   (E) $3,600

   (Hint: Let x equal the dollars that Barbara invests at 8%.)

5. How many ounces of soy sauce must be added to an 18-ounce mixture of peanut sauce and soy sauce consisting of 32% peanut sauce in order to create a mixture that is 12% peanut sauce?

   (A) 21
   (B) $24\frac{3}{4}$
   (C) $26\frac{2}{3}$
   (D) 30
   (E) $38\frac{2}{5}$

   (Hint: Equate the original amount of peanut sauce with the amount of peanut sauce after adding more soy sauce.)

Questions 6–10 are Data Sufficiency questions.

6. How long does it take Sam to eat an entire large pizza?

   (1) Thomas can eat the same large pizza in 8 minutes.
   (2) Sam and Thomas together can eat the same large pizza in 6½ minutes.

   (Hint: Ask yourself what values you need to solve a work equation.)

7. During the first three weeks of his 10-week diet program, Bob lost an average of five pounds per week. During the final seven weeks of the program, he lost an average of two pounds per week. How much weight had Bob lost after the seventh week of the diet program?

   (1) Bob lost an average of one pound per week during the fifth and sixth weeks of the program.
   (2) Bob lost the same amount of weight during the first three weeks of the program as during the last three weeks of the program.

   (Hint: From the information in the question stem, you can calculate how many pounds Bob lost altogether during his 10-week program.)

8. If 14 sculptors at a craft fair are also painters, how many painters are at the fair?

    (1) The number of painters and the number of sculptors add up to 44.

    (2) 7 of the sculptors are not painters.

    (Hint: Use a Venn diagram to help visualize each of three sets.)

9. Among all sales staff at Listco Corporation, college graduates and those without college degrees are equally represented. Each sales staff member is either a level 1 or level 2 employee. How many sales staff members without college degrees are level 2 employees?

    (1) Level 1 college graduates account for 15% of Listco's sales staff.

    (2) Listco employs 72 level 1 employees, 30 of whom are college graduates.

    (Hint: Use a 4-quadrant table to help organize the information.)

10. If Rachel's age is twice Steven's age, and if Rachel is exactly 11 years older than Timothy, is Steven older than Timothy?

    (1) Timothy's age subtracted from Rachel's age is greater than Steven's age.

    (2) One year from now Rachel's age will be twice Timothy's age.

    (Hint: Some of the information in the question stem is unnecessary and might be included to throw you off track.)

Answers and Explanations

1. **(B)** Let x = number of quarters, and express the other numbers in terms of x:

$$\begin{aligned} 2x &= \text{number of nickels} \\ 35 - 3x &= \text{number of dimes} \end{aligned}$$

Express all money values in cents; the total is 400:

$$\begin{aligned} 25(x) + 5(2x) + 10(35 - 3x) &= 400 \\ 25x + 10x + 350 - 30x &= 400 \\ 5x &= 50 \\ x &= 10 \end{aligned}$$

2. **(A)** Set up two motion equations, one for Gina and one for Jim (change 20 minutes to $\frac{1}{3}$ hour):

    Formula: Rate × Time = Distance

    Gina: $12 \times x$

    Jim: $36 \times (x - \frac{1}{3})$

Distance is constant, so equate Gina's distance with Jim's distance, then solve for x:

$$\begin{aligned} 12x &= 36\left(x - \frac{1}{3}\right) \\ 12x &= 36x - 12 \\ 12 &= 24x \\ x &= \frac{1}{2} \end{aligned}$$

Gina rode for $\frac{1}{2}$ hour at 12 mph, thereby traveling 6 miles. Accordingly, Jim also had traveled 6 miles when he caught up with her.

3. **(C)** It took Alfredo 25 minutes to ski back to the lodge. Set up two motion equations, one for Alfredo's drive up, the other for his skiing down. (The 15-minute drive = $\frac{1}{4}$ hour, and the 25-minute return trip $\frac{5}{12}$ hour):

   Formula: Rate × Time = Distance

   Drive Up: $24 \times \frac{1}{4} = 6$

   Ski Down: $x \times \frac{5}{12} = \frac{5}{12}x$

   The distances are equal:

   $$6 = \frac{5}{12}x$$
   $$x = \frac{72}{5}, \text{ or } 14\frac{2}{5}, \text{ or } 14.4$$

   Alfredo skied down the mountain at an average rate of 14.4 mph.

4. **(B)** If Barbara invests x additional dollars at 8%, her total investment will amount to $2400 + x$ dollars.

   $$\begin{aligned} .05(2400) + .08(x) &= .06(2400 + x) \\ 5(2400) + 8(x) &= 6(2400 + x) \\ 12000 + 8x &= 14400 + 6x \\ 2x &= 2400 \\ x &= 1200 \end{aligned}$$

5. **(D)** Letting x equal the number of ounces of soy sauce added to the mixture, $18 + x$ equals the total amount of the mixture after the soy sauce is added. The amount of peanut sauce (5.76 ounces) must equal 12% of the new total amount of the mixture, which is $18 + x$. You can express this as an algebraic equation and solve for x:

   $$\begin{aligned} 5.76 &= .12(x + 18) \\ 576 &= 12(x + 18) \\ 576 &= 12x + 216 \\ 360 &= 12x \\ x &= 30 \end{aligned}$$

   30 ounces of soy sauce must be added to achieve a mixture that includes 12% peanut sauce.

6. **(C)** This question focuses on the work formula. Given one worker's rate along with the aggregate rate of both workers, you can solve for the other worker's rate:

   $$\frac{A}{8} + \frac{A}{S} = 1$$

   You don't need to answer the question; in other words, you don't have to solve for S.

7

7. **(B)** Statement (1) alone is insufficient to answer the question, because you cannot determine Bob's weight loss during the fourth through seventh weeks. Statement (2) alone, however, suffices to answer the question. Given that Bob lost an average of 5 pounds per week during the first three weeks, his total weight loss during that period was 15 pounds. With statement (2), his total weight loss during all but the fourth through seventh weeks was 30 pounds. Given that he lost 29 pounds altogether during the 10-week program [(3)(5) + (7)(2)], he must have gained 1 pound during the fourth through seventh week. Accordingly, he had lost 14 pounds (–15 + 1) after the first seven weeks.

8. **(C)** Statement (1) alone provides no information about the number of painters in relation to the number of sculptors. Statement (2) alone provides no information about the total number of painters and sculptors. However, both statement together tell you the number of painters at the fair. Why? The 14 sculptors who are also painters along with the 7 that are not adds up to 21. Thus there must be 23 painters at the fair (9 of whom are not sculptors).

9. **(C)** Statement (1) provides no information about the number of sales staff members. Thus, you can easily eliminate answers (A) and (D). Statement (2), although providing the number of level 1 sales employees of each type, is insufficient alone to determine the numbers of the level 2 employees. However, statements (1) and (2) together suffice to answer the question. You can fill in a table as follows:

	Level 1	Level 2	
cg	30(15%)	70(35%)	50%
non-cg	42(21%)	58(29%)	50%
	72(36%)	128(64%)	

10. **(D)** Statement (1) says essentially: $R - T > S$. Given that R's age is twice S's age, you can substitute $2S$ for R in the inequality, then determine the relationship between S and T:

$$R - T > S$$
$$2S - T > S$$
$$S - T > 0$$
$$S > T$$

Thus, you can conclude from statement (1) alone that S is older than T. Given statement (2) alone, T's current age must be less than half of R's current age. (If you're not certain of this, use a few simple numbers to confirm it.) Given that S's age is exactly half of R's age, you can conclude from statement (2) alone that S is older than T.

Hour 8

Teach Yourself Geometry I

This hour you'll continue your preparation for the Quantitative section, by forging ahead to geometry. You'll learn how to handle GMAT geometry problems involving intersecting lines, triangles, and quadrilaterals. Here are your goals for this hour:

- Know the relationships among angles formed by intersecting lines
- Know the characteristics of any triangle
- Learn the Pythagorean Theorem and apply it to any right triangle
- Recognize Pythagorean triplets in order to quickly solve right triangle problems
- Know the relationship between area and perimeter of an equilateral triangle
- Know the distinguishing characteristics of squares, rectangles, parallelograms, rhombuses, and trapezoids
- Review the concepts and formulas you learn by applying them to a GMAT-style quiz

Lines and Angles

Lines and line segments are the basic building blocks of all GMAT geometry problems. In fact, some GMAT geometry problems involve nothing more than intersecting lines—and the angles they form. Here are four basic rules you need to remember about angles formed by intersecting lines:

1. Opposite angles are equal in degree measure, or *congruent* (≅). In other words, they're the same size.
2. If adjacent angles combine to form a straight line, their degree measures total 180. In fact, a straight line is actually a 180° angle.
3. If two lines are perpendicular (⊥) to each other, they intersect at right (90°) angles.
4. The sum of all angles formed by intersecting lines is 360°.

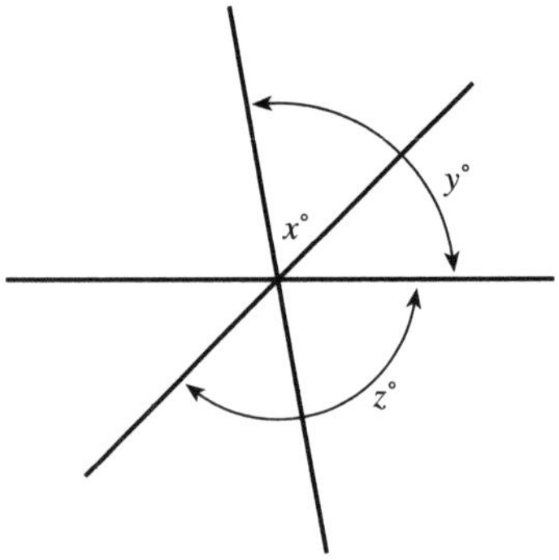

Note: Figure not drawn to scale.

QUESTION In the figure above, if $y = 100$ and $z = 135$, what is the value of x?

(A) 35
(B) 40
(C) 45
(D) 50
(E) 55

8

ANALYSIS The correct answer is **(E)**. Angles y and z exceed 180° by the value of x; that is, $y + z - x = 180$. Substitute 100 and 135 for y and z, respectively, in order to solve for x.

$$100 + 135 - x = 180$$
$$55 = x$$

TIP

> GMAT "wheel spoke" problems almost always involve overlapping angles. Check opposite angles to determine the amount of the overlap.

GMAT problems involving parallel lines also involve at least one *transversal*, which is a line that intersects each of two (or more) parallel lines. In this next figure, $l_1 \parallel l_2$, and l_3 transverses l_1 and l_2.

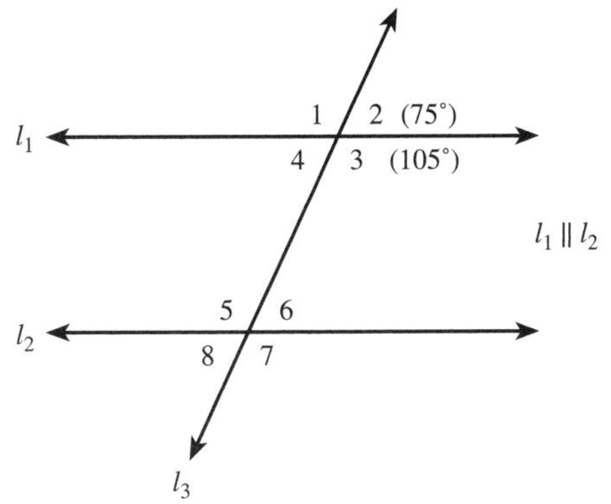

In this figure, because $l_1 \parallel l_2$, the upper cluster of angles (created by the intersection of l_1 and l_3) is identical to, or mirrors, the lower cluster (created by the intersection of l_2 and l_3). For example, $\angle 1$ is congruent (equal in size or degree measure) to $\angle 5$. Because opposite angles are congruent:

- All the *odd*-numbered angles are congruent (equal in size) to one another.
- All the *even*-numbered angles are congruent (equal in size) to one another.

Now try the Data Sufficiency question on the next page. (See pages 50–51 for directions.)

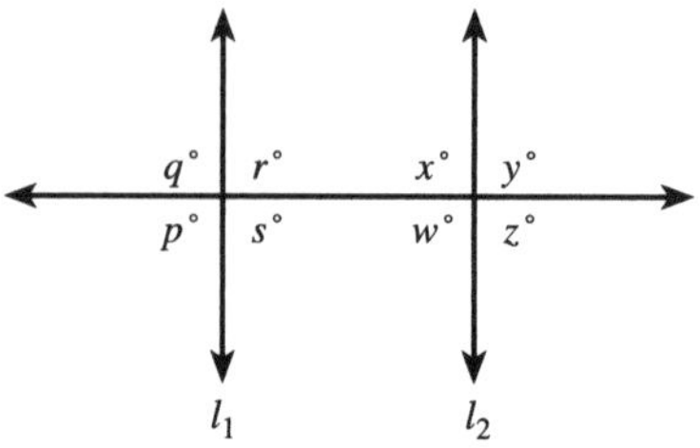

QUESTION In the figure above, is l_1 parallel to l_2?

(1) $q + y = s + w$

(2) $p + x = 180$

ANALYSIS The correct answer is **(B)**. Opposite angles are always congruent. Thus, $q = s$ and $y = w$. Accordingly, $q + y$ must equal $s + w$ in any event, and statement (1) alone does not suffice to answer the question. Given statement (2) alone, because p and x are supplementary, p must equal y as well as w (because $y + x = 180$ and $w + x = 180$). Thus, all corresponding angles are the same, and the two lines are parallel.

CAUTION

In transversal problems, you can substitute one angle for a corresponding angle (in another cluster), but *only* if the problem indicates that they're congruent *or* if you know for sure that you're dealing with parallel lines.

Triangles

Angles and Sides

Here are three basic characteristics—or properties—that apply to *all* triangles, regardless of shape or size. (There's a fourth property as well, involving a triangle's *area*. You'll examine that one separately, just a few pages ahead.)

1. *Length of the sides.* In any triangle, each side is shorter than the sum of the lengths of the other two sides.
2. *Angle measures.* In any triangle, the sum of the three interior angles is 180°.
3. *Angles and opposite sides.* In any triangle, the relative angle sizes correspond to the relative lengths of the sides opposite those angles. In other words, the smaller the

angle, the smaller the side opposite the angle (and vice versa). Accordingly, if two angles are equal in size, the sides opposite those angles are of equal length (and vice-versa).

CAUTION

Don't take this rule too far! The ratio among angle sizes does not necessarily correspond precisely to the ratios among the lengths of the sides opposite those angles. For example, if a certain triangle has angle measures of 30°, 60°, and 90°, the ratio of the angles is 1:2:3. However, this does *not* mean that the ratio of the lengths of the opposite sides is also 1:2:3 (it is *not*, as you will soon learn!).

Now try a Data Sufficiency question. (See pages 50–51 for directions.)

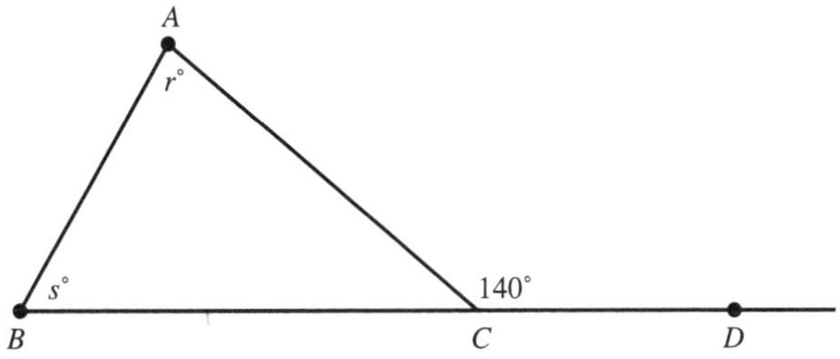

QUESTION In the figure above, is it true that $r > s$?

(1) $r = 70$

(2) AC is equal in length to line segment BC.

ANALYSIS The correct answer is **(D)**. Given that $\angle ACD = 140°$, $\angle ACB = 40°$ (because the sum of the two angles is 180°). Because the sum of the three angles of ΔABC is 180°, $r + s = 140$. Given statement (1) alone, you know that r also equals 70, and you can answer the question. (The answer is *no*; $r = s$.) Given statement (2) alone, the angles opposite AC and BC must be equal, and you can answer the question. (Again, the answer is *no*; $r = s$).

TIP

The measure of an exterior angle of a triangle (such as $\angle ACD$ in the last question) is equal to the sum of the measures of the two remote interior angles.

Area, Right Triangles, and the Pythagorean Theorem

Area of a Triangle

Here's a fourth property that applies to any triangle:

The area of any triangle is equal to $\frac{1}{2}$ the product of its base and its height (height is also called *altitude)*:

$$\text{Area} = \tfrac{1}{2} \times \text{base} \times \text{altitude (height)}$$
$$A = \tfrac{1}{2}(b)(h)$$

You can use any side as the base to calculate area.

CAUTION

Do not equate altitude (height) with the length of any particular side. Instead, imagine the base on flat ground, and drop a plumb line straight down from the top peak of the triangle to define height or altitude. The only types of triangles in which the altitude equals the length of one side are *right* triangles—as you'll see next.

Right Triangles

The only case where a triangle's altitude (height) equals the length of any of its sides is with a right triangle, in which one angle measures 90° and, of course, each of the other two angles measures less than 90°. The two sides forming the 90° angle are commonly referred to as the triangle's *legs* (*a* and *b* in the figure below), whereas the third (and longest side) is referred to as the *hypotenuse* (*c* in the figure below).

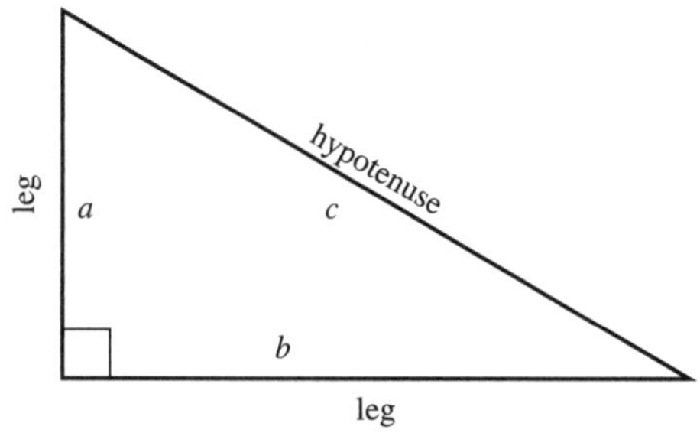

8

The *Pythagorean Theorem* expresses the relationship among the sides of any right triangle (a and b are the two legs, and c is the hypotenuse):

$$a^2 + b^2 = c^2$$

With any right triangle, if you know the length of two sides, you can determine the length of the third side with the Theorem.

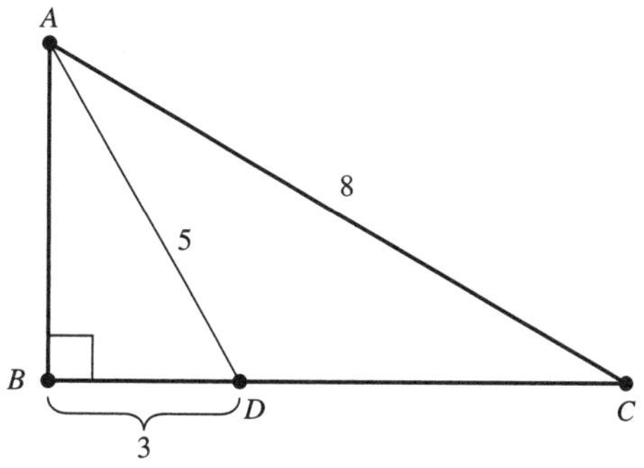

QUESTION In the figure above, what is the area of ΔABC?

(A) $4\sqrt{3}$

(B) $\frac{15\sqrt{2}}{2}$

(C) $8\sqrt{3}$

(D) 14

(E) 16

ANALYSIS The correct answer is **(C)**. Don't be intimidated by complex problems such as this one. You already have the tools to solve the problem. First determine what values you need to know to answer the question, then perform the steps to find each of those values. To calculate the area of ΔABC, you need to know its base (BC) and its height (AB). Determine AB by applying the Pythagorean Theorem to ΔABD:

$$3^2 + (AB)^2 = 5^2$$
$$(AB)^2 = 25 - 9$$
$$(AB)^2 = 16$$
$$AB = 4$$

Now find BC by applying the Theorem again, this time to ΔABC:

$$\begin{aligned} 4^2 + (BC)^2 &= 8^2 \\ (BC)^2 &= 64 - 16 \\ (BC)^2 &= 48 \\ BC &= \sqrt{48}, \text{ or } 4\sqrt{3} \end{aligned}$$

Now you can find the area of ΔABC:

$$\text{Area of } \Delta ABC = \frac{1}{2} \cdot 4\sqrt{3} \cdot 4 = 8\sqrt{3}$$

CAUTION

The Pythagorean Theorem applies only to *right* triangles, not to any others. Never apply the Theorem unless you're sure the triangle includes a 90° angle; and never try to calculate a triangle's area using the length of one side as the altitude unless you're sure the side is one of two that forms a right angle!

Pythagorean Triplets

A Pythagorean triplet is a specific ratio among the sides of a triangle that satisfies the Pythagorean Theorem. In each of the following triplets, the first two numbers represent the relative lengths of the two legs, whereas the third—and largest—number represents the relative length of the hypotenuse (the first four appear far more frequently on the GMAT than the last two):

ratio	*Theorem*
$1 : 1 : \sqrt{2}$	$1^2 + 1^2 = (\sqrt{2})^2$
$1 : \sqrt{3} : 2$	$1^2 + (\sqrt{3})^2 = 2^2$
$3 : 4 : 5$	$3^2 + 4^2 = 5^2$
$5 : 12 : 13$	$5^2 + 12^2 = 13^2$
$8 : 15 : 17$	$8^2 + 15^2 = 17^2$
$7 : 24 : 25$	$7^2 + 24^2 = 25^2$

Each triplet above is expressed as a *ratio* because it represents the relative proportion of the triangle's sides. All right triangles with sides having the same ratio or proportion have the same shape. For example, a right triangle with sides of 5, 12, and 13 is smaller but exactly the same shape (proportion) as a triangle with sides of 15, 36, and 39.

TIME SAVER

> To save valuable time on GMAT right triangle problems, learn to recognize given numbers (lengths of triangle sides) as multiples of Pythagorean triplets. In the Problem Solving question on page 157, for instance, you could have saved time by recognizing that ΔABD is a 3:4:5 triangle.

QUESTION Two boats leave the same dock at the same time, one traveling due east at 10 miles per hour and the other traveling due north at 24 miles per hour. How many miles apart are the boats after three hours?

(A) 68

(B) 72

(C) 78

(D) 98

(E) 110

ANALYSIS The correct answer is **(C)**. The distance between the two boats after three hours forms the hypotenuse of a triangle in which the legs are the two boats' respective paths. The ratio of one leg to the other is 10:24, or 5:12. So you know you're dealing with a 5:12:13 triangle. The slower boat traveled 30 miles (10 mph × 3 hours). 30 corresponds to the number 5 in the 5:12:13 ratio, so the multiple is 6 ($5 \times 6 = 30$). 5:12:13 = 30:72:78.

Other Special Right Triangles

In two (and only two) of the unique triangles we've identified as Pythagorean triplets, *all degree measures are integers:*

1. The corresponding angles opposite the sides of a $1:1:\sqrt{2}$ triangle are 45°, 45°, and 90°.
2. The corresponding angles opposite the sides of a $1:\sqrt{3}:2$ triangle are 30°, 60°, and 90°.

This next figure shows these two angle triplets and their corresponding side triplets.

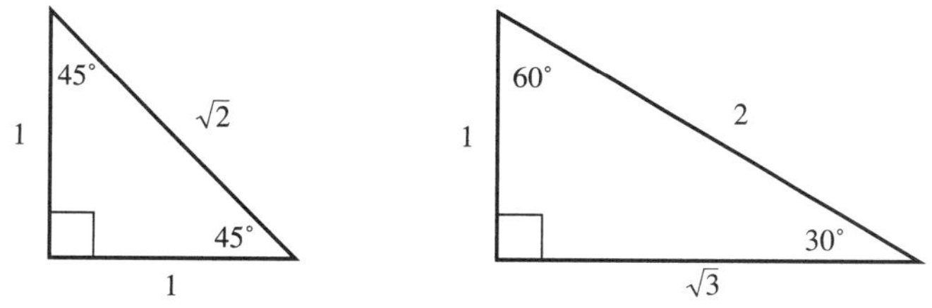

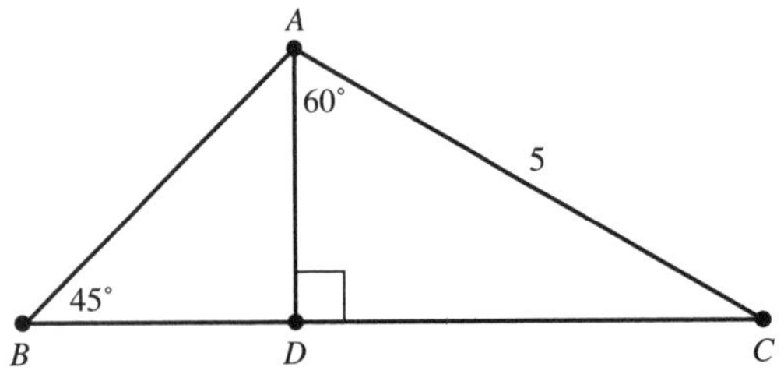

QUESTION In the figure above, what is the length of *AB*?

(A) $\frac{3\sqrt{3}}{2}$

(B) $\frac{7}{3}$

(C) $\frac{5\sqrt{2}}{2}$

(D) $2\sqrt{2}$

(E) $\frac{7}{2}$

ANALYSIS The correct answer is **(C)**. To find the length of *AB*, you first need to find *AD* and *BD*. The angles of ΔADC are 30°, 60°, and 90°. So you know that the ratio among its sides is $1:\sqrt{3}:2$. Given that $AC = 5$, $AD = \frac{5}{2}$ $(1:2 = \frac{5}{2}:5)$. Next, you should recognize ΔABD as a 45°-45°-90° triangle. The ratio among its sides is $1:1:\sqrt{2}$. You know that $AD = \frac{5}{2}$. Accordingly, $AB = \frac{5\sqrt{2}}{2}$.

NOTE

Two 45°-45°-90° triangles pieced together form a square, and two 30°-60°-90° triangles together form an equilateral triangle. This amazing phenomenon fascinates the test-makers, so it should interest you as well. (We'll look closer at equilateral triangles and at squares in just a bit.)

8

Isosceles Triangles

An *isosceles* triangle has the following three special properties:

1. Two of the sides are congruent (equal in length).
2. The two angles opposite the two congruent sides are congruent (equal in size or degree measure).
3. A line that bisects the angle formed by the equal sides bisects the opposite side.

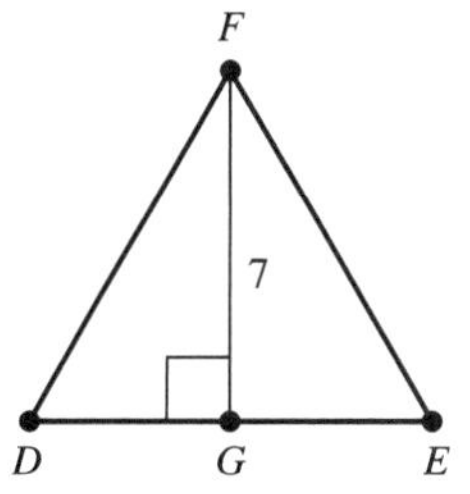

Note: Figure not drawn to scale

QUESTION If the area of ΔDEF in the figure above is 21, and if ΔFDG has the same area as ΔFEG, what is the length of EF?

(A) $\frac{10\sqrt{2}}{3}$

(B) $\frac{7\sqrt{3}}{2}$

(C) $\sqrt{51}$

(D) $4\sqrt{3}$

(E) $\sqrt{58}$

ANALYSIS The correct answer is **(E)**. The area of ΔDEF is given as 21, and its height is 7. To find EF, first determine DE (the triangle's base, or b):

$$A = \frac{1}{2}(b)(h)$$

$$21 = \frac{1}{2}(b)(7)$$

$$b = 6$$

Because ΔDEF is isosceles, FG bisects DE. So use $\frac{1}{2}b$ as a leg of either of two right triangles, DFG or FEG, and apply the Pythagorean Theorem to find EF.

$$(EF)^2 = 3^2 + 7^2$$
$$(EF)^2 = 9 + 49 = 58$$
$$EF = \sqrt{58}$$

Equilateral Triangles

An equilateral triangle has the following three properties:

1. All three sides are congruent (equal in length)
2. All three angles are 60°.
3. The area = $\frac{s^2\sqrt{3}}{4}$ [s = any side]

Any line bisecting one of the 60° angles divides an equilateral triangle into two right triangles with angle measures of 30°, 60°, and 90°; in other words, into two $1{:}\sqrt{3}{:}2$ triangles. (Remember the Pythagorean angle triplet a few pages back?)

Try this Data Sufficiency question. (See pages 50–51 for directions.)

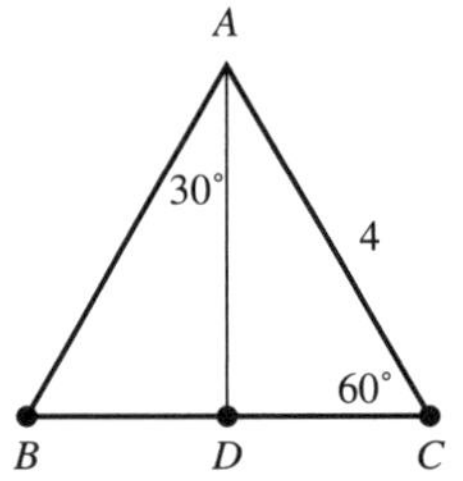

QUESTION What is the area of ΔABC in the figure above?

(1) $AD \perp BC$

(2) AB and AC are equal in length.

ANALYSIS The correct answer is **(D)**. Statement (1) alone establishes that both smaller triangles are 30°-60°-90° ($1{:}\sqrt{3}{:}2$) triangles, and that ΔABC is equilateral. Given that $AC = 4$, you can easily determine the area. Statement (2) alone establishes that $\angle ABC = \angle ACB$, and in turn the two smaller triangles are congruent ($1{:}\sqrt{3}{:}2$) triangles. Accordingly, statement 2 alone suffices to answer the question for the same reason as (1). (Although you don't need to do the math, the triangle's area is $\frac{4^2\sqrt{3}}{4} = 4\sqrt{3}$.)

NOTE

> On the GMAT, you might also encounter equilateral triangles in problems involving *circles* (one of next hour's topics).

Quadrilaterals

A *quadrilateral* is a four-sided figure. Here are the specific types of quadrilaterals you should know for the GMAT:

1. square
2. rectangle
3. parallelogram
4. rhombus
5. trapezoid

Each of these five figures has its own properties (characteristics) that should be second nature to by the time you take the GMAT. The two most important properties are:

Area (the surface covered by the figure on a plane)

Perimeter (the total length of all sides)

NOTE

> All quadrilaterals share one important property: The sum of the four interior angles of any quadrilateral is 360°.

The Square

This next figure shows a square. All squares share these properties:

1. All four sides are equal in length.
2. All four angles are right angles (90°).
3. The sum of all four angles is 360°.
4. Perimeter = $4s$
5. Area = s^2

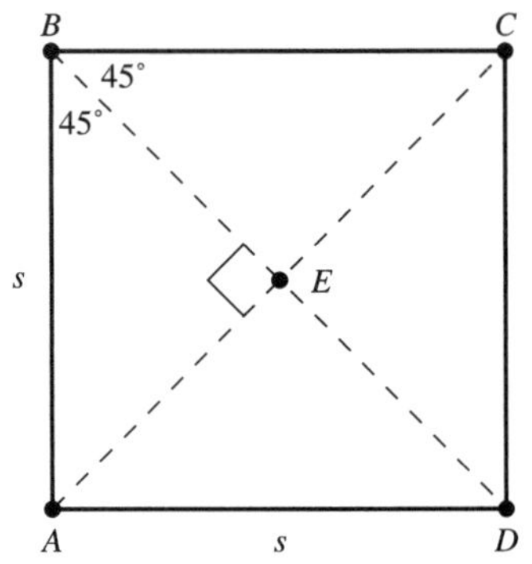

When you add diagonals to a square (dotted lines above), you create these additional relationships:

1. Diagonals are equal in length ($AC = BD$).
2. Diagonals are perpendicular; their intersection creates four right angles.
3. Diagonals bisect each 90° angle of the square; that is, they split each angle into two equal (45°) angles.
4. Divide the square of either diagonal by 2 to obtain square's area:

   $$\text{Area of square} = \frac{(AC)^2}{2} \text{ or } \frac{(BD)^2}{2}$$

   This formula applies only to squares, not to other quadrilaterals!
5. Diagonals create four distinct congruent (the same shape and size) triangles, each having an area $\frac{1}{2}$ the area of the square: ΔABD, ΔACD, ΔABC, and ΔBCD. Each triangle is a $1{:}1{:}\sqrt{2}$ triangle, with 45°-45°-90° angles.
6. Diagonals create four distinct congruent triangles, each having an area $\frac{1}{4}$ the area of the square: ΔABE, ΔBCE, ΔCDE, and ΔADE. Each triangle is a $1{:}1{:}\sqrt{2}$ triangle, with 45°-45°-90° angles.

Rectangles

This next figure shows a rectangle. All rectangles share these properties:

1. Opposite sides are equal in length
2. All four angles are right angles (90°)
3. The sum of all four angles is 360°
4. Perimeter $= 2l + 2w$

5. Area = $l \times w$
6. The maximum area of a rectangle with a given perimeter is a square
7. The minimum perimeter of a rectangle with a given area is a square

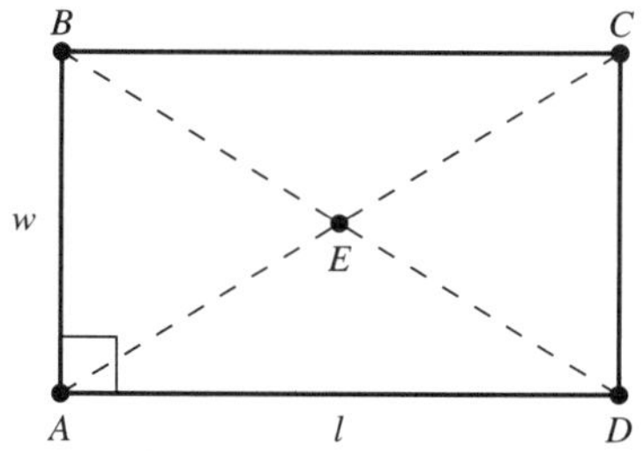

Here's what happens when you add diagonals to a rectangle (refer to the figure above):

1. Diagonals are equal in length ($AC = BD$).
2. Diagonals bisect each other ($AE = BE = CE = DE$).
3. Diagonals are *not* perpendicular (unless the rectangle is a square).
4. Diagonals do *not* bisect each 90° angle of the rectangle (unless the rectangle is a square).
5. Diagonals create four distinct congruent triangles, each having an area $\frac{1}{2}$ the area of the rectangle: ΔABD, ΔACD, ΔABC, and ΔBCD.
6. ΔABE is congruent to ΔCDE; both triangles are isosceles (but they are right triangles *only* if the rectangle is a square).
7. ΔBEC is congruent to ΔAED; both triangles are isosceles (but they are right triangles *only* if the rectangle is a square).
8. Each of the four small triangles mentioned in items 6 and 7 above has an area of $\frac{1}{4}$ the area of the rectangle.

CAUTION

Diagonals of rectangles are *not* perpendicular and do *not* bisect each 90° angle of the rectangle—*unless* the rectangle is a square (in which case they do both).

A typical GMAT rectangle question will also involve one or more triangles.

QUESTION A farmer uses 140 feet of fencing to enclose a rectangular field. If the ratio of length to width is 3:4, what is the distance from one corner of the field diagonally to the opposite corner?

(A) 40

(B) $25\sqrt{3}$

(C) 45

(D) 50

(E) $\frac{65\sqrt{3}}{2}$

ANALYSIS The correct answer is **(D)**. Given a 3:4 ratio, you can express the perimeter of the field in this manner:

$$\begin{aligned} 2(3x) + 2(4x) &= 140 \\ 14x &= 140 \\ x &= 10 \end{aligned}$$

The rectangle is 30' by 40'. You should recognize each triangle created by the diagonal as a 3:4:5 right triangle, with a diagonal (hypotenuse) of 50.

Parallelograms

The next figure shows a parallelogram. All parallelograms share these properties:

1. Opposite sides are parallel
2. Opposite sides are equal in length
3. Opposite angles are congruent (the same size or equal in degree measure)
4. The sum of all four interior angles is 360°
5. All four angles are congruent *only* if the parallelogram is a rectangle—that is, if the angles are right angles
6. Perimeter = $2l + 2b$
7. Area = base (b) × altitude (a)

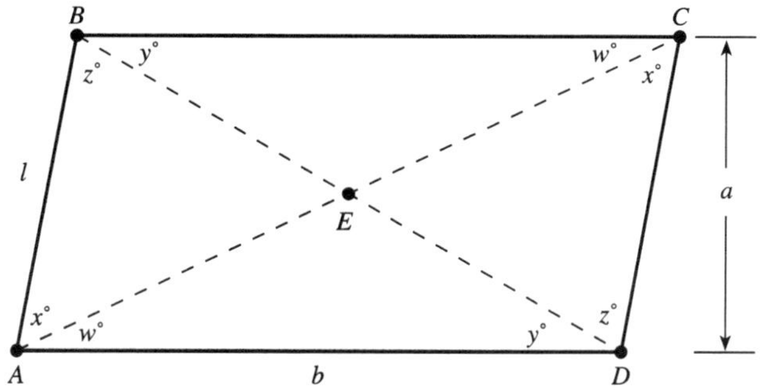

Here's what happens when you add diagonals to a parallelogram (refer to the figure above):

1. Diagonals bisect each other ($BE = ED$, $CE = AE$).
2. Diagonals (AC and BD) are *not* equal in length (unless the figure is a rectangle).
3. Diagonals are not perpendicular (unless the figure is a square or rhombus).
4. Diagonals do *not* bisect each angle of the parallelogram (unless it is a square or rhombus).
5. Diagonals create two pairs of congruent triangles, each having an area $\frac{1}{2}$ the area of the parallelogram: ΔABD is congruent to ΔBCD, and ΔACD is congruent to ΔABC.
6. ΔABE is congruent to ΔCED (they are mirror-imaged horizontally *and* vertically); the triangles are isosceles only if the quadrilateral is a rectangle.
7. ΔBEC is congruent to ΔAED (they are mirror-imaged horizontally *and* vertically); the triangles are isosceles only if the quadrilateral is a rectangle.
8. Each of the four small triangles has an area of $\frac{1}{4}$ the area of the parallelogram.

CAUTION

Diagonals of a parallelogram are *not* perpendicular and do *not* bisect each angle of the parallelogram—*unless* the parallelogram is either a square or rhombus (in which case they do both).

The Rhombus

The next figure shows a rhombus. All rhombuses share these properties:

1. All sides are equal in length.
2. Opposite sides are parallel.

3. The sum of all four angles is 360°.
4. No angles are right angles (angle measures ≠ 90°).
5. Perimeter = $4s$
6. Area = side (s) × altitude (a)

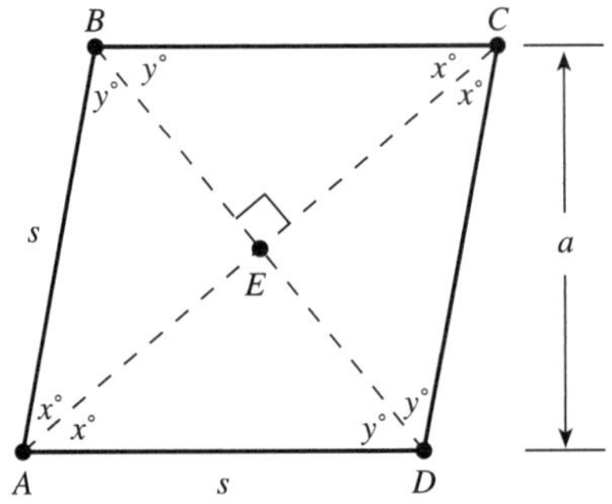

Here's what happens when you add diagonals (*AC* and *BD*) to a rhombus (refer to the figure above):

1. Area of the rhombus = $\frac{AC \times BC}{2}$ ($\frac{1}{2}$ the product of the diagonals); this formula applies to a rhombus and a square, but not to any other quadrilaterals!
2. Diagonals bisect each other ($BE = ED$, $AE = EC$).
3. Diagonals are perpendicular (their intersection creates four right angles).
4. Diagonals are *not* equal in length ($AC \neq BD$).
5. Diagonals bisect each angle of the rhombus.
6. Diagonals create four pairs of *congruent* (the same shape and size) isosceles triangles, each triangle having an area $\frac{1}{2}$ the area of the rhombus; none of these four triangles are right triangles.
7. Diagonals create four congruent (same shape and size) right triangles, each with an area one quarter that of the rhombus.

TIP

Every square is a rhombus, so if you know either diagonal of a square, you can apply the rhombus formula (the diagonals of a square are equal):

Area of a square = $\left(\frac{1}{2}\right)$(diagonal)(diagonal)

8

Trapezoids

This next figure shows a trapezoid. All trapezoids share these properties:

1. Only one pair of opposite sides are parallel ($BC \parallel AD$).
2. The sum of all four interior angles is 360°.
3. Perimeter $= AB + BC + CD + AD$
4. Area $= \frac{BC + AD}{2} \times$ altitude (a), one-half the sum of the two parallel sides multiplied by the altitude

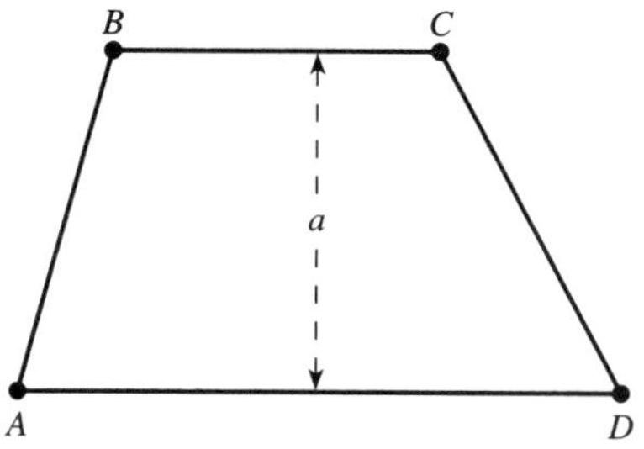

No predictable patterns emerge from the addition of two diagonals to a trapezoid.

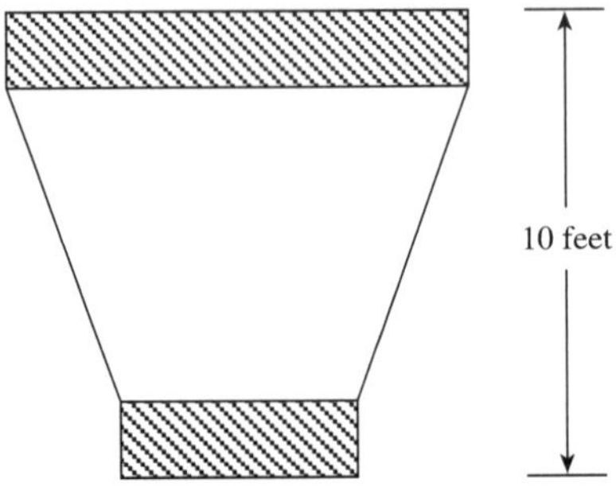

QUESTION To cover the floor of an entry hall, a 1-foot × 12-foot strip of carpet is cut into two pieces, shown as the shaded strips in the figure above, and each piece is connected to a third carpet piece as shown. If the 1-foot strips run parallel to each other, what is the total area of the floor?

(A) 44

(B) 48

(C) 54

(D) 56

(E) 60

ANALYSIS The correct answer is **(E)**. The altitude of the trapezoidal piece is 8. The sum of the two parallel sides of this piece is 12 feet (the length of the 1-foot × 12-foot strip before it was cut). You can apply the trapezoid formula to determine the area of this piece:

$$A = (8)\left(\frac{12}{2}\right) = 48$$

The total area of the two shaded strips is 12 square feet, so the total area of the floor is 60 square feet.

Workshop

In this hour's Workshop, you'll tackle a 10-question GMAT-style quiz, designed for you to review and apply the concepts and question types you learned about this hour.

ONLINE

Additional Quantitative questions are available online, at the authors' Web site: *http://www.west.net/~stewart/gmat*

Quiz

(Answers and explanations begin on page 173.)

DIRECTIONS: Attempt the following ten GMAT-style questions. Try to limit your time to 15 minutes. For each question, you'll see one or two hints to help you if you're having trouble.

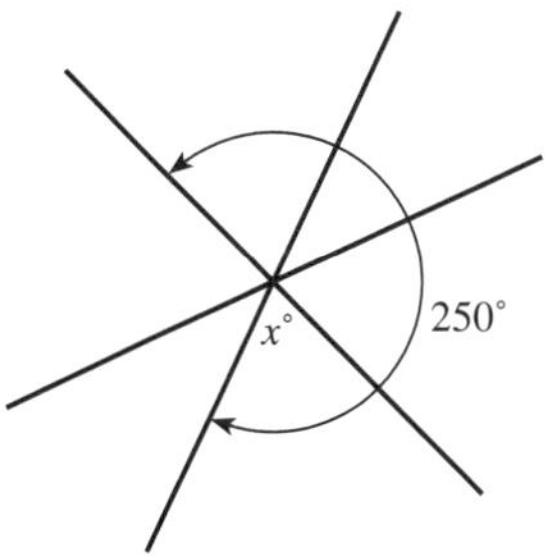

1. In the figure above, what is the value of x?

(A) 50
(B) 55
(C) 60
(D) 70
(E) 80

(Hint: The total degree measure of all angles with a common vertex is 360°.)

2. In triangle ABC, $AB = BC$ in length. If the degree measure of the interior angle at point B is b, which of the following represents the degree measure of the interior angle at point A?

(A) b
(B) $180 - b$
(C) $180 - \frac{b}{2}$
(D) $90 - \frac{b}{2}$
(E) $90 - b$

(Hint: The triangle is isosceles.)

3. In a parallelogram with an area of 15, the base is represented by $x + 7$ and the altitude is $x - 7$. What is the length of the parallelogram's base?

(A) 1
(B) 5
(C) 8
(D) 15
(E) 34

(Hint: The area of a parallelogram is the product of its base and altitude.)

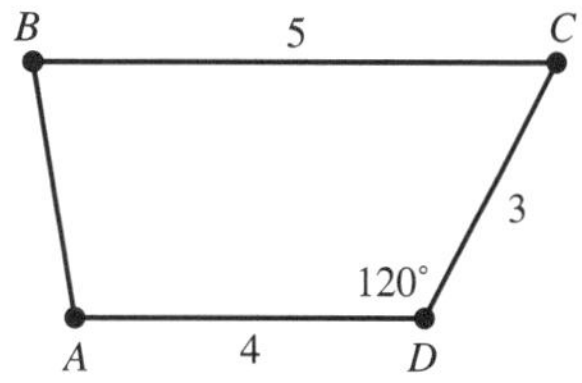

4. What is the area of trapezoid $ABCD$ in the above figure?

(A) $5\sqrt{2}$
(B) $\frac{9\sqrt{3}}{2}$
(C) $\frac{27\sqrt{3}}{4}$
(D) $13\frac{1}{2}$
(E) 16

(Hint: One of the Pythagorean angle triplets comes into play here.)

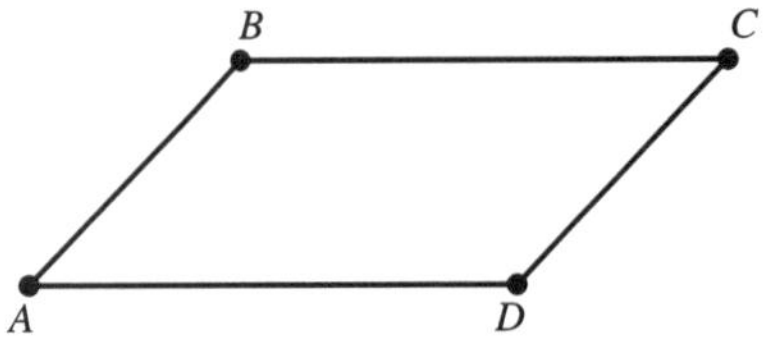

5. In parallelogram *ABCD* in the figure above, $\angle ABC$ is five times as large as $\angle BCD$. What is the degree measure of $\angle ABC$?

   (A) 30
   (B) 60
   (C) 100
   (D) 120
   (E) 150

   (Hint: The sum of the four angles of any parallelogram is 360°.)

Questions 6–10 are Data Sufficiency questions.

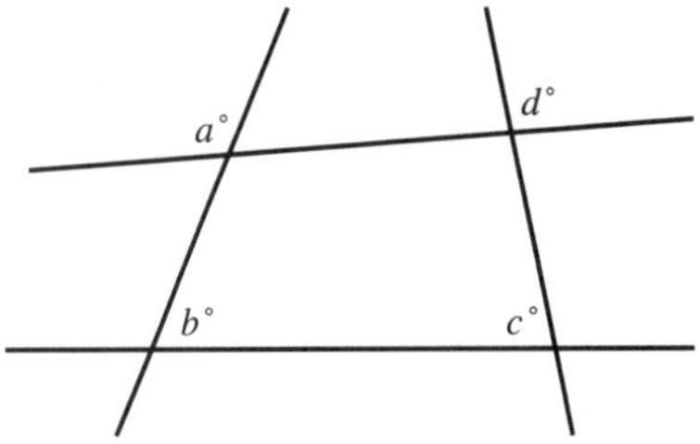

6. In the figure above, what is the sum of *a* and *b*?

   (1) $c = 70$
   (2) $d = 110$

   (Hint: Look for supplementary angles.)

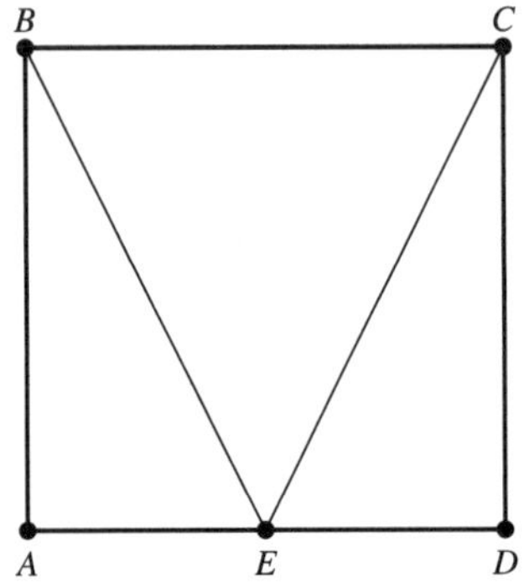

7. In rectangle *ABCD* in the figure above, if $AE = ED$ in length, is rectangle *ABCD* a square?

   (1) The length of *AE* multiplied by $\sqrt{5}$ is equal to the length of *BE*.
   (2) The area of triangle *BCE* is exactly half the area of rectangle *ABCD*.

   (Hint: Recall the properties that distinguish a square from other rectangles.)

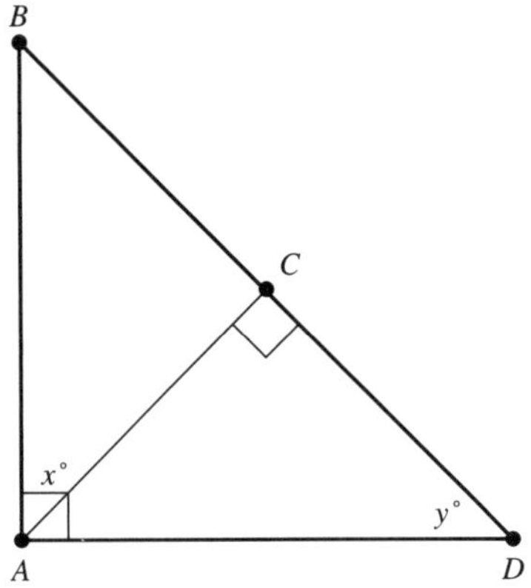

8. In the above figure, does $x = y$?

   (1) ΔACD is an isosceles triangle.
   (2) ΔABC is an isosceles triangle.

   (Hint: Angles opposite congruent sides are also congruent.)

9. Eight square window panes of equal size are to be pieced together to form a rectangular French door. What is the perimeter of the door, excluding framing between and around the panes?
   (1) Each pane is one square foot in area.
   (2) The area of the door, excluding framing between and around the panes, is eight square feet.

   (Hint: Consider all possible configurations of the eight square windows.)

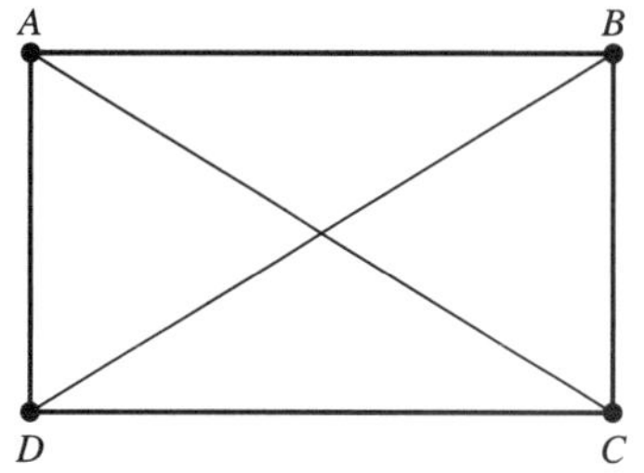

10. In the figure above, is $ABCD$ a rectangle?
   (1) $AC = BD$ in length.
   (2) AC bisects BD.

   (Hint: Recall the properties that distinguish a rectangle from all other quadrilaterals.)

Answers and Explanations

1. **(D)** The total degree measure of all angles is 360. The two angles not part of the 250° arc total 110°. These two angles along with angle x form a straight line (a 180° angle). Thus, $x = 70$.

2. **(D)** The triangle is isosceles, so $\angle A = \angle C$. Letting a, b, and c represent the degree measures of $\angle A$, $\angle B$, and $\angle C$, respectively, solve for a:

$$a + c + b = 180$$
$$2a + b = 180 \ [a = c]$$
$$a = \frac{180}{2} - \frac{b}{2}$$
$$a = 90 - \frac{b}{2}$$

3. **(D)** The area of a parallelogram = (base) × (altitude):

$$(x + 7)(x - 7) = 15$$
$$x^2 - 49 = 15$$
$$x^2 = 64$$
$$x = 8$$
$$\text{base} = x + 7 = 15$$

4. **(C)** The area of a trapezoid is $\frac{1}{2}$ the product of the sum of the two parallel sides ($BC + AD$) and the trapezoid's height. To determine the trapezoid's height, form a right triangle, as shown in the figure below. This right triangle conforms to the 30-60-90 Pythagorean angle triplet. Thus, the ratio of the three sides is $1{:}\sqrt{3}{:}2$. The hypotenuse is given as 3, so the

height is $3\frac{\sqrt{3}}{2}$. Calculate the area of the trapezoid as follows:

$$\frac{1}{2}(4+5)\cdot\frac{3\sqrt{3}}{2}=\frac{9}{2}\cdot\frac{3\sqrt{3}}{2}=\frac{27\sqrt{3}}{4}$$

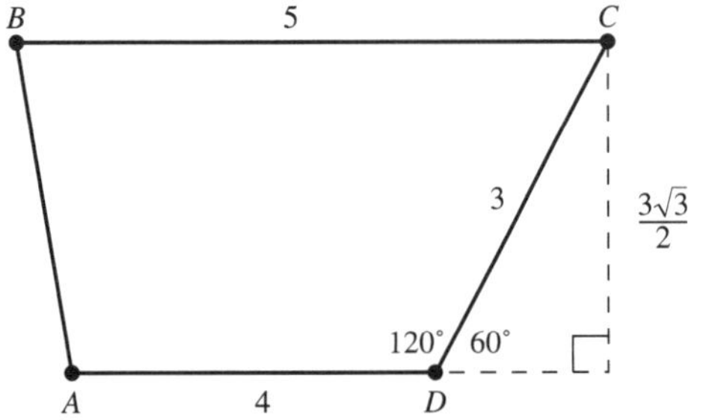

5. **(E)** The sum of the angles in a parallelogram is 360°. $\angle B$ and $\angle C$ together account for half the sum, or 180°. Letting x equal the degree measure of angle C:

$$5x + x = 180$$
$$6x = 180$$
$$x = 30$$
$$\angle B = 5x = (5)(30) = 150$$

6. **(C)** Both statements together establish that c and d are supplementary ($c + d = 180$) and, accordingly, that the two horizontally-oriented lines are parallel. As a result, a and b are also supplementary ($a + b = 180$).

7. **(A)** Given $AE \times \sqrt{5} = BE$ (statement 1), AB must be exactly twice the length of AE. Why? Because triangle ABE is a right triangle, the Pythagorean Theorem establishes that $(AE)^2 + (AB)^2 = (BE)^2$, or $1^2 + 2^2 = (\sqrt{5})^2$. Given that $AE = ED$, $AB = AD$, and the rectangle is indeed a square. Statement (1) alone suffices to answer the question. Given statement (2) alone, a bit of visualization reveals that the area of triangle BCE is always exactly half that of rectangle $ABCD$, regardless of where point E lies along line segment AD. Thus, statement (2) alone is insufficient to answer the question.

8. **(D)** Given statement (1) alone, since triangle ACD is a right isosceles triangle, the two angles other than the 90° angle must each measure 45°. Because $\angle BAD$ measures 90°, $x = 45$, and $x = y$. You can apply the same analysis to statement (2), and either statement alone suffices to answer the question.

9. **(E)** You could piece together the panes into either a single column (or row) of eight panes or into two adjacent columns (or rows) of four panes each. In the first case, the door's perimeter would be 18. In the second case, the door's perimeter would be 12. Thus, statement (1) alone is insufficient to answer the question. Statement (2) alone is insufficient for the same reason. Both statements together still fail to provide sufficient information to determine the shape (or perimeter) of the door.

10. **(C)** If a quadrilateral's diagonals are equal in length and bisect each other, then the quadrilateral must be a rectangle. Statement (1) alone does not allow you to determine any of the quadrilateral's angles. Statement (2) alone provides no useful information; $ABCD$ could be any shape at all. Thus, both statements together are needed to answer the question.

Hour 9

Teach Yourself Geometry II

This hour you'll continue to teach yourself geometry, focusing on problems involving polygons with five or more sides, circles, three-dimensional figures, and the coordinate plane. In this hour, you will learn:

- How to determine angle sizes of any polygon
- The characteristics of any circle, and the relationship between a circle's radius, diameter, circumference, and area
- How to apply the area and circumference formulas to GMAT circle questions
- How to handle hybrid problems, which combine circles with other geometric figures
- How to determine surface area and volume of rectangular solids, cubes, and right cylinders
- The relationship between the edges, faces, and volume of any rectangular solid
- How to solve coordinate geometry problems

Polygons

Last hour you concentrated on three-sided polygons (triangles) and four-sided polygons (quadrilaterals). Now, let's look at polygons having more than four sides. Consider these two:

(A)

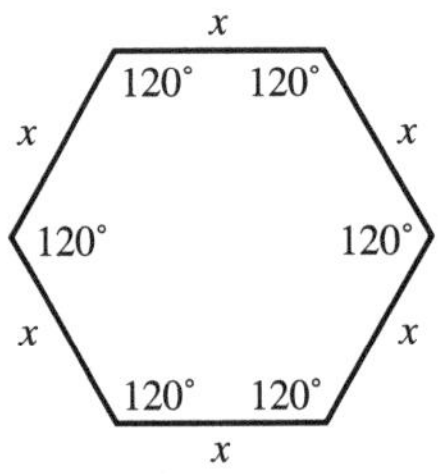

(B)

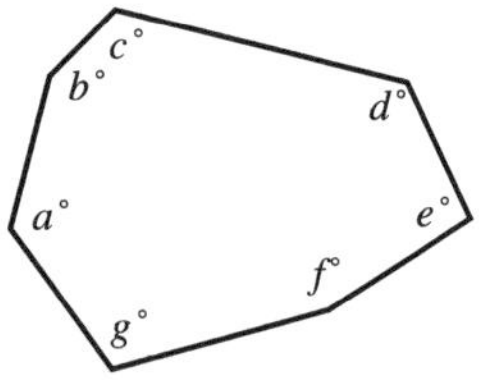

In polygon (A), which has six sides, notice that all angles are congruent (the same size) and that all sides are congruent (the same length). For the GMAT, remember these two rules about sides and angles of polygons:

1. If all angles of a polygon are congruent (the same size), then all sides are congruent (equal in length).
2. If all sides of a polygon are congruent (equal in length), then all angles are congruent (the same size).

NOTE

> A polygon in which all sides are congruent and all angles are congruent is called a *regular* polygon. A regular triangle is equilateral; a regular quadrilateral is square. (For the GMAT, you don't need to know the terminology—just the principle.)

You can use the following formula to determine the sum of all interior angles of *any* polygon, regular or otherwise (n = number of sides):

$(n - 2)(180°)$ = sum of interior angles

This formula applies to irregular polygons, such as (B) above, as well as regular polygons such as (A) above. You can find the average size of the angles by dividing the sum by the number of sides. For regular polygons, the average angle size is also the size of every angle.

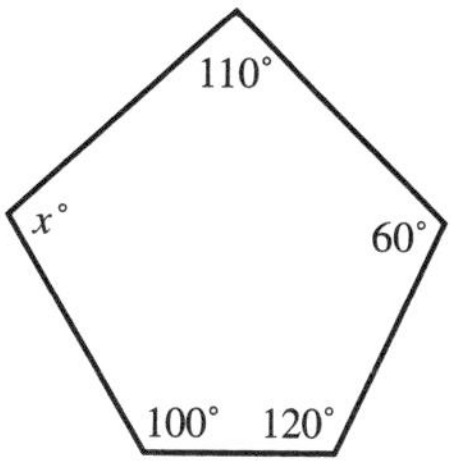

QUESTION In the figure above, what is the value of x?

(A) 100
(B) 110
(C) 125
(D) 135
(E) 150

ANALYSIS The correct answer is **(E)**. The figure has 5 sides, so it contains 540 degrees:

$$180(5 - 2) = 540$$

The sum of the five angles is 540, so solve for x:

$$540 = x + 110 + 60 + 120 + 100$$
$$540 = x + 390$$
$$150 = x$$

Circles

A *circle* is the set of all points that lie equidistant from the same point (the circle's *center*) on a plane. For the GMAT, you should know the following terms involving circles:

radius: the distance from a circle's center to any point on the circle

diameter: the greatest distance from one point to another on the circle

chord: a line segment connecting two points on the circle

circumference: the distance around the circle (its "perimeter")

arc: a segment of a circle's circumference (an arc can be defined either as a length or as a degree measure)

minor arc: the shortest arc between two given points on a circle's circumference

Properties of a Circle

There are six properties of any circle that you should know for the GMAT:

1. Every point on a circle's circumference is equidistant from the circle's center.
2. The total number of degrees of all angles formed from the circle's center is 360.
3. Diameter is twice the radius.
4. Circumference = $2\pi r$, or πd
5. Area = πr^2, or $\frac{\pi d^2}{4}$
6. The longest possible chord of a circle passes through its center and is the circle's diameter.

With the area and circumference formulas, you can determine a circle's area, circumference, diameter, and radius, as long as you know just one of these four values.

NOTE

The value of π is approximately 3.14, or $\frac{22}{7}$. On the GMAT, you probably won't have to work with a value for π any more precise than "a little over 3." In fact, in most circle problems, the solution is expressed in terms of π rather than numerically.

GMAT circle problems almost always involve other geometric figures as well, as you're about to see.

Circles with Triangles Inside of Them

One common type of GMAT circle problem is a "hybrid" involving a circle and a triangle. Look for any of the following three varieties on the GMAT:

1. A *right* triangle with one vertex at the circle's center and the other two on the circumference (ΔABO in the next figure).

   Given either that $\angle AOB = 90°$ or that $AB = r\sqrt{2}$, here's what else you know about ΔABO (r = radius):

   - $AO = r$, and $OB = r$, because OA and OB each equal the circle's radius.
   - $AO = OB$ (ΔABO is a right isosceles triangle)

- $\angle OAB = \angle OBA = 45^\circ$
- AB (the hypotenuse) = $r\sqrt{2}$, because the ratio of the triangle's sides is $1:1:\sqrt{2}$.
- Area of $\Delta ABO = \frac{r^2}{2}$

2. An *equilateral* triangle with one vertex at the circle's center and the other two on the circumference (ΔODC in the next figure).

   Given either that $\angle DOC = 60^\circ$ or that $DC = r$, you know that ΔODC is equilateral ($OD = OC = DC = r$, all angles are 60°).

3. A triangle *inscribed* inside a circle (all three vertices lie on the circle's circumference) in which one side equals the circle's diameter (ΔFGH in the next figure).

   ΔFGH must be a right triangle (it must include one 90° angle)—regardless where point G lies on the circle's circumference. If you don't believe it, go ahead and draw some more triangles, moving G around the circumference. (We know you will, anyway.)

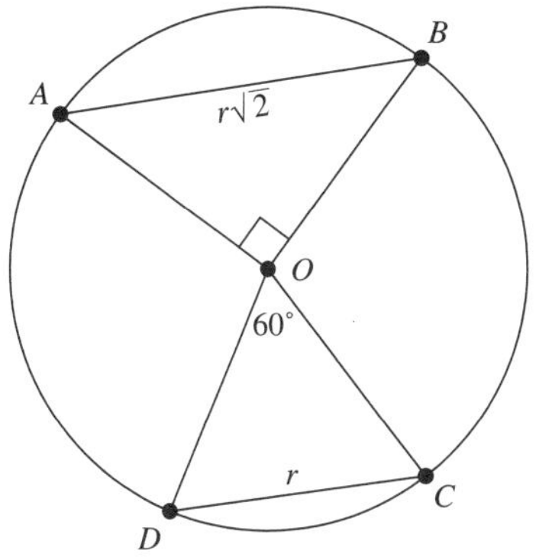

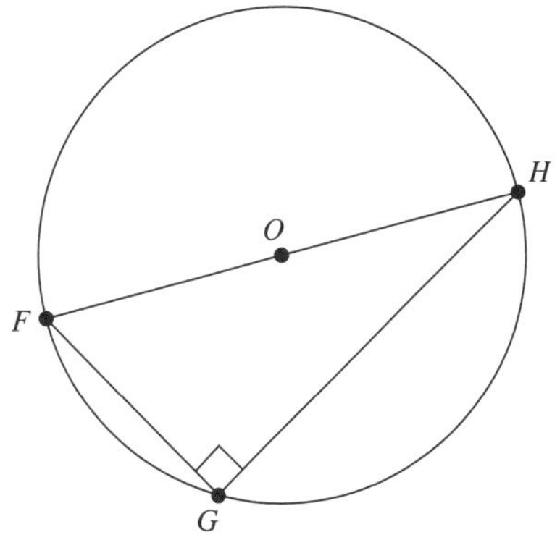

Now try the Data Sufficiency question at the top of the next page. (See pages 50–51 for directions.)

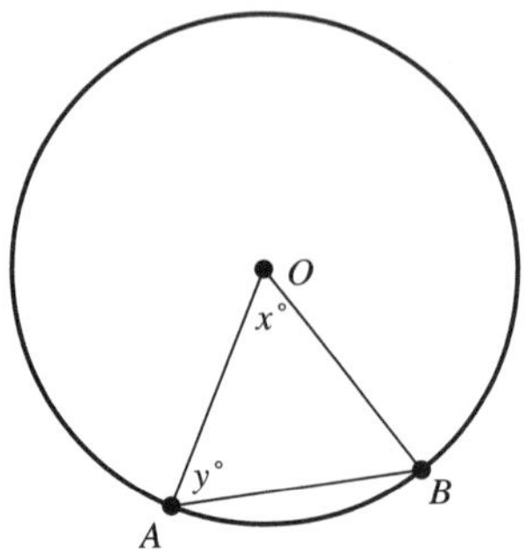

QUESTION In the figure above, if O lies at the center of the circle, what is the value of x?

(1) The length of AB equals the radius of the circle.

(2) $y = 60$

ANALYSIS The correct answer is **(D)**. OA and OB each equals the circle's radius. Given statement (1) alone, ΔOAB must be equilateral, and all angle measures are 60°. Statement (1) suffices to answer the question. Given statement (2) alone, ($y = 60$), a bit of intuition reveals that AB can only be one length relative to OA (because its length is bound by the circle). Could AB be any length other than the circle's radius (OA)? No. Any other relative length would result in a value for y either greater or less than 60. So the triangle must be equilateral, and $x = 60$.

Squares Inside Circles (and Vice Versa)

Another common type of GMAT circle problem is a hybrid involving a circle and a square. Look for either:

1. A circle with an *inscribed* square (left-hand figure at the top of the next page)
2. A circle with a *circumscribed* square (right-hand figure at the top of the next page)

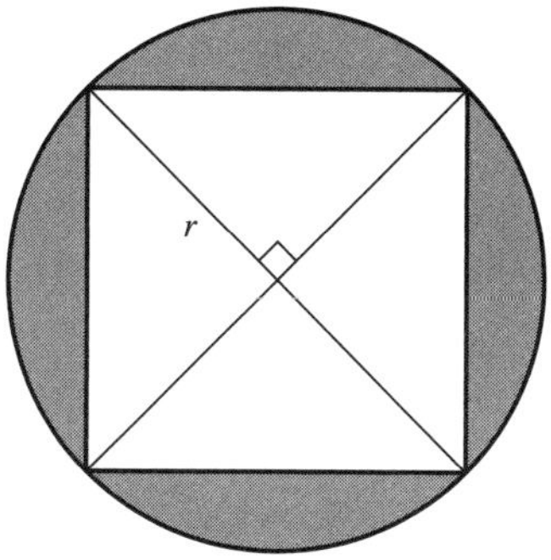

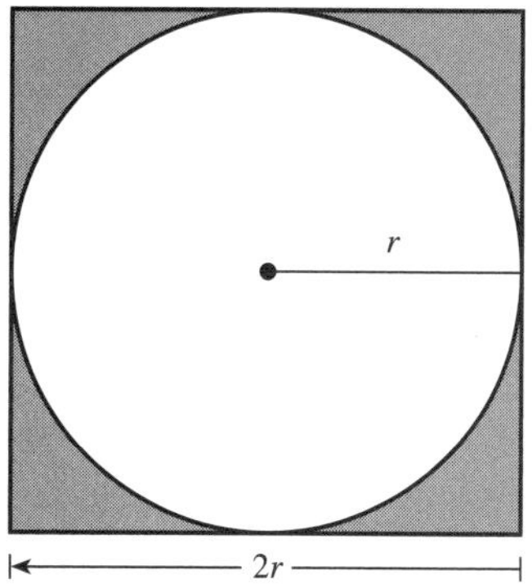

In either case, the square touches the circle at four and only four points. Here are the characteristics that emerge in each of these two figures:

In the left-hand figure:

Each of the four small triangles formed by the diagonals is a $1:1:\sqrt{2}$ triangle.

In each of the four small triangles, the ratio of the hypotenuse (same as the side of the square) to the legs (same as circle's radius) is $\sqrt{2}:1$.

The area of a square inscribed in a circle is $(r\sqrt{2})^2$, or $2r^2$.

The ratio of the inscribed square's area to the circle's area is $2:\pi$.

The *difference* between the two areas—the total shaded area—is $\pi r^2 - 2r^2$.

The area of each crescent-shaped shaded area is $\frac{1}{4}(\pi r^2 - 2r^2)$.

In the right-hand figure:

Each side of the square is $2r$ in length.

The square's area is $(2r)^2$, or $4r^2$.

The ratio of the square's area to that of the inscribed circle is $\frac{4}{\pi}:1$.

The *difference* between the two areas—the total shaded area—is $4r^2 - \pi r^2$, or $r^2(4 - \pi)$

The area of each separate (smaller) shaded area is $\frac{1}{4}$ of the difference identified above.

Because each side of the square is tangent to the circle, it is *perpendicular* to a line segment from the tangent point (where the line segment touches the circle) to the circle's center.

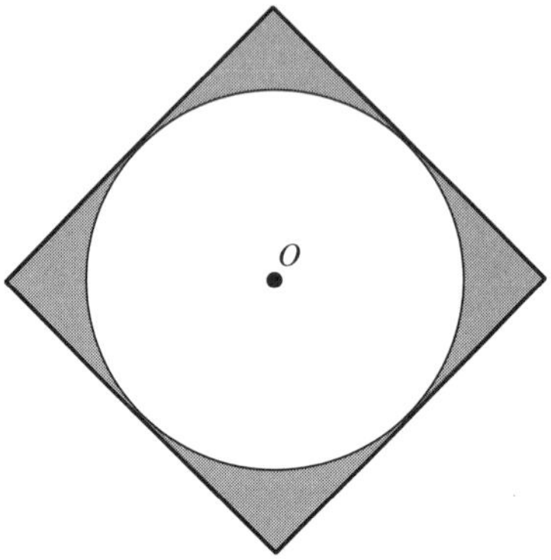

QUESTION If the area of circle O in the figure above is 64π, what is the perimeter of the square?

(A) 16

(B) 32

(C) 64

(D) 32π

(E) 64π

ANALYSIS The correct answer is **(C)**. The area of the circle = $64\pi = r^2\pi$. Thus, the radius of the circle = 8. The side of the square is 16—twice the circle's radius. Therefore, the perimeter of the square is $4 \times 16 = 64$.

Comparing Circles

A third type of circle problem calls for you to compare circles. The relationship between a circle's radius and area is exponential, not linear (because $A = \pi r^2$). So if one circle's radius is *twice* that of another's (as in the left-hand figure at the top of the next page), the ratio of the circles' areas is 1:4 ($\pi r^2 : \pi(2r)^2$). If the larger circle's radius is *three* times the length of that of the smaller circle (as in the right-hand figure at the top of the next page), the ratio is 1:9 ($\pi r^2 : \pi(3r)^2$). A 1:4 ratio between radii results in a 1:16 area ratio (and so forth).

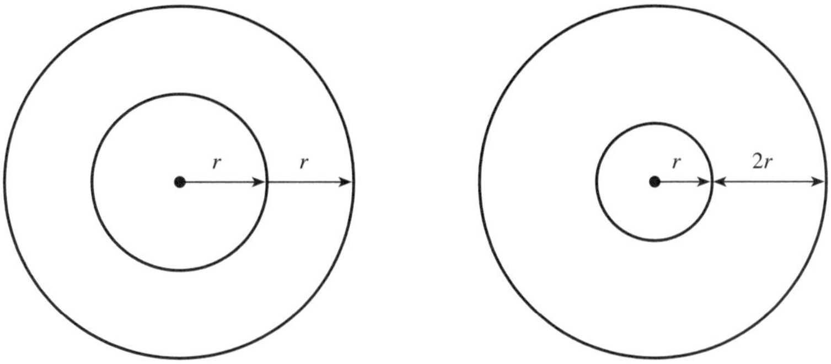

QUESTION If a circle whose radius is x has an area of 4, what is the area of a circle whose radius is $3x$?

(A) $\sqrt{13}$

(B) $4\sqrt{13}$

(C) 12

(D) 36

(E) 144

ANALYSIS The correct answer is **(D)**. The area of a circle is πr^2. The area of a circle with a radius of x is πx^2, which is given as 4. The area of a circle with radius $3x$ is $\pi(3x)^2 = 9\pi x^2$. Therefore, the area of the larger circle is 9 times the area of the smaller circle.

TIP A GMAT question might call for you to determine the difference in area, a segment of the area, or circumference of two circles, given their radii. No sweat! Just calculate each area (or circumference), then subtract.

Solids

If you understand how to determine areas of two-dimensional figures such as rectangles, triangles, and circles, you won't have any trouble handling problems involving three-dimensional objects—or *solids*. For the GMAT, you should know these three basic shapes:

1. Rectangular solids (boxes)
2. Cubes
3. Cylinders (tubes)

The following figure summarizes the formulas for determining surface area (*SA*) and volume (*V*). Memorize these formulas!

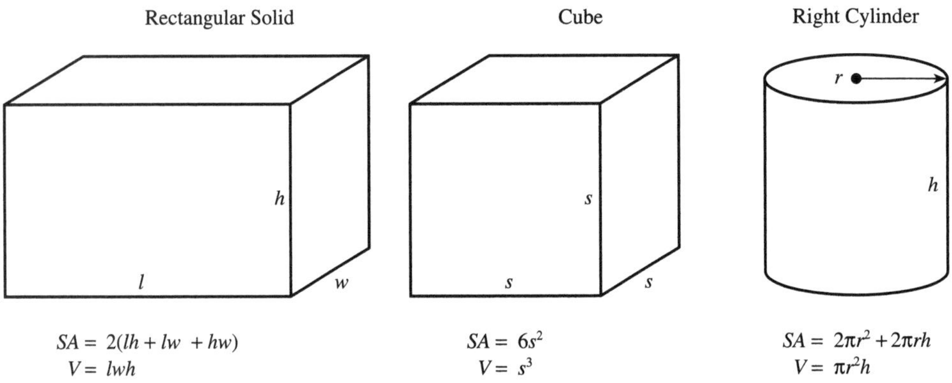

Rectangular Solids

The volume (*V*) of any rectangular solid (the left-hand solid in the figure above) is the product of its three dimensions: length, width, and height.

$$\text{Volume} = \text{length} \times \text{width} \times \text{height}$$
$$V = lwh$$

Each of three pairs of opposing faces are identical; in other words, they have the same dimensions and area. So the surface area of any rectangular solid can be expressed as follows:

$$\text{Surface Area} = 2lw + 2wh + 2lh = 2(lw + wh + lh)$$

QUESTION A rectangular box with a square base contains 24 cubic feet. If the height of the box is 18 inches, how many feet in length is each edge of the base?

(A) 4

(B) 6

(C) 8

(D) 12

(E) 16

ANALYSIS The correct answer is **(A)**. The volume of a rectangular box is the product of its length, width, and height. Since the height is 18 inches, or $1\frac{1}{2}$ feet, and the length and width of the square base are the same, we can use the same variable (such as x) to represent l and w in the volume formula, then solve for x:

$$x \cdot x \cdot 1\tfrac{1}{2} = 24$$
$$x^2 = 16$$
$$x = 4$$

Cubes

A *cube* (the middle solid in the previous figure) is a special type of rectangular solid in which all six faces, or surfaces, are square. Because all six faces of a cube are identical in dimension and area, given a length s of one of a cube's side—or edges—its surface area is six times the square of s, and its volume is the cube of s:

Surface Area = $6s^2$

Volume = s^3

Here's the relationship between the area of each square face of a cube and the cube's volume:

$$\text{Volume} = \left(\sqrt{\text{Area}}\right)^3$$
$$\text{Area} = \left(\sqrt[3]{\text{Volume}}\right)^2$$

QUESTION Find the edge, in inches, of a cube whose volume is equal to the volume of a rectangular solid 2 inches by 6 inches by 18 inches.

(A) 4

(B) 6

(C) 8

(D) 9

(E) 12

ANALYSIS The correct answer is **(B)**. First, determine the volume of the rectangular solid:

$$V = l \cdot w \cdot h = 2 \cdot 6 \cdot 18 = 216$$

Equate this volume with the volume of the cube and solve for *s* (the length of any edge of the cube):

$$V = s^3$$
$$216 = s^3$$
$$6 = s$$

Cylinders

The right-hand solid in the figure on page 184 is a "right" circular cylinder (the tube is sliced at 90° angles). This is the only kind of cylinder you need to know for the GMAT. The *surface area* of a right cylinder can be determined by adding together three areas:

1. the circular base
2. the circular top
3. the rectangular surface around the cylinder's vertical face (visualize a rectangular label wrapped around a soup can)

The area of the vertical face is the product of the circular base's circumference (i.e., the rectangle's width) and the cylinder's height. Thus, given a radius *r* and height *h* of a cylinder:

$$\text{Surface Area } (SA) = 2\pi r^2 + (2\pi r)(h)$$

Given a cylinder's radius and height, you can determine its *volume* by multiplying the area of its circular base by its height:

$$V = \pi r^2 h$$

QUESTION A certain cylindrical pail has a diameter of 14 inches and a height of 10 inches. If there are 231 cubic inches in a gallon, which of the following most closely approximates the number of gallons the pail will hold?

(A) 4.8

(B) 5.1

(C) 6.7

(D) 14.6

(E) 44

ANALYSIS The correct answer is **(C)**. The volume of the cylindrical pail is equal to the area of its circular base multiplied by its height:

$$V = \pi r^2 h = \left(\frac{22}{7}\right)(49)(10) = 1540 \text{ cubic inches}$$

The gallon capacity of the pail = $\frac{1540}{231}$, or about 6.7.

Coordinate Geometry

On the GMAT, you're likely to encounter one or two *coordinate geometry* questions, which involve the rectangular *coordinate plane* (or *xy*-plane) defined by two axes—a horizontal *x-axis* and a vertical *y-axis*. You can define any point on the coordinate plane by using two coordinates: an *x-coordinate* and a *y-coordinate*. A point's *x*-coordinate is its horizontal position on the plane, and its *y*-coordinate is its vertical position on the plane. You denote the coordinates of a point with (x,y), where x is the point's *x*-coordinate and y is the point's *y*-coordinate.

Coordinate Signs and the Four Quadrants

The center of the coordinate plane—the intersection of the *x* and *y* axes—is called the *origin*. The coordinates of the origin are (0,0). Any point along the *x*-axis has a *y*-coordinate of 0 $(x,0)$, and any point along the *y*-axis has an *x*-coordinate of 0 $(0,y)$. The coordinate signs (positive or negative) of points lying in the four quadrants I–IV in this next figure are as follows:

Quadrant I (+,+)

Quadrant II (–,+)

Quadrant III (–,–)

Quadrant IV (+,–)

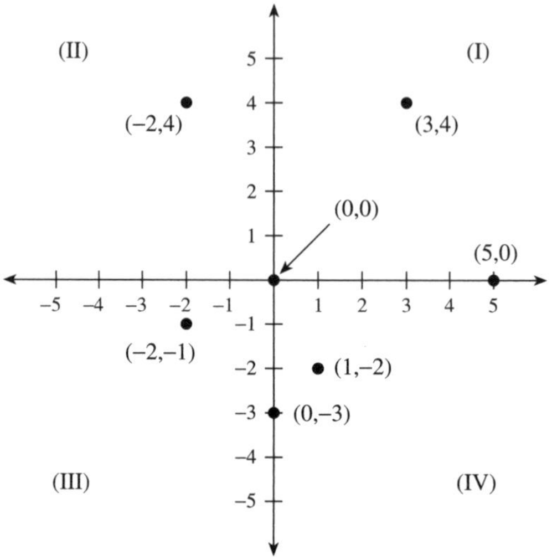

NOTE

Notice that we've plotted seven different points on this plane. Each point has its own unique coordinates. Before you read on, make sure you understand why each point is identified (by two coordinates) as it is.

Coordinate Triangle Problems

GMAT coordinate geometry problems can involve any 2-dimensional geometric figures you examined in this hour or the last one. But they usually involve either triangles, circles, or both. In triangle problems, your task is usually to determine the length of a sloping line segment (by forming a right triangle and applying the Pythagorean Theorem).

QUESTION On the *xy*-plane, what is the length of a line segment with end points defined by the (x,y) coordinate pairs $(-2,-1)$ and $(3,4)$?

(A) 4

(B) 5

(C) $4\sqrt{2}$

(D) 6

(E) $5\sqrt{2}$

ANALYSIS The correct answer is **(E)**. On the coordinate plane, construct a right triangle with the line segment as the hypotenuse. The length of the horizontal leg is 5 (the horizontal distance from –2 to 3). The length of the vertical leg is also 5 (the vertical distance from –1 to 4). So you're dealing with an isosceles right triangle. The ratios of the lengths of the three sides is $1:1:\sqrt{2}$. Since each leg (either of the short sides) is 5 in length, the length of the hypotenuse is $5\sqrt{2}$. The upper triangle in the following diagram illustrates the solution:

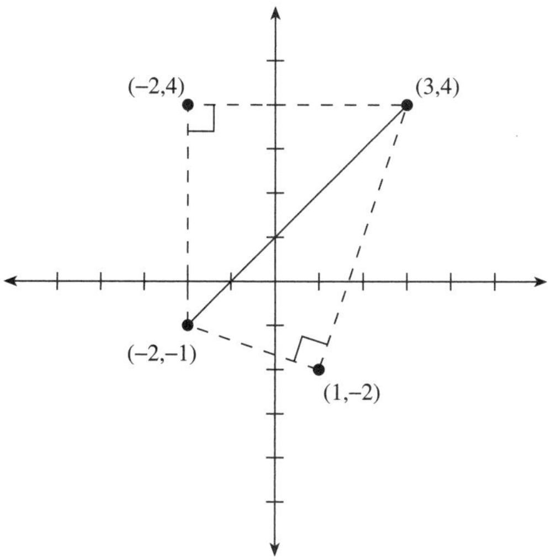

QUESTION On the *xy*-plane, what is the area of a triangle whose three vertices are defined by the (*x*,*y*) coordinate pairs (–2,–1), (3,4), and (1,–2)?

(A) 8

(B) 9

(C) 10

(D) 12

(E) 13

ANALYSIS The correct answer is **(C)**. The information in this question establishes the lower triangle in the preceding diagram. How do you know that the angle at point (1,–2) measures 90°? The slopes of the two dotted line segments are $-\frac{1}{3}$ and 3, so the segments are perpendicular. (You'll learn about slopes a few pages ahead.) The base and height of the triangle are represented by the dotted lines. The area of the triangle is, of course, $\frac{1}{2}bh$. So we need to determine b and h. Just as we did in the first question, think of b as the hypotenuse of a right triangle, this time with legs of 1 and 3 in length. Similarly, think of h as the hypotenuse of a right triangle whose legs are 2 and 6 in length. Do any of the convenient Pythagorean triplets allow us to shortcut applying the Pythagorean Theorem to determine each hypotenuse (the dotted line segments in the lower triangle)? No, not in either of these cases. So we need to find b and h the "long" way:

$$b^2 = 1^2 + 2^2$$
$$b^2 = 10$$
$$b = \sqrt{10}$$

$$h^2 = 2^2 + 6^2$$
$$h^2 = 40$$
$$h = \sqrt{40}, \text{ or } 2\sqrt{10}$$

We're not quite done. Now, we need to plug these values into our formula for the area of a triangle:

$$\text{Area} = \frac{1}{2}(\sqrt{10})(2\sqrt{10})$$
$$\text{Area} = 10$$

Coordinate Circle Problems

In circle problems, your task is usually to determine the circumference or area of a circle lying on the plane. By now you know that triangles pervade the area of geometry, and coordinate-plane circle problems are no exception.

QUESTION On the xy-plane, what is the area of a circle whose center is located at the point defined by the (x,y) coordinates (2,-1), if the point (-3,3) lies on the circle's circumference?

(A) 9π

(B) 75

(C) 25π

(D) 81

(E) 41π

ANALYSIS The correct answer is **(C)**. Construct a right triangle with the circle's radius as the hypotenuse. The length of the triangle's horizontal leg is 5 (the horizontal distance from –3 to 2), and the length of its vertical leg is 4 (the vertical distance from –1 to 3).

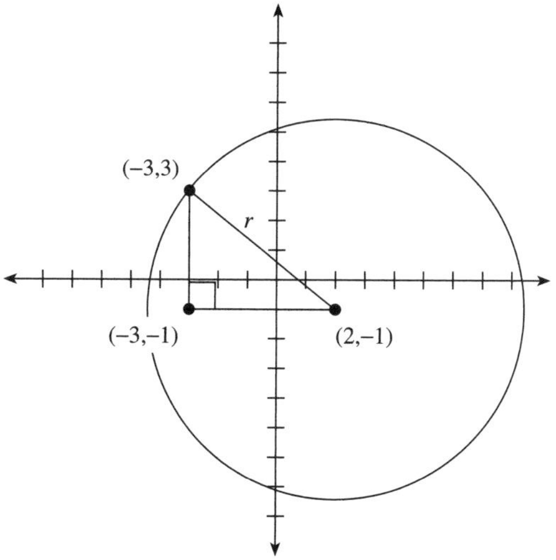

Be careful: These numbers do *not* conform to the Pythagorean triplet 3:4:5, because 4 and 5 are the lengths of the two *legs* here! Instead, you must calculate the length of the hypotenuse (the circle's radius) by applying the Pythagorean Theorem:

$$4^2 + 5^2 = r^2$$
$$16 + 25 = r^2$$
$$41 = r^2$$
$$\sqrt{41} = r$$

Now you can find the area of the circle:

$$\text{Area} = \pi\left(\sqrt{41}\right)^2$$
$$\text{Area} = 41\pi$$

CAUTION In any geometry problem involving right triangles, look out for the test-takers' Pythagorean triplet fake-out, in which you'll see the right ratio—but between the wrong sides!

Defining a Line on the Coordinate Plane

You can define any line on the coordinate plane with the following algebraic equation:

$$y = mx + b$$

In this equation:

m is the slope of the line

b is the y-intercept

x and y are the coordinates of any point on the line

Any (x,y) pair defining a point on the line can substitute for the variables x and y in this equation. The constant b represents the line's *y-intercept* (the point on the y-axis where the line crosses that axis). The constant m represents the line's *slope.*

TIP

Think of the slope of a line as a fraction in which the numerator indicates the vertical change from one point to another on the line (moving left to right) corresponding to a given horizontal change, which the fraction's denominator indicates. The common term used for this fraction is "rise-over-run."

Problems involving the algebraic equation for defining a line do *not* appear as frequently as the types we've already looked at. But you should be ready for one—just in case.

QUESTION On the xy-coordinate plane, two points—defined by the (x, y) pair $(-\frac{3}{2}, 0)$ and $(0, -2)$—both lie on the same line. Which of the following (x, y) pairs also lies on the same line?

(A) (–1, –1)

(B) (3, –3)

(C) (4, –4)

(D) (–5, 5)

(E) (–6, 6)

ANALYSIS The correct answer is **(E).** Given two points, you can determine the slope of the line:

$$\text{slope} = \frac{-2 \text{ (rise)}}{\frac{3}{2} \text{ (run)}} = -2\left(\frac{2}{3}\right) = -\frac{4}{3}$$

You know that the *y*-intercept is –2 (see the figure below). Thus, the equation that defines the line is $y = -\frac{4}{3}x - 2$. Among the answer choices, only (E) provides values for *x* and *y* that satisfy this equation:

$$6 = \left(-\frac{4}{3}\right)(-6) - 2$$

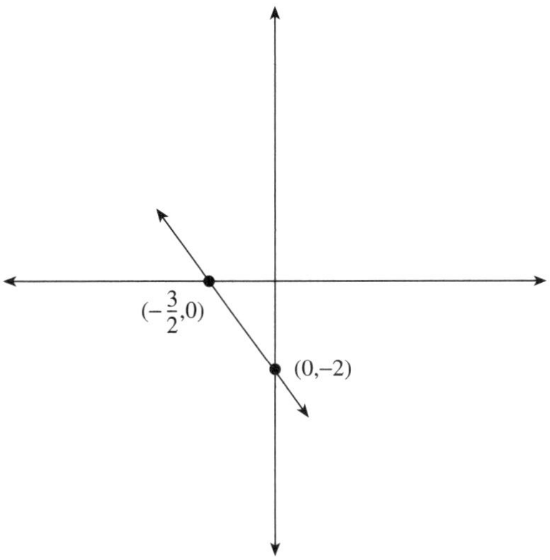

9

Workshop

In this hour's Workshop, you'll tackle a 10-question GMAT-style quiz, designed for you to review and apply the concepts and question types you learned about this hour.

ONLINE

Additional Quantitative questions are available online, at the authors' Web site: *http://www.west.net/~stewart/gmat*

Quiz

(Answers and explanations begin on page 196.)

DIRECTIONS: Attempt the following ten GMAT-style questions. Try to limit your time to 15 minutes. For each question, you'll see one or two hints to help you if you're having trouble.

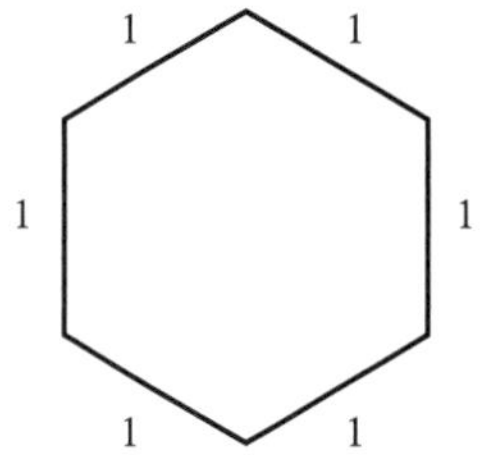

1. What is the area of the hexagon in the figure above?

   (A) $\frac{2\sqrt{3}}{3}$
   (B) $\sqrt{3}$
   (C) $\frac{3\sqrt{3}}{2}$
   (D) 4
   (E) $2\sqrt{2} + 1$

   (Hint: Divide the polygon into rectangles and triangles.)

2. The length of an arc of a certain circle is one fifth the circumference of the circle. If the length of the arc is 2π, what is the radius of the circle?

   (A) 1
   (B) 2
   (C) $\sqrt{10}$
   (D) 5
   (E) 10

   (Hint: You can find the radius if you know the circumference.)

3. If the volume of one cube is 8 times greater than that of another, what is the ratio of the area of one square face of the larger cube to that of the smaller cube?

   (A) 2:1
   (B) 4:1
   (C) 8:1
   (D) 12:1
   (E) 16:1

   (Hint: The relationship between volume and area is not linear.)

4. In a particular 4-sided pyramid, each side of the square base is 50 feet in length. If the apex of the pyramid is 60 feet from the ground, what is the total surface area of the pyramid in square feet, excluding the base? (Assume that all triangular faces are the same shape and size.)

   (A) 1625
   (B) $1475\sqrt{10}$
   (C) 5250
   (D) $2500\sqrt{5}$
   (E) 6500

   (Hint: First find the sloping height of each face.)

   (Hint: Look for Pythagorean triplets.)

5. On the coordinate plane, how many units is the point $(-4,-\frac{15}{2})$ from the origin, point (0,0)?

   (A) $\frac{29}{4}$
   (B) 8
   (C) $\frac{17}{2}$
   (D) 9
   (E) $6\sqrt{3}$

   (Hint: Look for a Pythagorean triplet.)

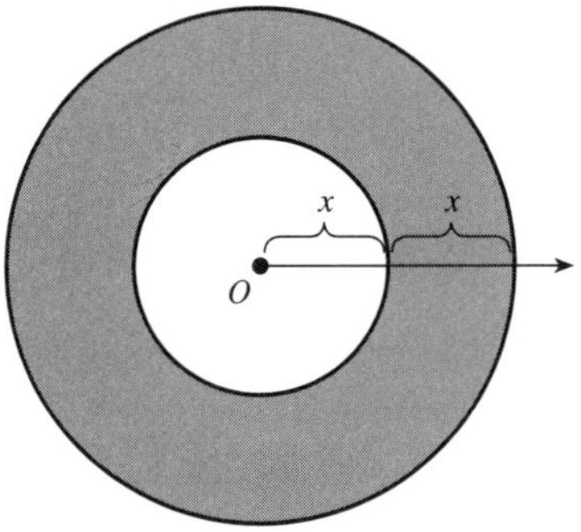

6. In the figure above, if $x = 1\frac{1}{2}$, what is the area of the shaded region?

   (A) $\frac{9}{4}\pi$
   (B) $\frac{9}{2}\pi$
   (C) 6π
   (Δ) $\frac{27}{4}\pi$
   (E) 9π

   (Hint: You can use ratios as a shortcut.)

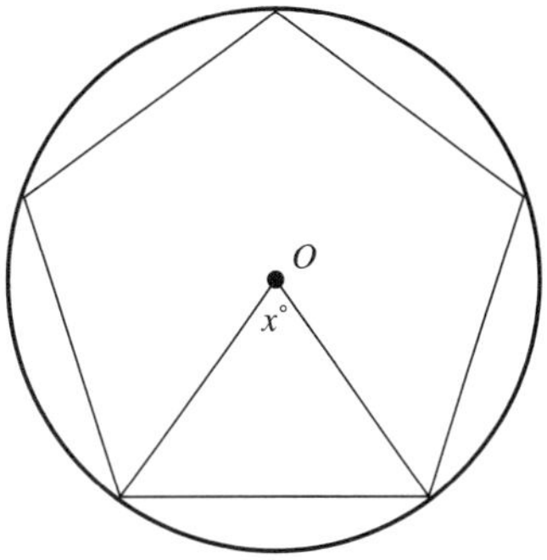

7. In the figure above, a pentagon whose sides are all equal in length touches a circle whose center is *0* at exactly five points. What is the value of *x*?

   (A) 54
   (B) 60
   (C) 72
   (D) 78
   (E) 84

Questions 8–10 are Data Sufficiency problems.

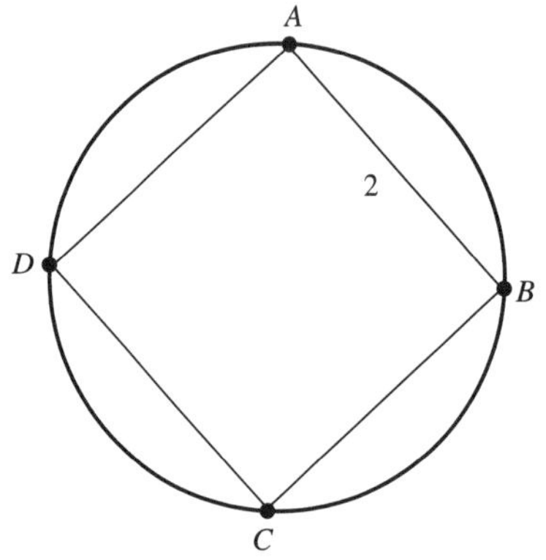

8. In the figure above, is rectangle *ABCD* a square?

   (1) The length of minor arc *AB* is equal to the length of minor arc *DC*.

   (2) The length of minor arc *AD* is $\frac{1}{2}\pi\sqrt{2}$.

   (Hint: Visualize all possible rectangular shapes.)

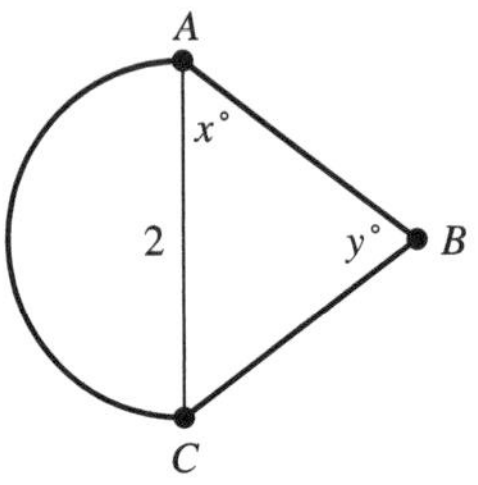

9. If a semicircle and triangle are pieced together to from the figure shown above, what is the total area of the figure?

   (1) The length of *AB* is 2.

   (2) $x = y$

   (Hint: Ask yourself what information you need to determine the area of a semicircle and the area of a triangle.)

10. How many boxes, each of which contains 64 cubic inches, will fit into a larger rectangular box?

    (1) Each of the small boxes is a cube.

    (2) The volume of the larger box is 1440 cubic inches.

    (Hint: Consider all possible shapes of a rectangular box.)

Answers and Explanations

1. **(C)** Each angle in the hexagon is 120°. You can divide up the figure as indicated to the right:

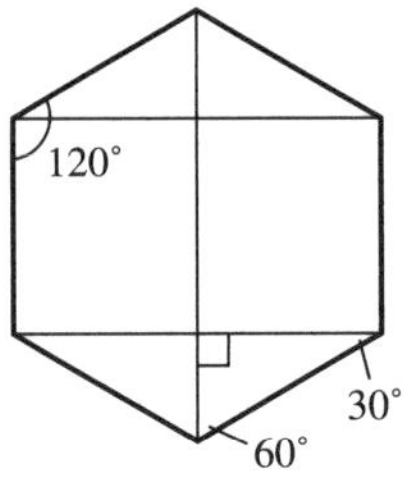

   Each of the four triangles is a 30-60-90 triangle, so the ratio of the sides of each is $1{:}\sqrt{3}{:}2$. The hypotenuse is 1, so the other two sides are $\frac{1}{2}$ and $\frac{\sqrt{3}}{2}$. The area of each triangle $= (\frac{1}{2})(\frac{1}{2})(\frac{\sqrt{3}}{2}) = \frac{\sqrt{3}}{8}$. The hexagon includes four such triangles, so the total area is $\frac{\sqrt{3}}{2}$. The area of each of the two rectangles is $(1)(\frac{\sqrt{3}}{2})$, so the area of both rectangles combined is $\sqrt{3}$. The total of all triangles and both rectangles is $\sqrt{3} + \frac{\sqrt{3}}{2}$, or $\frac{3\sqrt{3}}{2}$

2. **(D)** The circumference is five times the length of the arc:

$$5(2\pi) = 10\pi = \pi d$$
$$d = 10, \text{ and } r = 5$$

3. **(B)** The ratio of the two volumes is 8:1. Thus, the linear ratio of the cubes' edges is the cube root of this ratio: $\sqrt[3]{8}$, or 2:1. The area ratio is the square of the linear ratio, or 4:1.

4. **(E)** The altitude of the pyramid (60) and one-half the length of a side (25) form the legs of a right triangle whose hypotenuse is the sloping (angular) height of each face. This triangle is a 5:12:13 right triangle whose sides are 25, 60, and 65. (The sloping height of each triangular face is 65.) You can now determine the area of each triangular face:

$$A = \left(\frac{1}{2}\right)(50)(65)$$
$$A = 1625$$

Accordingly, the total surface area of the pyramid is 4 times this amount, or 6500 square feet.

5. **(C)** Plotting the points reveal a 8-15-17 triangle $(4^2 + \left(\frac{15}{2}\right)^2 = \left(\frac{17}{2}\right)^2)$, in which the x-axis and y-axis serve as the two legs of the triangle.

6. **(D)** The area of the smaller circle is $\pi\left(\frac{3}{2}\right)^2$, or $\frac{9}{4}\pi$. Given that the radius of the larger circle is twice that of the smaller one, the area ratio is 4:1. Accordingly, the area of the shaded region is 3 times the area of the smaller circle (4 times the area of the smaller circle minus the area of the smaller circle), or $\frac{27}{4}\pi$.

7. **(C)** Because the pentagon is regular (all five sides are equal in length), each angle measures 108°. A line segment from the circle's center to any of the pentagon's angles bisects that angle into two 54° angles. The figure below shows the triangle formed by two such line segments. The angle at the circle's center must measure 72° (54 + 54 + 72 = 180).

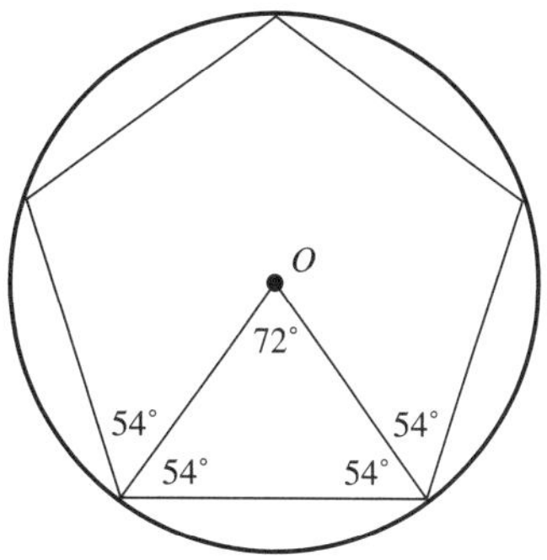

9

8. **(B)** Statement (1) alone is insufficient, because *AD* (and *BC*) could be either longer, equal to, or shorter than *AB* (and *DC*). Statement (2) alone does suffice to answer the question. Assume hypothetically that *ABCD* is a square. Given that $AB = 2$, the circle's radius is $\sqrt{2}$, and the circle's circumference is $2\pi\sqrt{2}$. Statement (2) provides that arc *AD* is exactly $\frac{1}{4}$ that circumference, so all four sides of the rectangle must be equal in length. Thus, given statement (2) alone, *ABCD* must indeed be a square.

9. **(C)** You can determine the area of the semicircle in any event—without either statement (1) or (2). So you need more information only to determine the triangle's area. Given statement (1) alone, the triangle could be any shape, so its area could vary. Given statement (2) alone, *AB* and *BC* each could be any length, and so the area of the triangle could vary. Thus, neither statement alone suffices to answer the question. Given both statements together, the triangle must be equilateral, and you can determine its area. (Although you don't need to do the math, the semicircle's area is $\frac{\pi}{2}$, the triangle's area is $\sqrt{3}$, and so the total area is $\frac{\pi}{2} + \sqrt{3}$.)

10. **(E)** Neither statement provides any information about the dimensions of the larger box. (It might be a cube, or it might be only one inch in height, or it might have any other shape.) Without this information, it's impossible to answer the question.

Part III

Learn to Answer GMAT Verbal Questions

Hour

Hour 10

Teach Yourself Sentence Correction I

This hour (as well as the next two) you'll teach yourself how to handle Sentence Correction questions, which appear in the Verbal section of the GMAT CAT. Here are your goals for this hour:

- Learn what Sentence Correction questions look like and how to answer them
- Learn tips for avoiding common Sentence Correction pitfalls and traps
- Learn to recognize and fix certain grammatical errors appearing in GMAT Sentence Correction questions
- Review the concepts you learn by attempting a GMAT-style quiz

Sentence Correction at a Glance

WHERE: In the GMAT CAT Verbal section, mixed in with Reading Comprehension and Critical Reasoning questions

HOW MANY: 14–15 out the 41 questions in the Verbal section (though not all of them are necessarily scored)

WHAT'S COVERED: Two areas of English language proficiency:

1. *correct expression*, measured by your ability to recognize errors in grammar and usage
2. *effective expression*, measured by your ability to improve sentences that are poorly worded or structured

WHAT'S NOT COVERED: Other areas of English language proficiency:

1. *punctuation* (except that comma placement can come into play if it affects the meaning of a sentence)
2. *vocabulary* (you won't have to memorize long lists of obscure and erudite words just for GMAT Sentence Correction)
3. *slang and colloquialisms* (informal expressions don't appear at all in Sentence Correction questions)

DIRECTIONS: These directions will appear on your screen before your first Sentence Correction question:

> This question presents a sentence, all or part of which is underlined. Beneath the sentence you will find five ways of phrasing the underlined part. The first of these repeats the original; the other four are different. If you think the original is best, choose the first answer; otherwise choose one of the others.
>
> This question tests correctness and effectiveness of expression. In choosing your answer, follow the requirements of Standard Written English; that is, pay attention to grammar, choice of words, and sentence construction. Choose the answer that produces the most effective sentence; this answer should be clear and exact, without awkwardness, ambiguity, redundancy, or grammatical error.

What Sentence Correction Questions Look Like

Part of a sentence (or the whole sentence) will be underlined. Answer choice (A) will simply restate the underlined part "as is." The other four choices present alternatives to the original underlined phrase. Here's what a typical Sentence Correction question looks like (we'll analyze this question just a few pages ahead):

QUESTION <u>Despite sophisticated computer models for assessing risk, such a model is nevertheless</u> limited in their ability to define what risk is.

(A) Despite sophisticated computer models for assessing risk, such a model is nevertheless

(B) Sophisticated computer models, which assess risk, are nevertheless

(C) Despite their sophistication, computer models for assessing risk are

(D) Assessment of risk can be achieved with sophisticated computer models, but these models are

(E) Assessing risk with sophisticated computer models is limited because such models are

NOTE

> You won't find informal or conversational sentences in GMAT Sentence Correction. Instead, you'll see that all sentences are rather formal in tone and that most involve academic topics. Don't worry: you won't need any knowledge of the topic at hand in order to handle a question. (Experts in computer modeling or risk assessment wouldn't hold any advantage in the sample question above, would they?)

What You Should Know about Sentence Correction Questions

Any portion of the sentence might be underlined. The underlined part may appear at the beginning, middle, or end of the sentence. Also, in some cases, the entire sentence will be underlined.

The first answer choice simply restates the underlined part "as is." The other four choices present alternatives to the original underlined phrase.

The best answer choice isn't always perfect. In some cases the best choice among the five may be a bit awkward or wordy—but nevertheless the only choice that is free of grammatical errors. Don't be stubborn and insist on finding an answer choice that makes for an ideal sentence that Emerson or Hemingway would be proud of. You're looking for the best version among the five, not the perfect version.

More than one answer choice may be grammatically correct. These questions cover not just grammar, but also effective expression. So don't select an answer choice just because it results in a grammatically correct sentence. Another answer choice may be clearer, more concise, or less awkward—and therefore better.

Punctuation doesn't matter. You won't find errors in punctuation in these sentences (except as part of larger errors involving sentence structure). The test-makers rely instead on your two GMAT essays to demonstrate your "punctuation prowess."

How to Approach a Sentence Correction Question

Here's a 4-step approach that will help you to handle any Sentence Correction question the GMAT CAT throws at you:

ACTION PLAN

1. **Read the original sentence carefully.**
2. **Plug your remaining choices, one at a time, into the original sentence, and read the entire *revised* sentence.**
3. **If you still haven't narrowed the choices down to a clear winner, compare the remaining candidates.**
4. **Verify your selection before confirming your response.**

Let's Apply the 4-Step Action Plan

It's time to return to the sample question you looked at a few pages back. This time around, we'll walk through the question using the 4-step approach you just learned.

QUESTION Despite sophisticated computer models for assessing risk, such a model is nevertheless limited in their ability to define what risk is.

(A) Despite sophisticated computer models for assessing risk, such a model is nevertheless

(B) Sophisticated computer models, which assess risk, are nevertheless

(C) Despite their sophistication, computer models for assessing risk are

(D) Assessment of risk can be achieved with sophisticated computer models, but these models are

(E) Assessing risk with sophisticated computer models is limited because such models are

1. Upon a first reading, doesn't "such a model" sound a bit awkward? That's a good clue that (A) is not the correct response. In fact, the original sentence contains two flaws. One is a grammatical error: the plural pronoun *their* is used to refer to the singular noun *model*. Either both should be plural or both should be singular; but they must match! The word *their* is not part of the underlined phrase, so look for an answer choice that uses *models* instead of *model*. (In grammatical terminology, the original sentence contains an error in "pronoun-antecedent agreement.") The other flaw is one of ineffective expression: the first clause (before the comma) is structured differently from the second clause, and the result is an awkward and confusing sentence. So you should look for an answer choice that makes the sentence clearer and perhaps a bit more concise—one that helps the sentence sound a bit better and "flow" a bit more smoothly.

2. Substitute each answer choice in turn for the underlined part.

   (B) does not contain any grammatical errors. But doesn't the phrase *which assess risk* appear to describe computer models in general rather than models for assessing risk? Surely, this isn't the intended meaning of the sentence. (B) is a perfect example of an answer choice that is wrong because it either distorts, confuses, or obscures the intended meaning of the sentence. Eliminate (B).

   (C) takes care of both problems with the original sentence. The plural noun *models* matches the plural pronoun *their,* and the underlined part has been reconstructed to provide a clearer and briefer sentence. (C) is probably the correct answer, but read the remaining choices anyway.

   (D) sounds pretty good when you read it as part of the sentence, doesn't it? No grammatical errors jump out at you. So is it a toss-up between (C) and (D)? Well, go on to (E) for now, then come back to the (C) versus (D) debate.

(E) incorrectly uses the phrase *is limited* to describe *assessing risk*. It is the computer models' ability, not assessing risk, that is limited. Eliminate (E).

3. Go back to (C) and (D). Is one less awkward than the other? More concise? Closer in meaning to the original version? Perhaps you noticed that the first clause in (D) (*assessment of risk can be achieved*) sounds a bit awkward. (The clause employs the so-called "passive" voice, an awkward construction that you'll learn more about next hour.) So, you should choose (C) over (D).

4. Check (C) one more time by plugging it into the sentence: *Despite their sophistication, computer models for assessing risk are limited in their ability to define what risk is.* Sounds great! Confirm your response, and move on to the next question.

NOTE

> Don't worry if you just encountered a few unfamiliar grammatical terms; when you look at the rules of English grammar later this hour as well as during the next two, you'll learn what those terms mean.

DO's and DON'Ts for Tackling Sentence Correction Questions

Do **Don't**

DON'T just skim the answer choices; one little word can make all the difference!

DO read the entire sentence with each version, in turn.

DON'T choose an answer just because it fixes every flaw in the original version.

DO trust your ear.

DON'T be thrown by a nonsensical answer choice.

DO eliminate answer choices that change the meaning of the original sentence.

DO resolve close judgment calls in favor of briefer answer choices.

DON'T assume the original sentence is wrong.

Finding—and Fixing—Grammatical Errors Involving Parts of Speech

For the rest of the hour, you'll examine grammatical errors involving parts of speech (adjectives, adverbs, pronouns, verbs). The error types covered here are the ones that appear most frequently in GMAT Sentence Correction sentences. In addition to learning how to fix each type of error, you'll see how each error might appear in a typical GMAT question.

TIP

By the way, immersing yourself in English grammar (as you're about to do) will help you not only for Sentence Correction questions, but also for the Analytical Writing Assessment (AWA) sections of the GMAT. So pay close attention; your efforts here will be doubly rewarded on exam day!

Error in Choice Between Adjective and Adverb

Adjectives describe nouns, while *adverbs* describe verbs, adjectives and other adverbs. Adverbs generally end with *-ly*, while adjectives don't. Look for adjectives incorrectly used as adverbs (and vice versa).

INCORRECT: The movie ended *sudden.*

CORRECT: The movie ended *suddenly.* (The adverb *suddenly* describes the verb *ended.*)

Although adverbs generally end with *-ly*, some adverbs don't. Also, if you're dealing with two adverbs in a row, sometimes the *-ly* is dropped from the second adverb. There are no hard-and-fast rules here. Trust your ear as to what sounds correct.

INCORRECT: The Canadian skater jumps *particularly highly.*
CORRECT: The Canadian skater jumps *particularly high.*

Now look at how the test-makers might try to slip one of these errors past you in a GMAT sentence. In the question on the next page, the original sentence is flawed, so Response (A) is incorrect. Your choice is between (C) and (D).

NOTE

To help you focus on the specific grammatical error at hand, we'll simplify the Sentence Correction format by listing just *three* answer choices, and by limiting the different kinds of errors altogether to one or two. Actual GMAT questions include five answer choices, of course.

QUESTION A recent report from the Department of Energy suggests that over the next two decades demand for crude oil will increase at an alarming fast rate, and greatly exceeds most economists' previous forecasts.

(A) increase at an alarming fast rate, and greatly exceeds

(B) ***

(C) increase at an alarmingly fast rate, greatly exceeding

(D) be alarmingly increasing and will greatly exceed

(E) ***

ANALYSIS The correct answer is **(C)**. The original sentence incorrectly uses the adjective *alarming* instead of the adverb *alarmingly* to describe the adjective *fast.* The original sentence also contains an additional, and more conspicuous, flaw. The phrase *and greatly exceeds* improperly suggests that the rate is increasing alarmingly at the present time. However, the sentence as a whole makes clear that this is a future event. (C) corrects both of these problems. Although (D) also corrects both problems, it creates a new flaw. The phrase *alarmingly increasing* is an awkward and inappropriate expression of the idea that the sentence attempts to convey.

TIP

Because this sort of error is generally easy to spot in a sentence, the GMAT test-makers will probably try to sneak it past you by including another (and possibly more conspicuous) flaw as well—in the hope that you'll carelessly overlook the incorrect adjective or adverb. Beat them at their own game by looking carefully at adjectives and adverbs, *especially when they appear in pairs* (as in the sample question above)!

Error in Choice of Adjective for Comparisons

As you read a GMAT sentence, pay close attention to any adjective ending in *-er*, *-ier*, *-est*, and *-iest*. Adjectives ending in *-er* or *-ier* should be used to compare *two* things, while adjectives ending in *-est* and *-iest* should be used in dealing with three or more things.

Another way of making a comparison is to precede the adjective with a word such as *more*, *less*, *most*, or *least*. But if both methods are used together, the sentence is incorrect.

INCORRECT: Frank is less intelligent than the other four students.

CORRECT: Frank is the *least* intelligent among the *five* students.

CORRECT: Frank is *less* intelligent than *any* of the other four students (The word *any* is singular, so the comparative form is proper.)

INCORRECT: Francis is *more healthier* than Greg.

CORRECT: Francis is *healthier* than Greg.

QUESTION The more busier the trading floor at the stock exchange, the less opportunities large institutional investors have to influence the direction of price by initiating large leveraged transactions.

(A) The more busier the trading floor at the stock exchange, the less opportunities

(B) A busier trading floor at the stock exchange results in less opportunities

(C) The busier the trading floor at the stock exchange, the fewer opportunities

(D) ***

(E) ***

ANALYSIS The corrrect answer is **(C)**. In the original sentence, the phrase *more busier* incorrectly uses both comparative methods. (C) corrects this flaw by using *busier*. The original sentence includes another flaw as well. The phrase *less opportunities* is incorrect; the word *fewer* should be used instead of *less* in referring to countable things. (C) corrects this flaw. However, (B) does not.

Error in Choice of Personal Pronoun

Personal pronouns are words such as *they*, *me*, *his*, and *itself*—words that refer to specific people, places and things. Pronouns take different forms depending on how they are used in a sentence.

You can generally trust your ear when it comes to detecting personal-pronoun errors. In some cases, however, your ear can betray you, so make sure you are "tuned in" to the following uses of pronouns.

INCORRECT: Either *him* or *Trevor* would be the best spokesman for our group.

INCORRECT: The best spokesperson for our group would be either *him* or Trevor.

CORRECT: Either Trevor or *he would be* the best spokesperson for our group.

10

CORRECT: The best spokesperson for our group *would be* either *he* or Trevor.
(Any form of the verb *to be* is followed by a subject pronoun, such as *he*.)

INCORRECT: One can't help admiring *them* cooperating with one another.

CORRECT: One can't help admiring *their cooperating* with one another.
(The possessive form is used when the pronoun is part of a "noun clause," such as *their cooperating*.)

INCORRECT: In striving to understand others, we also learn more about *us*.
CORRECT: In striving to understand others, *we* also learn more about *ourselves*.
(A reflexive pronoun is used to refer to the sentence's subject.)

CAUTION

What appears to be a reflexive pronoun may not even be a real word! Here's a list of "non-words" and improper phrases, any of which might masquerade as a reflexive pronoun in a GMAT sentence:

ourself, our own selves, theirselves, theirself, themself, their own self, their own selves

QUESTION Those of the legislators opposing the swampland protection bill have only theirselves to blame for the plight of the endangered black thrush bird.

(A) of the legislators opposing the swampland protection bill have only theirselves

(B) ***

(C) legislators which opposed the swampland protection bill, have only themselves

(D) legislators who opposed the swampland protection bill have only themselves

(E) ***

ANALYSIS The correct answer is **(D)**. The original sentence suffers from two flaws. First, *theirselves* is a non-word and should be replaced with the reflexive pronoun *themselves*. Second, the phrase *those of the legislators opposing*, while not grammatically incorrect, is awkward and confusing. (D) provides a briefer and clearer alternative phrase, as well as correcting the pronoun error. Answer choice (C) also corrects the pronoun error, but it creates a new problem: it uses the relative pronoun *which* instead of a preferred *who* to refer to *legislators*. (You'll learn about relative pronouns immediately ahead.)

NOTE

> In GMAT sentences, you'll find very few (if any) first-person or second-person personal pronouns. Why do the test-makers shun pronouns such as *we*, *you*, and *our*? Because GMAT sentences are academic in nature, not conversational or informal. (But you probably already noticed that, didn't you?)

Error in Choice of Relative Pronoun

The English language includes only a handful of *relative pronouns*. Here they are:

which	whom	whose	whoever
who	that	whichever	whomever

Don't worry about what the term "relative pronoun" means. Instead, just remember the following rules about when to use each one.

1. Use *which* to refer to things.
2. Use either *who* or *that* to refer to people.

    INCORRECT: Amanda, *which* was the third performer, was the best of the group.

    CORRECT: Amanda, *who* was the third performer, was the best of the group.

    CORRECT: The first employee *that* fails to meet his or her sales quota will be fired.

    CORRECT: The first employee *who* fails to meet his or her sales quota will be fired.

3. Whether you should use *which* or *that* depends on what the sentence is supposed to mean.

    ONE MEANING: The third page, *which* had been earmarked, contained several typographical errors.

    DIFFERENT MEANING: The third page *that* had been earmarked contained several typographical errors.

(The first sentence merely describes the third page as earmarked. The second sentence also suggests that the page containing the errors was the third earmarked page.)

4. Whether you should use *who* (*whoever*) or *whom* (*whomever*) depends on the grammatical function of the person (or people) being referred to. Confused? Don't worry; just take a look at the sample sentences here, then read the TIP that follows, and you shouldn't have any trouble deciding between *who* and *whom* on the GMAT.

   INCORRECT: It was the chairman *whom* initiated the bill.

   CORRECT: It was the chairman *who* initiated the bill.

   INCORRECT: First aid will be available to *whomever* requires it.

   CORRECT: First aid will be available to *whoever* requires it.

TIP

On the GMAT, to make sure that *who (whoever)* and *whom (whomever)* are being used correctly, try substituting a regular pronoun, then rearrange the clause (if necessary) to form a simple sentence. If a subject-case pronoun works, then *who* (*whoever*) is the right choice. On the other hand, if an object-case pronoun works, then *whom* (*whomever*) is the right choice. Here's how it works with the foregoing sentences:

It was the chairman *whom* initiated the bill.
He initiated the bill.
(*He* is a subject-case pronoun, so *whom* should be replaced with *who*.)

First aid will be available to *whomever* requires it.
She requires it.
(*She* is a subject-case pronoun, so *whomever* should be replaced with *whoever*.)

QUESTION The Civil War's bloodiest battle was initiated on behalf of those, the indentured black slaves, for who life was most precious.

(A) bloodiest battle was initiated on behalf of those, the indentured black slaves, for who life was most precious

(B) indentured black slaves, for whom life was most precious, initiated the war's bloodiest battle

(C) ***

(D) ***

(E) bloodiest battle was initiated on behalf of the indentured black slaves, for whom life was most precious

ANALYSIS The correct answer is **(E)**. The original sentence suffers from two flaws. First, the relative pronoun *who* should be replaced with *whom*. (Replace the last clause with: *Life was most precious for them.* The pronoun *them* is an object-case pronoun, so the correct choice is *whom*.) Secondly, the word *those*, probably intended to refer to the slaves, should be omitted because it is unnecessary and because it confuses the meaning of the sentence. The comma following *those* should also be omitted. (E) corrects both flaws. (B) also corrects both flaws, but it radically alters the sentence's meaning, improperly suggesting that the slaves initiated the bloodiest battle (rather than properly communicating that it was on the slaves' behalf that the battle was fought).

Error in Pronoun-Antecedent Agreement

An *antecedent* is simply the noun to which a pronoun refers. In GMAT sentences, make sure that pronouns agree in *number* (singular or plural) with their antecedents.

SINGULAR: Studying other artists actually helps a young *painter* develop *his* or *her* own style.

PLURAL: Studying other artists actually helps young *painters* develop *their* own style.

Singular pronouns are generally used in referring to antecedents such as *each*, *either*, *neither*, and *one*.

CORRECT: *Neither* of the two countries imposes an income tax on *its* citizens.

CORRECT: *One* cannot be too kind to *oneself*.

QUESTION <u>Many powerful leaders throughout history, such as President Nixon during the Watergate debacle, had become victimized by his own paranoia.</u>

(A) Many powerful leaders throughout history, such as President Nixon during the Watergate debacle, had become victimized by his own paranoia.

(B) Many powerful leaders throughout history, such as President Nixon during the Watergate debacle, have become victims of their own paranoia.

(C) Throughout history, many a powerful leader, such as President Nixon during the Watergate debacle, have by his or her own paranoia become a victim.

(D) ***

(E) ***

ANALYSIS The correct answer is **(B)**. The original sentence intends to make the point that *many leaders* (plural) *have* (plural verb) become victimized by *their* (plural pronoun) own paranoia. However, by using the singular *had* and *his*, the final clause seems to refer to Nixon instead of to leaders. (B) correctly uses the plurals *have* and *their*. In (C), the plural subject *leaders* has been transformed into a singular subject (*many a powerful leader*). This form is grammatically acceptable. However, the subject's verb, as well as any pronouns that refer to the subject, should now be singular as well. Although the singular *his or her* is correct, the plural verb *have* is incorrect. (C) also separates the words *have* and *become*. These two words are part of the same grammatical unit which should not be split.

Error in Subject-Verb Agreement (When the Verb Is Separated from Its Subject)

A verb should always "agree" in number—either singular or plural—with its subject. Don't be fooled by any words or phrases that might separate the verb from its subject. In each sentence below, the singular verb *was* agrees with its subject, the singular noun *parade*:

CORRECT: The *parade was* spectacular.

CORRECT: The *parade* of cars *was* spectacular.

CORRECT: The *parade* of cars and horses *was* spectacular.

CAUTION An intervening clause set off by commas can serve as an especially effective "smokescreen" for a subject-verb agreement error. Pay careful attention to what comes immediately before and after the intervening clause. Reading the sentence without the clause often reveals a subject-verb agreement error.

INCORRECT: John, as well as his sister, *were* absent from school yesterday.

CORRECT: *John*, as well as his sister, *was* absent from school yesterday.

QUESTION Grade school instruction in ethical and social values, particularly the values of respect and of tolerance, are required for any democracy to thrive.

(A) values of respect and of tolerance, are

(B) value of respect, together with tolerance, is

(C) values of respect and tolerance, is

(D) ***

(E) ***

ANALYSIS The correct answer is **(C)**. In the original sentence, the subject of the plural verb *are* is the singular noun *instruction*. The correct answer choice must correct this subject-verb agreement problem. Also, the second *of* in the underlined phrase should be omitted because its use results in an awkward and nonsensical clause which seems to suggest that *of tolerance* is a value. Both (B) and (C) correct the problem by changing *are* to *is* and by dropping the second *of*. However, (B) creates two new problems. First, using the word *value* instead of *values* distorts the meaning of the underlined phrase. Respect and tolerance are not referred to in (B) as values. However, the original sentence, considered as a whole, clearly intends to refer to respect and tolerance as examples of ethical and social *values*. Secondly, the phrase *together with tolerance* (set off by commas), adds an unnecessary clause and results in a sentence that is wordy and awkward. (C) is clearer and more concise.

TIP Keep a keen eye out for GMAT sentences that separate verbs from their subjects. In every one of these sentences, it's a sure bet that the test-makers are testing you on subject-verb agreement.

Error in Subject-Verb Agreement (Pronoun and Compound Subjects)

You can easily determine whether a personal pronoun such as *he, they,* and *its* is singular or plural. But other pronouns are not so easily identified as either singular or plural. Here are two lists, along with some sample sentences, to help you keep these pronouns straight in your mind:

Singular pronouns:

anyone, anything, anybody

each

either, neither

every, everyone, everything, everybody

nobody, no one, nothing

what, whatever

who, whom, whoever, whomever

Even when they refer to a "compound" subject joined by *and*, the pronouns listed above remain *singular.*

CORRECT: *Each adult and child* here *speaks* fluent French.

CORRECT: *Every* possible *cause and suspect was* investigated.

Plural pronouns:

both

few

many

several

some

others

It's especially easy to overlook a subject-verb agreement problem in a sentence involving a compound subject (multiple subjects joined by connectors such as the word *and* or the word *or*). If joined by *and*, a compound subject is usually plural (and takes a plural verb). But if joined by *or*, *either . . . or*, or *neither . . . nor*, compound subjects are usually singular.

PLURAL: The chorus *and* the introduction *need* improvement.

SINGULAR: *Either* the chorus *or* the introduction *needs* improvement.

SINGULAR: *Neither* the chorus *nor* the introduction *needs* improvement.

QUESTION Neither his financial patron <u>or Copernicus himself were expecting the societal backlash resulting from him</u> denouncing the Earth-centered Ptolemaic model of the universe.

(A) or Copernicus himself were expecting the societal backlash resulting from him

(B) ***

(C) nor Copernicus himself was expecting the societal backlash resulting from his

(D) nor Copernicus were expecting the societal backlash resulting from him

(E) ***

ANALYSIS The correct answer is **(C)**. The original sentence actually contains three grammatical errors! First, *neither* should be paired with *nor* instead of *or*. Secondly, the singular verb *was* should be used instead of the plural *were* because *neither . . . nor* calls for a singular verb when both parts of the subject (*patron* and *Copernicus*) are singular. Thirdly, the phrase *him denouncing* is improper; *denouncing* is a gerund (a verb turned into a noun by adding *-ing*), and gerunds always take possessive pronouns (*his* in this case). (C) corrects all three errors without creating any new ones. (D) corrects the first error, but not the other two. Also, notice that (D) deletes *himself* from the original sentence. In doing so, (D) actually obscures the intended meaning of the sentence, which makes it clear, through the use of *himself*, that the word "his" (appearing twice in the sentence) refers to Copernicus rather than to someone else. So (D) actually creates a new error!

Workshop

In this Workshop, you'll review the rules of grammar you learned this hour by attempting a GMAT-style Quiz.

NOTE

This Workshop will focus, of course, on the grammatical errors you examined this hour. But other types of errors will pop up as well. Don't worry: you'll learn all about them during the next two hours. So this Workshop is both a *review* and a *preview*!

Quiz

(Answers and explanations begin on page 218.)

Directions: This question presents a sentence, all or part of which is underlined. Beneath the sentence you will find five ways of phrasing the underlined part. The first of these repeats the original; the other four are different. If you think the original is best, choose the first answer; otherwise choose one of the others.

ONLINE

Additional Sentence Correction questions are available online, at the authors' Web site: *http://www.west.net/~stewart/gmat*

1. Raising a child alone and holding down a full-time job requires good organization skills.

   (A) requires good organization skills
   (B) require good organizational skills
   (C) requires the skill of good organization
   (D) require that one be skilled in organizing
   (E) requires good organizational skill

   (Hint: Subject and verb must agree in number.)

2. Contrary to popular myth, war heroes rarely earn their status by acting as if they themselves are invincible.

   (A) as if they themselves are invincible
   (B) as though they are invincible
   (C) as being invincible
   (D) as if they themself are invincible
   (E) as if they were invincible

   (Hint: Use the reflexive pronoun form when the subject acts upon itself.)

3. Even an introductory course in English literature can be challenging because they all require large amounts of reading.
   (A) they all require large amounts
   (B) it is necessary to do large amounts
   (C) these courses would require a great deal
   (D) it requires a large amount
   (E) it always entails a large quantity

   (Hint: Use "amount" to refer to degree; use "quantity" to refer to number.)

4. In Norse poetry, the stories rarely stand as substitutes or symbols for anything outside itself.
   (A) as substitutes or symbols for anything outside itself
   (B) as either substitutes nor symbols for anything else
   (C) neither as substitutes nor symbols for anything other than themselves
   (D) as substitutes or symbols for anything else
   (E) as substitutes or as symbols in place of something else

   (Hint: Use the reflexive pronoun form when the subject acts upon itself.)

5. It is our legislators who are to blame for our nation's dependency on oil.
   (A) It is our legislators who are to
   (B) Our legislators are whom we should
   (C) It is they, our legislators, who are to
   (D) To our legislators belong the
   (E) Our legislators hold the

   (Hint: The phrase "It is our legislators" is a noun clause; treat the clause as the subject of the sentence.)

6. Improved sonar technology, together with less stringent quotas, account for the recent increase in the amount of fish caught by commercial vessels.
   (A) account for the recent increase in the amount of
   (B) would account for a recent increase in
   (C) accounts for the recent increase in the number of
   (D) account for recent increases in amounts of
   (E) is accounted for by the recent increase in

   (Hint: Ask yourself whether the subject is singular or plural.)

Answers and Explanations

1. **(B)** The original version contains a subject-verb agreement error. The subject (*raising . . . and . . . holding*) is considered plural, so the plural form *require* should be used instead of the singular *requires*. Also, the adjective *organizational* should be used instead of the noun *organization*, since the word is intended to modify (describe) a noun (*skills*). (B) corrects both errors. (C) fails to correct the subject-verb agreement error. (C) is also wordy and awkward. (D) is grammatically correct but is wordy and a bit awkward. (E) fails to correct the subject-verb agreement error. Also, the use of *skill* instead of *skills* is questionable. (The idiom *organizational skills* is preferable in this context.)

2. **(E)** The original version intends to express a contrary-to-fact situation, so the subjunctive *were* (instead of *are*) is appropriate here. Also, the reflexive pronoun *themselves* is improper here. (Compare the phrase *consider themselves invincible*, which uses the reflexive form properly.) (E) corrects both problems. (B) does not use the subjunctive form. (C) uses an improper idiom (*as being*). (D) does not use the subjunctive form, and it includes the "non-word" *themself.*

3. **(D)** In the original version, the plural *they* should be replaced with the singular *it*, since the pronoun refers here to the singular *course*. Also, the plural *large amounts* is idiomatically improper to refer to reading; the proper idiom here is *a large amount*. (D) corrects both errors in the original version. (B) is nonsensical. (C) improperly uses the plural *these courses* instead of the singular *this course* or simply *it*. (C) also mixes the present tense (*can be*) with the subjunctive form (*would require*), confusing the time frame and meaning of the sentence. (E) improperly uses *quantity*, which can be used to refer to numbers of things, but not to volume (as in the volume of reading).

4. **(D)** The original version incorrectly uses *itself* (instead of *themselves*) to refer to the plural antecedent *stories*. Also, although *outside itself* is acceptable, *else* is also appropriate and is more concise. (D) remedies both problems with the original version. (B) uses the improper correlative *either . . . nor* (*nor* should be replaced with *or*). (C) reverses the meaning of the sentence with the correlative *neither . . . nor.* Also, to say that a story *rarely* stands *neither* as one thing *nor* as another is tantamount to using a confusing double negative. (E) is redundant; *in place of* merely expresses again the notion of a substitute or symbol (*for* would be better).

5. **(A)** The original sentence is not as concise as it could be. A better (more concise) alternative would be: *Our legislators are to*. Nevertheless, the original sentence is grammatically correct. (The idiomatic expression *It is . . . who* is proper.) (B) incorrectly uses the object pronoun *whom* instead of the subject pronoun *who*. [*They* (subject pronoun) are to blame.] (C) is grammatically correct but is wordy. (D) contains a subject-verb agreement error. The subject of *belong* is *blame* (not *legislators*). But one is singular, while the other is plural. The plural *belongs* should be use instead. (E) is idiomatically questionable. A person can be "held responsible," but can a person be said to *hold blame*? This questionable idiom obscures the meaning of the sentence.

6. **(C)** The original sentence contains a subject-verb agreement error. The plural verb *account* does not agree in number with its singular subject *technology*. The intervening clause (set off by commas) should not affect the verb's case, which

should be singular (*accounts*). (C) corrects this error. Notice that (C) changes *amount* to *number*; either word is acceptable here since in this context fish could be considered either by number or by weight—for example, tonnage. Although (B) seems to correct the agreement error by using the subjunctive verb form *would account* (this form could be either singular or plural), this subjunctive form alters the meaning of the original sentence, transforming it into a hypothetical, or conditional, statement. (D) fails to correct the subject-verb agreement error. Although (E) is grammatically correct, by using the passive voice without reconstructing the sentence, (E) completely distorts the meaning of the original sentence. (E) suggests that the increase in fish caught by commercial vessels is responsible for improved solar technology—instead of the other way around.

Hour 11

Teach Yourself Sentence Correction II

Now that you know what Sentence Correction questions are all about, you'll continue to focus on the particular errors of grammar and usage that appear most often on the GMAT. Here are your goals for this hour:

- Learn to recognize and fix certain grammatical errors appearing in GMAT Sentence Correction questions
- Learn to recognize and fix "ineffective expression" in GMAT Sentence Correction questions
- Review the concepts you learn by attempting a GMAT-style quiz

Finding—and Fixing—Problems with Grammar and Expression

This hour you'll continue to grapple with GMAT grammar! Last hour you focused on errors involving *words*—pronouns, verbs, and so forth. Now your focus will broaden to encompass grammatical errors as well as forms of ineffective expression involving *phrases* and *entire sentences.* As we did last hour, we're going to cut to the chase here by homing in on the particular errors that the test-makers will most likely test you on, and by showing you how these flaws might appear in typical GMAT questions.

NOTE

> To help you focus on the specific grammatical error or other flaw at hand, we'll simplify the Sentence Correction format here by listing just *three* answer choices, and by limiting the different kinds of flaws altogether to one or two (just as we did last hour). Actual GMAT questions include five answer choices, of course.

Two Main Clauses Connected Improperly

A *main clause* is any clause that can stand alone as a complete sentence. There's nothing wrong with combining two main clauses into one sentence—as long as the clauses are properly connected. On the GMAT, look for any of these three flaws:

1. no punctuation between main clauses
2. a comma between main clauses, but no connecting word (such as *and*, *or*, *but*, *yet*, *for*)
3. a confusing or inappropriate connecting word

QUESTION The Aleutian Islands of Alaska include many islands near the mainland, <u>the majority of them are</u> uninhabited by humans.

(A) the majority of them are

(B) ***

(C) yet the majority of them are

(D) ***

(E) so the majority of them are

ANALYSIS The correct answer is **(C)**. Notice that (C) includes a connecting word (*yet*) that gives the sentence a reasonable meaning—by underscoring the contrast between the mainland (which is populated) and the unpopulated nearby islands. Although (E) adds a connecting word (*so*), this word is inappropriate—inferring that the islands are unpopulated *because* they are near the mainland. The resulting sentence is nonsensical, so (E) can't be the best answer choice. (By the way: In the foregoing sentence, notice the appropriate use of *so* as a connector!)

Sentence Fragments (Incomplete Sentences)

It was probably your fifth- or sixth-grade teacher who first informed you that a sentence must include both a subject and a predicate. Well, your teacher was right, and the GMAT is here to remind you. Grammarians call incomplete sentences "sentence fragments."

> **FRAGMENT:** Expensive private colleges, generally out of financial reach for most families with college-aged children.
>
> **FRAGMENT:** Without question, responsibility for building and maintaining safe bridges.

Ordinarily, you probably don't have any trouble recognizing a sentence fragment. However, on the GMAT, an especially long fragment might escape your detection if you're not paying close attention.

QUESTION One cannot deny that, even after the initial flurry of the feminist movement subsided, Congresswoman Bella Abzug, undeniably her female constituency's truest voice, <u>as well as its most public advocate</u>.

(A) as well as its most public advocate

(B) who was her constituency's most public advocate

(C) ***

(D) was also its most public advocate

(E) ***

ANALYSIS The correct answer is **(D)**. If you use (D), the sentence can be distilled down to this: *One cannot deny that Bella Abzug was its [the feminist movement's] most public advocate.* Adding the verb *was* is the key to transforming the original fragment into a complete sentence. Neither (A) nor (C) provides the verb needed for a complete sentence.

TIP

> If you're not sure whether it's a complete sentence, ask yourself two questions:
>
> - What's the subject?
> - Where's the verb that establishes a predicate?

Part of a Sentence out of Balance with Another Part

An effective sentence gets its point across by placing appropriate emphasis on its different parts. If you're dealing with two equally important ideas, they should be separated as two distinct "main clauses," and they should be similar in length (to suggest equal importance).

UNBALANCED: Julie and Sandy were the first two volunteers for the fund-raising drive, <u>and</u> they are twins.

BALANCED: Julie and Sandy, <u>who</u> are twins, were the first two volunteers for the fund-raising drive.

COMMINGLED (CONFUSING): Julie and Sandy, <u>who</u> are twins, are volunteers.

SEPARATED (BALANCED): Julie and Sandy are twins, <u>and</u> they are volunteers.

On the other hand, if you're dealing with only one main idea, be sure that it receives greater emphasis (as a main clause) than the other ideas in the sentence.

EQUAL EMPHASIS (CONFUSING): Jose and Victor were identical twins, <u>and</u> they had completely different ambitions.

EMPHASIS ON SECOND CLAUSE (BETTER): <u>Although</u> Jose and Victor were identical twins, they had completely different ambitions.

QUESTION <u>Treating bodily disorders by non-invasive methods is generally painless, and these methods</u> are less likely than those of conventional Western medicine to result in permanent healing.

(A) Treating bodily disorders by non-invasive methods is generally painless, and these methods

(B) Treating bodily disorders by non-invasive methods is generally painless, but they

(C) ***

(D) ***

(E) Although treating bodily disorders by non-invasive methods is generally painless, these methods

ANALYSIS The correct answer is **(E)**. Notice that the original sentence contains two main clauses, connected by *and*. Two problems should have occurred to you as you read the sentence: (1) the connector *and* is inappropriate to contrast differing methods of treatment (it fails to get the point across), and (2) the second clause expresses the more important point but does not receive greater emphasis than the first clause. (E) corrects both problems by transforming the first clause into a subordinate one and by eliminating the connecting word *and*. What about answer choice (B)? Replacing *and* with *but* is not as effective in shifting the emphasis to the second clause as the method used in (E). Moreover, by replacing *these methods* with *they*, (B) creates a new grammatical problem: it is unclear whether *they* refers to *disorders* or to *methods*. (Grammarians would call this a "pronoun reference" problem. You'll explore this type of grammatical error in greater detail later this hour.)

Error in Verb Tense

Tense refers to how a verb's form indicates the *time frame* (past, present, or future) of the sentence's action. An incorrect sentence might needlessly *mix* tenses or *shift* tense from one time frame to another in a confusing manner.

INCORRECT: If it rains tomorrow, we cancel our plans.
CORRECT: If it rains tomorrow, we *will cancel* our plans.

INCORRECT: When Bill arrived, Sal still did not begin to unload the truck.
CORRECT: When Bill arrived, Sal still *had not begun* to unload the truck.

INCORRECT: The senator declared that he will oppose tobacco farm subsidies.
CORRECT: The senator declared that he *would oppose* tobacco farm subsidies.

11

QUESTION Companies that fail in their making cost-of-living adjustments of salaries of workers could not attract or retain competent employees.

(A) fail in their making cost-of-living adjustments of salaries of workers could not
(B) ***
(C) ***
(D) will fail to adjust worker salaries to reflect cost-of-living changes can neither
(E) fail to make cost-of-living adjustments in their workers' salaries cannot

ANALYSIS The correct answer is **(E)**. The original sentence mixes present tense (*fail*) with past tense (*could not attract*). Also, the phrases "fail in their making" and "of salaries of workers" are awkward and unnecessarily wordy. (E) renders the sentence consistent in tense by replacing *could* with *can*. (E) is also more concise than the original sentence. (D) improperly mixes future tense (*will fail*) with present tense (*can . . . retain*). (D) also uses *neither* to form the improper correlative pair *neither . . . or*. (The proper correlative is *neither . . . nor*.)

Unnecessary Use of the Passive Voice

In a sentence expressed in the *active voice*, the subject "acts upon" an object. Conversely, in a sentence expressed in the passive voice, the subject "is acted upon" by an object. The passive voice can sound a bit awkward, so the active voice is generally preferred.

PASSIVE (AWKWARD): The book was read by the student.

ACTIVE (BETTER): The student read the book.

PASSIVE (AWKWARD): Repetitive tasks are performed tirelessly by computers.

ACTIVE (BETTER): Computers perform repetitive tasks tirelessly.

Mixing the active and passive voices results in an even more awkward sentence.

MIXED (AWKWARD): Although the house was built by Gary, Kevin built the garage.

PASSIVE (LESS AWKWARD): Although the house was built by Gary, the garage was built by Kevin.

ACTIVE (BEST): Although Gary built the house, Kevin built the garage.

Although the active voice is usually less awkward than the passive voice, sometimes the passive voice is appropriate for emphasis or impact.

ACTIVE (LESS EFFECTIVE): Yesterday a car hit me.

PASSIVE (MORE EFFECTIVE): Yesterday I was hit by a car.

ACTIVE (LESS EFFECTIVE): Only the sun itself *surpasses* the Tetons in beauty.

PASSIVE (MORE EFFECTIVE): Sunrise over the Tetons *is surpassed* in beauty only *by* the sun itself.

CAUTION

Keep in mind that the passive voice is *not* grammatically wrong. So don't eliminate an answer choice merely because it uses the passive voice. Check for grammatical errors among all five choices. If the one that uses the passive voice is the only one without a grammatical error, then it's the best choice.

QUESTION It is actually a chemical in the brain that creates the sensation of eating enough, a chemical that is depleted by consuming simple sugars.

(A) It is actually a chemical in the brain that creates the sensation of eating enough, a chemical that is

(B) ***

(C) The sensation of having eaten enough is actually created by a chemical in the brain that is

(D) A chemical actually creates the sensation in the brain of having eaten enough, and this chemical is

(E) ***

ANALYSIS The correct answer is **(C)**. The original sentence isn't terrible, but it nevertheless includes two flaws. First, the awkward *eating enough* should be replaced; *having eaten enough* is the appropriate tense here. Both (C) and (D) correct this flaw. Second, notice that "a chemical" appears twice in the sentence. A more effective sentence would avoid repetition. Only (C) avoids repeating this phrase—by reconstructing the first clause. In doing so, (C) admittedly uses the passive voice. Nevertheless, (C) is more concise and less awkward overall than the original sentence. One more point about (D): it also creates a new problem. It separates *the sensation* from *of having eaten enough*, thereby creating an awkward and confusing clause. The phrase *in the brain* should be moved to either an earlier or later position in the sentence.

Error in Using the Subjunctive Mood

The *subjunctive mood* should be used to express a *wish* or a *contrary-to-fact* condition. These sentences should include words such as *if*, *had*, *were* and *should*.

INCORRECT: I wish it *was* earlier.

CORRECT: I wish it *were* earlier.

INCORRECT: Suppose he speeds up suddenly.

CORRECT: Suppose he *were* to speed up suddenly.

INCORRECT: If the college lowers its tuition, I would probably enroll.

CORRECT: *Should* the college lower its tuition, I *would* probably enroll.

CORRECT: *If* the college *were* to lower its tuition, I *would* probably enroll.

TIP

The subjunctive mood can be tricky because it uses its own idiomatic verb forms and because you can't always trust your ear when it comes to catching an error. Just remember: If the sentence uses a regular verb tense (past, present, future, etc.) to express a wish or contrary-to-fact condition, then it is grammatically incorrect, even if the subjunctive verb form is also used.

QUESTION The Environmental Protection Agency would be overburdened by its detection and enforcement duties <u>if it fully implemented all of its own regulations completely</u>.

(A) if it fully implemented all of its own regulations completely

(B) if it was to implement all of its own regulations completely

(C) were it to fully implement all of its own regulations

(D) ***

(E) ***

ANALYSIS The correct answer is **(C)**. The original sentence poses two problems. First, the sentence clearly intends to express a hypothetical or contrary-to-fact situation; yet the underlined phrase does not use the subjunctive *were*. Secondly, *fully* and *completely* are redundant; one of them should be omitted. (C) corrects both problems without creating a new one. (B) corrects the redundancy problem by deleting *fully*. However, it incorrectly uses *was* instead of the subjunctive *were*.

Error in Pronoun Reference

A pronoun (e.g., *she*, *him*, *their*, *its*) is a "shorthand" way of referring to an identifiable noun—person(s), place(s), or thing(s). Nouns to which pronouns refer are called *antecedents*. Make sure every pronoun in a sentence has a clear antecedent!

UNCLEAR: Minutes before Kevin's meeting with Paul, *his* wife called with the bad news. (Whose wife called—Kevin's or Paul's?)

CLEAR: *Kevin's* wife called with the bad news minutes before *his* meeting with Paul.

CLEAR: Minutes before Kevin's meeting with Paul, *Kevin's* wife called with the bad news.

Pronoun reference errors are usually corrected in one of two ways:

1. by placing the noun and pronoun as near as possible to each other, without other nouns coming between them (second sentence above)
2. replacing the pronoun with its antecedent (third sentence above)

Also look for the vague use of *it*, *you*, *that*, or *one*—without clear reference to a particular antecedent.

VAGUE: When one dives in without looking ahead, *you* never know what will happen. (Does *you* refer to the diver or to the broader *one*?)

CLEAR: *One* never knows what will happen when *one* dives in without looking ahead.

CLEAR: When *you* dive in without looking ahead, *you* never know what will happen.

VAGUE: When the planets are out of alignment, *it* can be disastrous. (*It* does not refer to any noun.)

CLEAR: Disaster can occur when the planets are out of alignment.

QUESTION E-mail accounts administered by <u>an employer belong to them, and they can be seized and used</u> as evidence against the employee.

(A) an employer belong to them, and they can be seized and used

(B) employers belong to them, who can seize and use it

(C) an employer belong to the employer, who can seize and use the accounts

(D) ***

(E) ***

ANALYSIS The correct answer is **(C)**. There are two pronoun problems in the original sentence. First, *them* is used vaguely, without clear reference to *employers*, which seems to be the intended antecedent. Adding to this confusion is the fact that the pronoun *them* is plural, yet its intended antecedent *employer* is singular. Second, the antecedent of *they* is unclear because *they* is separated from its intended antecedent *accounts* by two other possibilities (*them* and *employer*). (C) corrects the first problem by replacing the pronoun *them* with its (singular) antecedent *employer.* (C) also corrects the second problem by using *who*, which clearly refers to *employer*, since the two words appear immediately next to each other. (B) is riddled with problems! First, (B) does not correct the vague use of *them* (although the use of the plural *employers* is an improvement). Second, (B) leaves it unclear as to which noun *who* refers; presumably, *who* refers to *them*, yet the antecedent of *them* is uncertain. Third, although the pronoun *it* is intended to refer to *accounts*, the reference is unclear because the pronoun and antecedent are separated by other nouns. Finally, the pronoun *it* is singular, yet its antecedent *accounts* is plural (they should both be either singular or plural).

TIP

When you see a pronoun in a GMAT sentence, ask yourself: "To what noun does this pronoun refer?" If the answer is the least bit unclear, you can be certain that the sentence (or answer choice) is wrong.

Improper Placement of Modifiers

A *modifier* is a word or phrase that describes, restricts, or qualifies another word or phrase. Modifying phrases are typically set off with commas, and many such phrases begin with a relative pronoun (*which*, *who*, *that*, *whose*, *whom*). Modifiers should generally be placed as close as possible to the word(s) they modify. Positioning a modifier in the wrong place can result in a confusing or even nonsensical sentence.

MISPLACED: His death shocked the entire family, which occurred quite suddenly.

BETTER: His death, which occurred quite suddenly, shocked the entire family.

MISPLACED: Nearly dead, the police finally found the victim.

BETTER: The police finally found the victim, who was nearly dead.

UNCLEAR: Bill punched Carl while wearing a mouth protector.

CLEAR: While wearing a mouth protector, Bill punched Carl.

QUESTION <u>Exercising contributes frequently to not only a sense of well being but also to longevity.</u>

(A) Exercising contributes frequently to not only a sense of well being but also to longevity.

(B) ***

(C) Exercising frequently contributes not only to a sense of well being but to longevity.

(D) ***

(E) Frequent exercise contributes not only to a sense of well being but also to longevity.

ANALYSIS The correct answer is **(E)**. In the original sentence, *frequently* is probably intended to describe (modify) *exercising* (frequent exercise). But separating these words makes it appear as though *frequently* describes *contributing*, which makes no sense in the overall context of the sentence. The original sentence also contains a "parallelism" error. The phrase after *not only* should parallel the phrase after *but also*, so that the two phrases can be interchanged and still make sense grammatically. But in the original sentence, the two phrases are not parallel. (E) corrects both problems. In (E) it is clear that what is "frequent" is *exercise* (rather than *contributing*). Also, the phrases following each part of the *not only . . . but also* pair are now parallel. (Notice that each phrase begins with *to*.) (C) fails to clear up the confusion as to whether *frequently* describes *exercising* or *contributes*. Also, (C) improperly uses *not only . . . but* instead of the proper idiom *not only . . . but also*.

Improper Splitting of a Grammatical Unit

Splitting apart clauses or phrases (by inserting another clause between them) often results in an awkward and confusing sentence.

SPLIT: The value of the dollar *is not*, relative to other currencies, *rising* universally.

BETTER: The value of the dollar *is not rising* universally relative to other currencies.

SPLIT: The government's goal this year *is to provide* for its poorest residents *an economic safety net.*

SPLIT: *The government's goal* is to provide an economic safety net *this year* for its poorest residents.

BETTER: The government's goal this year is to provide an economic safety net for its poorest residents.

11

QUESTION Typographer Lucian Bernhard was influenced, perhaps more so than any of his contemporaries, by Toulouse-Lautrec's emphasis on large, unharmonious lettering.

(A) Typographer Lucian Bernhard was influenced, perhaps more so than any of his contemporaries, by Toulouse-Lautrec's emphasis on large, unharmonious lettering.

(B) Perhaps more so than any of his contemporaries, typographer Lucian Bernhard was influenced by Toulouse-Lautrec's emphasis on large, unharmonious lettering.

(C) ***

(D) ***

(E) Typographer Lucian Bernhard was influenced by Toulouse-Lautrec's emphasis on large, unharmonious lettering perhaps more so than any of his contemporaries.

ANALYSIS The correct answer is **(B)**. The original sentence awkwardly splits the main clause with an intervening subordinate one (set off by commas). Both (B) and (E) keep the main clause intact. However, (E) creates a pronoun reference problem. In (E) it unclear as to whom the pronoun *his* refers—Bernhard or Toulouse-Lautrec.

TIP

Whenever you see a clause set off by commas in the middle of the sentence, check the words immediately before and after the clause. If keeping those words together would sound better to your ear or would more effectively convey the sentence's main point, then the sentence (answer choice) is wrong, and you can safely eliminate it!

Dangling Modifier Errors

A *dangling modifier* is a modifier that doesn't refer to any particular word(s) in the sentence. The best way to correct a dangling-modifier problem is to reconstruct the sentence.

DANGLING: *Set by an arsonist*, firefighters were unable to save the burning building. (This sentence makes no reference to whatever was set by an arsonist.)

BETTER: Firefighters were unable to save the burning building from *the fire set by an arsonist.*

QUESTION By imposing artificial restrictions in price on oil suppliers, these suppliers will be forced to lower production costs.

(A) By imposing artificial restrictions in price on oil suppliers, these suppliers will be forced

(B) Imposing artificial price restrictions on oil suppliers will force these suppliers

(C) By imposing on oil suppliers artificial price restrictions, these suppliers will be forced

(D) ***

(E) ***

ANALYSIS The correct answer is **(B)**. The original sentence includes a dangling modifier. The sentence makes no reference to whomever (or whatever) is imposing the price restrictions. (B) corrects the problem by reconstructing the sentence. (B) also improves on the original sentence by replacing *restrictions in price* with the more concise *price restrictions*. (C) does not correct the dangling modifier problem. Also, the grammatical construction of the first clause in (C) is awkward and confusing.

Too Many Subordinate Clauses in a Row

A *subordinate clause* is one that does not stand on its own as a complete sentence. Stringing together two or more subordinate clauses can result in an awkward and confusing sentence.

AWKWARD: Barbara's academic major is history, *which* is a very popular course of study among liberal arts students, *who* are also contributing to the popularity of political science as a major.

BETTER: Barbara's academic major is history, which along with political science is a very popular course of study among liberal arts students.

QUESTION By relying unduly on anecdotal evidence, which often conflicts with more reliable data, including data from direct observation and measurement, a scientist risks losing credibility among his or her peers.

(A) By relying unduly on anecdotal evidence, which often conflicts with more reliable data, including data from direct observation and measurement, a scientist risks losing credibility among his or her peers.

(B) ***

(C) ***

(D) A scientist, by relying unduly on anecdotal evidence, which often conflicts with more reliable data, including data from direct observation and measurement, risks losing credibility among his or her peers.

(E) A scientist risks losing credibility among his or her peers by relying unduly on anecdotal evidence, which often conflicts with more reliable data, including data from direct observation and measurement.

ANALYSIS The correct answer is **(E)**. The original sentence contains four clauses (separated by commas). The first three are all subordinate clauses! The result is that you are left in suspense as to who unduly relies on anecdotal evidence (first clause) until you reach the last (and main) clause. The solution is to rearrange the sentence to join the first and last clause, thereby minimizing the string of subordinate clauses and eliminating confusion. Answer choice (E) provides this solution. Answer choice (D) solves the problem only partially—by moving only part of the main clause (the scientist) to the beginning of the sentence. In fact, in doing so, (D) probably creates more confusion. Do you agree?

NOTE

Subordination of a dependent clause to a main clause can be achieved through the use of:

- relative pronouns: *which, who, that*
- words establishing time relationship: *before, after, as, since*
- words establishing a causal relationship: *because, since*
- words of admission or concession: *although, though, despite*
- words indicating place: *where, wherever*
- words of condition: *if, unless*

Workshop

In this hour's Workshop, you'll review the rules of grammar and guidelines for effective expression you just learned, by attempting a GMAT-style quiz.

NOTE

This Workshop will focus, of course, on the grammatical errors you examined this hour. But other types of errors will pop up as well. Some you examined last hour, others you'll learn about next hour. So this Workshop serves as a *review* of Hours 10 and 11 as well as a *preview* of Hour 12!

Quiz

(Answers and explanations begin on page 237.)

DIRECTIONS: This question presents a sentence, all or part of which is underlined. Beneath the sentence you will find five ways of phrasing the underlined part. The first of these repeats the original; the other four are different. If you think the original is best, choose the first answer; otherwise choose one of the others.

ONLINE

Additional Sentence Correction questions are available on-line, at the authors' Web site: *http://www.west.net/~stewart/gmat*

1. Engineering teams monitor over a hundred former nuclear test sites for radiation levels, the civilian populace is banned from any area with sufficiently high levels.
   (A) for radiation levels, the civilian populace is banned
   (B) to measure its levels of radiation, yet the civilized populace is banned
   (C) for their radiation levels, without the civilian population banned
   (D) for their levels of radiation, and the civilian populace is banned
   (E) in order to determine radiation levels, and the civilian populace are banned

   (Hint: The original sentence can be split into two independent sentences.)

2. Upon Margaret Thatcher's winning the British general election, she had become Europe's first woman prime minister.
   (A) Upon Margaret Thatcher's winning
   (B) When Margaret Thatcher won
   (C) Whenever Margaret Thatcher won
   (D) At the time Margaret Thatcher won
   (E) With Margaret Thatcher's winning of

   (Hint: Use your ear to determine whether a sentence sounds right.)

3. Considered to be the most unforgiving course in the world, cyclists must train especially hard in order to meet the challenge.
   (A) Considered to be the most unforgiving course in the world, cyclists must train especially hard in order to meet the challenge.
   (B) Considered as the most unforgiving course in the world, the challenge is be met only by cyclists training especially hard.
   (C) Cyclists must train especially hard in order to meet the challenge of the course considered more unforgiving than any other course in the world.
   (D) The most unforgiving course in the world, the challenge for cyclists is to train especially hard for it.
   (E) Meeting the challenge requires cyclists to train especially hard for the most unforgiving course in the world.

   (Hint: To what course does this sentence refer?)

4. Neither result of the two experiments were what the researchers have expected.
   (A) Neither result of the two experiments were what the researchers have expected.
   (B) Of the two experiments, neither result was expected by the researchers.
   (C) Neither of the two experiments result in what the researchers expected.
   (D) Neither of the two experiments resulted in what the researchers had expected.
   (E) What the researchers have expected was the result of neither of the two experiments.

   (Hint: The original version has three distinct flaws.)

5. If empty space was nothing real, then any two atoms located in this "nothingness" would contact each other since nothing would be between them.
   (A) If empty space was
   (B) In the event that empty space is
   (C) If empty space is
   (D) That empty space were
   (E) Were empty space

   (Hint: the original version intends to express a contrary-to-fact situation.)

6. The need to foster allegiances between all the states was recognized by Madison and Hamilton, among others, during its burgeoning independence from England by the United States.
   (A) The need to foster allegiances between all the states was recognized by Madison and Hamilton, among others, during its burgeoning independence from England by the United States.
   (B) The need to foster allegiances was recognized by Madison and Hamilton, among others, between all the states during their burgeoning independence from England.
   (C) During the United States' burgeoning independence from England, Madison and Hamilton, among others, recognized the need to foster allegiances among all the states.
   (D) During the United States' burgeoning independence from England, among others, Madison and Hamilton recognized the need to foster allegiances among all the states.
   (E) The need recognized by Madison and Hamilton, among others, was to foster allegiances among all the states during their burgeoning independence from England.

   (Hint: To what does the pronoun "its" refer?)

7. If speaking too quickly, a court reporter can have trouble producing an accurate transcript based on that witness' testimony.
   (A) If speaking too quickly, a court reporter can have trouble producing an accurate transcript based on that witness' testimony.
   (B) Should he or she speak too quickly, a court reporter can have trouble producing an accurate transcript based on a witness' testimony.
   (C) A court reporter can have trouble if a witness speaks too quickly during testimony, possibly producing an inaccurate transcript.
   (D) An accurate transcript based on a witness' testimony can, if speaking too quickly, produce trouble for a court reporter.
   (E) A court reporter can have trouble producing an accurate transcript based on the testimony of a witness that speaks too quickly.

   (Hint: Who is it that speaks too quickly?)

Answers and Explanations

1. **(D)** In the original sentence, two main clauses are incorrectly separated by only a comma, without an appropriate connecting word. (B) inserts an inappropriate connecting word (*yet*) between the clauses, resulting in a sentence whose intended meaning is unclear. Also, the words *civilian* and *civilized* do not carry similar meanings. (C) seems to remedy the problem with the original sentence; it transforms the second main clause into a subordinate clause. However, the resulting sentence is ambiguous and confusing. (D) corrects the problem with the original sentence by inserting a connecting word (*and*) that seems to convey the intended meaning of the original sentence. In the first clause, both the additional word *their* and the use of *levels of radiation* instead of *radiation levels* are acceptable. (E) corrects the problem with the original sentence by inserting the connecting word *and*. However, the phrase *in order to determine* is unnecessarily wordy. Moreover, the word *is*, not *are*, should be used in conjunction with the singular noun *populace*.

2. **(A)** In the original version the noun clause *Margaret Thatcher's winning* correctly takes the possessive verb form. (B) improperly mixes the past tense (*won*) with the past perfect tense (*had become*). (C) mixes past tense with past perfect tense. (C) is also nonsensical; *whenever* suggests that Margaret Thatcher won the election (and became the first woman prime minister) numerous times. (D) mixes past tense with past perfect tense. Also, *at the time* obscures the meaning of the original version. In (E), the word *of* should be omitted. Also, the word *with* does not convey the sentence's meaning as clearly as the word *upon*.

3. **(C)** The first clause in the original version is a dangling modifier; what is considered *the most unforgiving course* is never mentioned in the sentence. The sentence should be reconstructed to eliminate this problem. Only (C) corrects this problem without creating another one. Both (B) and (D) misplace the modifier; in both versions, *the most unforgiving course* appears to refer to *challenge*, which makes no sense. (E) distorts the meaning of the original version. It is possible that *the challenge* in (E) refers to something completely unrelated to the course.

4. **(D)** In the original version, the shift in time frame from past (*were*) to present (*have expected*) is confusing and illogical. Also, the syntax obscures the intended meaning; specifically, one could interpret *neither result of the two experiments* to mean that *each* of the two experiments had two results; but this is clearly not the intended meaning. Finally, the plural verb *were* does not agree in number with its singular subject *neither result*. (D) remedies all of these problems. (B) is nonsensical, equating an experi-

ment with a result. (C) mixes present tense (*result*) with past tense (*expected*) in a confusing manner. (E) mixes present perfect tense (*have expected*) with past tense (*was*) in a confusing manner. (E) is also awkward.

5. **(E)** The subjunctive mood is appropriate for this sentence since it ostensibly involves a contrary-to-fact situation. However, the underlined part incorrectly uses the past tense *was*. To correct this problem, the underlined phrase should be replaced with either *If empty space were or Were empty space*. (E) employs the latter phrase. Both (B) and (C) incorrectly use the present tense *is* instead of a subjunctive form. (B) is also wordy. (D) is nonsensical (*That* should be replaced with *If*).

6. **(C)** The original version is flawed in three ways. First, it uses the awkward passive voice (. . . *was recognized by* . . .). Second, *between* is incorrectly used to refer to more than two states; *among* should be used instead. Third, the pronoun *its* (in the final clause) does not refer clearly to its intended antecedent United States. (The sentence should be reconstructed so that *its* follows *United States*.) (C) revamps the sentence, remedying all three problems with the original version. (B) is no better than the original version. It awkwardly splits the grammatical element *allegiances between*. Also, *between* is incorrect (*among* should be used instead). Finally, (B) uses the awkward passive voice. (D) remedies the problems with the original version, but the position of *among others* confuses the meaning of the sentence—by suggesting that the states' independence was from not just England but other countries as well. (E) is grammatically correct, but it's use of the passive voice (*The need recognized by* . . . *was* . . .) results in an awkward and confusing sentence.

7. **(E)** In the original version, the modifier *If speaking too quickly* is misplaced. As it stands, this phrase appears to refer to the court reporter. However, the sentence clearly intends that this phrase refer to the witness. The sentence must be reconstructed to position this modifier closer to the phrase that it modifies. (B), (C), and (D) are all constructed improperly. Each of them includes a misplaced modifier. (E) is the only choice that corrects the modifier problem with the original version without creating a new one. (E) reconstructs the original version so that *speaking too quickly* clearly refers to the witness.

Hour 12

Teach Yourself Sentence Correction III

This hour you'll continue to teach yourself how to handle Sentence Correction questions, switching your emphasis to the errors of expression most likely to be tested on the GMAT. Here are your goals for this hour:

- Learn to recognize and fix certain grammatical errors appearing in GMAT Sentence Correction questions
- Learn to recognize and fix "ineffective expression" in GMAT Sentence Correction questions
- Review the concepts you learn this hour by attempting a GMAT-style quiz

Finding—and Fixing—Errors of Expression

It's time, once again, to grapple with grammar—as well as to ferret out more forms of ineffective expression. As in the last two hours, we'll focus here on the flaws that show up most frequently on the GMAT. You'll see how each flaw might appear in a typical GMAT question. A bit later, you'll examine errors in word usage, idiom, and diction that commonly appear on the exam.

NOTE

> To help you focus on the specific grammatical error or other flaw at hand, we'll simplify the Sentence Correction format here by listing just *three* answer choices, and by limiting the different kinds of flaws altogether to one or two (just as we did during Hours 10 and 11). Actual GMAT questions will include five answer choices, of course.

Faulty Parallelism (Lists)

Sentence elements that are grammatically equal—such as a list, or "string," of items—should be constructed similarly; otherwise the result will be what is referred to as *faulty parallelism*. Whenever you see a string of items, look particularly for inconsistent or mixed use of:

- prepositions (such as *in*, *with* or *on*)
- gerunds (verbs with an *-ing* added to the end)
- infinitives (plural verb preceded by *to*)
- articles (such as *a* and *the*)

FAULTY: Flight 82 travels first to Boise, then to Denver, then Salt Lake City. (to precedes only the first two of the three cities in this list.)

PARALLEL: Flight 82 travels first to Boise, then Denver, then Salt Lake City.

PARALLEL: Flight 82 travel first to Boise, then to Denver, then to Salt Lake City.

FAULTY: Being understaffed, lack of funding, and being outpaced by competitors soon resulted in the fledgling company's going out of business. (Only two of the three listed items begin with the gerund *being*.)

PARALLEL: Understaffed, underfunded, and outpaced by competitors, the fledgling company soon went out of business.

PARALLEL: As a result of understaffing, insufficient funding, and outpacing by its competitors, the fledgling company soon went out of business.

FAULTY: Among *the* mountains, *the* sea and desert, we humans have yet to fully explore only the sea.

PARALLEL: Among *the* mountains, sea and desert, we humans have yet to fully explore only the sea.

PARALLEL: Among *the* mountains, *the* sea and *the* desert, we humans have yet to fully explore only the sea.

QUESTION Long before the abolition of slavery, many freed indentured servants were able to acquire property, <u>to interact with people of other races, and maintain</u> their freedom.

(A) to interact with people of other races, and maintain

(B) ***

(C) interact with people of other races, and maintain

(D) to interact with people of other races, as well as maintaining

(E) ***

ANALYSIS The correct answer is **(C)**. Notice the string of three items in this sentence. In the original version, the second item repeats the preposition *to*, but the third item does not. (C) corrects this faulty parallelism. (E) improperly mixes the use of a prepositional phrase (beginning with *to*) with a construction that instead uses a gerund (*maintaining*).

12

Repeating the same preposition, article, or other modifier before each item in a string can sometimes result in an awkward and unnecessarily wordy sentence. In other instances, repeating the modifier may be necessary to achieve clarity.

AWKWARD: Some pachyderms can go for days at a time without water or without food or without sleep.

BETTER: Some pachyderms can go for days at a time without water, food, or sleep.

UNCLEAR: Going for broke and broke usually carry identical consequences.

CLEAR: Going for broke and going broke usually carry identical consequences.

CAUTION

Just because all items in a string are parallel, don't assume that the string is problem-free!

Faulty Parallelism (Correlatives)

You just saw how items in a list can suffer from faulty parallelism. Now, look at how this grammatical error shows up in what are called *correlatives*. Here are the most commonly used correlatives:

- either . . . or . . .
- neither . . . nor . . .
- both . . . and . . .
- not only . . . but also . . .

Whenever you spot a correlative in a sentence, make sure that the element immediately following the first correlative term is parallel in construction to the element following the second term.

FAULTY: Those wishing to participate should *either* contact us by telephone *or* should send e-mail to us.

PARALLEL: Those wishing to participate should *either* contact us by telephone *or* send e-mail to us.

QUESTION Species diversity in the Amazon basin results <u>not from climate stability, as once believed, but</u> climate disturbances.

(A) not from climate stability, as once believed, but

(B) ***

(C) not only from climate stability, as once believed, but instead from

(D) ***

(E) not from climate stability, as once believed, but rather from

ANALYSIS The correct answer is **(E)**. As it stands, the original sentence might carry one of two very different meanings: (1) stability and disturbances *both* contribute to species diversity, or (2) disturbances, *but not* stability, contribute to species diversity. The reason for the ambiguity is the use of an improper correlative as well as faulty parallelism (*from* appears only in the first correlative term). The correct answer choice must make the sentence's meaning clear, probably by using one of two correlatives: *not only . . . but also* or *not . . . but rather . . . .* Also, the two correlative terms must be parallel. (E) corrects the faulty parallelism (*from* appears in each correlative term) and clears up the sentence's meaning. Although (B) corrects the parallelism problem, it uses the nonsensical (and improper) correlative *not only . . . but instead.*

Redundant Words and Phrases

Look for words and phrases that express the same essential idea twice. This syndrome is known as *redundancy.* In many cases, correcting the problem is as simple as omitting one of the redundant phrases.

REDUNDANT: *The reason that* we stopped for the night was *because* we were sleepy.

REDUNDANT: *Because* we were sleepy, we *therefore* stopped for the night.

BETTER: We stopped for the night because we were sleepy.

REDUNDANT: The *underlying* motive *behind* his seemingly generous offer was old-fashioned greed.

BETTER: The motive behind his seemingly generous offer was old-fashioned greed.

BETTER: The underlying motive for his seemingly generous offer was old-fashioned greed.

REDUNDANT: One of the fossils is twenty thousand years old *in age.*

BETTER: One of the fossils is twenty thousand years old.

REDUNDANT: The German Oktoberfest takes place *each October of every year.*

BETTER: The German Oktoberfest takes place *every October.*

REDUNDANT: *At the same time* that lightning struck, we *simultaneously* lost our electric power.

BETTER: At the same time that lightning struck, we lost our electric power.

REDUNDANT: *Both* unemployment *as well as* interest rates can affect stock prices.

BETTER: Both unemployment levels and interest rates can affect stock prices.

BETTER: Unemployment levels as well as interest rates can affect stock prices.

REDUNDANT: Not only does dinner smell good, but it *also* tastes good *too.*

BETTER: Not only does dinner smell good, but it tastes good too.

QUESTION Due to a negligible difference in Phase III results as between patients using the drug and those using a placebo, the Food and Drug Administration refused to approve it on this basis.

(A) Due to a negligible difference in Phase III results as between patients using the drug and those using a placebo, the Food and Drug Administration refused to approve it on this basis.

(B) The Food and Drug Administration refused to approve the drug based upon a negligible difference in Phase III results as between patients using it and those using a placebo.

(C) Due to a negligible difference in Phase III results as between patients using the drug and those using a placebo, the Food and Drug Administration refused to approve the drug.

(D) ***

(E) ***

ANALYSIS The correct answer is **(C)**. There are three distinct problems with the original version. First, *due to* and *on this basis* serve the same function—to express that the FDA's refusal was based on the Phase III results. (The redundancy is easy to miss since one phrase begins the sentence while the other phrase ends it.) Secondly, the intended antecedent of *it* is *the drug*, but the intervening noun *placebo* obscures the reference. Thirdly, the sentence is ambiguous. Did the FDA refuse to approve the drug, or did it approve the drug on some basis other than the one mentioned in the sentence? The sentence is ambiguous as to which meaning is intended. (C) corrects all three problems, simply by omitting *on this basis* and by replacing *it* with *the drug*. (B) corrects the first two problems—by omitting *due to* and reconstructing the sentence. But (B) fails to clarify the meaning of the sentence.

TIP

On the GMAT, be on the lookout for sentences having the following "themes" and keywords. Redundancies are most likely to spring up in these kinds of sentences.

- words establishing cause-and-effect (because, since, if, then, therefore)
- references to time (age, years, hours, days)
- words used in conjunctions (both, as well, too, also)

Superfluous (Unnecessary) Words

You just took a look at one variety of unnecessary verbiage: redundancy. Now look at some other kinds of sentences in which certain words can simply be omitted without affecting the meaning or effectiveness of the original sentence. Remember: Briefer is better!

Each sentence in the first group below contains an *ellipsis*: a word or phrase that can be omitted because it is clearly implied. (In the incorrect version, the ellipsis is italicized.)

SUPERFLUOUS: The warmer the weather *is*, the more crowded the beach *is*.

CONCISE: The warmer the weather, the more crowded the beach.

SUPERFLUOUS: He looks exactly like Francis *looks*.

CONCISE: He looks exactly like Francis.

SUPERFLUOUS: That shirt is the ugliest *shirt that* I have ever seen.

CONCISE: That shirt is the ugliest I have ever seen.

SUPERFLUOUS: If my alarm clock malfunctions, *then* I might be late for work.

CONCISE: If my alarm clock malfunctions, I might be late for work.

CONCISE: Were my alarm clock to malfunction, I might be late for work.

Each sentence in the next group includes a superfluous preposition. (In the incorrect version, the preposition is italicized.)

SUPERFLUOUS: The other children couldn't help *from* laughing at the girl with mismatched shoes.

CONCISE: The other children couldn't help laughing at the girl with mismatched shoes.

SUPERFLUOUS: One prominent futurist predicts a nuclear holocaust by the year *of* 2020.

CONCISE: One prominent futurist predicts a nuclear holocaust by the year 2020.

SUPERFLUOUS: They made the discovery *in* around December of last year.

CONCISE: They made the discovery around December of last year.

SUPERFLUOUS: The waiter brought half *of* a loaf of bread to the table.

CONCISE: The waiter brought half a loaf of bread to the table.

Superfluous words can also appear in a series of parallel clauses. Both versions of the next sentence use proper parallelism, but briefer is better—as long as the meaning of the sentence is clear.

SUPERFLUOUS: My three goals in life are to be healthy, *to be* wealthy, and *to be* wise.

CONCISE: My three goals in life are to be healthy, wealthy, and wise.

QUESTION Only through a comprehensive, federally funded vaccination program can a new epidemic of tuberculosis be curbed, just like the spread of both cholera as well as the spread of typhoid was curbed.

(A) as well as the spread of typhoid was curbed

(B) ***

(C) ***

(D) and typhoid

(E) as well as typhoid was curbed

ANALYSIS The correct answer is **(D)**. The original version includes no fewer than three distinct "verbiage" problems. First, the correlative *both . . . as well as* is redundant (and improper). Since *both* is not underlined, *as well as* should be replaced with *and*. Secondly, because the preposition *like* sets up an ellipsis, *were curbed* is implied and can be omitted. Thirdly, the second occurrence of *the spread of* can be omitted since it is implied through a parallel construction. (D) pares down the underlined phrase to its most concise form. (E) fails to correct the redundant correlative *both . . . as well as*. (E) also fails to omit the unnecessary *was curbed.*

Wordy and Awkward Phrases

Just because a sentence is grammatically acceptable, you shouldn't assume that there is no room for improvement. You've already seen that unnecessary words can sometimes be omitted, thereby improving a GMAT sentence. Now look at some phrases that can be *replaced* with clearer, more concise ones.

WORDY: Failure can *some of the time* serve as a prelude to success.

CONCISE: Failure can *sometimes* serve as a prelude to success.

WORDY: *As a result of Greg's being* a compulsive overeater, *it is not likely that he will* live past the age of fifty.

CONCISE: *Because Greg is* a compulsive overeater, *he is unlikely* to live past the age of fifty.

WORDY: Before the mother eats, she feeds *each and every one* of her offspring.

CONCISE: Before the mother eats, she feeds *each* of her offspring.

WORDY: There are fewer buffalo on the plains today than *there ever were* before.

CONCISE: There are fewer buffalo on the plains today than *ever* before.

WORDY: Discipline is crucial to *the attainment of* one's objectives.

CONCISE: Discipline is crucial to *attaining* one's objectives.

WORDY: Her husband was waiting for her on the platform *at the time of the train's arrival.*

CONCISE: Her husband was waiting for her on the platform *when the train arrived.*

AWKWARD: Calcification *is when* (or *is where*) calcium deposits form around a bone.

CLEARER: Calcification *occurs when* calcium deposits form around a bone.

AWKWARD: *There are* eight cats in the house, *of which* only two have been fed.

CLEARER: Of the eight cats in the house, only two have been fed.

AWKWARD: The wind poses a serious threat to the old tree, and *so does* the snow.

CLEARER: The wind and snow both pose a serious threat to the old tree.

QUESTION To avoid confusion between oral medications, different pills' coatings should have different colors, and pills should be different in shape and size.

(A) different pills' coatings should have different colors, and pills should be different in shape and size

(B) pills should differ in color as well as in shape and size

(C) ***

(D) pills should be able to be distinguished by their color, shape and size

(E) ***

ANALYSIS The correct answer is **(B)**. There are several problems with the original version. The first is that *different pills' coatings* is very awkward. Secondly, the word *coatings* is probably superfluous here; *color* suffices to make the point. Thirdly, *have different colors* is awkward (*differ in color* would be better). Fourth, the phrase *be different* is ambiguous (different from what?). Finally, a parallel series including color, shape and size would be more concise and less awkward than the construction used in the original version. (B) corrects all these problems. In (D), the phrase *be able to be distinguished* awkwardly mixes the active and passive voices. The phrase *be distinguishable* would be better.

> **NOTE** The wordy and awkward phrases that the GMAT CAT can throw at you are limited in variety only by the collective imagination of the test-makers. So the phrases we've provided here are just a small sampling.

Omission of Necessary Words

On the flip side of redundancy and wordiness is the error of *omission*. Excluding a necessary word can obscure or confuse the meaning of the sentence. Check for the omission of key "little" words—prepositions, pronouns, conjunctives, and especially the word *that*.

OMISSION: The lost hiker went without food, water, or shelter two days.

CLEARER: The lost hiker went without food, water, or shelter *for* two days.

OMISSION: Missing the deadline would be a disaster the first order.

CLEARER: Missing the deadline would be a disaster *of* the first order.

OMISSION: The newscaster announced the voting results were incorrect. (What did the newscaster announce: the results or the fact that the results were incorrect?)

CLEARER: The newscaster announced *that* the voting results were incorrect.

Look out especially for an omission that results in an illogical comparison, as in the following sentences. It can easily slip by you if you're not careful!

ILLOGICAL: The color of the blouse is different from the skirt.
(This sentence illogically compares a color with a skirt.)

LOGICAL: The color of the blouse is different from <u>that</u> of the skirt.

ILLOGICAL: China's population is larger than that of any country in the world.
(This sentence suggests illogically that China is not a country.)

ILLOGICAL: China's population is larger than any other country in the world.
(This sentence suggests illogically that "population" is a country.)

LOGICAL: China's population is larger than <u>that of</u> any <u>other</u> country in the world.

QUESTION Some evolutionary theorists believe the main reason humans began to walk in an upright posture is they needed to reach tree branches to obtain food.

(A) believe the main reason humans began to walk in an upright posture is they

(B) believe the main reason humans began to walk in an upright posture is that they

(C) ***

(D) ***

(E) believe that the main reason humans began to walk in an upright posture is that they

ANALYSIS The correct answer is **(E)**. The original version commits two omission errors involving the word *that*. (E) corrects these errors. (B) corrects only the first omission.

CAUTION

As you've just seen, one little word can make all the difference! Your mind can easily trick you by filling in a key word that is not actually there. The moral here is: Read every GMAT sentence slowly and carefully!

Workshop

In this hour's Workshop, you'll review the areas of grammar and proper expression you covered this hour by attempting a GMAT-style quiz.

NOTE

In this Workshop, you'll focus, of course, on the areas of grammar and expression covered this hour. But you'll also encounter many of the kinds of errors you learned about during Hours 10 and 11. So this Workshop serves as a final Sentence Correction review!

Quiz

(Answers and explanations begin on page 251.)

DIRECTIONS: This question presents a sentence, all or part of which is underlined. Beneath the sentence you will find five ways of phrasing the underlined part. The first of these repeats the original; the other four are different. If you think the original is best, choose the first answer; otherwise choose one of the others.

ONLINE

Additional Sentence Correction questions are available online, at the authors' Web site: *http://www.west.net/~stewart/gmat*

1. To indicate the fact that they are in opposition to a bill, legislators sometimes engage in filibusters.
   (A) To indicate the fact that they are in opposition to
   (B) To indicate the fact of their opposition to
   (C) To show their opposition to
   (D) To indicate they themselves are in opposition to
   (E) In indicating the fact that they are in opposition to

   (Hint: The correct answer should express the intended idea in a clear and concise manner.)

2. Harnessing the power of nature has resulted in our control over it rather than submitting to it.
   (A) our control over it rather than submitting to it.
   (B) us controlling as opposed to submitting to it.
   (C) control over it on our part instead of submission.
   (D) control, not submission, over it by us.
   (E) our controlling it instead of our submitting to it.

   (Hint: Check for proper parallelism.)

3. It is necessary for our society to reconsider its priorities regarding education, national defense and public health.
   (A) its priorities regarding
   (B) their priorities as to
   (C) priorities in respect of
   (D) its priorities amongst
   (E) its priorities as they concern

   (Hint: The word "regarding" means with respect to or concerning.)

4. Andrew Carnegie was a philanthropist around the turn of the twentieth century.
   (A) was a philanthropist around
   (B) lived philanthropically around
   (C) was a philanthropist who lived around
   (D) was a philanthropist which lived around
   (E) was a philanthropist at around

   (Hint: The correct version must be unambiguous in meaning.)

5. With laser technology, many forms of cancer can now be treated by means of using a quick and painless surgical procedure.
   (A) by means of using
   (B) by means of
   (C) with using
   (D) by means of the use of
   (E) through means of

   (Hint: Check for redundancy.)

6. Through careful examination, competent diagnosing and successful treatment, patients grow to trust their physicians.
   (A) diagnosing and successful treatment, patients grow to trust their physicians
   (B) diagnosis and treatment, if successful, lead patients to trust their physicians
   (C) and successful diagnosing and treatment, physicians develop trust in their patients
   (D) diagnosis and successful treatment, physicians help their patients grow to trust them
   (E) diagnosis and successful treatment, physicians develop in their patients growing trust

   (Hint: Check for proper parallelism.)

7. There is the gene that causes hemophilia, which if paired with a healthy gene the individual will not develop the disease's symptoms.
   (A) There is the gene that causes hemophilia, which if paired with a healthy gene the individual will not develop
   (B) The gene that causes hemophilia, which if paired with a healthy gene, then the individual will not develop
   (C) There is the gene that causes hemophilia, and if paired with a healthy gene the individual will not develop
   (D) Hemophilia is caused by a gene that, if paired with a healthy gene, will not develop in the individual
   (E) If paired with a healthy gene, the gene that causes hemophilia will not result in the individual's developing

   (Hint: The best version is the clearest, most concise expression of the intended idea.)

12

Answers and Explanations

1. **(C)** The original version is grammatically correct, but it is wordy. (C) provides a more concise alternative. In (B), *the fact of* is idiomatically improper and unnecessary (the phrase could be removed altogether). (D) misuses the reflexive verb *themselves*. In (E), the word *In* distorts the meaning of the original version.

2. **(E)** The original version includes a faulty parallel between the two phrases *our control over it* and *submitting to it*. *Our* should precede both terms, and the gerund form should be used in both terms, or not at all. (B) uses the wrong pronoun form; the possessive form (*our*) should be used instead of *us* preceding a gerund (*controlling*). (B) also lacks proper parallelism. (C) uses the idiom *on our part* awkwardly. (C) also lacks proper parallelism. (D) lacks proper parallelism (*submission over* makes no sense). (D) is also awkwardly constructed. (E) achieves grammatical parallelism through the use of *our controlling* and *our submitting*.

3. **(A)** The original version is correct; *its* is proper here because it refers to a singular thing (*society*); *regarding* is also proper here (*regarding* means "with respect to" or "concerning"). (B) uses the plural *their* instead of *its*, and its use of *as to* obscures the meaning of the original version, which intends to impose a choice on society among the three concerns listed. (C) uses the awkward and improper idiom *in respect of.* (D) uses the archaic (and improper) *amongst*. (E) confuses the meaning of the original version; *as they concern* nonsensically suggests that priorities concern the three areas listed.

4. **(C)** The original version is unclear as to the point it intends to make. (Is the point that Carnegie *lived* at that time or that he *engaged in philanthropy* at that time?) (C) clarifies the meaning of the sentence. (B) creates confusion by suggesting that Carnegie may have lived in some other manner during another time. (D) uses *which* incorrectly (*which* should be used to refer to things, not people). (E) fails to clarify the meaning of the original version, as well as using the improper idiom *at around.*

5. **(B)** The original version is redundant. Either *by means of* or *using* would be acceptable here—but not both. (B) corrects the redundancy by omitting *using*. (C) uses the wrong preposition (*with*); the proper idiom is *by using*. (D) is redundant in the same way as the original version. (E) uses the wrong preposition (*through*); the proper idiom is *by means of.*

6. **(D)** The original sentence suffers from faulty parallelism. The words *examination*, *diagnosing*, and *treatment* are not all grammatically parallel. One solution is to replace *diagnosing* with *diagnosis.* Also, notice that the first clause seems to refer nonsensically to *patients* because of this word's proximity to the clause. The solution is to reconstruct the sentence so that the clause is closer to *physicians* than to *patients*. (D) corrects both errors without creating any new ones. (B) creates an awkward, nonsensical sentence. (C) fails to correct the faulty parallelism. (C) also alters the meaning of the original sentence; *competent* and *successful* refer in (C) to both *diagnosis* and *treatment.* Also, the last clause in (C) is confusing. Are physicians trusting their patients, or vice versa? (E) corrects both errors in the original sentence. However, the grammatical element *develop growing trust* is split, resulting in the same confusion as in (C): Are physicians trusting their patients, or vice versa?

7. **(E)** The superfluous *there is* in the original version sets up an awkward construction. The sentence should be reconstructed, omitting *there is*. Among the other four versions, (E) is the best solution. (B) uses the correlative *if. . . then* awkwardly. (C) fails to correct the problem with the original version. In (D), the last clause is awkwardly constructed. The subject of *develops* is *individual* (the individual develops symptoms), but (D) improperly suggests that the *gene* develops the symptoms.

Hour 13

Teach Yourself Critical Reasoning I

This hour (as well as the next two hours) you'll teach yourself how to handle the Critical Reasoning questions that appear in the Verbal section of the GMAT CAT. Here are your goals for this hour.

- Learn what Critical Reasoning questions look like and how to deal with them
- Learn how to identify the main point or conclusion of an argument
- Learn how to find the unstated conclusion of a passage
- Review the skills you learn this hour by attempting a GMAT-style quiz

Critical Reasoning at a Glance

WHERE: In the GMAT CAT Verbal section, mixed in with Reading Comprehension and Sentence Correction questions

HOW MANY: 14–15 out of the 41 questions in the Verbal section

WHAT'S COVERED: You'll encounter 8 basic question types that test the following Critical Reasoning skills:

1. Identifying the main point or conclusion of an argument
2. Making inferences or drawing conclusions from given premises
3. Identifying assumptions in an argument
4. Assessing the effect of additional information on an argument
5. Identifying the unstated conclusion of an argument
6. Identifying the method of reasoning employed in an argument
7. Detecting reasoning errors
8. Recognizing arguments that have similar structure or employ a similar method

WHAT'S NOT TESTED: You won't have to know formal logic or the terminology of formal logic.

WHAT'S ASSUMED: You'll need to be familiar with the following ideas:

- Argument
- Issue
- Premise
- Conclusion
- Assumption

Don't worry: all you need to know about these ideas will be covered a few pages ahead.

DIRECTIONS: Here are the directions that will appear on your screen before your first Critical Reasoning question:

DIRECTIONS: For this question, select the best of the answer choices given.

What Critical Reasoning Questions Look Like

Critical Reasoning questions consist of a brief *passage* containing an argument followed by a *question* about the passage (called the *question stem*) and five *answer choices*. Here's what a typical Critical Reasoning question looks like:

QUESTION Eighty percent of the homeless people interviewed in a recent survey said that they prefer to eat and sleep on the streets rather than go to shelters. Surprisingly, this survey proves that contrary to popular opinion, homeless people prefer the discomfort and uncertainty of life on the streets to the comfort and security afforded by shelters.

Which of the following, if true, would cast most doubt on the conclusion of the above argument?

(A) Some of the people interviewed in the survey possessed warm clothing and adequate sleeping bags.

(B) The survey was conducted in several small rural communities.

(C) The only question asked in the survey was: "Which do you prefer more, eating and sleeping on the streets or eating and sleeping in shelters?"

(D) The survey was conducted by a homeless person.

(E) The survey was conducted concurrently in several different metropolitan communities during the winter.

NOTE We'll analyze this example just a few pages ahead to demonstrate the general approach you should take when dealing with Critical Reasoning questions.

What You Should Know About Critical Reasoning Questions

Critical Reasoning passages vary considerably in writing style and format. Passages also cover a broad range of topics.

There are only eight basic question types. However, there is extensive variation in the way in which each type is phrased. Don't worry: all of the question variations will be covered in the lessons that follow.

Prior knowledge of the topic at hand is never required to answer the question. All of the information you need to answer the question is contained in the passage. Critical Reasoning questions test your ability to recognize correct and incorrect reasoning; they do not test your knowledge of the topic under discussion.

Critical Reasoning questions on the GMAT CAT do not assume that you know the terminology of formal logic or that you have taken a course in logic. Specialized terms such as "syllogism," "valid," and "modus ponens" will not be used in asking questions. There are, however, some ideas that you'll be expected to understand. The bottom line is that you will be expected to be able to understand and critique the reasoning contained in arguments. To do this requires, at a minimum, that you are familiar with ideas such as argument, topic, issue, premise, conclusion, main point, and assumption. Before you go any further, take a few moments to review these basic ideas.

ARGUMENT: The word "argument" is used in two different ways. When we say that two or more people are "having an argument" or "are arguing," we mean merely that there is a discussion going on in which the participants disagree about some topic. This is not the sense of "argument" intended in GMAT CAT Critical Reasoning questions. In this context, to argue is to offer reasons in support of the truth of some claim or the correctness of some action. An argument, in this sense, is a sequence of statements, some of which are given as reasons or evidence for the truth or correctness of some claim.

PREMISE: A premise is a reason that is offered to support the truth or correctness of a claim. An argument may have any number of premises, but it must have at least one. Some of the premises of an argument might be unstated. Unstated premises in arguments are commonly referred to as assumptions.

CONCLUSION: A conclusion is any claim that is supported by reasons. An argument may have any number of conclusions, but it must have at least one. In complex arguments that have more than one conclusion, some will be intermediate conclusions and one will be the final conclusion.

INTERMEDIATE CONCLUSION: A claim that is supported by reasons and that, in turn, becomes a reason to support another conclusion in the argument.

FINAL CONCLUSION: The final conclusion is a claim that is supported by reasons but does not support any other claim in the argument. The final conclusion isn't always explicitly stated. In such cases, however, the author usually presents the reasons in such a way that there is really only one obvious conclusion that can be drawn from them. This implicit conclusion, even though unstated in the argument, is the main point or final conclusion of the argument.

TOPIC: The topic or subject of an argument is simply what the argument is about (e.g., censorship).

ISSUE: The issue of an argument is the question that is being addressed on the topic (e.g., Does national security justify censorship?).

MAIN POINT: The main point of an argument is the particular claim or position on the issue that the author argues for (e.g., National security does not justify censorship). The main point is typically expressed in the final conclusion of the argument.

ASSUMPTION: Assumptions are unstated premises that fill logical gaps in the stated argument. They are left unstated in most cases because the author believes that they are obvious or that they express claims that the audience already accepts as true or correct.

How to Tackle a Critical Reasoning Question

Here's a 5-step approach that will help you in handling any Critical Reasoning question.

ACTION PLAN

1. **Read the question stem first.** Determine which skill the question is testing so you're ready for the passage.
2. **Read the passage with the question stem in mind.** What to look for as you read the passage depends on the question; but in most cases you should try to identify the premises and the conclusion as you read; pay particular attention to key words that signal these elements.
3. **Formulate your own response to the question, if possible.** Doing so will force you to think actively about the question and the passage, and will help you to zero in on viable candidates while avoiding sucker-bait wrong answers.
4. **Scan the answer choices for one that resembles your "home grown" response.** If one of the five choices expresses essentially the same idea as your own response, it's a good bet that this is the correct answer. But unless you're pressed for time, don't confirm your answer yet; go on to step 5.
5. **Read all answer choices carefully.** Eliminate obvious wrong answer choices, then compare the quality of the viable choices.

Let's Apply the 5-Step Action Plan

Let's return to the sample question you looked at a few pages ago. This time we'll walk you through the problem using the 5-step approach you just learned.

QUESTION Eighty percent of the homeless people interviewed in a recent survey said that they prefer to eat and sleep on the streets rather than go to shelters. Surprisingly, this survey proves that contrary to popular opinion, homeless people prefer the discomfort and uncertainty of life on the streets to the comfort and security afforded by shelters.

Which of the following, if true, would cast most doubt on the conclusion of the above argument?

(A) Some of the people interviewed in the survey possessed warm clothing and adequate sleeping bags.

(B) The survey was conducted in several small rural communities.

(C) The only question asked in the survey was: "Which do you prefer more, eating and sleeping on the streets or eating and sleeping in shelters?"

(D) The survey was conducted by a homeless person.

(E) The survey was conducted concurrently in several different metropolitan communities during the winter.

ANALYSIS The correct answer is **(B)**. This question is of average difficulty. Approximately 60% of test-takers would respond correctly to this question. Here's how to analyze it with the 5-step approach:

1. This problem tests your ability to assess the effect of additional information on an argument. Your task in this case is to find a statement that weakens the argument; that is, one that makes it less likely that the conclusion is true. Notice that the question directs you to assume that the statements in the answers are true.

2. To solve this problem you're going to have to figure out which of the statements in the passage is the conclusion and which is the premise. This isn't too hard to do in this case. To make the argument clear, we'll list the premise first followed by the conclusion:

> *Premise:* Eighty percent of the homeless people interviewed in a recent survey said that they prefer to eat and sleep on the streets rather than go to shelters.
>
> *Conclusion:* Homeless people prefer the discomfort and uncertainty of life on the streets to the comfort and security afforded by shelters.

TIP

> It's a good idea to eliminate unnecessary verbiage whenever you restate an argument.

3. You'll learn later this hour that in this type of question (a "weaken-the-argument" question) the stated argument usually relies on at least one *unstated assumption*—a logical piece that is needed in order to bridge the gap between premise and conclusion. In most cases, the correct answer to a weaken-the-argument question is a statement that contradicts an important unstated assumption. In reading the sample question, did it occur to you that the conclusion depends on the assumption that the data gathered are drawn from a sample that is representative of the entire homeless community? If so, you'd be on the right track; look for an answer choice that refutes this assumption.

4. You're looking for an answer choice that essentially refutes the unstated assumption you formulated in step 3. Indeed, answer choice (B) provides such a statement.

Response (B) suggests that the data are drawn from a sample that is not representative of the entire homeless community. After all, small rural communities are significantly different from large metropolitan communities, and these differences could bias the sample considerably.

5. Let's go back and consider the other answers choices, to make sure that one of the other choices is not better than (B).

Response (A) does not suggest that the data are drawn from a sample that is not representative of the entire homeless community. In fact, (A) states something that we should expect to be the case if the sample is in fact representative of the entire homeless community. Had (A) stated that all or most or none of those interviewed possessed warm clothing and adequate sleeping bags, this would suggest that the sample was not representative, but this is not what (A) asserts. You can eliminate answer (A).

Response (C) does not suggest that the data are drawn from a sample that is not representative of the entire homeless community. (C) suggests that the survey may be unreliable because of the way in which the question was phrased, but it does not undermine the representativeness of the sample. You can eliminate answer (C).

Response (D) does not suggest that the data are drawn from a sample that is not representative of the entire homeless community. Clearly, the fact that the person conducting the survey was homeless does not, by itself, call the representativeness of the sample into question. You can eliminate answer (D).

Response (E) suggests that the data are drawn from a sample that is representative of the entire homeless community. Moreover, the fact that the survey was conducted during the winter gives even greater credence to the results. Rather than weaken the argument, (E) would strengthen it considerably. You can eliminate answer (E).

DO's and DON'Ts for Handling Critical Reasoning Questions

Here's a useful list of DO's and DON'Ts for Critical Reasoning questions. Some of these tips were touched on in the analysis of our sample question.

Do | **Don't**

DO identify the skill being tested before you read the passage; otherwise, you'll probably have to read the passage again.

DON'T let yourself get bogged down on a question; these questions can be confusing, so if you're still stuck after 1.5 minutes, take a reasoned guess and move on.

DO pay attention only to the skill that is being tested; disregard any reasoning flaws and errors that aren't relevant to the question.

DO focus your attention on the argument's logic.

DON'T choose an answer simply because you believe it is a true statement or because you agree with it.

DON'T reject an answer merely because you believe it is a false statement or because you disagree with it.

"Main Point" and "Conclusion" Questions

One of the Critical Reasoning skills you'll teach yourself this hour is how to identify the premises and conclusions of arguments. Even though you'll be tested only on your ability to correctly identify conclusions, figuring out which statements are premises as well as identifying which are conclusions is essential to answering most of the Critical Reasoning questions on the GMAT.

GMAT questions that ask you to identify the conclusion of an argument are typically worded in the following ways:

- Which of the following best expresses the main point of the passage?
- The conclusion of the argument is best expressed by which of the following?

Using Indicator Words to Identify Premises and Conclusions

In most cases, you can quickly identify an argument's conclusion simply by paying close attention to key words and phrases in the passage. Here is a list of words and phrases that are commonly used to indicate that the sentence that follows is a conclusion:

therefore/thus	proves/implies that
shows that	so
as a result	it is likely that
hence	suggests that
consequently	demonstrates that
it follows that	that's why

In cases where such words and phrases are absent, you can identify the conclusion by first identifying the premises and then looking for the sentence that they are intended to support. Here are some words and phrases commonly used to indicate that the sentence that follows is a premise:

since	for the reason that, is entailed by
for	assuming that
because, inasmuch as	is substantiated by, is shown by
follows from	as a result
given that, is suggested	on the supposition that by
is proved by	can be concluded from

Now, let's examine a few examples to see how these indicator words and phrases can help you identify the premises and conclusion of an argument.

> Einstein is as great a cult figure as Madonna, *so* T-shirts with Einstein's picture on them will sell as well as shirts with Madonna's picture.
>
> *Since* Einstein is as great a cult figure as Madonna, T-shirts with Einstein's picture on them will sell as well as shirts with Madonna's picture.

In the first example, the word *so* indicates the conclusion; in the second example, the word *since* indicates the premise. The argument in each of these examples is identical and can be rewritten as follows:

> *Premise:* Einstein is as great a cult figure as Madonna.
>
> *Conclusion:* T-shirts with Einstein's picture on them will sell as well as shirts with Madonna's picture.

Here's a more complicated example:

> *Inasmuch as* Einstein is as great a cult figure as Madonna, *it is likely that* T-shirts with Einstein's picture on them will sell as well as shirts with Madonna's picture, *so* we should add them to our inventory.

Each of the three italicized expressions in this example is an indicator. The first indicates a premise, the other two indicate conclusions. The word *so* indicates the final conclusion. The phrase *it is likely that* indicates the intermediate conclusion. You can rewrite this argument as follows to reveal its structure:

> *Premise:* Einstein is as great a cult figure as Madonna.
>
> *Intermediate conclusion:* T-shirts with Einstein's picture on them will sell as well as shirts with Madonna's picture.
>
> *Final conclusion:* We should add to our inventory T-shirts with Einstein's picture on them.

NOTE

> On the GMAT, if a question asks which answer choice best expresses the argument's conclusion, the best answer will express the final conclusion—not just an intermediate conclusion.

Here's another example of an argument that has an intermediate and a final conclusion:

> Sexual harassment against women is often fostered by economic motives *because* women generally have greater difficulty in finding jobs, and *for this reason* can be intimidated more easily.

This argument has two conclusions. The claim "[Women] can be intimidated more easily," is an intermediate conclusion supported by the premise "Women generally have greater difficulty in finding jobs." (signaled by the phrase *for this reason*). This intermediate conclusion in turn provides a reason (signaled by the word *because*) for the final conclusion that is stated in the first part of the sentence. You can rewrite the argument to reveal its structure as follows:

Premise: Women generally have greater difficulty in finding jobs.

Intermediate Conclusion: Women can be intimidated more easily than men.

Final Conclusion: Sexual harassment against women is often fostered by economic motives.

NOTE

In this example the intermediate and the final conclusion were identified using the *premise* indicators *because* and *for this reason.*

Using a Rhetorical Question to Signal a Conclusion

In addition to the use of indicator words and phrases, another common way to signal an argument's conclusion is to express it as a rhetorical question or as an answer to a rhetorical question. The purpose of such questions is not to solicit information, but rather to emphasize a particular point or to raise a particular issue. Rhetorical questions typically (but not always) appear at the beginning of the passage. The remaining sentences in the passage typically state reasons that support the position on the issue that the rhetorical question encompasses.

Identifying the Main Point or Conclusion of an Argument

Here's a 3-step approach that will help you identify the main point or conclusion of any argument:

ACTION PLAN

1. **Scan the passage looking for conclusion or premise indicator words or phrases.**
2. **If there are no indicator words or phrases in the passage, scan the passage looking for a rhetorical question.**
3. **If the passage has no indicator expressions or rhetorical questions, look at the first and last statements in the passage.**

Now let's look at a GMAT-style "conclusion" question. Try applying the 3-step approach indicated above, then read the analysis that follows the question.

QUESTION Who can disagree that immediate action must be taken to create a better code for hospital care and management? Recent studies showing that the death rate in U.S. hospitals is considerably higher than the overall U.S. death rate clearly demonstrate that hospitals are not providing proper care to patients.

Which of the following best expresses the conclusion of the argument above?

(A) The death rate in U.S. hospitals is too high.

(B) U.S. hospitals are not providing proper care to patients.

(C) Immediate action must be taken to lower the overall U.S. death rate.

(D) Hospital care and management in the U.S. is substandard.

(E) Codes that define hospital care and management standards need to be improved.

ANALYSIS The correct answer is **(E)**. There are two conclusions in this argument. The first appears at the end of the passage and is indicated by the phrase "clearly demonstrate that." The second conclusion is the first sentence, which is a rhetorical question. The conclusion at the end of the passage is an intermediate conclusion because it provides support for the conclusion expressed in the first sentence, which expresses the final conclusion. (E) is a good statement of the point that the first sentence (the rhetorical question) seeks to make.

"Unstated Conclusion" Questions

Unstated conclusion questions test your ability to follow a line of reasoning and reach the conclusion that most logically completes that line of reasoning. In such questions, an underlined blank replaces the last few words or the last sentence of the passage, and you must choose the answer that best fits in the blank. The best answer is the one that most logically completes the passage's reasoning process.

GMAT questions that ask you identify the unstated conclusion of an argument are typically worded in the following ways:

- Which of the following best completes the line of reasoning in the passage?
- Which of the following best completes the preceding argument?

Focusing on the Main Ideas

When dealing with unstated conclusion questions, one way to proceed is to first identify the passage's main ideas. Second, look for links between these ideas in the passage. Finally, look for an answer choice that ties together two of the main ideas that the passage does not link together.

Here's a simple example to illustrate this approach:

> All people who live in the tropics are friendly. Jamaicans live in the tropics. Therefore, ______________________________.

The main ideas in this example are: (1) people who live in the tropics, (2) friendly people, and (3) people who live in Jamaica. The first sentence of the passage links ideas (1) and (2). The second sentence links ideas (1) and (3). The unstated conclusion is a sentence that links ideas (2) and (3). In this example, the unstated conclusion is: Jamaicans are friendly.

Here's another example of this approach:

> Sexual preference is not something over which people have control. The only things people are accountable for are things over which they have control. Therefore, ______________________________.

The main ideas in this example are: (1) sexual preference, (2) behavior over which people have control, and (3) behavior people are accountable for. The first sentence of the passage links ideas (1) and (2). The second sentence links ideas (2) and (3). The unstated conclusion is a sentence that links ideas (1) and (3). In this example, the unstated conclusion is: People are not accountable for their sexual preference.

Focusing on the Pattern of the Argument

Another approach is to focus on the pattern of the argument in the passage, rather than on the ideas.

NOTE

> Of the two approaches discussed here, the one you use to solve a given problem is entirely dependent on the problem. Don't worry; careful study of the examples and exercises in this lesson will give you a good idea of when to use each.

Here's a simple example to illustrate this approach:

> Either we should get out of the stock market entirely or we should re-invest. We cannot afford to get out entirely. Therefore, ______________________________.

The basic pattern of this argument is:

> Either *A* or *B*. Not *A*. Therefore, ______________________________.

Common sense tells you that the statement that best completes this pattern is *B*. Consequently the unstated conclusion is *B* which in the example above is "we should re-invest."

Here's another simple example to illustrate this approach:

> If George had pie for dessert, then he didn't have ice cream. He had ice cream. So it follows that, ______________________________.

The pattern of this argument is:

> If *A*, then not *B*. *B*. Therefore, ______________________________.

Common sense tells you that the statement that best completes this pattern is *Not A*. Consequently, the unstated conclusion is *Not A,* which in the example above is "George didn't have pie for dessert."

Here's one more example of this approach:

> Senator Brown has consistently opposed national health care legislation, argued against affirmative action measures, and voted against NAFTA. Brown is supported by The Citizens for Responsible Government. Senator Black also opposes national health care legislation, thinks affirmative action programs should be abolished, and voted against NAFTA. Therefore, we can reasonably expect that ______________________________.

The pattern of this argument is:

> A has properties *W*, *X*, *Y*, and *Z*
>
> B has properties *W*, *X*, *Y*,
>
> Therefore, B is likely to have property ______.

Obviously, the property that best completes this pattern is *Z*. In the example above *Z* = the property of being supported by the Citizens for Responsible Government. So, the unstated conclusion is: Senator Black is supported by the Citizens for Responsible Government.

Identifying Unstated Conclusions

Here's a 4-step approach that will help you identify the unstated conclusion of an argument:

Action Plan

1. **Identify the passage's main ideas, or the argument's pattern.**
2. **Look for links between the main ideas expressed in the passage, or for logical relationships between the statements in the argument.**
3. **Look for an answer choice that links together two of the main ideas that the passage does not link together, or for a statement that best completes the argument's pattern.**
4. **If all else fails, look at the answer choices and ask yourself which is most strongly supported by the statements in the passage.**

Now, let's look at a GMAT-style example of an "unstated conclusion." Try tackling it using the 4-step approach you just learned. Then read the explanation that follows.

Question When we regard people to be morally responsible for their actions, we regard them as being the object of praise or blame with respect to those actions. But it seems evident that people cannot be the object of praise or blame for their actions unless they performed them of their own free will. Therefore, ____________________________.

Which of the following best completes the preceding argument?

(A) People are morally responsible only for actions that they perform of their own free will.

(B) People are not morally responsible for actions that they did not perform.

(C) People can be blamed or praised only for actions that they perform of their own free will.

(D) People are morally responsible only for actions for which they can be blamed or praised.

(E) People who are not morally responsible for their actions cannot be blamed or praised for their actions.

13

Analysis The main ideas in the passage are (1) actions for which one is morally responsible, (2) praiseworthy and blameworthy actions, and (3) actions performed of one's own free will. Notice that the passage's first sentence links ideas (1) and (2), and the second sentence of the passage links ideas (2) and (3). In this example, the conclusion that the author invites is one that ties together ideas (1) and (3). Looking at the answer choices with this in mind, the best response is **(A)**.

Workshop

In this Workshop, you'll review the techniques for identifying stated and unstated conclusions you learned this hour by attempting a GMAT-style quiz.

ONLINE

Additional Critical Reasoning questions are available online at the author's Web site: *http://www.west.net/~stewart/gmat*

Quiz

(Answers and explanations begin on page 270)

DIRECTIONS: Try these five GMAT-style Critical Reasoning questions. Try to limit your time to 8 minutes altogether.

1. As the bilateral trade deficit continues to widen, the United States and Japan are trying to blame each other for the problem. However, the U.S. cannot continue to hold Japan responsible by placing tariffs on electronic products and semiconductors, and, at the same time, expect the deficit problem to go away. Given all this, it's pretty clear that the trade deficit will continue since the administration has announced that it will continue its "get tough" policy against Japan by imposing more tariffs on Japanese goods.

   Which of the following best expresses the main point of the passage?

   (A) The bilateral trade deficit between the United States and Japan will continue.
   (B) The United States cannot hold Japan responsible for the bilateral trade deficit between these countries.
   (C) The trade deficit between Japan and the U.S. will not be solved by tariffs.
   (D) Neither Japan nor the U.S. is responsible for the trade deficit between these two countries.
   (E) The U.S. will continue its "get tough" policy against Japan.

   (Hint: Look for indicator words or phrases to help you identify the final conclusion of the argument.)

2. Can anyone seriously deny that unrestricted immigration will harm hundreds of thousands of American workers? If the United States allows unrestricted immigration, there will soon be a surplus of cheap labor. This will inevitably lead to lower wages. And if wages fall, it's only a matter of time until the standards of living of other workers are adversely affected.

   The conclusion of the argument is best expressed by which of the following?

   (A) Unrestricted immigration will result in a surplus of cheap labor.
   (B) A surplus of cheap labor will lead to lower wages for all workers.
   (C) A decrease in worker's wages should be avoided at all costs.
   (D) Unrestricted immigration will be detrimental to the standards of living of all workers.
   (E) Hundreds of thousands of American workers will be harmed by unrestricted immigration.

   (Hint: Look for a rhetorical question in the passage.)

3. Wearing seat belts in a car is like getting a vaccine to prevent measles. In both cases, it's good for our health and well-being, but it's a hassle and lots of people wouldn't do it unless they were forced to. All in all, however, it's good that we have a law requiring people to get vaccinated for measles. Likewise, it's good to have a law that requires people to wear seat belts in cars.

   The conclusion of the argument is best expressed by which of the following?

   (A) Wearing seat belts in cars is good for our health and well-being.
   (B) People will not wear seat belts unless they are forced to.
   (C) The law that requires people to get vaccinated for measles is a good idea.
   (D) The law that requires people to wear seat belts in cars is a good idea.
   (E) Wearing seat belts in cars is a hassle.

   (Hint: Ask yourself what point the author is trying to make.)

4. The meteor hypothesis is often cited to explain the extinction of dinosaurs. But, if dinosaurs were killed by the effects of dust raised by a giant meteor striking Earth, then higher than normal amounts of iridium will be found in sediments deposited 60 million years ago. This would result because iridium is an element common in meteors, but rare in the Earth's crust. So far, however, no large concentrations of iridium have been found anywhere on Earth despite years of investigation by scientists. Therefore ________________.

   Which of the following best completes the argument?

   (A) A giant meteor did not strike Earth 60 million years ago.
   (B) Dinosaurs were not killed by the effects of dust in the atmosphere.
   (C) Sediments deposited 60 million years ago do not contain high levels of iridium.

(D) The meteor hypothesis is most likely false.
(E) No explanation of the extinction of dinosaurs has yet been found.

(Hint: Identify the pattern of the argument.)

5. Given that American historical documents of the last quarter of the eighteenth century are filled with references to the effect that liberty is the "greatest good" or that the preservation of liberty is "the most valuable end of government," or that government exists "to secure the blessings of liberty," it can be inferred that liberty was of paramount importance to our nation's founders. And, it is for this reason, more than any other, that we should make every effort to preserve it.

   What is the main point of the argument?

   (A) Liberty is the "greatest good."
   (B) Liberty is an important American value.
   (C) Liberty was important to our nation's founders.
   (D) Government exists only to secure the liberty of its citizens.
   (E) Liberty should be preserved.

   (Hint: Look for indicator words and phrases to help you identify the final conclusion of the argument.)

Answers and Explanations

1. **(A)** The indicators in this passage are the phrases *"given all this," "it's pretty clear that"* and the word *"since,"* all of which appear in the last sentence. *"Given all this"* indicates that the preceding statements are intended as reasons for the statement that follows this phrase. The sentence following the phrase *"it's pretty clear that"* is the conclusion (i.e., the trade deficit will continue). The sentence following the word "*since*" states another reason in support of this conclusion. Moreover, since there is only one conclusion in the argument, it is the final conclusion or main point of the argument.

2. **(E)** The conclusion of this argument is expressed by the rhetorical question at the beginning of the passage. The sarcastic tone of the question indicates that the author believes that unrestricted immigration will harm hundreds of thousands of American workers. Answer choice (E) is a restatement of this idea.

3. **(D)**. In this argument an analogy is drawn between wearing seat belts and getting vaccinated. On the basis of several similarities between them, the author reasons that they are also similar in an additional way. The conclusion is signaled by the word "*likewise*," which indicates the additional feature they share.

4. **(D)**. The argument in this passage can be boiled down to the following: If the meteor theory is true, then higher than normal amounts of iridium will be found in sediments deposited 60 million years ago. No large concentrations of iridium have been found anywhere on Earth. Therefore, ________. The pattern of the argument is: *If A, then B. Not B. Therefore ________*. The statement that best completes this pattern is *"Not A."* Applying this analysis to the problem at hand, the sentence that best completes the argument is: The meteor hypothesis is most likely false.

5. **(E)** The indicators in this passage are the phrases *"given that"* and *"it can be inferred that"* in the first sentence, and the phrase *"it is for this reason that"* in the second sentence. The first of these is a premise indicator, the two remaining are conclusion indicators. The first conclusion ("liberty was of paramount importance to our nation's founders") is the intermediate conclusion since it functions as a reason for the second conclusion ("we should make every effort to preserve [liberty]"). Since the second conclusion does not support any other statement in the argument, it is the final conclusion, and, consequently, the main point of the argument.

Hour 14

Teach Yourself Critical Reasoning II

Now that you know what Critical Reasoning questions look like and how to identify premises and conclusions, you'll turn your attention to three additional Critical Reasoning skills you'll need for high scores on the GMAT CAT. In this hour you will learn:

- How to make inferences from given premises
- How to identify assumptions needed to make an argument correct
- How to assess the effect additional information has on an argument's conclusion
- How to apply the skills you learn this hour to a GMAT-style quiz

"Inference" Questions

Inference questions test your ability to draw conclusions from given information. To be more precise, these questions test your ability to determine what conclusion must be true, or is most likely true, given that the statements in the passage are true. In problems of this type, the information in the passage functions as the premises of the argument and the candidate conclusions are among the answer choices.

Types of Inference Questions

Inference questions are worded in a variety of ways. Here are examples of the three basic types:

- If all the statements in the passage are true, which one of the following must also be true?
- Which one of the following conclusions is most strongly supported by the statements in the passage?
- Which of the following statements can be properly inferred from the passage?

The difference between the first two of these types of questions is important. The conclusion that *must be true* given the information stated in the passage is the one that cannot conceivably be false, given this information. The conclusion that is *most strongly supported* by the information stated in the passage is the one that is most unlikely to be false (in other words, most likely true), given this information. Questions that ask for what can be "properly inferred" or "properly drawn" from the passage are somewhat tricky. Without getting too technical, questions asking for the conclusion you can "properly" infer or draw from the statements in a passage can be understood in two ways. They can be asking either for the conclusion that *must be true*, or for the conclusion that the passage *most strongly supports*.

NOTE

For an inference to be "proper," it must be made in accordance with acceptable inference rules or meet certain standards of acceptable inference. In deductive reasoning, these rules and standards are designed to ensure that the truth of the premises guarantees the truth of the conclusion, whereas in inductive reasoning, the rules and standards are designed to ensure that the truth of the premises makes it highly likely that the conclusion is true.

Degrees of Support

In the context of critical reasoning, the word "support" means "increases the likelihood that the conclusion is true." Thus, to say that the premises support the conclusion is to say that they increase the likelihood that it is true. Given this, you can see that premises can provide varying *degrees* of support for conclusions, ranging from very little to maximum support. The premises provide maximum support if the conclusion cannot conceivably be false given that the information stated by the premises is true. Obviously, maximum support is the highest degree of support possible. Lesser degrees of support will reflect the degree of likelihood that the conclusion is true given that the premises are true. Thus, some premises will provide a *stronger* degree of support for a conclusion than others.

What this boils down to is that inference questions are aimed at testing your ability to make correct judgments about the *degree of support* premises provide for conclusions. As the previous example illustrates, the way in which this is typically done on the GMAT is to provide you with some information in a passage and a list of possible conclusions in the answer choices, and have you select the answer that is most strongly supported by this information.

Dealing with "Must Be True" Inference Questions

Here's a 2-step approach to help you deal with questions that ask you to find the statement that *must* be true given the information stated in the passage:

ACTION PLAN

1. **Read the passage very carefully.** If necessary, jot down the premises on your scratch paper, parsing out key information and deleting unnecessary verbiage.
2. **Read each answer choice.** Ask yourself whether an answer choice can conceivably be false given that the sentences in the passage are true. The correct answer is the one that *cannot conceivably be false* given the information stated in the passage.

Here's a simple example to illustrate this approach:

Example:

Cheating on your taxes is lying, and lying, as we all know, is morally wrong.

If the statements in the passage are true, which one of the following *must* also be true?

(A) Cheating on your taxes is illegal.

(B) Cheating is morally wrong.

(C) Cheating on your taxes is morally wrong.

(D) Lying is cheating.

(E) Cheating is immoral.

1. Jot down the premises as follows:

Premise: Cheating on your taxes is lying.

Premise: Lying is morally wrong.

2. Read each answer in turn and determine whether it can conceivably be false given the information stated in the premises.

Look at answer choice (A). Can it conceivably be false given the stated information? The answer is yes, because the given information does not explicitly mention anything about what is legal or illegal.

TIP

Don't make any superfluous assumptions. Focus only on the information *explicitly* stated in the passage.

Look at answer choice (B). Can it conceivably be false given the stated information? Again, the answer is yes, because the given information does not state that all kinds of cheating are lying. It states only that a particular kind of cheating (cheating on your taxes) is lying.

Look at answer choice (C). Can it conceivably be false given the stated information? In this case, the answer is no, because if all tax cheating is lying, and all lying is morally wrong, then all tax cheating must be morally wrong. Response **(C)** is the correct answer.

TIP

Once you have found an answer that must be true given the information, you need not continue with other answer choices. This type of question has only *one* correct answer.

A variation of this type of question asks not for the single statement that must be true, but rather for the answer that is the exception (that is, the statement that need not be true given the stated information). In this case, the question is worded as follows:

If the preceding statements are true, all of the following statements must also be true *except*:

In this version of the question, four of the five answer choices must be true and only one need not be true. Your job is to find the one that need not be true given the information in the passage. The procedure for dealing with this type of question is the same as previously described. The only difference is that the correct answer is the one that *could conceivably be false* given the stated information.

Dealing with "Most Strongly Supported" Inference Questions

Here's a 2-step approach to help you deal with questions that ask you to find the statement that is *most strongly supported* given the information stated in the passage:

ACTION PLAN

1. **Read the passage very carefully.** If necessary, jot down the premises on your scratch paper, parsing out key information and deleting unnecessary verbiage.
2. **Read each answer choice.** Determine how likely an answer choice is true given the information stated in the passage. Use a simple four-point scale to score each of the answers. For example, 1 = very unlikely, 2 = not very likely, 3 = somewhat likely, 4 = very likely. Using this scale the correct answer is the one that gets the *highest score*.

NOTE

> You can also use this procedure to deal with questions that ask you to find the conclusion that can be *properly inferred* from the information in the passage. The only change you need to make is to expand the four-point scale to a five-point scale, assigning 5 to answers that *must* be true.

Here's an example of this approach:

Example:

Dogs taken to humane shelters are routinely checked for rabies. The dog that bit James was also obtained from the humane shelter the day before it bit him.

If the statements in the passage are true, which of the following is most strongly represented?

(A) Humane shelter technicians never make mistakes when testing dogs for rabies.

(B) The dog contracted rabies after it was released from the shelter but before it bit James.

(C) The dog does not have rabies.

(D) James has rabies.

(E) The humane shelter technicians are incompetent.

1. Here's the key information stated in the passage:

Premise: Dogs taken to humane shelters are routinely checked for rabies.

Premise: The dog that bit James was obtained from the humane shelter.

Premise: The dog was obtained from the humane shelter the day before it bit James.

2. Using the 4-point scale, here's the score for each of the answer choices:

(A) is not very likely true, because the information in the passage really doesn't address the issue of whether the testing procedures are reliable. The score for (A) is 2.

CAUTION Don't make any superfluous assumptions. Focus only on the information explicitly stated in the passage.

(B) is not very likely true. Although it is possible that the dog contracted rabies during this brief period, without additional information regarding the dog's whereabouts during this period, it is difficult to assess the likelihood that this is the case. Given the information in the premises, the score for (B) is (2).

(C) is very likely true. The fact that the dog was tested for rabies just a short time before the incident makes it very likely that the dog was not rabid at the time of the incident. The score for (C) is 4.

CAUTION Unless otherwise directed, assume the information stated in the passage is true.

(D) is very unlikely true. The likelihood that (D) is true is a function of the likelihood that (C) is true, so if it is very likely that the dog does not have rabies, then it's very likely that James does not have rabies. The score for (D) is 1.

(E) is not very likely true. Although it is possible that the technicians are incompetent, the information stated in the premises does not support that claim. The score for (E) is 2.

CAUTION When using this approach you must read and score *all* of the answer choices.

Reviewing the scores, response (C) gets the highest score. (C) is the most strongly supported, and thus **(C)** is the correct answer.

Now let's look at a GMAT-style inference question. Try tackling this question using the 2-step method you just learned. Then, read the explanation that follows.

QUESTION There are more than two hundred nuclear power plants in this country. Each of them has operated for at least twenty years. None has reported any major problems, and every one of them has a superb safety record with no fatalities and no major injuries reported.

If all of the statements in the passage are true, which of the following conclusions is most strongly supported?

(A) Nuclear power plants do not pose a danger to humans.

(B) This country's nuclear power plants are safer than nuclear power plants in other countries.

(C) There will be a nuclear power plant failure in this country within the next five years.

(D) Power generated in nuclear power plants is a safe and reliable form of energy.

(E) Few people will be killed or injured in nuclear power plants in this country this year.

ANALYSIS The conclusion that is most strongly supported is **(E)**. Given the information stated in the passage, the score for (E) is 4 because no reasons are stated to suggest that the trends of the last twenty years will change. The score for (A) is 1 mainly because the information stated in the passage does not address the general issue of whether nuclear power plants pose dangers to humans. All that is addressed in the passage is the safety of nuclear power plant workers. The score for (B) is 1 because there is no information in the passage that compares this country's nuclear power plants with those of other countries. The score for (C) is 1 because nothing that is stated in the passage supports this claim. The score for (D) is 3. The evidence stated in the passage supports (D). But, since the evidence is applicable only to nuclear power in this country and not to nuclear power in general, (D) is only *somewhat* likely to be true.

CAUTION

> Keep in mind that you're *not* merely trying to figure out the likelihood of each answer; you're trying to figure out the likelihood of each answer *given that the information in the passage is true*.

"Unstated Assumption" Questions

An assumption is an unstated premise that fills in a logical gap in the stated argument. In other words, it's a missing piece of information that is required to support the conclusion. Assumption questions test your ability to supply the unstated information that is required to support the conclusions of arguments.

Assumption questions are typically worded as follows:

- The conclusion of the argument is properly drawn if which one of the following is assumed?
- For the argument to be logically correct, it must make which of the following assumptions?
- Which of the following is an assumption on which the argument depends?

Notice that the above questions ask you either for the assumption that makes the argument *logically correct* or for the assumption that allows the conclusion to be *properly drawn.* The exact conditions that must be satisfied for an argument to be "logically correct," or for the conclusion to be "properly drawn," differ depending on the argument type. As a general rule, however, the more unlikely it is for the conclusion to be false given that the premises are true, the more "logically correct" the argument and the more "properly drawn" is the conclusion. Therefore, the assumption that will make the argument logically correct, or the conclusion "properly drawn", is a statement that, when taken with the stated premises, significantly increases the likelihood that the conclusion is true. Moreover, given several choices, the statement that increases this likelihood most is the best choice.

Starting with the Answer Choices

When dealing with assumption questions, one approach is to use the answer choices to help you figure out the assumption. To do this, first identify the premises and the conclusion. Next, look at the answer choices and ask yourself which most increases the likelihood that the conclusion is true.

Here's a simple example to illustrate this approach:

Example:

Fred is a philosophy major, that's why I'm sure he'll score high on the GMAT.

For the argument to be logically correct, it must make which of the following assumptions?

(A) Philosophy majors have good verbal skills.

(B) Philosophy majors have good critical reasoning skills.

(C) Philosophy majors score high on the GMAT.

First, jot down the argument to reveal its structure as follows:

Assumption: ____________________________.

Stated Premise: Fred is a philosophy major.

Conclusion: Fred will score high on the GMAT.

Second, look at the answer choices and ask which *most* increases the likelihood that the conclusion is true?

(C) is the best choice because it increases the likelihood that the conclusion is true more than the other two choices.

Starting with the Argument

Another approach is to try to figure out the assumption *before* you look at the answer choices. In this approach, you use the stated information in the argument as a guide to the unstated assumption. Typically, assumptions in arguments serve to connect key ideas in the author's reasoning or fill logical gaps in the pattern of the reasoning. Consequently, this approach focuses on either identifying the argument's key ideas or the logical pattern of the argument. To do this, first identify the premises and the conclusion. Next, identify the key ideas in the argument or the pattern of the argument. The assumption required to make the argument logically correct is one that either links key ideas that are not linked in the premises and conclusion or that completes the argument's logical pattern.

CAUTION

Determining whether to identify the keys ideas or to identify the pattern of the argument depends upon the argument at hand. Don't worry; careful study of the examples and exercises in this lesson will give you a good idea of which to do in each case.

Here's a simple example that illustrates this approach:

People enjoy stories written by Mark Twain because they enjoy humorous stories.

Here's the argument:

Assumption: ______________________________.

Premise: People enjoy humorous stories.

Conclusion: People enjoy stories written by Mark Twain.

The key ideas in the argument are (1) things people enjoy, (2) humorous stories, and (3) stories written by Mark Twain. The stated premise links ideas (1) and (2). The conclusion links ideas (1) and (3). Since ideas (2) and (3) are not linked in the argument, the assumption required to make the argument logically correct must link these two ideas. The statement that does this is: Stories written by Mark Twain are humorous.

Dealing with Assumption Questions

Combining the two approaches discussed earlier, here's a 4-step approach to help you identify the assumption that makes an argument logically correct:

ACTION PLAN

1. **Identify the stated premises and the conclusion of the argument.**
2. **Read each answer choice. Look for the one that *most* increases the likelihood that the conclusion is true.**

As an alternative to step 2, do steps 3 and 4.

3. **Identify the key ideas in the argument or identify the argument's logical pattern.**
4. **Look for an answer choice that links key ideas that are not linked in the stated premises and conclusion, or that completes the argument's logical pattern.**

Now let's look at a GMAT-style assumption question. Try tackling it using the methods you just learned. Then, read the explanation that follows.

QUESTION

Captive animals exhibit a wider range of physical and behavioral traits than animals in the wild. That's why researchers who study captive animals are able to study a wider range of genetic possibilities than researchers who study wild animals.

For this argument to be logically correct, it must make which one of the following assumptions?

(A) Animals in zoos exhibit a wider range of physical and behavioral traits than wild animals.

(B) Animals that permit researchers to study a wide range of genetic possibilities are better research subjects than animals that do not.

(C) The wider the range of the physical and behavioral traits in a population of animals, the greater the range of their genetic possibilities.

(D) Captive animals are studied more than wild animals.

(E) Wild animals exhibit a narrow range of physical and behavioral traits.

ANALYSIS Following the procedure, here's the answer and explanation:

The best answer is **(C)**.

Here's why:

First, here's the argument:

Assumption: ______________________________.

Premise: Captive animals exhibit a wider range of physical and behavioral traits than animals in the wild.

Conclusion: Researchers who study captive animals are able to study a wider range of genetic possibilities than researchers who study wild animals.

Second, looking at each of the answer choices to determine which most increases the likelihood that the conclusion is true, we get the following:

Answer (A) does not increase the likelihood that the conclusion is true because (A) is just a restatement of the premise. Answer (B) does not increase the likelihood that the conclusion is true because the information stated in (B) is irrelevant to the conclusion. Answer (C) increases the likelihood that the conclusion is true; in fact, given (C) and the stated premise, the conclusion *must* be true. Answer (D) does not increase the likelihood that the conclusion is true because the information stated in (D) is irrelevant to the conclusion. Answer (E) does not increase the likelihood that the conclusion is true because (E) is a restatement of the premise. Since **(C)** increases the likelihood that the conclusion is true more than any other answer choice, it is the best answer.

"Additional Information" Questions

Questions that test your ability to assess the effect of new information on an argument are the most common Critical Reasoning question type on the GMAT. The passage states an argument. The answer choices state additional information. Your task is to assess the effect this additional information has on the argument.

There are just two types of "additional information" questions:

1. Those that ask you to choose the answer that strengthens the argument.
2. Those that ask you to choose the answer that weakens the argument.

It is important to remember that there are just two types of questions: strengthen questions and weaken questions. But on the GMAT these questions are worded in many different ways.

Weaken questions are worded as follows:

- Which of the following, if true, would refute the argument in the passage?
- Which one of the following, if true, casts the most doubt on the argument?
- Which one of the following, if accepted by the authors, would require them to reconsider their conclusion?
- Which of the following, if true, most seriously calls the preceding conclusion into question?
- Which of the following, if true, most seriously undermines the author's contention?
- Which of the following, if true, most substantially weakens the argument?

Strengthen questions are worded as follows:

- Which of the following, if true, most strengthens the argument?
- Which of the following would provide the most support for the conclusion?
- Which of the following supports the conclusion in the passage?
- The conclusion in the argument would be more reasonable if which one of the following were true?
- Which of the following, if true, would confirm the author's conclusion?

Determining Argument Strength and Weakness

The strength of an argument is determined by the degree of likelihood that the conclusion is true given that the premises are true. The higher this degree of likelihood, the stronger the argument. Conversely, the lower this degree of likelihood, the weaker the argument.

For example, compare the following arguments:

1. 90% of all men are forgetful, Adam is a man, therefore Adam is forgetful.
2. 50% of all men are forgetful, Adam is a man, therefore Adam is forgetful.

The first argument is stronger than the second. In the first, the likelihood that the conclusion is true given that the premises are true is 90%. If you had to make a bet whether Adam is forgetful and you knew the information stated in the premises, you'd probably wager a lot on it. In the second argument, the likelihood that the conclusion is true given that the premises are true is 50%. In this case, you'd probably wager a lot less.

Of course, in both cases you could lose your wager. For example, if it turned out that Adam was a mnemonist (a memory expert), then both wagers would be bad bets. In other words, this *additional information* about Adam would weaken both arguments considerably. You can see that it would do this by considering how much less you'd be willing to wager if you knew this. On the other hand, if it turned out that Adam had advanced Alzheimer's disease (a result of which is severe memory loss), then both wagers would be good bets. In other words, this additional information about Adam would strengthen both arguments considerably. Again, you can see that it would do this by considering how much more you'd be willing to bet if you knew this.

The bottom line is arguments can be strengthened or weakened by additional information. Arguments are strengthened by the new information if the likelihood that the conclusion is true (given that the premises are true) is increased by the addition of the new information. Arguments are weakened by the new information if the likelihood that the conclusion is true (given that the premises are true) is decreased by the addition of the new information.

Weakening an Argument

There are basically three ways to weaken an argument: (1) undermine a major assumption of the argument, (2) attack one of the premises of the argument, or (3) suggest an alternative conclusion that you can infer from the given premises. When dealing with problems that ask you to choose a statement that weakens an argument, the correct answer does one of these three things.

Here's a 3-step approach to help you deal with questions that ask you to find the statement that weakens an argument:

ACTION PLAN

1. **Identify the argument's premises and conclusion.**
2. **Identify the argument's major assumption.**
3. **Look for an answer choice that does one of the following:**
   - A. **undermines the major assumption**
   - B. **attacks a stated premise**
   - C. **suggests an alternative conclusion that you can infer from the stated premises**

   The correct answer is one that does any one of these.

Here's a simple example that illustrates this 3-step approach:

> The current regime is oppressive since it is holding thousands of people in jail without due process of law.

Which of the following, if true, most weakens this argument?

A. The current regime has only been in power for two weeks.
B. Most of the prisoners are political prisoners.
C. Many non-oppressive regimes hold people in jail without due process of law.

1. Here's the argument:

> *Premise:* The current regime is holding thousands of people in jail without due process of law.
>
> *Conclusion:* The current regime is oppressive.

2. Here's the major assumption:

> All regimes that hold people in jail without due process of law are oppressive.

3. Here's the reason (C) is the best choice:

> Answer **(C)** undermines the argument's major assumption.

Now let's look at a GMAT-style "weaken-the-argument" question. Try applying the approach you just learned, then read the explanation that follows.

QUESTION Mountain lion sightings in outlying areas of Los Alamos have increased dramatically over the past two years. Hence, the population of mountain lions must be increasing.

Which of the following, if true, most effectively weakens the above argument?

(A) People have become more active in outdoor activities during the past two years.
(B) Mountain lion habitat has dramatically diminished over the past two years.
(C) Human population in the outlying areas of Los Alamos has dramatically increased over the past two years.
(D) There has been a dramatic increase in the number of television programs about mountain lions during the past two years.
(E) Reports of people and animals being killed by mountain lions have increased dramatically over the past two years.

ANALYSIS The best answer is **(C)**. Here's why:

1. Here's the argument:

Premise: Mountain lion sightings in outlying areas of Los Alamos have increased dramatically over the past two years.

Conclusion: The population of mountain lions must be increasing.

2. Here's the major assumption:

The population of humans in the outlying areas of Los Alamos has remained constant over the past two years.

3. Here's the reason (C) is the best choice:

None of the answer choices undermines the major assumption. However, (C) provides an alternative conclusion that you can infer from the premise, so (C) is the best answer.

Strengthening an Argument

There are two ways to strengthen an argument, (1) offer support for the argument's major assumption, or (2) provide additional evidence for the conclusion (that is, evidence beyond what the given premises state). When dealing with problems that ask you to choose a statement that strengthens an argument, the correct answer does one of these two things.

Here's a 3-step approach to help you deal with questions that ask you to find the statement that strengthens an argument:

ACTION PLAN

1. **Identify the argument's premises and conclusion.**
2. **Identify the argument's major assumption.**
3. **Look for an answer choice that does either of the following:**

   A. **provides support for the major assumption**

   B. **provides additional evidence for the conclusion**

   The correct answer is one that does either of these.

Here's a simple example that illustrates this approach:

> Since we need to improve our minds in order to live full and happy lives, it follows that we cannot just play all the time.

Which of the following, if true, most strengthens the argument?

A. People who play all the time lead empty, unfulfilling lives.
B. The only way to improve your mind is through study and hard work.
C. Most people do not live full and happy lives.

1. Here's the argument:

> *Premise:* We need to improve our minds in order to live full and happy lives.
>
> *Conclusion:* We cannot just play all the time.

2. Here's the major assumption:

> Play does not improve our minds.

3. Here's the reason (B) is the best choice:

> Answer (B) provides support for the argument's major assumption.

Now, let's tackle a GMAT-style "strengthen-the-argument" question. Try applying the approach you just learned, then read the explanation that follows.

QUESTION The portrayal of violence on television and in movies has increased dramatically over the past 10 years. It is primarily for this reason that we have seen a dramatic increase in the rate of violent crime during the last decade.

Which one of the following, if true, most strengthens the argument?

(A) Liberal sentencing policies over the past 10 years have resulted in reduced sentences for perpetrators of violent acts.
(B) Persons who commit violent acts are less prone to being influenced by portrayals of violence.
(C) Recent studies have shown that repeated exposure to portrayals of violence significantly increases the tendency to commit violent acts.
(D) The number of homeless people has increased dramatically during the last decade.
(E) Due to severe overcrowding during the past decade, prisons have been forced to release violent criminals before they have served their full sentences.

ANALYSIS The best answer is **(C)**. Here's why:

1. Here's the argument:

Premise: The portrayal of violence on television and in movies has increased dramatically over the past 10 years.

Conclusion: We have seen a dramatic increase in the rate of violent crime during the last decade.

2. Here's the major assumption:

Exposure to portrayals of violence results in violent acts.

3. Here's the reason (C) is the best choice:

Answer choices (A), (D), and (E) provide plausible alternative reasons for the increase in violence and, as such, might be considered as providing additional support for the conclusion. However, neither (A), (D), nor (E) directly support the argument's main contention that increased portrayals of violence are the "primary" reason for the increase in violent acts. Answer choice (B) weakens the argument because it undermines the argument's major assumption, so you can eliminate it. Answer choice (C) supports the argument's major assumption and thus is the best answer.

Workshop

In this workshop, you'll review the lessons you learned this hour by attempting a GMAT-style quiz.

ONLINE Additional Critical Reasoning questions are available online at the author's Web site: *http://www.west.net/~stewart/gmat*

Quiz

(Answers and explanations begin on page 292.)

DIRECTIONS: Try these five GMAT-style Critical Reasoning questions. Try to limit your time to 8 minutes altogether.

1. If our society continues to have large numbers of homeless people living on the streets, then we will continue to have street crime. But, there is no immediate prospect of ending the problem of homeless people living on the streets, because that would be an extremely difficult undertaking even if there were great public support, which there clearly isn't.

   Which of the following conclusions can be properly inferred from the statements in the passage?

   (A) The number of homeless people in our society will increase.
   (B) Most people are interested in solving the problem of street crime.
   (C) The main victims of street crime are homeless people.
   (D) Our society will continue to have street crime.
   (E) The problem of homelessness cannot be solved.

   (Hint: Look for the answer choice that is most likely true given the information in the passage.)

2. Non-human primates are excellent animal models for the study of human disease because of their close genetic relationship to humans. Indeed, comparisons of the chromosomes and DNA of non-human primates and humans reveals a startling similarity in their structure and primitive origin, and testifies to the commonality of the genetic material between these phylogenetically related species.

   Which one of the following is an assumption upon which the argument depends?

   (A) Animals that are related genetically to humans make good models for studying human disease.
   (B) The genetic makeup of humans and non-human primates is very similar.
   (C) The more similar in structure and primitive origin of the chromosomes and DNA of species, the more commonalities in their genetic material.
   (D) Phylogenetically related species make good models for studying one another.
   (E) Non-human primates are closely related to humans.

   (Hint: Look for an unstated link between key ideas.)

3. Does having a large amount of money guarantee happiness? Results of a recent survey overwhelmingly confirm that having a sizable quantity of money is the key to happiness. In the survey, 78 percent of those who responded who also claimed

that they possessed a large amount of money said that they were happy.

Which of the following, if true, most seriously calls the survey finding into doubt?

(A) No clear quantitative definition of a large amount of money was provided to the respondents.
(B) No clear qualitative definition of *happiness* was provided to the respondents.
(C) Most of the respondents who claimed to have a large amount of money, in fact, did not.
(D) Many people are happy even though they do not possess a great deal of money.
(E) Many people who have a great deal of money are not happy.

(Hint: This is a weaken question. Look for an answer choice that attacks a premise of the argument.)

4. Whether we like it or not, we must either become energy self-sufficient or resign ourselves to the threat of international blackmail. Given these alternatives, it's obvious that we have no choice but to become energy self-sufficient.

The conclusion in the argument would be more reasonable if which one of the following were true?

(A) At the current rate of use, global energy sources will be depleted within the next century.
(B) We have the required natural energy sources to be energy self-sufficient.
(C) We have the required technological knowledge to develop our energy resources.
(D) There are no other countries that we can rely upon, without fear of threat, to meet our future energy needs.
(E) Our current natural energy sources are insufficient to meet our present energy needs.

(Hint: This is a strengthen question. Look for an answer choice that provides support for a major assumption of the argument.)

5. Since the transitional government has declared that they are not terrorists and will not use terrorist tactics to remain in power after the transition, we can be assured that they do not condone terrorist acts.

For the argument to be logically correct, it must make which of the following assumptions?

(A) Only terrorists condone acts of terrorism.
(B) Governments that don't condone acts of terrorism can be trusted to keep their word.
(C) Few transitional governments condone acts of terrorism.
(D) All terrorists engage in acts of terrorism.
(E) Terrorism is a tactic that many governments use to remain in power.

(Hint: Look for an unstated link between key ideas.)

Answers and Explanations

1. **(D)** Here's the key information in the passage:

    Premise: If our society continues to have homeless people living on the streets, then we will continue to have street crime.
    Premise: We will continue to have homeless people living on the streets.

    Here's the score for each answer choice:

    The score for (A) is 2. The information given in the passage does not support this claim. The score for (B) is 2. The information given in the passage does not support this claim.

    The score for (C) is 2. The information given in the passage does not support this claim. The score for (D) is 5. Given the information in the passage (D) must be true. The score for (E) is 2. The information given in the passage does not support this claim.

2. **(A)** Here's the argument:

    Assumption: ________________.
    Premise: Non-human primates are closely related genetically to humans.
    Conclusion: Non-human primates are excellent animal models for the study of human disease.

    The key ideas in this argument are (1) non-human primates, (2) animals that are related genetically to humans, and (3) animals that are models for the study of human disease. The stated premise links ideas (1) and (2). The conclusion links ideas (1) and (3). The assumption in the argument must relate ideas (2) and (3). Among the answer choices, only answer (A) links these two ideas.

3. **(C)** Here's the argument:

    Premise: 78 percent of the respondents said that they were happy.
    Premise: The same 78 percent of the respondents claimed that they possessed a large amount of money.
    Conclusion: Having a sizable quantity of money is the key to happiness.

    Answer choice (C) directly attacks the second premise listed above thereby seriously calling the survey finding into doubt. If (C) is true, the second premise listed above is false. As a consequence, the argument falls apart because the connection between having money and being happy in the argument is completely severed. Answer choices (A) and (B) state possible problems that could have an adverse effect on the reliability of the survey, but neither of these responses directly attacks the truth of a stated premise, nor do they undermine the major assumption or suggest an alternative conclusion that could be inferred from the premises. Answer (D) is consistent with the conclusion of the argument.

The conclusion does not state that everyone who is happy has a large amount of money; it states that persons who have a large amount of money are happy. Response (D) doesn't weaken the argument because it does not suggest an alternative conclusion that could be inferred from the premises nor does it undermine the major assumption of the argument or attack a stated premise. Answer (E) contradicts the conclusion of the argument. The conclusion states that persons who have a large amount of money are happy; response (E) states the opposite of this claim.

4. **(D)** Here's the argument:

   Premise: We must either become energy self-efficient or resign ourselves to the threat of international blackmail.
   Conclusion: We must become energy self-efficient.

   In this argument, there are two underlying assumptions:

   (1) The only alternatives available to us are the two stated in the premise.
   (2) We don't want to resign ourselves to the threat of international blackmail.

   Answer choice (D) provides support for the first assumption by ruling out a third possible alternative.

5. **(A)** Here's the argument:

   Assumption: ________________.
   Premise: The transitional government has declared that they are not terrorists.
   Conclusion: The transitional government does not condone terrorist acts.

   The key ideas in the argument are (1) the transitional government, (2) terrorists, and (3) groups that condone acts of terrorism. The stated premise links ideas (1) and (2). The conclusion links ideas (1) and (3). The assumption required to make the argument logically correct must link ideas (2) and (3). Of the answer choices, only (A) links ideas (2) and (3).

Hour 15

Teach Yourself Critical Reasoning III

This hour you'll teach yourself three new Critical Reasoning skills. Along with the skills you examined in Hours 13 and 14, these skills form the basis for top scores on the GMAT analytical section. In this hour you will learn:

- How to recognize reasoning errors
- How to identify the method of arguments
- How to recognize similarities between arguments
- How to apply the skills you learn this hour to a GMAT-style quiz

"Reasoning Error" Questions

Reasoning error questions test your ability to recognize various flaws or mistakes in reasoning. There are a great many different types of reasoning mistakes, but all of them involve practices that fail to meet the standards of good reasoning. Basically, these standards require that the premises of arguments provide grounds for believing that the conclusion is true, and they also require that criticisms or refutations of arguments focus on showing that the premises somehow fail to do this. Arguments that employ devices aimed at getting you to accept conclusions that are unwarranted by the premises, as well as refutations of arguments that employ devices that are aimed at getting you to reject the conclusion for reasons other than that it is unwarranted by the premises, violate the standards of good reasoning. The word "fallacy" is used to describe the error or mistake such arguments contain. Because there are so many different fallacies to keep track of, each has been given a name. The good news is that you won't be required to identify the fallacy by its traditional name; instead, you must simply select the best description of the reasoning error from the answer choices.

Reasoning error questions are typically worded as follows:

- Which of the following is the best statement of the flaw in the argument?
- Which one of the following indicates an error in the reasoning leading to the conclusion in the argument?
- Which one of the following questionable argumentative techniques does this passage employ?

Unfortunately, there is no magic pill you can take to learn the various reasoning errors that will be covered on the GMAT. The best way to study for these questions is to familiarize yourself with as many of the specific errors as possible. To help you do this, read the following discussion of the errors and study the examples.

NOTE

For purposes of clarity, in the following discussion each fallacy will be given a name. Remember, however, that you are *not* required to identify fallacies by name on the test, so try to focus on the mistake in each case rather than on trying to memorize the name.

Statistical Fallacies

Fallacies of hasty generalization. The two most common statistical reasoning errors are the fallacy of the biased sample and the fallacy of the small or insufficient sample. The fallacy of the biased sample is committed whenever the data for a statistical inference are drawn from a sample that is not representative of the population under consideration. The fallacy of the small or insufficient sample is committed whenever too small a sample is used to be representative of the population or whenever greater reliability is attributed to the conclusion than the sample size warrants. These two fallacies are commonly referred to as fallacies of "hasty generalization."

Example 1:

> In a recent survey conducted on the Internet, 80 percent of the respondents indicated their strong disapproval of government regulation of the content and access of web-based information. This survey clearly shows that legislation designed to restrict the access or to control the content of Internet information will meet with strong opposition from the electorate.

This argument draws the data for its inference from a sample that is not representative of the entire electorate. Because the survey was conducted on the Internet, not all members of the electorate have an equal chance of being included in the sample. Moreover, people who use the Internet are more likely to have an opinion on the topic than people who do not. For these reasons, the sample is obviously biased.

Example 2:

> I met my new boss at work today and she was very unpleasant. Twice when I tried to talk with her, she said that she was busy and told me not to interrupt her again. Later, when I needed her advice on a customer's problem, she ignored me and walked away. It's obvious that she has a bad attitude and is not going to be easy to work with.

The data for this argument's inference are insufficient to support the conclusion. Three observations of a person's behavior are necessarily representative of that person's behavior in general. Obviously, the boss could just have been having a bad day or been engrossed in other things.

TIP

> To recognize statistical reasoning errors, look for an argument in which the author reaches a general conclusion on the basis of a small number of cases, or from information that is biased in favor of the conclusion.

Causal Reasoning Fallacies

The "after this, therefore because of this" fallacy. This reasoning error is by far the most common causal fallacy, and the one most likely to appear on the GMAT CAT. This is the fallacy of concluding that because event *Y* occurred after some other event *X*, *X* must have caused *Y*. Many common superstitions are examples of this fallacy (for example, believing that the cause of your misfortune is the fact a black cat crossed your path just before your misfortune occurred.). The reasoning error in arguments of this type is that the evidence stated in the premises is insufficient to warrant the conclusion. Moreover, typically in these arguments the causal connection between the two events is implausible given our general understanding of the world.

Example 1:

> Ten minutes after walking into the auditorium, I began to feel sick to my stomach. There must have been something in the air in that building that caused my nausea.

Example 2:

> The stock market declined shortly after the president's election, thus indicating the lack of confidence that the business community has in the new administration.

Both examples conclude that there is a causal connection between two events simply on the basis of one occurring before the other. In the first example, the only reason given for claiming that the air in the auditorium caused the feeling of nausea is that the feeling of nausea happened shortly after entering the auditorium. In the second example, the only evidence offered to support the claim that the president's election caused the decline in the stock market is the fact that the election preceded the decline. Although the election might have been a causal factor in the stock market's decline, to argue that it is the cause merely because the election preceded the decline is to commit the "after this, therefore because of this" fallacy.

TIP

To recognize this error, look for an argument in which the author's *only* reason for concluding that one event is the cause of another is that it occurred before the other.

The "necessary vs. sufficient" fallacy. Another common causal fallacy occurs when one confuses a necessary condition for the occurrence of some event with a sufficient condition for the event's occurrence. Typically, the source of this fallacy is a misunderstanding of the meaning of conditional statements.

Example 1:

> The car will start only if the battery isn't dead, so the car will start if the battery isn't dead.

Example 2:

If you read this book carefully, you'll get a good score on the GMAT. Therefore, you won't get a good score on the GMAT unless you read this book carefully.

In the first example, the confusion of necessary condition with sufficient condition is obvious. While having a "live" battery is certainly necessary for starting the car's engine, it is not sufficient to do this. Many other conditions in addition to a "live" battery must be satisfied to bring this event about.

NOTE

Take special notice of the difference between "only if" and "if" in this example. "*A* only if *B*" is *not* equivalent in meaning to "*A* if *B*." The former means that *B* is a necessary condition for *A*; the latter means that *B* is a sufficient condition for *A*. The former is equivalent to "If *A* then, *B*"; the latter is equivalent to "If *B*, then *A*."

The premise in the second example states that reading this book carefully is a sufficient condition for getting a good score on the GMAT. The conclusion states that reading this book carefully is a necessary condition for getting a good score on the GMAT. In other words, the premise claims that anyone who reads this book carefully will get a good score; the conclusion claims that anyone who gets a good score has read this book carefully. Obviously, these are quite different claims.

TIP

To recognize this error, look for an argument that contains a conditional premise or conclusion or both. Then look to see whether a condition mentioned in one of the statements has been switched from a necessary to a sufficient condition or from a sufficient to a necessary condition in one or the other.

Unwarranted Assumption Fallacies

Unwarranted assumptions are assumptions that have no merit or independent justification. In other words, they are assumptions that are gratuitous, unfounded, or lacking in plausibility.

The "black and white" fallacy. This is a very common unwarranted-assumption fallacy. This error occurs when one assumes, without warrant, that there are only two alternatives, then reasons that because one of the alternatives is false or unacceptable, the other must be true or accepted. Typically, arguments that suffer from this fallacy offer no evidence to support the claim that only two alternatives are available, and a little thought reveals that this claim is not self-evident.

CAUTION

In cases where there are, in fact, only two alternatives, and this fact is obvious or justifiable, this pattern of reasoning is highly effective and acceptable.

Example:

> Either we put convicted child molesters in jail for life or we risk having our children become their next victims. We certainly can't risk this, so we had better lock up these criminals for the rest of their lives.

The argument assumes that only two alternatives are possible. The passage presents no evidence to support this claim, and a little thought reveals that the claim obviously has no validity. Although child molestation is a difficult problem to deal with, it is unlikely that the only solution to the problem is the one that the argument mentions. It is also unlikely that the advocated solution is the only way that we can protect children from becoming the victims of convicted offenders.

TIP

To recognize this error, look for an argument in which the author incorrectly assumes that we are forced to choose between alternatives (usually two), and that since one of them is clearly unacceptable, we must accept the other.

Irrelevant Appeals Fallacies

Irrelevant appeals attempt to persuade us to accept a conclusion by appealing to matters that are not relevant to the truth or correctness of the conclusion. Such appeals are considered reasoning errors because they violate the requirement that the reasons offered in support of a claim provide evidence that the claim is true or correct. In other words, such appeals mistakenly view the goal of argumentation to be simply persuasion rather than the attainment of the truth.

Appeal to ignorance. This appeal is commonly used to get us to accept a claim for which there is little or no evidence. The basic form of this error is to argue that a claim is true (or false) solely on the grounds that no one has demonstrated or can demonstrate that the claim is false (or true).

Example:

> Scientists have not established any causal link between smoking and lung cancer, hence we must simply accept the fact that smoking does not cause lung cancer.

Inability to prove that something is true (or false) cannot, by itself, be taken as evidence that it is false (or true). If this were accepted as a principle of reasoning, it would follow, for example, that our inability to prove that UFOs don't exist would lead immediately to the conclusion that UFOs exist.

TIP

> To recognize this error, look for an argument in which the author reasons that our lack of knowledge that some claim is true (or false) is grounds for accepting the claim as false (or true).

Appeal to authority. Another device used to gain acceptance of a claim is to cite an authority. In place of evidence that supports the claim, authors resort to the testimony or expertise of others to support the claim. Appealing to an authority is not always incorrect. As a matter of fact, people often rely on other people or sources when accepting claims. We do this, for example, when appealing to scientists, textbooks, doctors, and other experts to support our beliefs. This practice becomes incorrect when the competence, reliability, qualifications, motives, prejudices, and so on, of the persons or sources we are relying on is questionable.

Example:

> Geena Goodlooks is one of this country's most respected and honored actresses. You can be certain that when she says welfare reform is needed, it has to be true.

In this argument, you have to wonder about the relevance of Geena's testimony to the truth of the claim that it supports. The argument offers no evidence that justifies its reliance on her testimony on this topic. Obviously, the fact that she is a "respected and honored" actress hardly qualifies her as an expert on the need for welfare reform.

TIP

> To recognize this error, look for an argument in which the *only* reason given for accepting the conclusion is that some individual, group, or publication that is not qualified, or is biased, claims that it is true.

Reasoning Errors Involving the Use of Language

The fallacy of equivocation. This reasoning error occurs when a key word or phrase that has more than one meaning is employed in different meanings throughout the argument. Because the truth of the premises and the conclusion is in part a function of the meanings of the words in the sentences that express them, a shift in meaning of key terms in the argument can lead the audience to accept conclusions that are not supported by the premises.

Example:

> Logic is the study of arguments, and since arguments are just disagreements, it follows that logic is just the study of disagreements.

In this example, the word "argument" is used in two different meanings. In the first premise, "argument" means a discourse in which reasons are offered in support of a claim; the second premise defines "argument" as "a disagreement." If you adopt the second meaning, the first premise is false; if you adopt the first meaning, the second premise is false. Either way, the premises simply fail to support the conclusion.

TIP

To recognize this reasoning error, look for an argument in which the author uses a key term or phrase in different meanings in the premises and conclusion.

Faulty Analogy Fallacies

Reasoning by analogy typically proceeds by comparing two things, then reasoning that because they are alike in various ways, and because one of them has a certain characteristic, it is likely that the other has this characteristic as well. The fallacy of faulty analogy is committed either:

- when we overlook or ignore relevant dissimilarities between the things being compared, or
- when the similarities between the things compared are not relevant to the characteristic being inferred in the conclusion.

Example:

> "Joyce and Oona have similar tastes in fashion, music, movies, and books, and both are vegetarians. Since Joyce is a big fan of the famous French chef Julia Child, it's likely that Oona is too."

In this example, numerous similarities between Joyce and Oona are taken as the basis for the inference, and, all other things being equal, the stated conclusion is the correct one to draw. However, if Joyce and Oona, for all their shared characteristics, fail to share similar tastes in food (perhaps Oona likes Thai cuisine, while Joyce prefers French cuisine), this (relevant) dissimilarity between them will weaken the argument considerably.

Example:

> "Professors O'Toole and Stewart are alike in many ways. Both of them are young, handsome, and well liked by their students. O'Toole is an easy grader, so it is likely that Stewart is an easy grader as well."

In this example, the stated similarities between Professors O'Toole and Stewart are irrelevant to the characteristic stated in the conclusion. Obviously, age and appearance have no relevance to one's grading practices. Moreover, a professor may be well liked for many other reasons besides being an easy grader.

TIP

> To recognize the faulty analogy fallacy, look for an argument that draws a conclusion about one thing on the basis of its resemblance to something else. The fallacy occurs when the resemblance is not relevant to the similarity stated in the conclusion.

Fallacies of Refutation

Fallacies of refutation are committed in criticizing the arguments of others. Refutation reasoning errors occur whenever the critic focuses on aspects of the argument that are irrelevant to the reasoning employed in the argument or the truth of the claims that make up the argument. The basic tactic in criticisms that commit errors of this type is to scrupulously avoid attacking the argument, and instead attack the author, or a deliberately weakened version of the author's argument.

Attacking the author. Attacks that focus on the argument's author rather than the author's argument take three forms. The attack focuses either on the character, the motives, or the behavior of the person presenting the argument. The aim of the attack in all three cases is to discredit the conclusion of the person's argument. Assaults of this type are rarely, if ever, relevant to the reasoning employed in the argument or the truth or correctness of the conclusion. They are irrelevant for the simple reason that an arguer's personal character, motives, or behavior are rarely relevant to the correctness of his or her reasoning or the truth of the statements employed in the reasoning. Criticisms that employ attacks of these types are commonly known as *ad hominem* arguments (which means "against the person").

Example:

> When you realize that the man who is trying to convince you that he would be the best president this country has ever seen is, in fact, a womanizer and an illegal drug user, it's not difficult to draw the conclusion that his arguments are completely unacceptable.

This attack criticizes the presidential candidate's arguments by pointing out repugnant characteristics of the candidate. No attempt is made to consider or attack the candidate's arguments.

Example:

> The radio and television industry has been lobbying against proposed changes in the laws governing the use of publicly owned transmission frequencies. But just keep this in mind: No matter how good the industry's arguments might be, broadcasters stand to lose a great deal if the proposed changes become law.

In this case the radio and television industry's arguments are dismissed out of hand on the grounds that broadcasters have a vested interest in the outcome. The tactic exhibited in this example is commonly called "poisoning the well" because it condemns the argument's source to discredit the argument.

Example:

> My esteemed colleague accuses me of misappropriating taxpayers' funds for my own personal use. Well, it might interest you to know that he has the unenviable distinction of having spent more on so-called fact-finding trips to exotic locations all around the world than anyone else in Congress.

In this example, the politician makes no attempt to attack the colleague's argument; rather, the focus of the attack is to accuse the person of similar questionable behavior or wrongdoing. Because of this, the reasoning error in this example is commonly called the "you too!" or "two wrongs don't make a right" fallacy.

TIP

> To recognize refutation errors of this type, look for an argument in which the focus of the criticism is the author of the argument rather than the argument.

Now let's look at a GMAT-style "reasoning error" question. Try tackling this question using the information you just learned. Then, read the explanation that follows.

QUESTION Great scientists are produced either by heredity or environment. But, it's obvious that the intelligence of great scientists is not a product of their early training or their experience. So it follows that great scientists are born, not made.

Which of the following is the best statement of the flaw in the argument?

(A) The author incorrectly claims that training and experience cannot contribute to making one a great scientist.

(B) The author incorrectly assumes that there are only two ways of producing a great scientist.

(C) The author reasons that the conclusion is true on the grounds that it has not been proven false.

(D) The author's conclusion is based on too small a sample.

(E) The author's conclusion is more general than the evidence presented warrants.

ANALYSIS The correct answer is **(B)**. The argument rests on the unwarranted assumption that only two alternative explanations are available, but a little thought reveals that great scientists could be produced by a combination of these two ways.

"Method of Argument" Questions

The method of an argument is simply the way in which the author goes about establishing the conclusion, or in the case of a critical response to an argument, the way in which the author attempts to defeat the conclusion. Method questions test your ability to recognize various reasoning strategies or techniques. You're not required to identify the method by name, but only to select from the answer choices the best description of the argument's general reasoning strategy.

Method questions are typically worded as follows:

- Which of the following most accurately characterizes the argumentative strategy used in the passage?
- The argument proceeds by:
- Which one of the following argumentative techniques is used in the passage?
- The method of the argument is to:
- The argument employs which one of the following reasoning techniques?

As with the reasoning errors you studied earlier this hour, the best way to study for method questions is to familiarize yourself with as many of the reasoning techniques and strategies as possible. You'll learn a lot about reasoning methods as you read the following brief discussions of some of the more common techniques and study the examples.

CAUTION The following methods of establishing or defeating conclusions are not necessarily effective or logically correct. Don't get confused. The issue in questions of this type is merely to identify the method that the author employs, not to determine whether the method is effective or logically correct.

Reasoning by Analogy

A common method to establish a conclusion is to use an analogy. Starting with a claim or situation that is familiar and unproblematic, the author argues that the issue in question is very much like the familiar case, and hence that what is true of it is probably true of the case in question.

Example:

> The mushrooms that we saw in the forest yesterday are the same color, size, and shape as those that we saw in the grocery store today. Obviously, the mushrooms sold in the grocery store aren't poisonous, hence it is likely that the ones we saw in the forest aren't poisonous either.

Statistical Reasoning

Many arguments use statistics to establish claims. These arguments usually begin with a statistical claim to the effect that some percentage of a certain group has a certain characteristic. The argument typically concludes that because a given individual is in the group, the individual is likely (or unlikely) to have the selected characteristic.

Example :

> Only two percent of all vegetarians contract colon cancer. Because Sally is a vegetarian, it is unlikely that she'll get colon cancer.

Example :

> Eighty percent of all logic students scored high on the GMAT. Fred is a logic major, so he probably scored high on the GMAT.

Reasoning from Experience

People often use past experience as a reason for believing that something is the case or will be the case. This method of reasoning typically begins with an experience that the author or someone else has had. This experience then functions as a premise from which the author argues that some, as yet unexperienced, event or situation will occur.

Example:

> We have observed the sun rising countless times in the past, hence we can be assured that the sun will rise tomorrow.

A variation of this method of reasoning is to argue that some general claim is true on the basis of the observation of several instances of the claim. Arguments that employ this method typically begin with premises that state the observed instances; the conclusion typically asserts that what is true of the observed instances is true of all or most instances.

Example:

> Don't worry! All the lettuce that we checked in the shipment was in excellent condition, so you can be assured that all the lettuce is okay.

Causal Reasoning

Authors typically attempt to establish causal conclusions (conclusions that assert a causal relation between two events) by using eliminative reasoning. Arguments that employ this method usually proceed by isolating a common feature shared by a number of events by a process of elimination. The premises typically describe testing procedures aimed at determining which, if any, of a set of properties are causally related to the event in question. Through experiment or observation, the author attempts to eliminate each of these features as a causal candidate. The feature that resists these attempts is concluded to be the cause of the event under consideration.

Example:

> Six customers of a fast-food restaurant developed food poisoning shortly after eating lunch there. An investigation revealed that they had all drunk different beverages, but not all had eaten salads, soups, or french fries. However, they had all eaten chicken sandwiches prepared with different breads. The health department concluded that the cause of the food poisoning was poorly cooked chicken.

QUESTION All of the lawyers I've ever met were pushy, money hungry, and self-centered. Since your blind date is a lawyer, you can bet he'll be aggressive, cheap, and inattentive.

The argument proceeds by:

(A) reaching a general conclusion on the basis of a biased sample

(B) reaching a conclusion on the basis of previous experience

(C) isolating a feature through a process of elimination and concluding that this feature is causally related to the event under consideration

(D) attacking the motive of the argument's author

(E) attacking the character of the argument's author

The correct answer is **(B).** In this argument, the author reasons from previous experience with lawyers that other lawyers have similar characteristics.

"Parallel Argument" Questions

Parallel argument questions test your ability to recognize similarities between arguments. There are three kinds of questions. Some ask you to find the argument that has the same pattern as the argument in the passage. Others ask you to find the argument that employs the same method of reasoning, and others ask you to find the argument that contains the same reasoning error as the argument in the passage.

Questions that ask you to find the argument that has the *same pattern of reasoning* as the argument in the passage are typically worded as follows:

- The argumentative pattern of which one of the following most closely parallels that of the argument in the passage?
- The pattern of reasoning displayed in the argument in the passage is most closely paralleled in which of the following arguments?
- Which of the following arguments contains a flawed pattern of reasoning parallel to that contained in the preceding argument?
- Which of the following, in its logical features, most closely parallels the reasoning in the passage?

Questions that ask you to find the argument that employs the *same method of reasoning* as the argument in the passage are typically worded as follows:

- Which of the following most closely parallels the argumentative strategy of the argument presented in the passage?

- In which of the following is the method of reasoning most parallel to that in the preceding argument?

Questions that ask you to find the argument that contains the *same reasoning error* as the argument in the passage are typically worded as follows:

- Which one of the following arguments contains a flaw that is most similar to the one in the preceding argument?
- The faulty reasoning in which one of the following is most parallel to that in the preceding argument?

Dealing with Parallel Method and Parallel Reasoning Error Questions

Since you've already covered most of what you need to know in order to deal with parallel method and parallel reasoning error questions in the previous sections, we'll deal with these first.

Here's a 2-step approach to help you answer parallel argument questions that ask you to find an argument that has the same method or same reasoning error as the argument in the passage.

ACTION PLAN

1. **Identify the method or the reasoning error in the passage's argument.**
2. **Read the answer choices looking for an argument that employs a similar method or has a similar reasoning error.**

Example:

> Shortly after James visited his friend in the hospital, he became ill. This proves that going to the hospital when you're not sick is a bad idea because you never know what you're going to catch there.

Which one of the following arguments contains a flaw that is most similar to the one in the preceding argument?

(A) I have no idea what George did, but moments after he came into the room Joyce got up and ran out in a big hurry. He must have done something terribly wrong to make her act that way.

(B) 90% of those who smoke heavily also drink heavily. This proves that heavy smoking leads to heavy drinking.

(C) Whenever Sam drinks alcohol, he's a pain to be around. He's unhappy, wants to quit school, and says he's going to be a beach bum. Once he stops drinking, everything is fine again. That's why I'm sure it's the booze that makes him act this way.

1. The reasoning error in the passage is the "after this, therefore because of this" fallacy. The *only* reason given for the claim that James' illness was caused by his visit to the hospital is that his visit preceded his illness.

2. Answer choice (A) commits the same fallacy. The *only* reason given for the claim that George's entrance into the room caused Joyce to leave in a hurry is that she left moments after George came in.

Dealing with Parallel Pattern Questions

To get a basic idea of what is meant by logical "structure" or "pattern," consider the following pair of arguments:

All men are mortal. Socrates is a man. Hence, Socrates is mortal.

Every dog has a master. Fido is a dog. Therefore, Fido has a master.

Although these arguments are obviously about different topics, they are similar in the way in which they present information about their topics. Each begins with a general statement claiming that all individuals in a certain class have a certain characteristic, followed by a particular statement claiming that a certain individual belongs to the class mentioned previously, and concluding that the individual has the characteristic mentioned previously. Because of these similarities, the "pattern" or "structure" of these two arguments is the same. The basic pattern of these examples looks like this:

Premise: All A *are* B.

Premise: C *is an* A.

Conclusion: C *is a* B.

CAUTION

The argument's content (what the argument is about) is irrelevant when trying to determine the argument's pattern; it is not what the argument says that is important, but rather the way in which the argument says it.

The order of the premises and conclusion (which is stated first or second or third and so on) is irrelevant when trying to determine the similarity of the pattern of arguments. For example, look at the following pair of arguments that have the same pattern but which present their premises and conclusions in different orders:

People who are happy are content; hence, since Mary is happy, she must be content.

John must be tall because he is a basketball player and all basketball players are tall.

The similarity in the pattern of these two arguments becomes readily apparent when you restate them and reorganize them.

Here's the pattern of the first one:

> **NOTE**
> The quantity *all* is understood in the first premise of the first example.

Premise: All people who are happy are content.

Premise: Mary is happy.

Conclusion: Mary is content.

Here's the pattern of the second:

Premise: All basketball players are tall.

Premise: John is a basketball player.

Conclusion: John is tall.

Determining an argument's pattern is relatively easy so long as you focus on the way in which the argument is expressed rather than on what the argument expresses. In other words, focus on the syntax of the sentences that comprise the argument rather than on what the sentences mean.

Here's a 3-step approach to help you deal with parallel argument questions that ask you to find an argument that has the same pattern as the argument in the passage.

ACTION PLAN

1. **Identify the pattern of the argument in the passage. To do this, you must pay close attention to words such as *all*, *some*, and *no* (and their synonyms), and words and phrases such as *and*, *or*, *if*, *then*, and *if and only if*, and *not* (and their synonyms).**
2. **Focus on the terms or the sentences that are prefixed or connected by these words and phrases, and using abbreviations for them, jot down the premises and the conclusion of the argument on your scratch paper.**
3. **Look at each of the answer choices, and find the one with exactly the same pattern.**

Look at this example:

Example:

If you are wise, then you are patient. If you are patient, then good things happen to you. So, if you are wise, good things happen to you.

Which of the following arguments has the same pattern?

(A) If Cosmo is a comedian, then he is funny. Cosmo isn't very funny, so he's not a comedian.

(B) If Kelly graduates in June, she'll get a job. If she gets a job, she'll buy a new car. Therefore, if Kelly graduates in June, she'll buy a new car.

(C) If you take the high road, I'll take the low road. So, if I take the low road, I'll get there before you.

1. Here are the terms (in italics) to special pay attention to:

If you are wise, *then* you are patient. *If* you are patient, *then* good things happen to you. So, *if* you are wise, *then* good things happen to you.

2. Here's the abbreviated argument:

If W, *then* P. *If* P, *then* G. So, *If* W, *then* G.

NOTE

The abbreviations are: *W* = you are wise, *P* = you are patient, *G* = good things happen to you.

3. Looking at the answer choices, it's pretty obvious that (B) has the same pattern.

CAUTION

Be careful with sentences that express conditional statements. In answer choice (B) the word "then" is not explicitly stated, but it is understood.

Now let's look at a GMAT-style "parallel argument" question. Try tackling this question using the 3-step method you just learned. Then read the explanation that follows.

QUESTION Either the safe was already open or the burglar opened it. But it wasn't opened by the burglar unless he knew the combination. So either it was already open or the burglar knew the combination.

The pattern of reasoning displayed in the argument in the passage is most closely paralleled in which of the following arguments?

(A) Either the Slugs or the Snails will win the Fruit Bowl. The Snails won't win unless they beat the Slugs. Hence, if the Slugs win the Fruit Bowl, the Snails didn't beat them.

(B) Either the National Gun Lobby (NGL) supports gun control laws or the number of crimes involving handguns will continue to rise. The reasons for this are simple. Either gun control laws are passed or the number of crimes involving handguns will continue to rise. But gun control laws won't be passed unless the NGL supports them.

(C) God is either unwilling or unable to prevent evil. But He's not unable unless He is not omnipotent. Hence, He is not omnipotent.

(D) Professor Lascola is either a realist or an empiricist. But he is not an empiricist if he believes that some concepts are innate. So, if he believes that some ideas are innate, he is not a realist.

(E) Either smoking is harmful or the surgeon general's warnings about smoking cigarettes are incorrect. But studies have shown conclusively that smoking is harmful, hence the surgeon general's warnings are correct.

ANALYSIS

The correct answer is **(B)**. Here's why:

Here are the terms (in italics) to pay attention to:

Either the safe was already open *or* the burglar opened it. But it was*n't* opened by the burglar *unless* he knew the combination. So, *either* it was already open *or* the burglar knew the combination.

Here's the abbreviated argument:

Either O *or* B. *Not* B *unless* C. Therefore, O *or* C.

NOTE

The abbreviations are: *O* = the safe was already open, *B* = the burglar opened the safe, *C* = the burglar knew the combination. Also, pay attention to the way the contraction in the second premise is abbreviated here.

Here's the pattern of answer choice (B):

Either P *or* C. *Not* P *unless* S. Therefore, *either* S *or* C.

NOTE

The abbreviations are: *P* = gun control laws are passed, *C* = the number of crimes involving handguns will continue to rise, *S* = The NGL supports gun control laws.

CAUTION

Remember, the order of the premises and the conclusion is irrelevant when trying to determine the similarity of the pattern of arguments.

Workshop

In this Workshop, you'll review the skills you learned this hour by attempting a GMAT-style quiz.

ONLINE

Additional Critical Reasoning GMAT-style questions are available online at the author's Web site: *http://www.west.net/~stewart/gmat*

Quiz

(*Answers and explanations begin on page 316.*)

DIRECTIONS: For each of the following, select the *best* answer. Try to limit your time to 8 minutes altogether.

1. There's no doubt that lowering property taxes will result in the curtailment of many vital services. But, there's no other alternative because if you want to make an omelet, you have to break a few eggs.

   The argument employs which one of the following reasoning techniques?

   (A) reasoning from experience
   (B) reasoning by analogy
   (C) eliminative reasoning
   (D) conditional reasoning
   (E) disjunctive reasoning

   (Hint: Think about the author's reason for mentioning the omelet.)

2. Failure to comply with the directions contained in this chain letter will result in bad consequences. Jane received this letter and passed it on in the required 72-hour period. A week later, she won $6 million in the lottery. Sam received it, but did not comply with the directions. Within a week after receiving it, he was trampled to death by a renegade elephant at the circus.

   The faulty reasoning in which one of the following is most parallel to that in the preceding argument?

   (A) The portrayal of violence on television and in the movies is the main cause of violence in our nation. Hence, to get rid of violence in our nation, we must censor television shows and movies.
   (B) Mandatory life sentences for three-time felons is a bad idea. People who think that such sentences are a good idea think that they will stop violent crime. But if we really want to stop violent crime, instead of locking people up, we should eliminate the root cause of violent crime by ceasing to glamorize violence in movies and on television.
   (C) It has been well established that smoking marijuana leads to heroin use, and that heroin use leads to drug addiction. Drug addiction, in turn, leads to crime to support the drug habit. The epidemic of drug-related crime is threatening the very core of our existence as a nation. Hence, to stop this threat, we must not legalize marijuana use.
   (D) Parents are wrong to criticize their children for coming home late, smoking, watching too much television, and getting poor grades. After all, they do all these things and besides they're not all that smart themselves.
   (E) Statistics show that nearly every heroin user started out by using marijuana. This is convincing proof that smoking marijuana is the main cause of heroin addiction.

   (Hint: First identify the reasoning error in the passage, then find the answer choice that has the same error.)

3. I'm well aware that the very idea of deliberately injuring a laboratory animal is extremely repulsive. But if we don't experiment on living animals, then we won't be able to learn how to treat humans with injuries. So, like it or not, it must be done.

   Which of the following is the best statement of the flaw in the argument?

   (A) The author assumes without justification that there are only two alternatives open to us.
   (B) The author assumes that humans are like laboratory animals.
   (C) The author reasons that our lack of knowledge of human injuries is grounds for injuring laboratory animals.
   (D) The author employs the term "injury" in two different meanings.
   (E) The author's conclusion is a restatement of the premise.

   (Hint: The argument relies on an unwarranted assumption.)

4. Kelly has been counseling families for ten years and has never yet seen a family that does not exhibit some form of dysfunction. That's why she concludes that there are no fully functional families.

   Kelly's argument proceeds by:

   (A) reaching a conclusion on the basis of a biased sample
   (B) reaching a conclusion on the basis of too small a sample
   (C) reaching a conclusion on the basis of past experience
   (D) isolating a feature through a process of elimination and concluding that this feature is causally related to the event under consideration
   (E) attacking the character of the argument's author

   (Hint: Think about what leads Kelly to believe that there are no fully functional families.)

5. If the acid crystallizes, then either the solution is too weak or we made a mistake. I'm sure we didn't make a mistake. So, it follows that if the acid crystallizes, the solution is too weak.

   Which of the following, in its logical features, most closely parallels the reasoning in the passage?

   (A) If Jones is a liberal, then he favors a reduction in income tax or a reduction in inheritance tax. Jones is not a liberal. So it follows that he doesn't favor a reduction in income or inheritance tax.
   (B) Mars or Jupiter can be settled if the moon can be settled. Jupiter can't be settled. So it follows that if we can settle the moon, Mars can be settled.
   (C) If man has talent, then he can do anything his talent allows. But if he has no talent, then it follows that he can do nothing at all.
   (D) If summers are too hot or winters are too cold, the potatoes won't grow. This winter wasn't too cold. So, it follows that if the potatoes grow, the summer won't be too hot.
   (E) If John loves Mary, he will marry her or tell her why he won't marry her. But he doesn't really love her. So it follows that he'll tell her why he won't marry her.

   (Hint: Identify the pattern of the argument in the passage, then look for a similar pattern among the answer choices.)

Answers and Explanations

1. **(B)** In this argument, an analogy is drawn between making an omelet and lowering property taxes. It is argued that in each case to get what you want you have to put up with something you don't want.

2. **(E)** The reasoning error in the passage is to conclude that the Jane's good fortune and Sam's misfortune were caused by the ways they responded to the chain letter. The only reason offered in support of this conclusion is that their manner of

response to the letter preceded what happened to them. The argument in answer choice (E) suffers from the same error. The only reason offered in (E) for the claim that smoking marijuana causes heroin addiction is that statistics show marijuana use precedes heroin use.

3. **(A)** The unwarranted assumption in this argument is that there are only two alternatives available. Either we experiment on living animals or we fail to learn how to treat humans with injuries.

4. **(C)** Kelly's conclusion is based on her many years of experience counseling families.

5. **(B)** Here are the terms (in italics) to pay attention to in this argument:

    If the acid crystallizes, *then either* the solution is too weak *or* we made a mistake. I'm sure we did*n't* make a mistake. So, it follows that *if* the acid crystallizes, the solution is too weak.

    Here's the abbreviated argument:

    If C, *then* W *or* M. *Not* M. Therefore, *if* C, *then* W.

The abbreviations are: *C* = the acid crystallizes, *W* = the solution is too weak, *M* = we made a mistake.

The pattern of the argument in answer choice (B) is exactly the same as the above pattern. You can convince yourself of this by abbreviating the argument in (B). However, when you do this pay close attention to the first premise. You will need to restate it in the *If* ____, *then* ____. form.

Hour 16

Teach Yourself Reading Comprehension

This hour you'll teach yourself how to handle the Reading Comprehension questions that appear in the Verbal Ability section of the GMAT. Here are your goals for this hour:

- Learn what Reading Comprehension passages look like
- Learn some techniques for reading more effectively
- Teach yourself how to deal with the different question types and identify the test-makers' favorite wrong-answer ploys
- Review what you learned this hour by attempting a GMAT-style quiz

GMAT Reading Comprehension at a Glance

WHERE: In the GMAT Verbal section, mixed in with Sentence Correction and Critical Reasoning questions

HOW MANY: 12 questions, based on 4 passages (3 questions per passage)

BASIC FORMAT: 3 short passages (150–200 words) with 3 questions each, and 1 longer passage (275–325 words) with 3 questions

SUGGESTED TIME: 5–6 minutes per question set (20–24 minutes altogether)

GROUND RULES:

- Consider each question independently of all others.
- Answer each question based only on what is stated or implied in the passage; don't bring your outside knowledge of the subject matter (if any) to bear in answering the questions

WHAT'S COVERED: You'll be tested on the following reading skills:

- Recognizing the main point or primary purpose of the passage
- Recalling information explicitly stated in the passage
- Making inferences from specific information stated in the passage
- Recognizing the purpose of specific passage information
- Recognizing the author's tone or attitude as revealed in the language of the passage
- Applying and extrapolating from the ideas presented in the passage

DIRECTIONS: Here are the directions for GMAT Reading Comprehension. You'll encounter these directions just before your first group of Reading Comprehension questions:

DIRECTIONS: The questions in this group are based on the content of a passage. After reading the passage, choose the best answer to each question. Answer all questions on the basis of what is stated or implied in the passage.

What Reading Comprehension Sets Look Like

Following are two short reading passages, each followed by one question. You'll encounter two more questions for each passage a bit later this hour. Right now just try to get a sense for what typical passages and questions look like.

NOTE

Passage lines are always numbered as shown here because questions occasionally refer to portions of the passage by line number.

The encounter that a portrait records is most tangibly the sitting itself, which may be brief or extended, collegial or confrontational. Cartier-Bresson has expressed his passion for portrait photography by characterizing it as "a duel without rules, a delicate rape." Such metaphors contrast quite sharply with Richard Avedon's conception of a sitting. While Cartier-Bresson reveals himself as an interloper and opportunist, Avedon confesses—perhaps uncomfortably—to a role as diagnostician and (by implication) psychic healer: not as someone who necessarily transforms his subjects, but as someone who reveals their essential nature. Both photographers, however, agree that the fundamental dynamic in this process lies squarely in the hands of the artist.

A quite-different paradigm has its roots not in confrontation or consultation but in active collaboration between the artist and sitter. This very different kind of relationshipwas formulated most vividly by William Hazlitt in his essay entitled "On Sitting for One's Picture" (1823). To Hazlitt, the "bond of connection" between painter and sitter is most like the relationship between two lovers. Hazlitt fleshes out his thesis by recalling the career of Sir Joshua Reynolds. According to Hazlitt, Reynold's sitters were meant to enjoy an atmosphere that was both comfortable for them and conducive to the enterprise of the portrait painter, who was simultaneously their host and their contractual employee.

1. The author of the passage quotes Cartier-Bresson (lines 6–7) in order to
   - (A) refute Avedon's conception of a portrait sitting
   - (B) provide one perspective of the portraiture encounter
   - (C) support the claim that portrait sittings are, more often than not, confrontational encounters
   - (D) show that a portraiture encounter can be either brief or extended
   - (E) distinguish a sitting for a photographic portrait from a sitting for a painted portrait

The decline of the Iroquois Indian nations began during the American Revolution of 1776, when disagreement among them as to whether they should become involved in the war began to divide the Iroquois. Because of the success of the revolutionaries and the encroachment upon Iroquois lands that followed, many Iroquois resettled in Canada, while those who remained behind lost the respect they had enjoyed among other Indian nations. The introduction of distilled spirits resulted in widespread alcoholism, leading in turn to the rapid decline of both the culture and population. The influence of the Quakers impeded, yet in another sense contributed, to this decline. By establishing schools for the Iroquois and by introducing them to modern technology for agriculture and husbandry, the Quakers instilled in the Iroquois some hope for the future yet undermined the Iroquois' sense of national identity.

Ironically, it was Handsome Lake who can be credited with reviving the Iroquois culture. Lake, the alcoholic half-brother of Seneca Cornplanter, perhaps the most outspoken proponent among the Iroquois for assimilation of white customs and institutions, was a former member of the Great Council of Iroquois nations. Inspired by a near-death vision in 1799, Lake established a new religion among the Iroquois which tied the more useful aspects of Christianity to traditional Indian beliefs and customs.

1. The passage mentions all the following events as contributing to the decline of the Iroquois culture EXCEPT:
   (A) new educational opportunities for the Iroquois people
   (B) divisive power struggles among the leaders of the Iroquois nations
   (C) introduction of new farming technologies
   (D) territorial threats against the Iroquois nations
   (E) discord among the nations regarding their role in the American Revolution

What You Should Know About GMAT Reading Comprehension

Passages appear on the left side of the computer screen, and questions appear (one at a time) on the right side. You'll have to scroll vertically to read each entire passage, even the short ones (as in the simulated "screen shot" on page 10).

Reading Comprehension questions are designed to test a lot more than just your short-term memory and your knack for finding information quickly. Although your ability to recall what you've read is part of what's being tested, all but the easiest questions also gauge your ability to assimilate, interpret, and apply the ideas presented.

Some questions require that you focus on an isolated sentence or two; others require that you assimilate information from various parts of the passage. Understandably, questions that cover disparate parts of passage tend to be tougher than the ones that you can answer just be reading a particular sentence or two.

Questions about information appearing early in the passage *tend* to come before other questions. But this isn't a hard-and-fast rule; so don't assume you can simply scroll down the passage to answer each question in turn.

Tougher questions include not only a "best" response but also a tempting second-best response. Recognizing the difference in quality between the two most viable responses is the key to answering these questions correctly.

Reading Comprehension questions are not designed to test your vocabulary. Sure, you'll find the occasional erudite word (such as "interloper" and "paradigm" in the portraiture passage on page 321). But the test-makers don't intentionally load the passages with tough vocabulary. Also, if a reading passage introduces a technical term, don't worry—the passage will supply all you need to know about the term to respond to the questions.

Reading Comprehension passages are condensed from larger works in the humanities, social sciences, and physical sciences. Specific sources include professional journals, dissertations, and periodicals of intellectual interest. The test-makers edit the source material in order to pack it with test-worthy material.

Prior knowledge of a passage's subject matter is not important. All questions are answerable based solely on the passage's information. The exam includes passages from a variety of disciplines, so it is unlikely that any particular test-taker knows enough about two or more of the areas included on the test to hold a significant advantage over other test-takers.

How to Approach a Reading Comprehension Set

Here's a 6-step plan for handling any GMAT Reading Comprehension set.

ACTION PLAN

1. **Read the first question (including the answer choices), *before* you begin reading the passage.** Try to anticipate what the passage is about and the sort of information you should be on the lookout for in order to answer the first question.

2. **Begin reading the passage, actively thinking about a possible thesis (main idea) and how the author attempts to support that thesis.** Also, begin your reading with an eye for information useful in answering the first question.
3. **When you think you've learned enough to take a stab at the first question, go ahead and choose a *tentative* answer.** You probably won't have to read very far to at least take a reasoned guess at the first question. But don't confirm you're response yet!
4. **Read the remainder of the passage, formulating an outline as you go.** As you read, try to: (1) separate main ideas from supporting ideas and examples; (2) determine the basic structure of the passage (e.g., chronology of events, classification of ideas or things, comparison between two or more ideas, events, or things); and (3) determine the author's attitude or opinion about the subject. Make notes on your scratch paper as needed to see the "flow" of the passage and to keep the passage's details straight in your mind.
5. **Sum up the passage; formulate a brief thesis (main idea) statement.** Take a few seconds to review your outline, then in your own words express the author's main point—in one sentence. Jot it down on your scratch paper. Your thesis statement should reflect the author's attitude (e.g., critical, supportive, neutral) toward the ideas presented in the passage.
6. **Confirm your response to the first question, then move on to the remaining question(s), considering *all* of the answer choices for each question.** Later this hour you'll learn some tips to help you tackle different question types and to zero in on the best answer choices.

Let's Apply the 6-Step Action Plan

Let's tackle the first passage and question (involving portraiture) you encountered earlier, applying the 6-step approach you just learned.

1. The first question tells you a lot about what you might expect in the passage. In all likelihood, the passage will be primarily about the portraiture experience, and the author will probably provide different viewpoints and insights on this experience, from the perspective of particular artists.
2. The first four sentences (lines 1–9) reinforce your initial prediction about the passage's content. Based on these initial lines, it appears that author will indeed be comparing and contrasting different views of the portraiture experience. At this point you don't know whether the passage will involve the views of any artist other than Cartier-Bresson and Richard Avedon, nor do you know whether the author has any opinion on

the subject. But you should be on the lookout for answers to these unknowns during step 4.

3. Consider Question 1 based on what you've read so far. The author points out in lines 4–9 that Cartier-Bresson's conception is quite different from that of Avedon. Answer choices (A), (B) and (C) all appear to be viable choices, at least based on lines 4–9. But whether the author's purpose here is to *refute* Avedon's view (answer choice A), *support* Cartier-Bresson's view (answer choice C), or simply *provide* one of at least two perspectives without taking sides (answer choice B) remains to be seen. You'll have to read on to find out. In any event, you can probably eliminate (D) and (E), since neither one seems relevant to the Cartier-Bresson quotation. Don't confirm a response yet; go on to step 4.

4. Your goal in step 4 is to formulate a mental outline of the passage as your read from start to finish. You might want to jot down some key word and phrases to help you see how the ideas flow and to keep the four individuals discussed in the passage straight in your mind. Here's a good outline of the passage:

¶1 Contrast → CB: confrontation (rape)
→ Avedon: diagnosis (consultation
* but CB & Avedon agree artist is key

¶2 3-D view → Hazlitt (writer): collaboration (lovers)
→ e.g. Reynolds (host/contractor)

5. Now let's sum up the passage based on the outline you formulated in step 4. It's a good idea to jot it down. Notice that the thesis is neutral; the author does not side with any viewpoint presented in the passage.

Thesis: Portraiture is social experience, but artists differ regarding their role.

TIMESAVER

Make outlines and summaries as brief as possible. Don't write complete sentences; just jot down key words.

6. Having read the entire passage, return to the question. Nowhere in the passage does author attempt to either refute or support any of the viewpoints presented. So you can eliminate (A) and (C). Accordingly, (B) is the best response to the question. Notice also that (B) is consistent with our thesis statement. Regardless of the particular question, you can eliminate any answer choice that is inconsistent with your thesis statement.

NOTE

Just ahead we'll analyze two more questions about the portraiture passage, as we identify various question types and wrong-answer ploys.

DO's and DON'Ts to Help You Read More Effectively

Here's a useful list of DO's and DON'Ts to help you improve your concentration and efficiency as you read the passages.

Do	**Don't**

DO read actively, not passively, with pencil in hand. Pause after each logical "block" (perhaps after each paragraph) to think briefly about what basic points the author makes in the block, how these points are connected to earlier ones, and where the discussion is likely to go from here. Jot down a brief outline as you go.

DON'T get bogged down in details as you read the passage, especially the long passage. Gloss over the details (lists, statistics and other numbers, dates, titles, and so forth). Just take note of where the details were, so you can find them quickly if you need them to answer a particular question.

DON'T confirm your answer to any question without first reading the entire passage. Even if the question seems clearly to involve only a portion of the passage, it is always possible that relevant information will appear elsewhere as well.

DO pay attention to the overall structure, or "flow," of the passage. The passage might be organized as a chronology of events, a critique of a theory, a comparison of two or more things, or a classification system. Understanding how the passage "flows" will help you to locate details more quickly and to zero in on the best answer to the questions.

DO summarize the passage after reading it. Take a few seconds to recap the main thrust of the passage. Chances are, you'll be able to respond correctly to at least one of the questions based solely on the passage the main idea, or thesis.

DON'T do more vertical scrolling than necessary. You'll need to scroll to read the entire passage. But try to minimize scrolling by developing a good outline, so you won't have to reread the passage to search for information needed to respond a question. Besides, scrolling and rereading use up valuable time and add to eye strain and fatigue.

Six Question Types and How to Handle Them

Now that you know what Reading Comprehension questions look like and how to read the passages efficiently, it's time look at the questions themselves in greater detail. A GMAT reading question may ask you to perform any of the following six basic tasks:

1. recognize the passage's *main idea* or the author's *primary purpose*
2. recall *explicit details* contained in the passage
3. *interpret* or draw an *inference* from specific passage information
4. understand the author's *purpose* in including a *specific detail*
5. recognize the *author's attitude* or position regarding the passage's ideas
6. *apply* passage ideas or *extrapolate* from them

Here you'll learn tips for tackling each question type, by revisiting the questions in the two sample reading sets you encountered earlier this hour.

NOTE

Question types 1, 2 and 3 listed above appear more frequently on the exam than the other three types.

1. "Main Idea" and "Primary Purpose" Questions

These questions test your ability to recognize the central idea of a passage or to determine the author's broad purpose or concern. To get these question correct, you'll need to see the forest from the trees—the larger ideas from the supporting points and other details. Here are some tips for tackling these questions:

- Formulate your own main idea and primary purpose in advance; by doing so, you'll be far less tempted by the other (wrong) answer choices.
- Every passage has a main idea and a primary purpose. But don't expect the author to state either one explicitly in one nice tidy sentence; the test-makers won't make it that easy for you.
- Any idea addressed only in one portion of the passage *cannot* be a main idea or part of the author's overall concern.

- Eliminate answer choices that are either too *narrow* or too *broad* in scope, or that inaccurately express of *distort* any idea presented in the passage.
- The main idea and primary purpose must be consistent with the author's attitude (tone, opinion, perspective).

Here's a main-idea question based on the portraiture passage you read earlier (see page 321):

QUESTION Which of the following best expresses the passage's main idea?

(A) The success of a portrait depends largely on the relationship between artist and subject.

(B) Portraits, more than most other art forms, provide insight into the artist's social relationships.

(C) The social aspect of portraiture sitting plays an important part in the sitting's outcome.

(D) Photographers and painters differ in their views regarding their role in portrait photography.

(E) The paintings of Reynolds provide a record of his success in achieving a social bond with his subjects.

ANALYSIS The correct answer is **(C)**. Although this passage doesn't seem to convey a strong central idea or thesis, the author seems to be most concerned with emphasizing that a portrait sitting is a social encounter, not just an artistic exercise, and that artists consider their relationship with their sitters to be somehow significant. For this reason, response (C) is a good statement of the author's main point.

Answer choice (A) also has merit. In fact, but for (C), (A) would be the best response because it embraces the passage as a whole and properly focuses on the author's primary concern with exploring the relationship between the artist and the sitter. However, the passage does not discuss how or whether this relationship results in a "successful" portrait; thus, (A) *distorts* the passage's information.

Answer choice (D) has merit in that the author does claim that the Reynolds paradigm (described in the second paragraph) is "quite different" from the two paradigms that the first paragraph discusses. The latter does indeed involve a painter (Reynolds) whereas the other two paradigms involve photographers (Cartier-Bresson and Avedon). However, the author does not generalize from this fact that a portrait artist's approach or view depends on whether the artist is a painter or a photographer. Thus, (D) is a bit *off focus* as well as calling for an *unwarranted generalization*.

Responses (B) and (E) are qualitatively the worst responses among the five choices. (B) *distorts* the information in the passage and departs from the topic at hand. Although the passage does support the notion that a portrait might reveal something about the relationship between the artist and the sitter, the author neither states nor implies that a portrait reveals anything about the artist's other relationships. Moreover, nowhere in the passage does the author compare portraiture with other art forms.

Response (E) is *too narrow* and refers to information *not mentioned* in the passage. The passage is not just about Reynolds, but about the portraiture encounter in general. Also, the author does not comment on Reynold's "success" or about how his relationship with his sitters might have contributed to his success.

CAUTION

> When handling main-idea and primary-purpose questions, never jump at the first viable answer choice; determining the best answer to these questions always requires comparing the quality of at least two viable choices.

2. "Explicit Detail" Questions

Explicit detail questions are designed to measure your ability to recall detailed information (facts, lists, examples) and to locate specific passage information quickly. The question might either ask which choice (among the five) is mentioned or which choice (among the five) is not mentioned. Here are a few tips for tackling these questions:

- A good outline will help you to quickly locate the key details in passage to answer the question.
- Beware of answer choices that include details that appear in the passage but are unrelated to the question
- Beware of answer choices that bring in details not mentioned in the passage
- Beware of answer choices that contradict information stated in the passage
- As you read the passage, be on the lookout for *lists* of characteristics or examples. Chances are you'll encounter an explicit detail question covering that list.
- Don't rely on your memory to answer these questions; go back to the passage and read around the excerpt to which the question refers (from the preceding sentence to the following sentence).

Here's the explicit detail question you encountered earlier along with the Iroquois passage (see page 322).

QUESTION The passage mentions all the following events as contributing to the decline of the Iroquois culture EXCEPT:

(A) new educational opportunities for the Iroquois people

(B) divisive power struggles among the leaders of the Iroquois nations

(C) introduction of new farming technologies

(D) territorial threats against the Iroquois nations

(E) discord among the nations regarding their role in the American Revolution

ANALYSIS The correct answer is **(B)**. Nowhere in the passage does the author mention any power struggles among the leaders of the Iroquois nations. Although the first paragraph does refer to a dispute among the Iroquois leaders, the dispute involved the role that the Iroquois should play in the American Revolution. Thus, (B) confuses the information in the passage by referring to unrelated details. The passage explicitly refers to the events mentioned in choices (A), (C), (D) and (E) as factors contributing to the decline of the Iroquois culture.

CAUTION In explicit detail questions, don't expect the answer choices to restate the passage's details word-for-word; expect instead to see paraphrasing of the language used in the passage.

3. Inference Questions

Inference questions require you to draw simple conclusions, going just beyond what the author explicitly states to infer what would most likely be true given what is explicitly stated. Inference questions usually require that you piece together (logically speaking) only a few sentences.

Here are some tips to help you ferret out the best answer to an inference question:

- Eliminate answer choices that require you to make unwarranted assumptions or reach unsupported conclusions.
- Eliminate answer choices that require you to bring in extraneous information.
- Eliminate answer choices that are contrary to or contradict information stated in the relevant lines or paragraph.
- Eliminate answer choices that confuse information stated in the relevant lines or paragraph.

- Eliminate answer choices that distort or over-generalize information stated in the relevant lines or paragraph

Here's an inference question based on the portraiture passage you read earlier (see page 321):

QUESTION Which of the following characterizations of the portraiture experience as viewed by Avedon is most readily inferable from the passage?

(A) a collaboration

(B) a mutual accommodation

(C) a confrontation

(D) an uncomfortable encounter

(E) a consultation

ANALYSIS The correct answer is **(E)**. In the first sentence of the second paragraph, the author distinguishes a "quite-different paradigm" (that is, the case of Reynolds) from the conceptions of Cartier-Bresson and Avedon in that the Reynolds paradigm "has its roots not in confrontation or consultation but in active collaboration between artist and sitter." The third sentence of the passage makes clear that Cartier-Bresson conceives the encounter as "confrontational"; thus, you can *reasonably infer* that the author characterizes an Avedon sitting as a "consultation."

Response (B) is also a good response but nevertheless not as good as (E). Although the term "mutual accommodation," which does not appear in the passage, is not altogether inconsistent with Avedon's view, the term suggests a relationship in which both artist and painter allow for the other's needs or desires. Such a description is closer to Hazlitt's analogy of two lovers than to Avedon's view of the artist as diagnostician and psychic healer.

Response (A) also has merit, yet it is not as good a response as either (B) or (E). Admittedly, the idea of "a collaboration" is not in strong opposition to the idea of "a consultation." However, the author explicitly ascribes this characterization to the Reynolds paradigm, not to Avedon's view. Thus, (A) *confuses the passage's information.*

Responses (C) and (D) are the qualitatively worst responses among the five. (C) *confuses the passage's information.* The quotation in the first paragraph makes it clear that Cartier-Bresson (not Avedon) conceives the encounter as "confrontational." (D) also *confuses the passage's information.* According to the passage, Avedon confesses "uncomfortably" to his role as diagnostician and psychic healer. It does not necessarily follow, however, that Avedon finds his encounters with his sitters to be uncomfortable.

CAUTION

Don't overlook the obvious! Inference questions often require you to make only very "tight" inferences; in other words, the passage will suggest the conclusion so strongly that no other interpretation is reasonable. Don't fight the passage by looking for a more subtle or deeper interpretation.

4. "Purpose of Detail" Questions

A purpose-of-detail question might ask why the author mentions some particular detail, quotes some individual, gives certain examples, or discusses some related topic. In each case, the object is to figure out the purpose of the material in the passage. Here are a few tips for dealing with these questions:

- As your read the passage, continually ask yourself what role or function specific information plays in the context in which the passage mentions it. It's more important for you to understand why the author mentions details than to remember the details themselves (you can always look them up later).
- Read the sentences immediately preceding and following the detail; that should suffice to handle the question.
- Eliminate any answer choice involving an inference that the passage does not support, distorts the author's purpose, confuses information in the passage, or runs contrary to information in the passage.

Here's the purpose-of-detail question you encountered earlier along with the portraiture passage (page 321).

QUESTION The author of the passage quotes Cartier-Bresson (lines 6–7) most probably in order to

(A) refute Avedon's conception of a portrait sitting

(B) provide one perspective of the portraiture encounter

(C) support the claim that portrait sittings are, more often than not, confrontational encounters

(D) show that a portraiture encounter can be either brief or extended

(E) distinguish a sitting for a photographic portrait from a sitting for a painted portrait

ANALYSIS The correct answer is **(B)**. We've already analyzed this question (see page 325). Note the wrong-answer ploys built into this question:

(A) exaggerates the author's purpose as well as the meaning of the information in the passage.

(C) distorts the author's point.

(D) confuses the information in the passage.

(E) distorts the author's purpose and is unsupported by the passage.

NOTE Don't expect the author to state outright why he or she is mentioning the particular detail that the question involves. You'll need to infer the purpose.

5. "Author Attitude" Questions

Author attitude questions are designed to test your ability to sense the author's emotional involvement with the topic, position on an issue, or agreement or disagreement with the certain ideas discussed in the passage. For example, the author might be indifferent, resigned, critical, enthusiastic, defensive, or optimistic in discussing the subject. Here are a few tips for dealing with these questions:

- As you read the passage be on the lookout for descriptive words or phrases that convey the author's attitude. A lack of emotion-laden words indicates a neutral, academic, or indifferent attitude toward the subject. Words that convey a light mood would likely indicate an optimistic, enthusiastic, positive attitude, whereas those that convey a dark or brooding mood would likely indicate a negative, critical, resigned attitude.
- Be on the lookout for answer choices that confuse the author's attitude with the attitude of some other individual discussed in the passage
- Eliminate answer choices that run contrary to the author's emotional tone
- Eliminate answer choices that are too extreme (in either a negative or positive direction)

Here's an author-attitude question based on the Iroquois passage you read earlier (see page 322).

QUESTION The author's attitude toward the influence of the Quakers on the Iroquois nations is best described as which of the following?

(A) critical

(B) laudatory

(C) congratulatory

(D) enthusiastic

(E) defensive

ANALYSIS The correct answer is **(A)**. Choices (B), and (C) are *too positive* and *distort* the author's attitude. While the author does indicate that Quaker's influence "impeded" the decline of the Iroquois nation and "instilled in the Iroquois some hope for the future," thereby approving and congratulating their influence, the author also points out that their influence "contributed to" the decline and "undermined the Iroquois' sense of national identity." (D) and (E) *run contrary* to the author's emotional tone. Nothing in the passage supports these interpretations of the author's attitude.

TIP

Since most GMAT reading passages draw from academic and other scholarly publications, it is unlikely that the authors of these articles will display strong emotions or political incorrectness in their writing. So you can easily eliminate any answer choice that is extremely negative, positive, or politically incorrect.

6. Application and Extrapolation Questions

These questions require you to apply the author's ideas to new situations, or to speculate as to how the passage would continue. These questions usually involve relatively broad inferences. You might be asked to interpret how the author's ideas might apply to other situations, or be affected by them. To do this requires that you're able to make logical connections between the author's stated ideas and other ideas not explicitly discussed in the passage. Or you might be asked to assess the author's attitude (agreement or disagreement) toward some new situation. In dealing with these questions:

- Be on the lookout for wrong-answer choices that require you to make an inference that is not supported by the passage.
- Eliminate answer choices that run contrary to or contradict the author's main idea or attitude.
- Eliminate answer choices that distort the author's attitude.
- Look out for wrong answer choices that are based on information not stated in the passage
- Here's an application question based on the Iroquois passage you read earlier (see page 322).

QUESTION Assuming that the reasons asserted by the author for the decline of the Iroquois culture are historically representative of the decline of cultural minorities, which of the following developments would most likely contribute to the demise of a modern-day ethnic minority?

(A) A bilingual education program in which children who are members of the minority group learn to read and write in both their traditional language and the language prevalent in the present culture.

(B) A tax credit for residential-property owners who lease their property to members of the minority group.

(C) Increased efforts by local government to eradicate the availability of illegal drugs.

(D) A government-sponsored program to assist minority-owned businesses in using computer technology to improve efficiency.

(E) The declaration of a national holiday commemorating a past war in which the minority group played an active role.

ANALYSIS The correct answer is **(D)**. According to the author, the Quakers' introduction of new technology to the Iroquois was partly responsible for the decline of the Iroquois culture in that it contributed to the tribe's loss of national identity. (D) presents a similar situation.

(A) is the second-best answer but the passage does not fully support this answer choice. Insofar as the children referred to in answer choice (A) learn the language of the prevailing culture, assimilation and a resulting loss of ethnic identity might tend to occur. However, this sense of identity might be reinforced by their learning to read and write in their traditional language as well. Therefore, (A) is not as likely to lead to the demise of the minority group as (D), at least based on the Iroquois' experience as discussed in the passage.

(B) is too general and the passage does not support it. Whether a government incentive to provide housing for members of the minority group actually undermines the group's sense of ethnic identity would probably depend on whether the incentives result in integration or segregation. Moreover, because the passage does not address whether the Iroquois became geographically integrated (assimilated), it does not support (B).

(C) is contrary to the passage's information. The scenario posed in (C) would actually contribute to the minority group's retaining its ethnic identity, at least based on the information in the passage. According to the passage, the introduction of spirits to the Iroquois population led to rampant alcoholism, which in turn contributed to the culture's decline. Similarly, widespread drug abuse might have a similar effect today. Accordingly, any effort to curb such abuse-as answer choice (C) suggests-would tend to impede a decline rather than contribute to it.

(E), like (C), runs contrary to the passage's information. Also, the passage does not support (E). Any ceremony or holiday calling attention to the ethnic population as a distinct group and helping to bring the population together as a group under a shared experience would tend to reinforce a sense of identity. Moreover, the passage does not refer to any developments during the time of the Iroquois decline that might be similar in any way to scenario (E); accordingly, the passage does not support (E).

NOTE

Application and extrapolation questions, by their nature, are relatively difficult. So you'll encounter one of these only if you're moving up the ladder of difficulty (by answering prior reading questions correctly).

Workshop

In this Workshop you'll apply what you've learned about GMAT Reading Comprehension to two sets of GMAT-style questions.

ONLINE

Additional reading passages and questions are available at the authors' Web site: http://www.west.net/~stewart/gmat.

Quiz

DIRECTIONS: Attempt the following two GMAT-style Reading Comprehension sets, each of which includes 3 questions. *Read the first question before you read the passage.* Try to limit your time to 12 minutes altogether (6 minutes per set). For each question, we've included a hint to help you if you're having trouble.

(Answers and explanations begin on page 339.)

Questions 1–3 are based on the following passage:

Dorothea Lange was perhaps the most notable of the photographers commissioned during the 1930s by the Farm Security Administration (FSA), part of a federal plan to revitalize the nation's economy and to communicate its human and social dimensions. The value of Lange's photographs as documents for social history is enhanced by her technical and artistic mastery of the medium. Her well-composed, sharp-focus images reveal a wealth of information about her subjects and show historical evidence that would scarcely be known but for her camera. Her finest images, while according with conditions of poverty that prompted political response, portray people who appear indomitable, unvanquished by their reverses. "Migrant Mother," for example, portrays a sense of the innocent victim, of perseverance, of destitution as a temporary aberration calling for compassion, solutions, and politics to alter life for the better. The power of that photograph, which became the symbol of the photographic file of the FSA, endures today.

The documentary book was a natural genre for Lange and her husband Paul Taylor, whose narrative accompanied Lange's FSA photographs. In *An American Exodus,* produced by Lange and Taylor, a sense of the despair of Lange's subjects is heightened by the captioned quotations of the migrants. Taken from 1935 to 1940, the *Exodus* pictures became the accepted vision of the migration of Dust Bowl farm workers into California.

1. According to the passage, the photograph entitled "Migrant Mother"
   (A) appeared in the documentary book *An American Exodus*
   (B) was accompanied by a caption written by Lange's husband
   (C) was taken by Lange in 1935
   (D) portrays the mother of a Dust Bowl farm worker
   (E) is considered by the author to be one of Lange's best photographs

   (Hint: This is an explicit detail question. As you read the passage take note of any specific information about the "Migrant Mother" photograph.)

2. The passage provides information for responding to all of the following questions EXCEPT:
   (A) What was the FSA's purpose in compiling the photographic file to which Lange contributed?
   (B) How did the FSA react to the photographs taken by Lange under its commission?
   (C) In what areas of the United States did Lange take her photographs appearing in *An American Exodus*?
   (D) Why did Lange agree to work under the commission of the FSA?
   (E) What qualities make Lange's photographs noteworthy?

   (Hint: As you read each answer choice, ask yourself whether the subject sounds familiar; if it doesn't, trust your short-term memory and select that answer choice. If you made a mini-outline of the passage as you read, use it to refresh your memory.)

3. Among the following characterizations, the passage is best viewed as
   (A) a survey of the great photographers of the Depression era
   (B) an examination of the photographic techniques of Dorothea Lange
   (C) an argument for the power of pictures to enact social change
   (D) a discussion of the goals and programs of the FSA's photographic department
   (E) an explanation of Lange's interest in documenting the plight of Depression victims

   (Hint: This is a primary purpose question. To zero in on the best response, ask yourself what the author spends most time discussing.)

Questions 4–6 are based on the following passage:

Radiative forcings are changes imposed on the planetary energy balance; radiative feedbacks are changes induced by climate change. Forcings can arise from natural or anthropogenic causes. For example, the concentration of sulfate aerosols in the atmosphere can be altered by volcanic action or by the burning of fossil fuels. The distinction between forcings and feedbacks is sometimes arbitrary; however, forcings are quantities normally specified in global climate model simulations, while feedbacks are calculated quantities. Examples of radiative forcings are greenhouse gases (such as carbon dioxide and ozone), aerosols in the troposphere, and surface reflectivity. Radiative feedbacks include clouds, water vapor in the troposphere, and sea-ice cover.

The effects of forcings and feedbacks on climate are complex and uncertain. For example, clouds trap outgoing radiation and thus provide a warming influence. However, they also reflect incoming solar radiation and thus provide a cooling influence. Current measurements indicate that the net effect of clouds is to cool the Earth. However, scientists are unsure if the balance will shift in the future as the atmosphere and cloud formation are altered by the accumulation of greenhouse gases. Similarly, the vertical distribution of ozone affects both the amount of radiation reaching the earth's surface and the amount of reradiated radiation that is trapped by the greenhouse effect. These two mechanisms affect the Earth's temperature in opposite directions.

4. It can be inferred from the information in the passage that "burning of fossil fuels" (line 9)
   (A) is an anthropogenic cause of radiative forcings
   (B) results in both radiative forcings and radiative feedbacks
   (C) does not affect atmospheric forcings or feedbacks
   (D) is a significant type of radiative forcing
   (E) is an anthropogenic cause of radiative feedbacks

   (Hint: There's a logical connection between the second sentence [lines 4–6] and the third sentence [lines 6–9].)

5. According to the passage, radiative forcings and radiative feedbacks can generally be distinguished in which of the following ways?
   (A) whether the radiative change is global or more localized
   (B) the precision with which the amounts of radiative change can be determined
   (C) that altitude at which the radiative change occurs
   (D) whether the amount of radiative change is specified or calculated
   (E) whether the radiative change is directed toward or away from the earth

   (Hint: Be sure to read the entire passage before confirming your answer choice.)

6. The author discusses the effect of clouds on atmospheric temperature most likely in order to show that
   (A) radiative feedbacks can be more difficult to isolate and predict than radiative forcings
   (B) the climatic impact of some radiative feedbacks is uncertain
   (C) some radiative feedbacks cannot be determined solely by global climate model simulations
   (D) the distinction between radiative feedbacks and radiative forcings is somewhat arbitrary
   (E) the effects of radiative forcings on planetary energy balance are both complex and uncertain

(Hint: Use your mini-outline to quickly locate the relevant part of the passage. Then read the sentence that precedes it through the one that follows it, asking yourself why the author discusses the effect of clouds on atmospheric temperature.)

Answers and Explanations

1. **(E)** The author cites "Migrant Mother" as an example of "[h]er finest images" (line 15)—i.e., as an example of her best photographs. (A) calls for speculation. The photograph might have appeared in Lange's book; however, the passage does not explicitly indicate so. (B) calls for speculation. Lange's husband wrote narrative captions for the photographs appearing in *Exodus*. However, there is no indication in the passage that "Migrant Mother" was accompanied by a caption or even that it appeared in the book. (C) provides information not mentioned in the passage. Although it is reasonable to assume that the photograph was taken by Lange during the 1930s, the passage neither states nor implies what year the photo was taken. (D) calls for speculation. According to the passage, the photographs appearing in *Exodus* "became the accepted vision of the migration of Dust Bowl farm workers to California" (lines 36–38). However, the author does not indicate either that "Migrant Mother" appeared in the book or that the woman portrayed in the photograph was indeed the mother of a Dust Bowl farm worker.

2. **(D)** The passage provides absolutely no information about Lange's motives or reasons for accepting her FSA commission. (A) is answered implicitly in the first sentence of the passage: "...the FSA, part of a federal plan to revitalize the economy and to communicate its human and social dimensions." Thus, the photographic file was compiled in furtherance of that purpose. (B) is answered implicitly by the last sentence of the first paragraph. The FSA thought highly enough of one of Lange's photographs to use it as a symbol for its photographic file. (C) is

answered implicitly in the second paragraph. According to the passage, the *Exodus* pictures recorded the migration of Dust Bowl farm workers into California. Thus, some (and probably all or nearly all) of these photographs were taken in the "Dust Bowl" region of the U.S. and/or in California. (E) is answered in the first paragraph, where the author mentions Lange's "well-composed, sharp-focus" images (line 11).

3. **(C)** Admittedly, (C) is not an ideal characterization of the passage, which seems more concerned with Lange's work than with making a broader argument about the power of pictures. Nevertheless, the author does allude to Lange's ability to convey a need for social change through her photographs. Accordingly, the passage can be characterized as presenting one example (Lange) to support the broader point suggested by Response (C). (A) is far too broad. The only photographer discussed in the passage is Lange. (B) is too narrow. Although the author mentions some of Lange's techniques (e.g., her "well-composed, sharp-focus images"), the author does not examine them in any detail. (D) distorts the passage and is too broad. First, the passage does not indicate that a distinct photographic department within the FSA existed; in this sense, (C) distorts the information in the passage. Second, although the author alludes to the overall purpose of the FSA (in the first sentence), there is no further discussion of its goals or program, other than the discussion of Lange's involvement in compiling its photographic file; in this sense, (C) is far too broad. (E) distorts the passage. There is no discussion in the passage of Lange's motive or reasons for photographing Depression victims other than that she was commissioned by the FSA to do so.

4. **(A)** The author states in the first paragraph that "[f]orcings can arise from natural or anthropogenic causes." In the following sentence the author describes two specific causes of forcings, presumably to illustrate the point of the previous sentence. It can be reasonably inferred by considering both sentences together that the first example (volcanic activity) is a natural cause, while the second (the burning of fossil fuels) is an anthropogenic cause. (B) is only partly supported by the passage. Although it can be inferred that the burning of fossil fuels causes radiative forcings, the author neither states nor suggests that this activity also causes radiative feedbacks. (C) contradicts the information presented in this part of the passage, which states explicitly that the concentration of sulfate aerosols is affected ("can be altered") by burning of fossil fuels. Thus, although burning of fossil fuels may not affect radiative feedbacks, it can be inferred that such activity does affect radiative forcings. (D) is nonsensical. The burning of fossil fuels is a cause, not a type, of radiative forcing. (E) confuses forcings with feedbacks.

5. **(D)** According to the passage, radiative "forcings are quantities normally specified in global climate model situations, while feedbacks are calculated quantities" (lines 11–14). (A) is wholly unsupported by the passage. The author never discusses the geographic extent of radiative changes in any context. (B) is not supported by the passage. The fact that feedbacks are "calculated quantities" while forcings are "specified" quantities does not in itself suggest that one can be more precisely determined than the other. (C) and (E) confuse the information in the passage in a similar way. The subject of altitude is discussed in the second paragraph as a factor influencing the relative effects upon ozone changes (a radiative forcing) of radiation directed toward the earth and radiation directed away from the earth. This area of discussion involves forcings only and not feedbacks.

6. **(B)** Response (B) restates the author's point in the first sentence of the second paragraph. Immediately thereafter, the author discusses clouds as an example of this point—it is difficult to predict the impact of greenhouse gases on clouds and thus on temperature. (A) is unsupported by the passage. In the second paragraph, the author discusses two particular examples of radiative changes—one involving radiative forcings and the other involving radiative feedbacks. The author's purpose in discussing these two phenomena is to illustrate the author's previous point that "[t]he effects of some forcings and feedbacks on climate are complex and uncertain" (lines 21–22). However, the author makes no attempt to compare the relative complexity or uncertainty of these two effects. (C) confuses the information in the passage and is somewhat nonsensical. It is forcings (not feedbacks) that are specified in (not determined by) global climate model simulations (lines 11–13). Moreover, (C) is wholly unsupported by the information in the second paragraph—nowhere does the author discuss or mention global climate simulations in relation to the effects of clouds on atmospheric temperatures. (D) is supported by the passage but does not respond to the question. In the first paragraph, the author attempts to distinguish between forcings and feedbacks and does indeed mention that the distinction can be somewhat arbitrary. However, this point is completely unrelated to the discussion in the second paragraph. (E) is the second-best response. Radiative forcings are defined in the first sentence of the passage as "changes imposed on the planetary energy balance." (E) is indeed one of the author's points in the second paragraph. However, (E) does not respond to the question, which deals with feedbacks rather than forcings.

Part IV

Learn to Answer GMAT Analytical Writing Questions

Hour

Hour 17

Teach Yourself How to Write GMAT "Issue" Essays

In this hour, you'll learn about the AWA testing format and word processor. Then you'll learn everything you need to know about writing a high scoring essay for the Analysis-of-an-Issue section of the GMAT CAT. Highlights of this hour include the following:

- How to use the CAT word processor
- How to evaluate and score your own practice essays
- How to organize and compose a high-scoring Analysis-of-an-Issue essay
- Practice writing a sample Issue essay

ONLINE

Before you forge ahead, we recommend that you download via the Internet the complete bank of 230 official AWA questions. For how to do it, see *Appendix C.* Although you don't need the question bank, you'll get more out of the next two hours if you have the questions in hand.

Analytical Writing Assessment at a Glance

HOW MANY: Two 30-minute essays (Section 1 and Section 2 of the GMAT)

WHERE: The very beginning of the exam (before the Quantitative and Verbal sections)

TIME ALLOWED: 30 minutes per essay (60 minutes altogether)

GROUND RULES:

1. No break is provided between the two 30-minute AWA sections.
2. The CAT system does not allow you to spend more than 30 minutes on either essay.
3. The CAT system does not allow you to return to either of the two AWA essays once you've moved on. (But if you've finished an essay early, you can proceed immediately to the next section by clicking on the NEXT button.)
4. You're allowed a maximum of 5 minutes after the second AWA section before moving on to the multiple-choice sections. (The CAT clock is always running, so the next section will start after 5 minutes—with or without you.)
5. Scratch paper and pencils are provided (just as in the other exam sections).

WHAT'S COVERED: You'll encounter two types of essay questions. They can appear in either order on your exam—as Section 1 and Section 2.

- *Analysis-of-an-Issue.* You respond to a statement concerning an issue of general interest.
- *Analysis-of-an-Argument.* You critique a stated argument.

NOTE

The CAT system stores in its test bank 115 distinct Issue questions and 115 distinct Argument questions, and the system will randomly select one question of each type for you.

SKILLS TESTED:

Content. Your ability to present cogent, persuasive, and relevant ideas and arguments through sound reasoning and supporting examples

Organization. Your ability to present your ideas in an organized and cohesive fashion

Language. Your control of the English language, including diction (word choice and usage) and syntax (sentence structure)

Grammar. Your facility with the conventions (grammar and punctuation) of Standard Written English

NOTE

Which of these areas is most important? Unofficial statements by GMAC representatives suggest that the first two areas are more important than the last two. But in our conversations with former GMAT readers, they've admitted to us that writing style, grammar, usage, and diction—in other words, your ability to communicate ideas effectively in writing—may influence graders just as much as the ideas themselves.

SCORING SYSTEM: Two readers will read and score your Issue essay, and two *other* readers will read and score your Argument essay. Each reader will employ a "holistic" grading method in which he or she will assign a single score from 0 to 6 (0, 1, 2, 3, 4, 5 or 6) based on the overall quality of your writing. Your final Writing Assessment score is the average of the four readers' grades (in half-point intervals). Average scores falling midway between half-point intervals are rounded *up*.

SCORING CRITERIA: GMAT readers follow the official scoring criteria that are printed in the official *GMAT Bulletin.* Here are two scorecards based on the official scoring criteria, to show you what the readers will be looking for when they read your essays.

TIP

As you practice writing GMAT essays, use these scorecards to gauge your performance. Answer "yes," "no," or "maybe" to each question. For each "yes" answer, give yourself a mark of 1. For each "no" answer, give yourself a mark of 0. For each "maybe" answer, give yourself a mark of .5. Total the marks to calculate your score (on a scale of 0–6).

Scorecard for an Issue Essay:

- Do you show that you understand and appreciate the complexities of the issue?
- Is your essay well organized, with a clear introduction and conclusion, and logical flow from one point to the next?
- Do you use persuasive examples and/or insightful reasons to support your position?
- Do you present a well-reasoned, articulate analysis of the issue?
- Do you cover the specific tasks called for in the instructions, without digressing from the task or from the issue at hand?
- Do you demonstrate a good command of Standard Written English?

Scorecard for an Argument Essay:

- Do you show that you understand the argument and follow its line of reasoning?
- Do you identify the major problems with the argument, using relevant and reasonable support for your critique?
- Do you develop your ideas logically and connect them smoothly with clear transitions?
- Is your essay well organized, with a clear introduction and conclusion?
- Do you perform all relevant tasks mentioned in the instructions, without digressing from these tasks or from the argument?
- Do you demonstrate a good command of Standard Written English?

ONLINE

> The AWA scoring criteria are published in the official GMAT Bulletin and at the official GMAT Web site, at www.gmat.org. A quicker way to find the scoring criteria on-line is through a link at our Web site (www.west.net/~stewart/awa).

The AWA Word-Processing Features

During Hour 1, you examined the features of the computer interface that are common to all sections of the exam. (These features are illustrated in the "screen shot" on page 10.) Now let's look at the CAT word processing features and limitations.

Navigation and Editing—Available Keyboard Commands

Here are the navigational and editing keys available in the CAT word processor:

Backspace removes the character to the left of the cursor

Delete removes the character to the right of the cursor

Home moves the cursor to the beginning of the line

End moves the cursor to the end of the line

Arrow Keys move the cursor up, down, left, or right

Enter inserts a paragraph break (starts a new line)

Page Up moves the cursor up one page (screen)

Page Down moves the cursor down one page (screen)

Common Keyboard Commands Not Available

Certain often-used features of standard word processing programs are not available in the CAT word processor. For example, no keyboard commands are available for:

TAB—disabled (does not function)

Beginning/end of paragraph (not available)

Beginning/end of document (not available)

Mouse-Driven Editing Functions

In addition to editing keys, the CAT word processor includes mouse-driven CUT, PASTE, and UNDO. The CAT word processor stores only your most recent delete, cut, or paste.

CAUTION

Drag-and-drop cut-and-paste and multiple UNDO are not available.

The vertical scroll bar. Once you key in ten lines or so, you'll have to scroll to view your entire response. If you don't know how to scroll, the computer tutorial preceding the test will show you how.

TIP

Notice that a vertical scroll bar also appears to the right of the AWA topic and question. Be sure to scroll all the way down to make sure that you've read the entire question.

Spell checking, fonts, attributes, hyphenation. The CAT word processor does not include a spell checker, nor does it allow you to choose typeface or point size. Neither manual nor automatic hyphenation is available. Attributes such as bold, italics, and underlining are not available.

TIP

As for words that you would otherwise italicize or underline (such as titles or foreign words), it's okay to leave them as is. The readers understand the limitations of the CAT word processor.

The Analysis-of-an-Issue Section

The Analysis-of-an-Issue section is designed to test your ability to communicate your opinion on an issue effectively and persuasively. Your task is to analyze the issue presented, considering various perspectives, and to develop your own position on the issue. *There is no "correct" answer.*

What Analysis-of-an-Issue Questions Look Like

Each Issue question consists of a brief statement (in quotation marks) of opinion about a particular issue, followed by a directive (instructions) for responding to the statement. Here's an example. This question is similar to the ones on the actual GMAT. In fact, it's an amalgam of three or four of the official questions. Keep in mind, however, that it is not one of the official 115 questions, so you won't see this on e on the actual exam. (We're not permitted to reprint the actual test questions.)

QUESTION

"In any large business organization, teamwork is the ultimate key to the organization's success."

In your view, how accurate is the foregoing statement? Use reasons and/or examples from your experience, observation, and/or reading to explain your viewpoint.

What You Should Know About Analysis-of-an-Issue Questions

1. **The directives vary among the 115 Issue questions, but only slightly.** The directives for the 115 Issue questions are all similar, but they aren't all exactly the same. Nearly all of the 115 questions will include essentially one of the following directives (the first one appears most frequently, by far):

    - Discuss the extent to which you agree or disagree with this statement
    - Assess the accuracy of this statement
    - Explain the meaning of this quotation (or statement)

2. **There are common themes among the 115 topics in the test bank.** Although each of the 115 official Issue topics is unique, their basic themes cover a lot of common ground. We've categorized all 115 topics for you, each according to theme, or issue. Understandably, more topics involve business issues than any other type.

NOTE

The categories here are not mutually exclusive; some topics could fall into more than one category. (Question numbers here correspond to the sequence of 115 official questions, as provided by ETS.)

Theme:	*Question numbers:*
Business—organizational structure/behavior, management	10, 14, 25, 33, 35, 55, 56, 76, 107
Business—productivity, efficiency, and teamwork	5, 17, 21, 30, 36, 51, 68, 69, 72, 79, 98
Business—advertising and marketing	44, 85, 86, 91
Business—labor and employment issues	9, 19, 27, 48, 50, 60, 93, 94, 96, 109, 110
Business—ethics	18, 45, 64, 70, 84
Business—its overall role and objectives in society	42, 59, 66, 82, 87, 90, 101
Government's role in regulating business, commerce, speech	1, 61, 71
Government's role in ensuring the welfare of its citizens	13, 22, 34, 41, 47, 82, 92, 114
Bureaucracy and "the system"	46, 53, 63
"Global village" issues	2, 15, 40, 65, 106
Technology and its impact on business and society	8, 20, 26, 102, 108, 112, 115
Culture and social mores, attitudes, values	16, 32, 38, 54, 57, 67, 78, 80, 105, 113

Theme:	*Question numbers:*
Education	12, 23, 28, 37, 62, 97, 99, 100
Learning lessons from history	43, 88, 89, 103
Keys to individual success	6, 11, 29, 39, 49, 52, 81
Individual power and influence	4, 24, 74
Personal qualities and values	31, 73, 75, 77, 95, 104, 111

TIME SAVER

If you have time to prepare further for the Issue section, prioritize your preparation by concentrating on the issues in this list with which you are least comfortable or familiar. Don't leave it to chance that the CAT system will deal your favorite hand of cards to you!

3. **There is no "correct" answer to any Issue question.** Each one of the 115 Issue topics states a position on a particular issue. You won't encounter any statement among the 115 that is clearly irrefutable or clearly wrong. The test-makers have written the topics this way to gauge your ability to argue persuasively for or against a position, as well as to qualify, or "hedge," your position.
4. **There is no prescribed or "correct" length for your response.** The CAT system imposes neither a minimum nor maximum length for an AWA response (aside from the practical limitation associated with a 30-minute time limit.) Do GMAT graders prefer brief or longer essays? Well, it all depends on the essay's quality. An essay that is concise and to-the-point may be more effective than a long-winded, rambling one. In contrast, a somewhat lengthy essay that is nevertheless articulate and that includes many insightful ideas will score higher than a brief essay that lacks substance.

   Our experience in writing AWA essays (and we have lots of it, since we've written model responses to all 230 AWA questions!) is that you can score a 6 with a 300–325 word essay. How do we know? Each essay you'll read in hours 17 and 18 is in that range and former GMAT graders awarded us scores of 6 for each one.

CAUTION

ETS has published only one model ("6") response to an official Issue question. The response is 472 words in length, and ETS admits that it's "ambitious" and not normally what ETS graders look for in a "6" essay. So don't take the ETS model as your cue. Get real, and use ours instead.

5. **There is no prescribed or "correct" number of paragraphs for your response.** There is no "correct" or "best" number of paragraphs for an Issue essay. In our view, however, your essay should include separate "introductory" and "summary" para-

graphs, as well as at least two "body" paragraphs in which you develop your position. You should skip a line between paragraphs, since the TAB key will be disabled.

CAUTION

Don't take the single ETS model essay as your cue. It contains 7 paragraphs—far too many for most test-takers to organize and compose in 30 minutes (and do it well). What's more, it includes tabs at each paragraph break, even though the CAT word processor doesn't allow for tabs! Again, get real, and go with 4–5 paragraphs.

How to Approach an Analysis-of-an-Issue Question

In scoring your Issue essay, GMAT readers will consider how effectively you:

- Recognize and deal with the complexities and implications of the issue
- Organize, develop, and express your ideas
- Support you ideas (with reasons and examples)
- Control the elements of Standard Written English (grammar, syntax, diction, word usage, punctuation)

To make sure you accomplish all four tasks effectively within the 30-minute time limit, follow this 6-step approach to any of the official Issue topics.

ACTION PLAN

1. **Brainstorm, and get your pencil moving (3–4 minutes).** Try to come up with a few reasons in favor of each side of the issue, as well as a few examples supporting each side.
2. **Adopt a position, and organize your ideas (2–3 minutes).** Arrange your ideas into two or three body paragraphs, then decide on a logical order in which to present them.
3. **Type the body of your response (15–20 Minutes).** Skip any introduction for now. Try to stick to your outline, but be flexible (through the magic of word processing, you can iron out the wrinkles as you go).
4. **Write a brief concluding (summary) paragraph (2–3 minutes).** Unless your essay has a clear end, the reader might think you didn't finish in time; so be sure to make time to wrap up your essay.
5. **Write a brief introductory paragraph (2–3 minutes).** Wait until the end to write your introduction. Why? If your position on the issue evolves as you com-

pose the body of your essay (it could happen), you won't have to rewrite your introduction.

CAUTION

Don't begin your essay by simply restating the issue! Doing so waves a "red flag" at the graders, whose first impression will be that you're short on ideas of your own. Show the reader from the very first sentence that you're thinking for yourself.

6. **Proofread your essay (3–4 minutes) and revise as needed.** Rework awkward sentences so they flow more naturally. Check for errors in diction, usage, and grammar. Check the flow of your essay, paying particular attention to transitions. Check your introductory and concluding paragraphs to make sure they're consistent with each other and with the specific topic.

TIMESAVER

To score a 6, your essay doesn't not have to be flawless. The graders won't mark you down for the occasional awkward sentence and minor error in punctuation, grammar, or usage. So as you compose your essay, keep moving. Don't get hung up on whether each sentence is something Hemingway or Steinbeck would be proud of.

Let's Apply the 6-Step Action Plan to a Simulated Question

Let's apply the 6-step approach to the simulated question you encountered on page 350.

1. Here's what your notes might look like after 1 or 2 minutes of brainstorming. Notice that they're not in any particular order, and that it appears that we haven't made up our minds yet as to where we stand on the issue:

PRO	CON
division of labor requires coop.	innovative product
coworker conflict	→ but R&D requ. coop.
→ nothing gets done	CEO vision (e.g., Apple)
→ attrition	→ but how to implement?
football team/military analogy?	competition/entry barriers
	extrinsic < econ. conditions; laws/regul.

2. Using these notes as a starting point, adopt a position, then prioritize, then organize. Here's how you might do it on your scratch paper (we've decided to take a position in which we fundamentally agree with the statement):

```
PRO ①  no worker is an island  <  programmers
                                   R & D
                                   sales force?

PRO ②  peer conflict → low prod.  (e.g., my job)

CON ③  ✓ CEO – Apple   (how to implement)
       ✓ entry barriers   (not in info. age)
       ✓ ad gimmick   (how to implement)
       ✓ extrinsic   (uncontrollable, so not key)
```

3. Let's compose the body of our response. As you read these two paragraphs, notice that we haven't included every single point from our outline. That's because you probably won't have time in 30 minutes to cover every point you want to make. Also notice that we've underlined certain transitional words and phrases—just to help you see how the ideas flow from one to the next. The stripped-down CAT word processor doesn't allow you to underline or highlight text in any way.

Body Paragraphs:

First, cooperative interaction is an integral part of nearly all company jobs—including jobs performed in relative isolation and those in which technical knowledge or ability, not the ability to work with others, would seem to be most important. For example, scientists, researchers, and even computer programmers must collaborate to establish common goals and coordinate efforts. Even in businesses where individual tenacity and ambition of salespeople would seem to be the key for a firm's success, sales personnel must coordinate efforts with support staff and managers.

Secondly, in my experience the kinds of problems that ultimately undermine an organization are those such as low employee morale, attrition, and diminishing productivity. These problems, in turn, almost invariably result from ill-will among coworkers and their unwillingness to communicate, cooperate, and compromise. Thus, problems in working together as a team pose the greatest threat to an organization's success.

> Some might argue that the leadership and vision of a company's key executives is of paramount importance. Yet chief executives of our most successful corporations would no doubt admit that without the cooperative efforts of their subordinates, their personal vision would never become reality. Others might cite the heavy manufacturing and natural-resource industries, where the value of tangible assets—raw materials and capital equipment—are often the most significant determinant of business success. However, such industries are diminishing in significance as we move from an industrial society to an information age.

4. Let's compose a brief summary to assure the reader we've organized our time well and finished our essay. Notice that this brief summary does not introduce any new reasons or examples; it's just a quick recapitulation.

   Final (Summary) Paragraph:

   > In sum, although leadership, individual ambition, and even the value of tangible assets play crucial roles in the success of many large business organizations, teamwork is the single ingredient common to all such organizations. It is, therefore, the key one.

5. Let's compose a brief introduction. Notice that we're making it clear right at the outset that we appreciate the complexity of the issue and that we have a point of view.

   Introductory Paragraph:

   > Whether a particular business ultimately succeeds or fails depends, of course, on a myriad of factors—ranging from economic conditions to the extent of competition, even to the charisma and clout of the CEO. Nevertheless, because teamwork is an essential ingredient for any large business to succeed, it is in my view the pivotal factor in most cases.

6. Don't forget to proofread for errors, check for cohesiveness, and rework any awkward sentences. (The essay we've just composed is already polished.)

NOTE

Now that you've seen our entire sample essay, keep in mind:

- None of the points we made are irrefutable, because the issue is far from "black-and-white." It's all a matter of opinion. That's what the Issue essay is all about.
- Our response is relatively simple in style and language and brief enough (about 325 words) to compose and type in 30 minutes.
- We didn't compose this essay under the pressure of time, so don't expect yours to turn out as polished.

DO's and DON'Ts for Your Analysis-of-an-Issue Essay

Do — **Don't**

DON'T waste time second-guessing what the reader might agree (or disagree) with. Instead, just be sure to acknowledge various perspectives on the issue and develop a well-supported position on it.

DO "hedge" your position by qualifying your viewpoint and acknowledging others. In doing so, you won't appear wishy-washy, but rather thoughtful and scholarly!

DON'T be reluctant to take a strong stance on an issue; but avoid coming across as fanatical or extreme. Approach the Issue essay is an intellectual exercise, not as a forum for sharing your personal belief system.

DON'T dwell on the details, but don't try to cover everything. Try to cover as many points in your outline as you have time for, devoting no more than a few sentences to each point you want to make. At the same time, don't worry if you're forced to leave the secondary and more tangential points on your scratch paper. GMAT readers understand your time constraints.

DON'T overdo it when it comes to drawing on personal experiences to support your position. Try instead to demonstrate a breadth of both real-world experience and academic knowledge.

DON'T approach the Issue task as a trivia contest. Bolster your position with names and events with which the readers are likely to have at least some familiarity, not by recounting statistics, quoting obscure sources, or citing little-known historical events.

DO explain how each example you mention illustrates your point. Anyone can simply list a long string of examples and claim that they illustrate a point. But the readers are looking for incisive analysis, not fast typing.

Workshop

For this hour's workshop, you'll compose an response to a GMAT-style Issue topic, using a word processor.

ONLINE

At our Web site (www.west.net/~stewart/gmat) you'll find our own essay responses to several official Issue questions. If you want more practice, compose responses to these questions, then compare your responses with our samples.

Quiz

DIRECTIONS: Compose an essay in which you perform the following writing task. Use a word processor, but be sure to use only the word-processing functions available for the GMAT CAT (see pages 348–350).

(Assess your performance by referring to our scorecard on page 348. Then review our sample response below.)

Analysis of an Issue

Time—30 Minutes

> "The natural environment can best be protected and preserved not by government penalties and other regulatory measures but rather through the voluntary efforts of private business, particularly large corporations."

Discuss the extent to which you agree or disagree with the statement above. Use relevant reasons and/or examples to explain your viewpoint.

Sample Response (Analysis of an Issue)

Imposing penalties and other regulatory measures on those who pollute or destroy the environment is one way to preserve our environment. I agree with the speaker, however, that it is not necessarily the best way. Laws might elicit grudging compliance; but other approaches—those that instill a sense of genuine commitment—are likely to be more effective in the long term.

Admittedly, motivating environmental protection by way of government regulation will serve environmental goals up to a point. However, many businesses will attempt to avoid conformance by concealing their activities, lobbying legislators to modify regulations, or moving operations to jurisdictions that allow their environmentally harmful activities. Others might calculate the trade-off between accepting punishment and polluting, then budget in advance for anticipated penalties and openly violate the law. My intuition is that this practice is a standard operating mode among some of our largest manufacturers.

A better way to insure environmental protection is to inculcate a sense of genuine commitment in our corporate culture—through education and shareholder involvement. When key corporate executives are committed to values, the regulations associated with those values become a codification of conscience rather than obstacles to circumvent. Moreover, commitment-driven actions are likely to benefit the environment over and above what the law requires. For example, while a particular regulation might permit a certain amount of toxic effluents, businesses committed to environmental protection might avoid harmful emissions altogether.

Instilling a genuine sense of commitment through education and shareholder action is not just a better approach in theory, it is also less costly overall than a compliance-driven approach. Regulatory systems inherently call for legislative committees, investigations, and enforcement agencies, all of which add to the tax burden of the citizens whom these regulations are designed to protect. Also, delays typically associated with bureaucratic regulation can thwart the purpose of the regulations, because environmental problems can quickly become grave indeed.

In sum, environmental regulations are essentially expensive Band-Aids. A commitment-based approach, involving education and shareholder activism, can instill in corporate culture a sense an environmental conscience, resulting in far more effective environmental protection.

NOTE

> Our essay meets the ETS criteria for a top score of 6, yet it is brief enough to easily compose and type within 30 minutes. Keep in mind that we did not compose this essay under timed conditions, so your essay might deserve a score of 6 even if it is less polished than our sample.

Hour 18

Teach Yourself How to Write GMAT "Argument" Essays

This hour you'll continue to prepare for the GMAT essays, by taking a close-up look at the Analysis-of-an-Argument writing task. You'll also learn some tips for writing style that apply to both GMAT essays. Here are your goals for this hour:

- Learn how to organize and compose a high-scoring Argument essay
- Learn some tips for developing a persuasive and effective writing style
- Practice writing a 30-minute Argument essay

The Analysis-of-an-Argument Section

The Analysis-of-an-Argument section is designed to test your critical reasoning and analytic (as well as writing) skills. Your task is to critique the stated argument, but not to present your own views on the argument's topic. While there is no one correct answer, your essay must effectively analyze and critique the argument presented in the passage.

What Analysis-of-an-Argument Questions Look Like

Each Argument question consists of a one-paragraph argument, followed by a directive for critiquing the argument.

Here's an example. This question is similar to the ones on the actual GMAT. Keep in mind, however, that it is not one of the official questions, so you won't see this one on the actual exam.

QUESTION

"Most environmentalists believe that the 'information superhighway' does not pose a serious threat to the environment. But what they fail to see is that the information superhighway will enable millions of people to work at home, far from the office. In other words, it will enable them to flee the cities and the suburbs and take up residence in areas that have hitherto been unpopulated and unspoiled. This dispersal of the populace portends an environmental disaster of the first magnitude."

Discuss how logically convincing you find this argument. In your discussion, you should analyze the argument's line of reasoning and use of evidence. It may be appropriate in your critique to call into question certain assumptions underlying the argument and/or to indicate what evidence might weaken or strengthen the argument. It may also be appropriate to discuss how you would alter the argument to make it more convincing and/or discuss what additional evidence, if any, would aid in evaluating the argument.

What You Should Know about Analysis-of-an-Argument Questions

1. **The directive is exactly the same for every Argument question.** All 115 official Argument questions include exactly the same directive. The directive in the Simulated Question above is essentially the same as the one appearing in the official questions.

2. **Your analysis must focus strictly on important logical features of the argument.** The official instructions admonish you NOT to present your own views on the topic. Your personal opinions about an issue to which the argument might allude are neither relevant nor useful in the Argument section.

   It is impossible to overstate the importance of this point! Do not confuse your task in the Argument section with your task in the Issue section. Consider, for example, the simulated argument question you looked at a few moments ago. An Issue question involving the environment might call for you to present various viewpoints about:

   - how best to protect it
   - the severity of the threat discussed relative to other threats
   - who should take responsibility for protecting it

   However, such viewpoints are irrelevant to the Argument section, in which you must focus strictly on the internal cogency (logical justification) of the stated argument.

3. **The test-makers have intentionally "loaded" each argument with flaws (fallacies and other weaknesses), which you must address effectively to score high.** In contrast to the instructions for the Issue writing task, the instructions for the Argument task do not state: "There is no correct response." Why not? Well, in creating each argument, the test-makers made sure to incorporate certain logical problems (fallacies and other weaknesses) into the argument, in order to give the test-taker something to write about. If you fail to identify and address the more fundamental problems that were "built into" the argument, you won't attain a high score.

   Here's a list of the six most common fallacies found in the official Argument passages:

   - The "biased or insufficient sample" fallacy
   - The fallacy of faulty analogy
   - The "after this, therefore because of this" fallacy
   - The "black and white" fallacy
   - The fallacy of equivocation
   - The "all things are equal" fallacy

NOTE

For a complete description of these fallacies, see Hour 15.

4. **There is no prescribed or "correct" length for your response.** The length of your essay will depend in great part on the completeness of your analysis of the argument. Keep in mind the criteria for a high scoring essay (page 348) and try to accomplish *all* of them in the most concise fashion possible. Typically this can be done in a 300–350 word essay.
5. **There is no prescribed or "correct" number of paragraphs for your response.** There is no "correct" or "best" number of paragraphs for an Argument essay. In our view, however, your essay should include separate "introductory" and "conclusion" paragraphs, as well as at least two "body" paragraphs in which you develop your critique of the argument. As mentioned earlier, you should skip a line between paragraphs, since the TAB key will be disabled.

How to Approach an Analysis-of-an-Argument Question

To score high on the Argument section, you need to accomplish these four basic tasks:

1. Analyze the argument's line of reasoning and use of evidence
2. Evaluate the cogency (logical justification) of the argument
3. Support your critique with sound reasons and/or relevant examples
4. Discuss what is required to make the argument more persuasive and/or what would help you better evaluate its conclusion

To make sure you accomplish all four tasks in the 30 minutes allotted, follow this 4–step approach.

ACTION PLAN

1. **Analyze the argument (4–6 minutes).** Look especially for unwarranted assumptions and inadequate evidence in support of the argument's conclusion (jot down every flaw or weakness that occurs to you).
2. **Organize your essay (3–5 minutes).** Using your notes from step 1 as a guide, arrange your ideas into paragraphs (probably four to six, depending on the number of flaws built into the argument).
3. **Type your essay (15–20 minutes).** Try to stick to your outline, and make a conscious effort to use transitional words and phrases to indicate to the reader *exactly* what you're doing in each paragraph.

4. **Proofread your essay (2–3 minutes).** Check for errors in diction, usage, and grammar. Check the flow of your essay, paying particular attention to transitions. If you have time, rework awkward sentences so they flow more naturally.

Let's Apply the 4–Step Action Plan to a Simulated Question

Let's apply the 4–step approach to the simulated question you looked at on page 362.

1. After spending 4–6 minutes analyzing the argument, your notes might look like the ones in the next figure (except for the margin annotations, which we added during step 2).
2. Using your notes as a guide, here's how you might organize your essay into a 4-paragraph format.

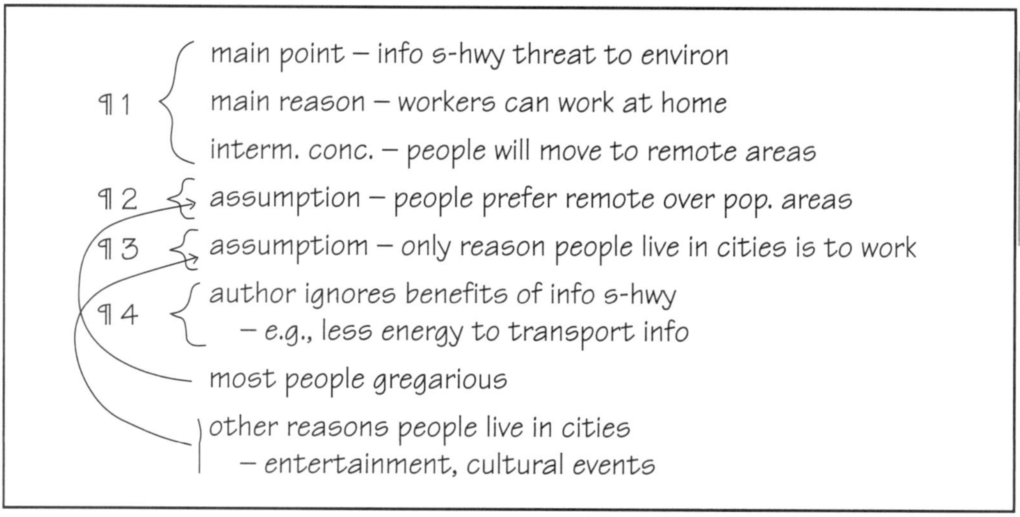

3. Here's the essay (se page 366). Notice that once again we've underlined certain transitional words and phrases to help you see how the ideas flow from one to the next.
4. Don't forget to proofread for errors, check for cohesiveness, and rework awkward sentences. (The essay we've composed is already polished.)

The author concludes that the information superhighway poses a serious threat to the environment because it will emancipate millions of people from traditional work places. The author's line of reasoning is that once emancipated, these workers will migrate into previously unpopulated and unspoiled areas, resulting in an environmental disaster of the first magnitude. This argument is unconvincing for several reasons.

First of all, the author's prediction of environmental disaster is based upon the questionable assumption that most people would prefer to live in unpopulated and remote areas. However, the author offers no evidence to support this crucial assumption. Moreover, given that most people are gregarious by nature, the truth of this claim is highly unlikely.

Secondly, the author assumes that most people live in cities and suburbs only because of the proximity to work and that, given the opportunity, they would move. Again, however, the author provides no evidence to support this questionable assumption. It seems equally reasonable to assume that people live in cities and suburbs for other reasons as well, such as the proximity to entertainment and cultural events.

Finally, the author fails to consider the environmental benefits this technology might bring. For example, transmitting information uses much less energy than transporting commuters, so it will save precious natural resources and be less polluting. It may turn out that the environmental advantages of this technology far outweigh the disadvantages. Because the author's argument lacks a complete analysis of the situation, the author's forecast of environmental disaster cannot be taken seriously.

In conclusion, to convince me that the information superhighway poses a threat to the environment, the author would have to provide evidence that, given the opportunity, most people would in fact move to remote and unspoiled areas. Additionally, the author would have to show that the adverse effects of this migration would outweigh the benefits of this technology. Without this additional evidence, I am not convinced that the information superhighway poses a serious threat to the environment.

NOTE

This response is simple in style and language and brief enough (about 325 words) to compose and type in 30 minutes. The response received a score of 6 (the highest possible score) from a former GMAT reader, who evaluated it just for us. We didn't compose this essay under the pressure of time, so don't expect yours to turn out as polished.

DO's and DON'Ts for Your Analysis-of-an-Argument Essay

Do **Don't**

DON'T merely restate of rehash the stated argument; the only way to score points is to tell the reader what's wrong with the argument; so keep your introductory paragraph brief.

DO analyze the argument's line of reasoning and use of evidence. Remember: unless you've recognized and discussed at least two or three logical flaws, you've missed something and you won't score a 5 or 6.

DO support your critique with sound reasons and/or relevant examples.

DON'T present your own views on the topic. Your personal opinions about the issue discussed in the argument are neither relevant nor useful for the Argument writing task.

DO discuss what is required to make the argument more persuasive and/or what would help you better evaluate its conclusion. Use the last paragraph of your essay to accomplish this.

DON'T introduce any new flaws in the concluding paragraph. Your job here is simply to reiterate the main points of your critique and to indicate what would be required to make the argument more convincing.

DO use transitional words or phrases to connect the various points of your critique.

18

Finding an Appropriate and Persuasive Style

According to GMAC officials, GMAT readers are instructed to place less weight on writing style and mechanics than on content and organization. But this doesn't mean that your writing style won't influence the reader or affect your AWA score. You can bet that it will! If your writing style is poor, the grader will be predisposed to award a lower score, regardless of the ideas you present and how you organize them. To score high on your GMAT essays, your writing must be:

- Concise (direct and to-the-point, not wordy or verbose)
- Correct in grammar, mechanics, and usage (conforming to the requirements of Standard Written English)
- Persuasive in style (using rhetorical devices effectively)
- Varied in sentence length and structure (to add interest and variety as well as to demonstrate maturity and sophistication in writing style)

All of this is easier said than done, of course. Don't worry if you're not a "natural" when it comes to writing effective prose. Few GMAT test-takers are. Nevertheless, you *can* improve your style in a few weeks to prepare for the GMAT. Here are some specific style-related guidelines for writing AWA essays.

DO's and DON'Ts for AWA Writing Style

Do **Don't**

DO maintain a somewhat formal tone; avoid slang and colloquialisms. If your essay sounds conversational in tone, it's probably a bit too informal for the GMAT. Avoid colloquialisms and jargon, whether in quotes or not. Otherwise, instead of hitting a "home run" with your essay, you'll be "out of luck" with the GMAT readers, and you'll have to "snake" your way in to a "bottom-barrel" MBA program. Get the idea?

DON'T try to make your point with humor or sarcasm. Avoid puns, double-meanings, and humor. Not that the GMAT readers don't have a sense of humor. It's just that they leave it at the door when they go to work for ETS.

DON'T overuse Latin and other non-English terms. One of the primary skills being tested in the AWA sections is your capacity with Standard Written English. So try to avoid non-English words. However, the occasional use of Latin terms and acronyms—for example, *per se, de facto, ad hoc, i.e.,* and *e.g.*—is perfectly acceptable. Non-English words used commonly in academic writing—such as *vis-à-vis, caveat* and *laissez faire*—are also acceptable. Just don't overdo it.

NOTE

The rules of Standard Written English require that Latin and other foreign terms be italicized (or underlined). But the CAT word processor doesn't allow you to incorporate these attributes or special diacritic marks (as in vis-à-vis). So leave such words as is, but be sure they are terms that most educated people are familiar with.

Do **Don't**

DON'T try too hard to impress the reader with your vocabulary. There's noth-ing wrong with demonstrating a well-educated vocabulary. But don't put the reader off by using obscure words that he is she is unlikely to be familiar with. Avoid technical terminology understood only by specialists and scholars in a specific field. In particular, don't assume that the GMAT readers know the language of economists.

DO refer to yourself, at your option. Self-references—singular as well as plural—are perfectly acceptable, though optional. Just be consistent:

"*I* disagree with . . . "

"In *my* view, . . . "

"Without additional evidence, *we* cannot assume that. . . . "

DO be sure your references to the source of the statement or argument are appropriate. The first time you refer to the source of an Argument, be specific and correct—for example:

"In this editorial . . . "

"The ad . . . "

"The vice president . .. "

"ACME Shoes . . . "

In your Issue essay try using "speaker," "statement" or "claim" in referring to the source of the statement. Also, it's okay to save keystrokes by using an occasional pronoun. Just be sure your pronouns are appropriate and consistent:

"The speaker argues . . . *Her* line of reasoning is . . . ; but *she* overlooks . . . "

"To strengthen *its* conclusion, the board must . . . *It* must also . . . "

DO use transition words and phrases to help your essay flow naturally from one idea to the next. Take another look at the underlined words in our two sample essays on pages 355–356 and 366. Make sure to connect your ideas with words such as these, to convince the reader that you can organize your thoughts under time pressure.

18

ONLINE

You'll get many ideas for enhancing your writing style by perusing our sample essays on-line (at www.west.net/~stewart/gmat). By reading these sample essays, the devices they employ can become part of your writing style as well. Print out the essays, highlight your favorite "buzz" words and phrases, then review them later and add them to your own GMAT essay inventory!

Workshop

For this hour's workshop, you'll compose an essay response to a GMAT-style Argument, using a word processor.

ONLINE

> At our Web site (www.west.net/~stewart/gmat) you'll find our own essay responses to several official AWA Arguments. If you want more practice, compose responses to these Arguments, then compare your responses with our samples.

Quiz

> **DIRECTIONS:** Compose an essay in which you perform the following writing task. Use a word processor, but be sure to use only the word-processing functions available for the GMAT CAT (see Hour 17).

(Assess your performance by referring to our scorecard on page 348. Then review our sample response on page 371.)

Analysis of an Argument

Time—30 Minutes

"Eighty percent of the homeless people interviewed in a recent survey said that they prefer to eat and sleep on the streets rather than go to shelters. Surprisingly, this survey proves that contrary to popular opinion, homeless people prefer the discomfort and uncertainty of life on the streets to the comfort and security afforded by shelters."

Discuss how logically convincing you find this argument. In your discussion, you should analyze the argument's line of reasoning and use of evidence. It may be appropriate in your critique to call into question certain assumptions underlying the argument and/or to indicate what evidence might weaken or strengthen the argument. It may also be appropriate to discuss how you would alter the argument to make it more convincing and/or discuss what additional evidence, if any, would aid in evaluating the argument.

Sample Response (Analysis of an Argument)

Based upon a survey in which 80 percent of the homeless respondents said that they prefer to eat and sleep on the streets rather than go to shelters, the author concludes that all homeless people share this preference. This argument is unconvincing for several reasons.

First of all, the author's conclusion goes beyond the evidence. Only 80 percent of the respondents indicated a preference for eating and sleeping on the streets. Yet the author concludes that all homeless people share this preference. This conclusion is not warranted by the evidence.

Secondly, it is possible that the homeless people interviewed are not representative of the entire population of homeless people. For example, perhaps the survey was conducted in a small rural community rather than a large metropolitan one, or perhaps it was conducted during summer rather than winter. Either fact would raise doubts about the reliability of the survey.

Thirdly, the argument fails to mention how many homeless people were interviewed in the survey or how they were selected. If, for example, only ten people were interviewed, this would be too small a sample to support the conclusion in this case. Lacking information about the sampling method used in the survey, it is impossible to assess the persuasiveness of the argument.

Finally, the author assumes that shelters are more comfortable and secure than the streets. No evidence is offered to support this assumption. It may be the case that the shelters are overcrowded and crime-ridden. If this were so, it would go a long way toward explaining the results of the survey.

In conclusion, the argument is unconvincing as it stands. To make the argument more persuasive, the author would have to modify the conclusion to bring it into line with the evidence and provide information that would ensure that the survey was reliable. Additionally, the author would have to provide evidence to support the assumption that shelters are more secure and comfortable than the streets.

NOTE

Our essay meets the ETS criteria for a top score of 6, yet it is brief enough to easily compose and type within 30 minutes. Keep in mind that we did not compose this essay under timed conditions, so your essay might deserve a score of 6 even if it is less polished than our sample.

Part V

Practice with Sample Exams

Hour

Hour 19

Sample Test #1 (Analytical Writing Assessment)

This hour you'll begin taking the first of two full-length sample GMAT CATs. You'll start by composing two AWA essays under timed conditions. You'll complete this sample test in Hours 20 and 21. Here are your goals for this hour:

- Using a word processor, compose an essay response to a simulated Analysis-of-an-Issue question
- Using a word processor, compose an essay response to a simulated Analysis-of-an-Argument question
- Review our sample responses (they begin on page 439)

NOTE

These two AWA topics are similar to the ones you'll encounter on the GMAT. But they are not among the topics in ETS' official AWA question bank. (To obtain the 230 official AWA questions, see Appendix C.)

Here are the directions that will appear at the top of your computer screen for both AWA sections.

DIRECTIONS: Read the statement and the instructions that follow it, and then make any notes that will help you plan your response. Begin typing in the box at the bottom of the screen.

Section 1—Analysis-of-an-Issue

Time—30 Minutes

1 Question

> "Just as governmental bureaucracies are not doing enough today to respond to the needs of individual citizens, big business is not doing enough today to respond to the needs of individual customers."

Discuss the extent to which you agree or disagree with the foregoing statement. Support your position with reasons and/or examples from your experience, observation, and/or reading.

Section 2—Analysis-of-an-Argument

Time—30 Minutes

1 Question

> "A survey of 300 students questioned at random from 9:00 to 11:00 AM in front of the Student Union building at Grant University revealed that only 30 percent of them plan to vote in the next national election. Apparently, the candidates and issues in the election don't excite university students since roughly 70 percent of them don't plan to participate."

Discuss how logically convincing you find this argument. In your discussion, you should analyze the argument's line of reasoning and use of evidence. It may be appropriate in your critique to call into question certain assumptions underlying the argument and/or to indicate what evidence might weaken or strengthen the argument. It may also be appropriate to discuss how you would alter the argument to make it more convincing and/or discuss what additional evidence, if any, would aid in evaluating the argument.

Hour 20

Sample Test #1 (Quantitative Ability)

This hour you'll continue taking your first sample GMAT CAT by completing a full-length Quantitative Ability section, which includes a total of 37 questions. Here are your goals for this hour:

- Take the test under timed conditions
- Check the answer key on page 387
- Assess your performance by checking the score conversion chart on page 474
- Review the explanations (they begin on page 441)

NOTE

The difficulty level of questions here is evenly distributed across various levels and will generally increase as you progress. Keep in mind, though, that the GMAT CAT does not necessarily follow this pattern, but instead will determine the difficulty level of each question based on your responses to prior questions.

NOTE

Although the CAT allows you 75 minutes to respond to 37 Quantitative questions, you should limit your time on this practice section to 60 minutes. (Solving math problems on the CAT takes longer than solving similar problems on a pencil-and-paper exam.)

Practice Test

Time—75 Minutes (but see the second note above)

37 Questions

Directions for Problem Solving Questions

(These directions will appear on your screen before your first Problem Solving question.)

Solve this problem and indicate the best of the answer choices given.

Numbers: All numbers used are real numbers.

Figures: A figure accompanying a problem solving question is intended to provide information useful in solving the problem. Figures are drawn as accurately as possible EXCEPT when it is stated in a specific problem that its figure is not drawn to scale. Straight lines may sometimes appear jagged. All figures lie on a plane unless otherwise indicated.

To review these directions for subsequent questions of this type, click on HELP.

Directions for Data Sufficiency Questions

(These directions will appear on your screen before your first Data Sufficiency question.)

This data sufficiency problem consists of a question and two statements, labeled (1) and (2), in which certain data are given. You have to decide whether the data given in the statements are *sufficient* for answering the question. Using the data given in the statements *plus* your knowledge of mathematics and everyday facts (such as the number of days in July or the meaning of *counterclockwise*), you must indicate whether:

(A) statement (1) ALONE is sufficient, but statement (2) alone is not sufficient to answer the question asked;
(B) statement (2) ALONE is sufficient, but statement 1 alone is not sufficient to answer the question asked;
(C) BOTH statements (1) and (2) TOGETHER are sufficient to answer the question asked; but NEITHER statement ALONE is sufficient;
(D) EACH statement ALONE is sufficient to answer the question asked;
(E) statements (1) and (2) TOGETHER are NOT sufficient to answer the question asked, and additional data specific to the problem are needed.

Numbers: All numbers used are real numbers.

Figures: A figure accompanying a data sufficiency problem will conform to the information given in the question, but will not necessarily conform to the additional information in statements (1) and (2).

Lines shown as straight can be assumed to be straight and lines that appear jagged can also be assumed to be straight.

You may assume that positions of points, angles, regions, etc., exist in the order shown and that angle measures are greater than zero.

All figures lie in a plane unless otherwise indicated.

Note: In data sufficiency problems that ask you for the value of a quantity, the data given in the statements are sufficient only when it is possible to determine exactly one numerical value for the quantity.

To review these directions for subsequent questions of this type, click on HELP.

1. Which of the following has the largest numerical value?

   (A) $\frac{3}{5}$

   (B) $\frac{\frac{2}{3}}{\frac{11}{9}}$

   (C) $\sqrt{.25}$

   (D) $(.81)^2$

   (E) $\frac{.2}{.3}$

2. The sum of Alan's age and Bob's age is 40. The sum of Bob's age and Carl's age is 34. The sum of Alan's age and Carl's age is 42. How old is Bob?

   (A) 12
   (B) 16
   (C) 18
   (D) 20
   (E) 24

3. If x and y are integers, is $x + y - 1$ divisible by 3?

   (1) When x is divided by 3, the remainder is 2.

   (2) When y is divided by 6, the remainder is 5.

4. Four knots—*A*, *B*, *C*, and *D*—appear in that order along a straight length of rope. Is the distance between *B* and *D* the same as the distance between *A* and *B*?

   (1) The distance between *A* and *C* is less than the distance between *B* and *D*.

   (2) Half the distance between *A* and *D* is the same as the distance between *C* and *D*.

5. Is $x > y$?

   (1) x is the arithmetic mean of all two-digit prime numbers less than 23.

   (2) y is the sum of all factors of 60 that are greater than -1 but less than 6.

6. If a total of 55 books were sold at a community book fair, and if each book was either hardback or paperback, how many hardback books were sold at the book fair?

   (1) The total proceeds from the sale of paperback books, each of which was sold for 75 cents, was \$19.50.

   (2) The proceeds from the book fair totaled \$48.50.

IMPORTS AND EXPORTS FOR
COUNTRY X AND COUNTRY Y, 1985–1990

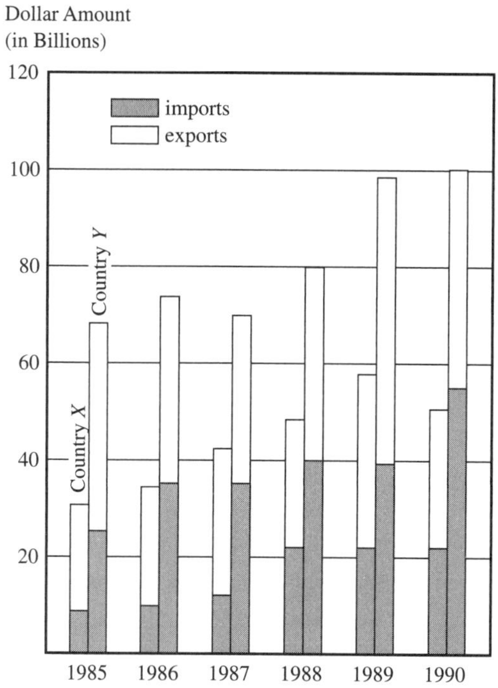

7. According to the chart above, during the year that Country *X*'s exports exceeded its own imports by the greatest dollar amount, Country *Y*'s imports exceeded Country *X*'s imports by approximately

(A) \$23 billion
(B) \$75 billion
(C) \$90 billion
(D) \$110 billion
(E) \$160 billion

8. A certain zoo charges exactly twice as much for an adult admission ticket as for a child's admission ticket. If the total admission price for a family of two adults and two children is \$12.60, what is the price of a child's ticket?

(A) \$1.60
(B) \$2.10
(C) \$3.20
(D) \$3.30
(E) \$4.20

9. If the legislature passes a particular bill by a ratio of 5 to 4, and if 900 legislators voted in favor of the bill, how many voted against it?

(A) 400
(B) 500
(C) 720
(D) 760
(E) 800

10. M is $P\%$ of what number?

(A) $\frac{MP}{100}$

(B) $\frac{100P}{M}$

(C) $\frac{M}{100P}$

(D) $\frac{P}{100M}$

(E) $\frac{100M}{P}$

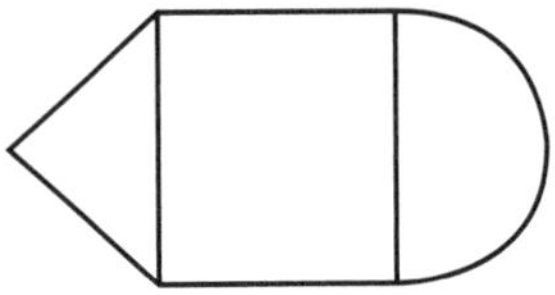

11. Three carpet pieces—in the shapes of a square, a triangle, and a semicircle—are attached to one another, as shown in the figure above, to cover the floor of a room. If the area of the square is 144 feet and the perimeter of the triangle is 28 feet, what is the perimeter of the room's floor, in feet?

    (A) $32 + 12\pi$
    (B) $40 + 6\pi$
    (C) $34 + 12\pi$
    (D) $52 + 6\pi$
    (E) $52 + 12\pi$

12. If (b ■ a ■ c) is defined as being equal to $ab - c$, what is the numerical value of (4 ■ 3 ■ 5) + (6 ■ 5 ■ 7)?

    (A) 6
    (B) 11
    (C) 15
    (D) 30
    (E) 40

13. Two competitors battle each other in each match of a tournament with nine participants. What is the minimum number of matches that must occur for every competitor to battle every other competitor?

    (A) 27
    (B) 36
    (C) 45
    (D) 64
    (E) 81

14. What is the value of x?

    (1) $4x^2 - 4x = -1$
    (2) $2x^2 + 9x = 5$

15. If $\frac{2y}{9} = \frac{y-1}{3}$, then $y =$

    (A) $\frac{1}{3}$
    (B) $\frac{4}{9}$
    (C) $\frac{9}{15}$
    (D) $\frac{9}{4}$
    (E) 3

16. Each computer in a computer lab is equipped with either a modem, a sound card, or both. What percentage of the computers are equipped with modems, but not sound cards?

    (1) Twenty percent of the computers are equipped with both modems and sound cards.
    (2) Twenty-five percent of the computers are equipped with sound cards, but not with modems.

17. Lisa has 45 coins, which are worth a total of \$3.50. If the coins are all nickels and dimes, how many more dimes than nickels does she have?

    (A) 5
    (B) 10
    (C) 15
    (D) 20
    (E) 25

18. In an election between two candidates—Lange and Sobel—70% of the voters voted for Sobel. Of the election's voters, 60% were male. If 35% of the female voters voted for Lange, what percentage of the voters were males who voted for Sobel?

    (A) 14%
    (B) 16%
    (C) 26%
    (D) 44%
    (E) 65%

19. If q workers can paint a house in d days, how many days will it take $q + 2$ workers to paint the same house, assuming all workers paint at the same rate?

    (A) $d + 2$
    (B) $d - 2$
    (C) $\frac{q + 2}{qd}$
    (D) $\frac{qd + 2d}{q}$
    (E) $\frac{qd}{q + 2}$

20. If $m = n$ and $p < q$, then

    (A) $m - p < n - q$
    (B) $p - m > q - n$
    (C) $m - p > n - q$
    (D) $mp > nq$
    (E) $m + q < n + p$

21. ABC Company pays an average of \$140 per vehicle each month in outdoor parking fees for three of its eight vehicles. The company pays garage parking fees for the remaining five vehicles. If ABC pays an average of \$240 per vehicle overall each month for parking, how much does ABC pay per month in garage parking fees for its vehicles?

    (A) \$300
    (B) \$420
    (C) \$912
    (D) \$1420
    (E) \$1500

22. If $abc \neq 0$, and if $0 < c < b < a < 1$, is

    $$\frac{a^4b^3c^2}{b^2cd^2} < 1?$$

    (1) $a = \sqrt{d}$
    (2) $d > 0$

23. If the price of a candy bar is doubled, by what percent will sales of the candy bar decrease?

    (1) For every ten cent increase in price, the sales will decease by 5 percent.
    (2) Each candy bar now costs sixty cents.

24. What is the numerical value of the second term in the following sequence: $x, x + 1, x + 3, x + 6, x + 10, x + 15, \ldots$?

    (1) The sum of the first and second terms is one-half the sum of the third and fourth terms.
    (2) The sum of the sixth and seventh terms is 43.

25. On the xy-plane, what is the area of a right triangle, one side of which is defined by the two points having the (x,y) coordinates (2,3) and (–4,0)?

(1) The triangle's sides cross the y-axis at exactly two points altogether.

(2) The y-coordinate of the triangle's third vertex is zero.

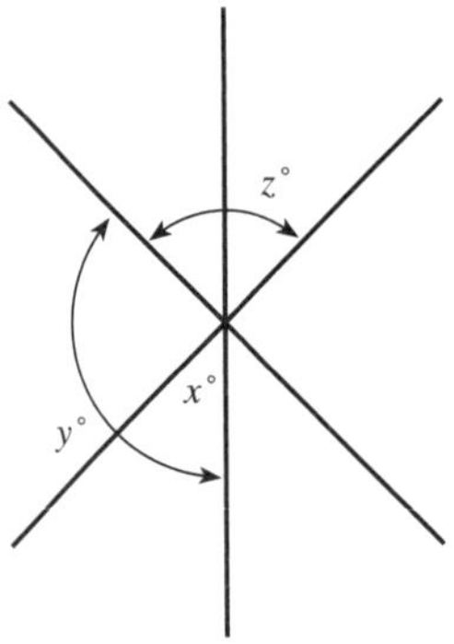

26. In the figure above, what is the value of x?

(1) $y = 130$

(2) $z = 100$

27. If $xy < 0$, and if x and y are both integers, what is the difference in value between x and y?

(1) $x + y = 2$

(2) $-3 < x < y$

28. A photographic negative measures $1\frac{7}{8}$ inches by $2\frac{1}{4}$ inches. If the longer side of the printed picture is to be 4 inches, how many inches long will the shorter side of the printed picture be?

(A) $2\frac{3}{8}$

(B) $2\frac{1}{2}$

(C) 3

(D) $3\frac{1}{8}$

(E) $3\frac{3}{8}$

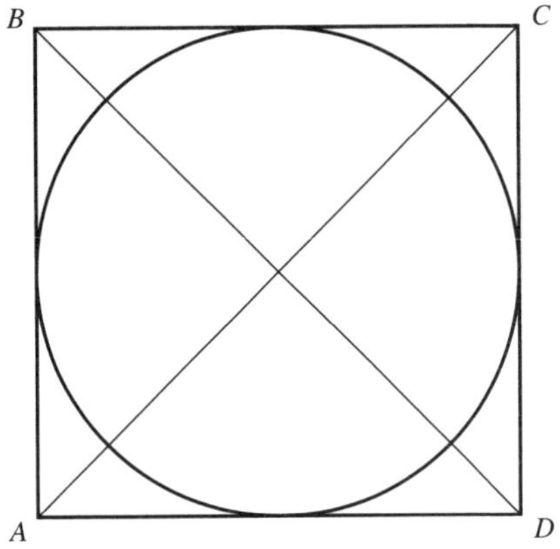

29. If the circumference of the circle above is 16π, and if the length of AC equals the length of BD, what is the length of AC?

(A) $4\sqrt{2}$

(B) 16

(C) $16\sqrt{2}$

(D) 32

(E) 16π

Questions 30 and 31 refer to the following chart.

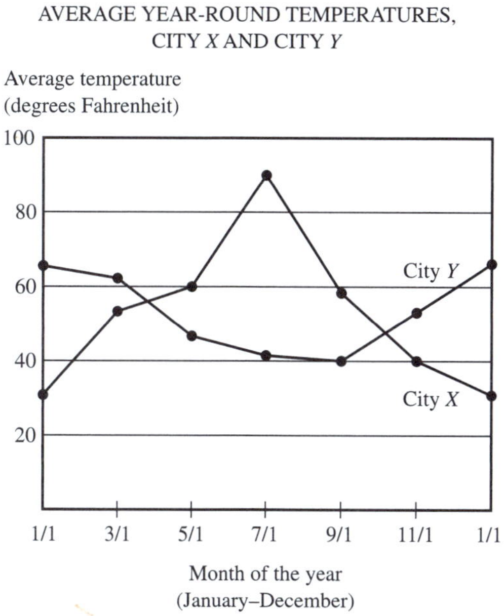

30. With respect to the two-month period over which the average daily temperature in City *X* increased by the greatest percentage, City *Y*'s average daily temperature was approximately
   (A) 38 degrees
   (B) 42 degrees
   (C) 52 degrees
   (D) 64 degrees
   (E) 68 degrees

31. During the time periods in which City *Y*'s average daily temperature was increasing while City *X*'s was decreasing, the average daily temperature in City *Y* exceeded that in City *X* by approximately
   (A) 0 degrees
   (B) 4 degrees
   (C) 10 degrees
   (D) 15 degrees
   (E) 19 degrees

32. Two ships leave from the same port at 11:30 a.m. If one sails due east at 24 miles per hour and the other due south at 10 miles per hour, how many miles apart are the ships at 2:30 p.m.?
   (A) 45
   (B) 62
   (C) 68
   (D) 78
   (E) 84

33. The average of seven numbers is 84. Six of the numbers are: 86, 82, 90, 92, 80, and 81. What is the seventh number?
   (A) 79
   (B) 85
   (C) 81
   (D) 77
   (E) 76

34. $\sqrt{\frac{y^2}{2} - \frac{y^2}{18}} =$

(A) 0

(B) $\frac{2y}{3}$

(C) $\frac{10y}{3}$

(D) $\frac{y\sqrt{3}}{6}$

(E) $\frac{y\sqrt{5}}{3}$

35. A certain cylindrical tank set on its circular base is 7.5 feet in height. If the tank is filled with water, and if the water is then poured out of the tank into smaller cube-shaped tanks, how many cube-shaped tanks are required to hold all the water?

(1) The length of a cube-shaped tank's side is equal to the radius of the cylindrical tank's circular base.

(2) If 3 cube-shaped tanks are stacked on top of one another, the top of the third cube stacked is the same distance above the ground as the top of the cylindrical tank.

36. A solution of 60 ounces of sugar and water is 20% sugar. How much water must be added to make a solution which is 5% sugar?

(A) 20 ounces
(B) 80 ounces
(C) 100 ounces
(D) 120 ounces
(E) 180 ounces

37. Dan drove home from college at an average rate of 60 miles per hour. On his trip back to college, his rate was 10 miles per hour slower and the trip took him one hour longer than the drive home. How far is Dan's home from the college?

(A) 65 miles
(B) 100 miles
(C) 200 miles
(D) 280 miles
(E) 300 miles

Answer Key

1. E
2. B
3. C
4. D
5. C
6. A
7. A
8. B
9. C
10. E
11. B
12. D
13. B
14. A
15. E
16. C
17. A
18. D
19. E
20. C
21. E
22. A
23. C
24. D
25. B
26. C
27. E
28. C
29. C
30. D
31. C
32. D
33. D
34. B
35. C
36. E
37. E

Hour 21

Sample Test #1 (Verbal Ability)

This hour you'll complete your first sample GMAT CAT by taking a full-length Verbal Ability section, which includes a total of 41 questions. Here are your goals for this hour:

- Take the test under timed conditions
- Check the answer key on page 406
- Assess your performance by checking the score conversion chart on page 474
- Review the explanations (they begin on page 448)

NOTE

The difficulty level of questions here is evenly distributed across various levels. Keep in mind, though, that the GMAT CAT does not necessarily follow this pattern, but instead will determine the difficulty level of each question based on your responses to prior questions.

NOTE

Although the CAT allows you 75 minutes to respond to 41 Verbal questions, you should limit your time on this practice section to 60 minutes. (Working through a computer-based test takes longer than working through a paper-based exam.)

Practice Test

Time—75 Minutes (but see the second note above)

41 Questions

DIRECTIONS:

Directions for Sentence Correction Questions

(These directions will appear on your screen before your first Sentence Correction question.)

This question presents a sentence, all or part of which is underlined. Beneath the sentence you will find five ways of phrasing the underlined part. The first of these repeats the original; the other four are different. If you think the original is best, choose the first answer; otherwise, choose one of the others.

This question tests correctness and effectiveness of expression. In choosing your answer, follow the requirements of standard written English; that is, pay attention to grammar, choice of words, and sentence construction. Choose the answer that produces the most effective sentence; this answer should be clear and exact, without awkwardness, ambiguity, redundancy, or grammatical error.

Directions for Critical Reasoning Questions

(These directions will appear on your screen before your first Critical Reasoning question.)

For this question, select the best of the answer choices given.

Directions for Reading Comprehension Questions

(These directions will appear on your screen before your first group of Reading Comprehension questions.)

The questions in this group are based on the content of a passage. After reading the passage, choose the best answer to each question. Answer all the questions following the passage on the basis of what is *stated* or *implied* in the passage.

1. To ensure the integrity of fossil evidence found at climatically unstable archeological sites, the immediate coating of newly exposed fossils with a specially formulated alkaline solution is as crucial, if not more crucial than, the prompt removal of the fossil from the site.

   (A) crucial, if not more crucial than, the
   (B) crucial as, if not more crucial than, the
   (C) crucial as, if not more than the
   (D) crucial, if not more crucial, than the
   (E) crucial, if not more crucial, as the

2. According to Newtonian physics, the greater the distance between two particles, given the so-called gravitational constant, the less will be the gravitational force between them.

   (A) the greater the distance between two particles, given the so-called gravitational constant, the less will be the gravitational force between them
   (B) the greater the distance the less the gravitational force between two particles, given the so-called gravitational constant
   (C) given the so-called gravitational constant, more distance between two particles will result in a lesser gravitational force between them
   (D) the less of a gravitational force between two objects, the more of a distance between them, given the so-called gravitational constant
   (E) given the so-called gravitational constant, the greater the distance between two particles, the smaller the gravitational force between them

3. Who the terrorists are, as well as who their recent terrorist activities were aimed at, are currently under investigation by the bureau.

   (A) Who the terrorists are, as well as who their recent terrorist activities were aimed at, are
   (B) The terrorists, as well as at whom their recent terrorist activities were aimed at, are
   (C) Who the terrorists are, as well as at whom their recent terrorist activities were aimed, is
   (D) Who they are and who the recent terrorist activities were aimed at are
   (E) Who the terrorists are and who their recent terrorist activities were aimed at are

4. Softec, a small computer software company, has introduced more new software products than any of its competitors during the past year. This is undoubtedly the reason that it enjoyed greater financial success than its competitors during this period.

   Which of the following, if true, would provide the most support for the conclusion above?

   (A) The software products introduced by Softec were favorably reviewed by most major computer magazines.
   (B) None of Softec's competitors introduced new software products during this period.
   (C) Softec and its competitors are equally well managed companies with insignificant differences in their marketing strategies.
   (D) Software innovations and applications are now the major driving force of the computer revolution.
   (E) Softec is one of the leading innovators in the fastest growing segment of the computer software market.

5. Many rare or endangered plant species are sources of drugs and chemicals that have proven to be useful in medicine and in agriculture. It is likely, therefore, that many plants that are now extinct would have served as the source of useful drugs and chemicals as well. Thus, if we want to ensure that drugs and chemicals from plants are available in the future, we must make every effort to preserve these precious natural resources.

   Which of the following is an assumption on which the above argument depends?

   (A) Only rare or endangered plant species have proven to be useful as sources of drugs and chemicals.
   (B) Extinct plant species would have provided useful drugs and chemicals.
   (C) Efforts are not now being made to preserve plant species.
   (D) Using plants as a source of drugs and chemicals will not threaten their survival.
   (E) All plant species are sources of useful drugs and chemicals.

Questions 6–8 are based on the following passage.

The German empire was largely a creation of the political genius of Bismarck. Not since Napoleon had Europe seen such a dominant and effective leader. In 1847 he had entered politics and found it to his liking and quickly rose up the ranks. Upon becoming Minister-President of Prussia, he made a famous pronouncement: "The great questions of the day will not be decided by speeches and the resolutions of majorities . . . but by iron and blood." He quickly went about showing what he meant by using war to unify the German states. There were victorious wars against Denmark and Austria. These victories threatened France, and another war ensued in 1870. Napoleon III and his army, which was thought to be the finest fighting machine in Europe, surrendered in humiliation. The Franco-Prussian war brought the

German states together, and Bismarck took full advantage of the opportunity this afforded, arguing for the creation of a new German empire with the Prussian king, Wilhelm I (Wilhelm II's grandfather), as emperor. The states agreed and made their proclamation on French soil in the Hall of Mirrors at Versailles. This, combined with a heavy war indemnity and the loss of the rich iron-mining and manufacturing territory of Alsace and Lorraine, was a grievous insult to the people of France.

6. The passage mentions all of the following events as leading to the creation of the new German empire EXCEPT:
   (A) the defeat of Napoleon III in the Franco-Prussian war
   (B) Bismarck's election to the post of Minister-President of Prussia
   (C) France's loss of the territory of Alsace and Lorraine
   (D) the defeat of Denmark and Austria by the unified German states
   (E) Bismarck's pronouncement that "iron and blood" would settle the great questions of the day

7. Each of the following can be inferred from the passage EXCEPT:
   (A) Wilhelm II's father was not named Wilhelm
   (B) the German states were unified for military purposes
   (C) the people of France were insulted by Bismarck
   (D) Napoleon III and his army were not the finest fighting machine in Europe
   (E) the wars against Austria and Denmark were fought by Prussia

8. The primary purpose of the passage is to
   (A) document Bismarck's rise to power.
   (B) document Bismarck's role in the creation of the German empire.
   (C) argue that Bismarck was a more dominant and effective leader than Napoleon.
   (D) argue that Bismarck used war as a means to settle political differences.
   (E) describe the sequence of events leading up to the Franco-Prussian war.

9. <u>The severity of the weather can some of the time prevent airplanes departing on time.</u>
   (A) The severity of the weather can some of the time prevent airplanes departing on time.
   (B) The severity of the weather sometime can prevent airplanes from their timely departing.
   (C) Severe weather can sometimes prevent airplanes from departing on time.
   (D) Airplanes departing in a timely manner can sometimes be prevented by severe weather.
   (E) Timely departures for airplanes are sometimes prevented as a result of severe weather.

10. New genetic testing procedures have been developed that can detect the presence or absence of dirolin in foods. Dirolin is the toxin that causes food poisoning in humans. While rarely fatal if identified and treated in its early stages, food poisoning causes severe intestinal illness and vomiting. It is for this reason that the Department of Public Health and Safety should require that all processed foods be subjected to the new testing procedures.

    Which one of the following, if true, would require the author to reconsider the conclusion?

    (A) A recent Disease Control Agency report states that reported cases of food poisoning have declined steadily over the past decade.
    (B) Death as a result of food poisoning is extremely rare in modern first-world countries.
    (C) Current processing procedures employed in preparing foodstuffs are extremely effective in preventing and detecting dirolin contamination.
    (D) The bacillus that produces dirolin can be easily treated with modern antibiotics.
    (E) Improper preserving and processing procedures are responsible for the presence of dirolin in prepared foods.

11. Blood pressure varies over a 24-hour period, with a low point occurring when resting in a reclining position. Memory recall varies with blood pressure such that whenever blood pressure is lowered, recall time is lengthened. This correlation suggests that low blood pressure is the cause of slow recall and, consequently, that recall time should shorten when blood pressure is raised. However, tests show that recall time does not shorten when blood pressure is raised.

    If the statements above are true, they provide the most support for which one of the following?

    (A) Persons with neither high nor low blood pressure have normal memory recall time.
    (B) Low blood pressure is not the cause of increase in memory recall time.
    (C) There is no relation between blood pressure and memory recall time.
    (D) Persons with high blood pressure will have fast memory recall.
    (E) High blood pressure causes a decrease in memory recall time.

12. Over twenty million illegal immigrants live in the United States, <u>including greater than a million alone in California</u>.

    (A) including greater than a million alone in California
    (B) including in California greater than a million
    (C) including more in California than a million
    (D) including more than a million in California alone
    (E) including greater than a million such illegal immigrants in California

13. For generations after Napoleon, who posed for his portrait with hand in vest, men, especially Civil War generals, similarly posed for their portraits.

    (A) For generations after Napoleon, who posed for his portrait with hand in vest, men, especially Civil War generals,
    (B) Generations of men after Napoleon, who posed for his portrait with hand in vest, especially Civil War generals,
    (C) After Napoleon posed for his portrait with hand in vest, generations of men, especially Civil War generals,
    (D) For generations after Napoleon posed for his portrait with hand in vest, Civil War generals especially, and men in general
    (E) Generations of men after Napoleon, especially Civil War generals, who posed for his portrait with hand in vest

14. The space program's missions to Mars have confirmed that the soil composition on that planet is similar to that on our planet.

    (A) to that on our planet
    (B) to our planet
    (C) with the soil on our planet
    (D) to this composition on our planet
    (E) to our planet's soil's composition

Questions 15–17 are based on the following passage.

The number of disorders for which DNA tests exist has grown steadily. Testing is now being done to look for the presence of flaws in single genes—flaws that lead to disorders such as cystic fibrosis, hemophilia, muscular dystrophy, and spinal muscular atrophy. However, even if we know that a certain mutant gene is present, it is not possible to predict how that gene will finally be expressed and what the outcome on health will be, either at the time of birth or later on as the individual develops and matures. Different mutations in the same gene can have different effects—from being virtually unnoticeable to causing severe and devastating health problems.

The newest wave of testing goes beyond single gene disorders and looks for genes that can predispose a person to a disorder. Some of the first susceptibility genes found have been for familial colon cancer, coronary heart disease, breast cancer, and Alzheimer's disease. These are complex conditions that result from the interaction of several different genes with environmental factors—diet, exercise, exposure to viruses, or environmental chemicals. The presence of a susceptibility gene can increase the chances that a disorder can develop but it does not mean that it will. And the absence of a susceptibility gene does not mean a person will be spared.

15. According to the passage, flaws in single genes
    (A) predispose a person to a health disorder
    (B) always have the same effect
    (C) are called "susceptibility" genes
    (D) cause severe and devasting health problems
    (E) do not cause predictable health problems

16. The passage mentions all of the following disorders as being related to susceptibility genes EXCEPT:
    (A) breast cancer
    (B) coronary heart disease
    (C) spinal muscular atrophy
    (D) Alzheimer's disease
    (E) familial colon cancer

17. It can be inferred from the passage that
    (A) neither flawed genes nor susceptibility genes lead to predictable health problems.
    (B) the absence of a mutant gene insures that an individual will not have devastating health problems.
    (C) susceptibility genes are the cause of breast cancer and Alzheimer's disease.
    (D) a healthy diet, plenty of exercise, and minimizing exposure to viruses and harmful chemicals is the best way to avoid developing breast cancer.
    (E) a mutant gene is more likely to cause a serious health problem than a susceptibility gene.

18. In Los Alamos the majority of residents are professionals whose incomes exceed $120,000. Moreover, they always elect conservative candidates in their elections. Los Brunos is also populated with professionals who earn high incomes; therefore it is likely that ____________.

    Which of the following sentences best completes the argument?
    (A) Los Brunos residents have incomes above $120,000.
    (B) Los Brunos residents always elect conservative candidates.
    (C) Poor people do not live in Los Brunos.
    (D) People who earn high incomes are usually conservative.
    (E) The majority of residents of Los Brunos are doctors and lawyers.

19. In a recent medical experiment, twenty volunteers who were not immune to yellow fever lived for an extended period of time in a mosquito-proof environment with patients who had advanced cases of yellow fever. During this period, the volunteers were in constant contact with these patients, yet none of the volunteers developed the disease. This experiment was repeated in a non-mosquito-proof environment, and several of the volunteers were bitten by mosquitoes. In this instance, the ones bitten all developed yellow fever. That mosquito bites, and not contact with persons who have this disease, is the cause of yellow fever can be confidently concluded on the basis of these two experiments.

The argument above employs which one of the following methods of argumentation?

(A) Establishing a causal conclusion through a process of elimination of all but one of the candidate causes
(B) Establishing a causal conclusion on the basis of the identification of an event that precedes the effect
(C) Establishing a causal conclusion on the basis of an analogy between two different environments
(D) Establishing a causal conclusion on the basis of a significant correlation between two circumstances
(E) Employing the expert testimony of the experimenters as grounds for the conclusion

20. A recipe for cooking potatoes states that potatoes should be cooked in boiling water for twenty minutes to be properly prepared. This holds only for potatoes that have been diced into one-inch cubes—smaller cubes would require proportionately less cooking time and larger ones proportionately more. It is important that potatoes not be overcooked, since this greatly diminishes their food value. Undercooking also should be avoided because undercooked potatoes cannot be properly digested.

If the above statements are true, which of the following conclusions is most strongly supported?

(A) Whole potatoes, when properly cooked, cannot be properly digested.
(B) Potatoes that are diced into one-half-inch cubes and cooked in boiling water for twenty minutes will likely have little food value.
(C) Potatoes that are properly digestible must be cooked in boiling water for at least twenty minutes.
(D) Boiling in water is the only method of cooking potatoes that will ensure high food value and proper digestibility.
(E) To be prepared properly, potatoes must be boiled in water for at least twenty minutes.

21. The overall demand for used computers has risen dramatically in the past few years. Most of this increase is due to the explosion of entertainment software products aimed at young first-time computer users. As is to be expected, this demand has exerted an upward pressure on prices of used computers. As a result, we can expect that an increasing number of computer owners will be selling their old computers in order to buy the latest models.

Which of the following, if true, would most help to support the conclusion in the argument above?

(A) Computer technology is progressing so rapidly that computers purchased a year ago are now virtually obsolete.
(B) Exciting new software is being developed that can only run on the latest computer models.
(C) Most computer users do not know how to upgrade their old computers to accommodate the latest software products.
(D) It is less expensive to buy a new computer than to buy the components and build one yourself.
(E) The primary reason computer owners have not bought new computers or used computers that are newer models is that their old computers have little or no resale value.

22. A pluralistic democracy, in greater degree than any system of government, diffuses power away from a center.

(A) in greater degree than any
(B) which more than any
(C) to a greater extent than any
(D) as opposed to any other
(E) more than any other

23. Whether the universe is bound is frequently asked but impossible to answer.

(A) Whether the universe is bound is frequently asked but impossible to answer.
(B) A question asked frequently is whether the universe is bound, and it is impossible to answer.
(C) As to whether the universe is bound is frequently asked but impossibly answered question.
(D) Whether the universe is bound is frequently asked but impossible answered.
(E) Whether or not the universe is bound is a question asked frequently but a question impossible to answer.

24. The need of third world countries for trained workers are partially met by the efforts of the Peace Corps.

(A) The need of third world countries for trained workers are
(B) Trained workers for the needs of third world countries are
(C) Third world countries' need for trained workers is
(D) The need for trained workers in third world countries is
(E) The trained worker needs of countries of the third world are

25. Last month video production giant MovieCo announced that it was declaring bankruptcy due to insolvency. Today, another major video production studio—Vidfilms—filed for bankruptcy citing rising production costs as the primary reason for its failure. These facts clearly show that the video production business is in serious trouble and would make a poor investment for the future.

    The reasoning in the above argument is most vulnerable to criticism on which of the following grounds?

    (A) The argument employs circular reasoning in which the conclusion is merely a restatement of the information stated in the premises.
    (B) The argument reaches a general conclusion on the basis of a small number of specific instances.
    (C) The argument explains one event as being caused by another event simply because one preceded the other.
    (D) The argument depends upon the assumption that there are only two possible alternatives, and having eliminated one, concludes that the other must be the case.
    (E) The argument involves an equivocation, in that the word "bankruptcy" is allowed to shift its meaning in the course of the argument.

26. Recent reports from waste management companies indicate that disposable plastic containers make up an increasingly large percentage of the waste they collect. As a result, landfills and incineration sites now deal almost exclusively with the disposal of plastics, whereas glass and metal containers previously made up the bulk of their refuse. It is evident from this radical change in disposal patterns that the use of plastic containers has virtually replaced the use of glass and metal containers.

    Which of the following, if true, would most seriously call into question the conclusion above?

    (A) Metal and glass containers are more expensive to manufacture than plastic containers.
    (B) An increasing proportion of metal and glass containers is now being recycled.
    (C) Plastic containers can be used over and over again before being discarded.
    (D) Plastic containers decompose faster than metal and glass containers.
    (E) Environmentalists have been unsuccessful in their attempts to decrease the production of plastic containers.

27. Humans naturally crave to do good, act reasonably and <u>to think decently, these</u> urges must have a global purpose in order to have meaning.

    (A) to think decently, these
    (B) think decently, yet these
    (C) to decently think, and these
    (D) thinking decently, but these
    (E) think decent, these

Questions 28–30 are based on the following passage.

Economists and other social scientists have demonstrated that the research and development activities of private firms generate widespread benefits enjoyed by consumers and society at large. As a result, the overall economic value to society often exceeds the economic benefits enjoyed by innovating firms as a result of their research efforts. This excess of the social rate of return over the private rate of return enjoyed by innovating firms is described by economists as a positive externality or spillover. These spillovers imply that private firms will invest less than is socially desirable in research, with the result that some desirable research projects will not be undertaken, and others will be undertaken more slowly, later, or on a smaller scale than would be socially desirable.

Spillovers occur for a number of reasons. First, spillovers occur because the workings of the market or markets for an innovative product or process create benefits for consumers and non-innovating firms. Second, spillovers occur because knowledge created by one firm is typically not contained within that firm, and thereby creates value for other firms and other firms' customers. Finally, because the profitability of a set of interrelated and interdependent technologies may depend on achieving a critical mass of success, each firm pursuing one or more of these related technologies creates economic benefits for other firms and their customers.

28. According to the passage, a spillover is
    - (A) the economic value to society of research and development projects
    - (B) the economic benefits to innovating firms resulting from their research and development efforts
    - (C) the excess of the private rate of return on investment over the social rate of return
    - (D) the benefits to consumers as a result of private firms' research and development programs
    - (E) the excess in the economic value to society over the economic value to private firms' that results from their research and development efforts

29. Which of the following statements about spillovers finds the least support in the passage?
    - (A) Research and development projects undertaken by innovating firms provide benefits to non-innovating firms.
    - (B) Socially desirable research projects may not be undertaken by private firms.
    - (C) Knowledge gained by the research and development efforts of private firms will benefit only those firms.
    - (D) Innovative technologies produced by innovating firms create benefits for other firms engaged in related technologies.
    - (E) The economic value to society of private firms research and development activities is often greater than the economic benefit to the innovating firm.

30. The passage provides information for responding to all of the following questions EXCEPT:
    (A) What are the underlying causes of spillovers?
    (B) What benefits do non-innovating firms enjoy from the research and development efforts of innovating firms?
    (C) What is a "positive externality"?
    (D) Why do private firms invest less in research and development than is socially desirable?
    (E) Why is knowledge that is acquired by an innovating firm typically not contained within that firm?

31. In the context of illegal drug trafficking, deterrence is a particularly unconvincing rationale for the death penalty. The main reason is that drug trafficking is extremely lucrative and may well be worth the gamble. This is true especially for the economically disenfranchised members of our society. Also, given the extremely high level of violence associated with illegal drug trafficking, the criminal justice system's penalties are unlikely to be a more effective deterrent than the violence to which one exposes himself or herself upon entering the trade.

    The conclusion of the above argument is best expressed by which of the following?
    (A) Drug trafficking is extremely lucrative and is worth the gamble, even if the price of being caught and convicted is the death penalty.
    (B) The death penalty will not deter drug trafficking.
    (C) The death penalty should be imposed on drug traffickers.
    (D) The violence of the drug scene is not an effective deterrent to stop drug traffickers from entering the trade.
    (E) Most drug traffickers are economically disenfranchised members of our society.

32. Unequal pay for men and women is a completely indefensible practice and one that must be stopped immediately. After all, can anyone seriously doubt that women have as much right to self-esteem as men? Surely this fact alone is reason enough to justify their right to earn as much money as men.

    Which of the following is an assumption on which the above argument depends?
    (A) A person who has less money than another has less self-esteem.
    (B) People who do not have jobs lack self-esteem.
    (C) Women and men who perform similar jobs should earn similar salaries.
    (D) Equal pay for equal work is a constitutionally guaranteed right of all workers.
    (E) High self-esteem is as important to women as it is to men.

33. Abraham Lincoln knew instinctively that when its people obey and revere the law a democracy flourishes.
    (A) when its people obey and revere the law a democracy flourishes
    (B) when its people obey and they revere the law a democracy flourishes
    (C) when the law is obeyed and revered by its people a democracy flourishes
    (D) a democracy flourishes when its people obey and revere the law
    (E) when the people who obey and revere the law a democracy flourishes

34. The California gold rush, the historical development instilling the greatest sense of manifest destiny in the populace, wore not the clothing of political ideology but rather a suit spun of gold and greed.
    (A) The California gold rush, the historical development instilling the greatest sense of manifest destiny in the populace, wore not the clothing of political ideology but rather a suit spun of gold and greed.
    (B) The historical development which most greatly instilled a sense of manifest destiny in the populace wore not the clothing of political ideology but instead a suit spun of gold and greed; it was the California gold rush.
    (C) The historical development most instilling in the populace a sense of manifest destiny was the California gold rush, wearing a suit of greed and gold, not the clothing of political ideology.
    (D) It was the California gold rush, not the clothing of political ideology, but rather a suit of gold and greed, that most greatly instilled in the populace a sense of manifest destiny.
    (E) The greatest sense of manifest destiny in the populace was instilled by the California gold rush, which wore a suit of gold and greed rather than the clothing of political ideology.

35. People in the north central region of the United States use certain utterances that distinguish their speech from other regions.
    (A) distinguish their speech from
    (B) distinguishes their manner of speaking from
    (C) distinguishes their speech from those of
    (D) distinguish the way they speak from
    (E) distinguish their speech from that of

36. Lying is morally justified only if it is done to save a person's life. But most people lie not because a life is in danger but only to avoid the unpleasant consequences of telling the truth. Thus, most lies that are told are morally unjustified.

In which of the following is the pattern of reasoning most parallel to that in the argument above?

(A) Capital punishment is justified if it deters people from taking another's life. But it has been demonstrated conclusively that capital punishment is not an effective deterrent. Thus, capital punishment is not justified.

(B) Capital punishment is justified only if we are certain that the convicted offender is actually guilty of the crime. But there are many cases in which persons who are not guilty are convicted of capital offenses. Therefore, in many cases capital punishment is unjustified.

(C) Capital punishment is morally wrong only if it does not promote the greatest good for the greatest number of people. But sacred religious texts do not condemn capital punishment as being morally wrong. Thus, capital punishment promotes the greatest good for the greatest number of people.

(D) If the defendant in a murder trial is determined to be guilty beyond a reasonable doubt, then the maximum penalty allowed under the law can be imposed. But most defendants in murder trials are not determined to be guilty beyond a reasonable doubt. Therefore, the maximum penalty is seldom imposed.

(E) Corporal punishment for persons who commit violent crimes is justified if and only if the punishment will alter the persons' behavior in the future. But most persons who commit violent crimes are corporally punished not in order to alter their future behavior, but only to exact revenge. Therefore, most instances of corporal punishment are unjustified.

Questions 37–39 are based on the following passage.

Opponents of affirmative action claim that it forces employers to "give preference" to less qualified minorities. Equating affirmative action with quotas, they argue that color-blind laws are fairer than those that take race into account. But affirmative action is not a quota system or a form of reverse discrimination. Nor does it give preferential treatment to unqualified minorities and women. Quotas have always been used as a method of exclusion, not inclusion. Before the Civil Rights Act, quotas were used to keep out qualified members of unpopular racial or religious groups. That is why they are intensely disliked by the public, and have been strongly disfavored by the Supreme Court.

Goals and timetables found in affirmative action plans are not the same thing as quotas. They are a nondiscriminatory way of making sure that those who were previously excluded are finally brought into the workplace, and a way of measuring whether discrimination is being reduced. Without them, employers with a history of discriminatory practices would continue "business as usual." With them, employers must make efforts to recruit and hire qualified women and/or minorities for vacant positions from which they were previously excluded. This is the opposite of discrimination. Employers and universities have always engaged in forms of "preferential treatment." It was only when race and gender became a factor in the effort to end discrimination that preferences became a problem. Yet there are many examples of long-accepted preferential treatment. University preference of veterans over non-veterans, or of children of alumnae over other youth is one example; employers hiring the sons and daughters of their economic and social equals (the "old boys club") is another. Requiring that qualified minorities and women be actively recruited and, whenever appropriate, hired is the only way that previously excluded minorities and women can gain a toehold in companies, occupations and schools that were previously reserved for white men. It's fairness itself.

37. Which of the following best expresses the main point of the passage?
    - (A) Quotas have traditionally been a method of exclusion, not inclusion.
    - (B) Affirmative action is the only way previously excluded minorities and women can be fully integrated into the society.
    - (C) Affirmative action is not a form of discrimination.
    - (D) Affirmative action plans use quotas as a means to include, not exclude, women and minorities in hiring.
    - (E) Affirmative action does not give preferential treatment to unqualified women and minorities, nor is it a quota system or a form of reverse discrimination.

38. It can be inferred from the passage that the author maintains that quotas are:
    - (A) a means of discriminating against those who are otherwise qualified for vacant positions
    - (B) a way of insuring that employers with a history of discriminatory practices do not continue "business as usual"
    - (C) a way of measuring whether discriminatory practices have been reduced
    - (D) a means of insuring that employers make efforts to recruit and hire qualified women and minorities for vacant positions from which they were previously excluded
    - (E) a means of including unqualified candidates for vacant positions and excluding qualified candidates for those positions

39. The passage mentions all of the following as examples of preferential treatment EXCEPT:
    (A) universities practice of giving preference to people who served their country in time of war over those who did not
    (B) employers giving preference to their own sons or daughters over the children of their economic and social equals
    (C) employers giving preference to the children of people who have similar interests, education, and political views to their own
    (D) universities giving preference to persons whose parents attended the university
    (E) employers giving preference to the offspring of their economic peers

40. Every philosopher of science of the twentieth century who was either a realist or an empiricist was influenced by a group of philosophers known collectively as the logical positivists. The philosophical writings of this group deal primarily with the methodology of science and the question as to whether our belief that scientific theories are true can be justified. Their arguments on the latter topic are so compelling that no one who is influenced by them holds that scientific theories can be proven to be true.

    If the statements above are true, which one of the following conclusions must be true on the basis of them?
    (A) No twentieth-century philosophers of science who are realists maintain that scientific theories can be proven to be true.
    (B) Every twentieth-century philosopher of science who believes that scientific theories cannot be proven to be true was influenced by the logical positivists.
    (C) The logical positivists were the only twentieth-century philosophers to influence philosophers of science who believe that scientific theories cannot be proven to be true.
    (D) Every philosopher of science in the twentieth century who was influenced by the logical positivists believes that scientific theories are false.
    (E) Every twentieth-century philosopher of science who was not influenced by the logical positivists believes that scientific theories can be proven to be true.

41. International environmental regulations do not protect hybrid species, <u>but they are protected by way of domestic laws</u>.
    (A) but they are protected by way of domestic laws
    (B) although domestic laws do
    (C) and so domestic laws only protect hybrid species
    (D) yet the laws of domestic protection will so protect
    (E) which require legal protection domestically

Answer Key

1. B
2. E
3. C
4. C
5. D
6. D
7. C
8. B
9. C
10. C
11. B
12. D
13. C
14. A
15. E
16. C
17. A
18. B
19. A
20. B
21. E
22. E
23. A
24. D
25. B
26. B
27. B
28. E
29. C
30. E
31. B
32. A
33. D
34. A
35. E
36. B
37. E
38. A
39. B
40. A
41. B

Hour 22

Sample Test #2 (Analytical Writing Assessment)

This hour you'll begin your second sample GMAT CAT. You'll start by composing two AWA essays under timed conditions. You'll complete this sample test in Hours 23 and 24. Here are your goals for this hour:

- Using a word processor, compose an essay response to a simulated Analysis-of-an-Issue question
- Using a word processor, compose an essay response to a simulated Analysis-of-an-Argument question
- Review our sample responses (they begin on page 456)

NOTE

These two AWA topics are similar to the ones you'll encounter on the GMAT. But they are not among the topics in ETS' official AWA question bank. (To obtain the 230 official AWA questions, see Appendix C.)

Here are the directions that will appear at the top of your computer screen during both AWA sections.

DIRECTIONS: Read the statement and the instructions that follow it, and then make any notes that will help you plan your response. Begin typing in the box at the bottom of the screen.

Section 1—Analysis-of-an-Issue

Time—30 Minutes

1 Question

> "Exposure to higher forms of art clearly enrich any society. Therefore, the government should subsidize the production of high art."

Discuss the extent to which you agree or disagree with the foregoing statement. Support your position with reasons and/or examples from your experience, observation, and/or reading.

Section 2—Analysis-of-an-Argument

Time—30 Minutes

1 Question

> "Pregnant women are advised to limit their caffeine intake on the grounds that caffeine causes birth defects in rats. This warning followed a study conducted at a major university in which pregnant rats were force-fed massive amounts of caffeine—the human equivalent of up to 24 cups a day of strong coffee. Some of the offspring of these rats were born with missing toes."

Discuss how logically convincing you find this argument. In your discussion, you should analyze the argument's line of reasoning and use of evidence. It may be appropriate in your critique to call into question certain assumptions underlying the argument and/or to indicate what evidence might weaken or strengthen the argument. It may also be appropriate to discuss how you would alter the argument to make it more convincing and/or discuss what additional evidence, if any, would aid in evaluating the argument.

Hour 23

Sample Test #2 (Quantitative Ability)

This hour you'll continue taking your second sample GMAT CAT by completing a full-length Quantitative Ability section, which includes a total of 37 questions. Here are your goals for this hour:

- Take the test under timed conditions
- Check the answer key on page 419
- Assess your performance by checking the score conversion chart on page 474
- Review the explanations (they begin on page 458)

NOTE

The difficulty level of questions here is evenly distributed across various levels and will generally increase as you progress. Keep in mind, though, that the GMAT CAT does not necessarily follow this pattern, but instead will determine the difficulty level of each question based on your responses to prior questions.

NOTE

Although the CAT allows you 75 minutes to respond to 37 Quantitative questions, you should limit your time on this practice section to 60 minutes. (Solving math problems on the CAT takes longer than solving similar problems on a pencil-and-paper exam.)

Practice Test

Time—75 Minutes (but see the second note above)

37 Questions

Directions for Problem Solving Questions

(These directions will appear on your screen before your first Problem Solving question.)

Solve this problem and indicate the best of the answer choices given.

Numbers: All numbers used are real numbers.

Figures: A figure accompanying a problem solving question is intended to provide information useful in solving the problem. Figures are drawn as accurately as possible EXCEPT when it is stated in a specific problem that its figure is not drawn to scale. Straight lines may sometimes appear jagged. All figures lie on a plane unless otherwise indicated.

To review these directions for subsequent questions of this type, click on HELP.

Directions for Data Sufficiency Questions

(These directions will appear on your screen before your first Data Sufficiency question.)

This data sufficiency problem consists of a question and two statements, labeled (1) and (2), in which certain data are given. You have to decide whether the data given in the statements are *sufficient* for answering the question. Using the data given in the statements *plus* your knowledge of mathematics and everyday facts (such as the number of days in July or the meaning of *counterclockwise*), you must indicate whether:

(A) statement (1) ALONE is sufficient, but statement (2) alone is not sufficient to answer the question asked;
(B) statement (2) ALONE is sufficient, but statement (1) alone is not sufficient to answer the question asked;
(C) BOTH statements (1) and (2) TOGETHER are sufficient to answer the question asked; but NEITHER statement ALONE is sufficient;
(D) EACH statement ALONE is sufficient to answer the question asked;
(E) statements (1) and (2) TOGETHER are NOT sufficient to answer the question asked, and additional data specific to the problem are needed.

Numbers: All numbers used are real numbers.

Figures: A figure accompanying a data sufficiency problem will conform to the information given in the question. but will not necessarily conform to the additional information in statements (1) and (2).

Lines shown as straight can be assumed to be straight and lines that appear jagged can also be assumed to be straight.

You may assume that positions of points, angles, regions, etc., exist in the order shown and that angle measures are greater than zero.

All figures lie in a plane unless otherwise indicated.

Note: In data sufficiency problems that ask you for the value of a quantity, the data given in the statements are sufficient only when it is possible to determine exactly one numerical value for the quantity.

To review these directions for subsequent questions of this type, click on HELP.

1. If $\frac{a}{b} \cdot \frac{b}{c} \cdot \frac{c}{d} \cdot \frac{d}{e} \cdot x = 1$, then $x =$

   (A) $\frac{a}{e}$

   (B) $\frac{e}{a}$

   (C) e

   (D) $\frac{1}{a}$

   (E) $\frac{be}{a}$

2. Among four women—*A, B, C* and *D*—three must be selected randomly to serve on a certain committee. Two of three men—*X, Y* and *Z*—must be selected randomly to serve on the same committee. What is the probability that neither *A* nor *X* will be selected for the committee?

   (A) $\frac{1}{18}$

   (B) $\frac{1}{12}$

   (C) $\frac{1}{6}$

   (D) $\frac{1}{5}$

   (E) $\frac{2}{9}$

3. Who takes less time to drive to work, Maria or Lupe?

   (1) Maria drives to work in 20 minutes.

   (2) Lupe and Maria drive the same distance to work.

4. How many buses are required to transport 175 students to the museum?

   (1) No two buses have the same carrying capacity.

   (2) The average capacity of a bus is 55 students.

5. What is the minimum value of $|a + b|$?

   (1) $|a| = 3$

   (2) $|a - b| = 1$

6. If $x < 0$, what is the value of x?

   (1) $x^2 - x - 6 = 0$

   (2) $(x - 3)(x + 2) = 0$

7. If *J* is a set of six integers, what is the median of *J*?

   (1) The difference between the smallest and largest integers in set *J* is 40.

   (2) The arithmetic mean (average) of the six integers in set *J* is 15.

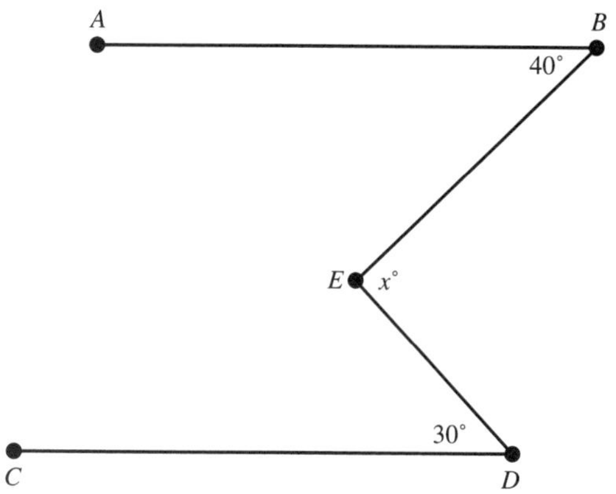

(*Note:* Figure not drawn to scale.)

8. In the diagram above, if *AB* is parallel to *CD*, what is the value of *x*?
   (A) 40
   (B) 50
   (C) 60
   (D) 70
   (E) 80

9. Kirk sent $54 to the newspaper dealer for whom he delivers papers, after deducting a 10% commission. How many papers did he deliver if papers sell for 40 cents each?
   (A) 135
   (B) 150
   (C) 160
   (D) 540
   (E) 600

10. Lyle is 23 years old and Melanie is 15 years old. If Lyle and Melanie were both born on July 15, how many years ago was Lyle twice as old as Melanie?
   (A) 5
   (B) 7
   (C) 8
   (D) 9
   (E) 16

11. If $x + y = a$, and if $x - y = b$, then $x =$
   (A) $a + b$
   (B) $a - b$
   (C) $\frac{1}{2}(a + b)$
   (D) $\frac{1}{2}ab$
   (E) $\frac{1}{2}(a - b)$

12. A county animal shelter houses two different types of animals—dogs and cats. If *d* represents the number of dogs, and if *c* represents the number of cats, which of the following expresses the portion of animals at the shelter that are dogs?
   (A) $d + \frac{c}{d}$
   (B) $\frac{d + c}{c}$
   (C) $\frac{d}{c}$
   (D) $\frac{c}{d}$
   (E) $\frac{d}{d + c}$

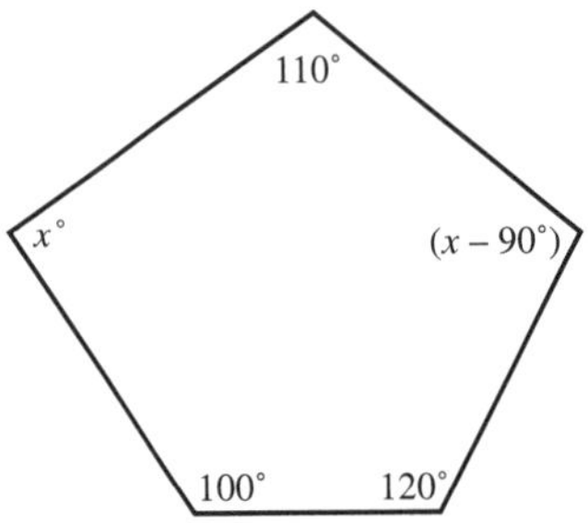

(*Note:* Figure not drawn to scale.)

13. In the figure above, what is the value of x?
    (A) 100
    (B) 110
    (C) 125
    (D) 135
    (E) 150

HARVESTED CROP REVENUES (YEAR X)
(percent of total revenue among four counties)

	non-subsidized farms	subsidized farms
Willot County	7%	
Tilson County		12%
Stanton County		
Osher County	8%	
(Total Percentages)	30%	

14. Based on the table above, if the total harvested crop revenues for Willot and Tilson counties combined equaled those for Stanton and Osher counties combined, then Stanton County's subsidized farm revenues accounted for what percentage of the total harvested crop revenues for all four counties?
    (1) During year *X*, Osher County's total harvested crop revenues totaled twice those of Tilson county.
    (2) During year *X*, Tilson County's farms contributed 18% of all harvested crop revenues for the four counties.

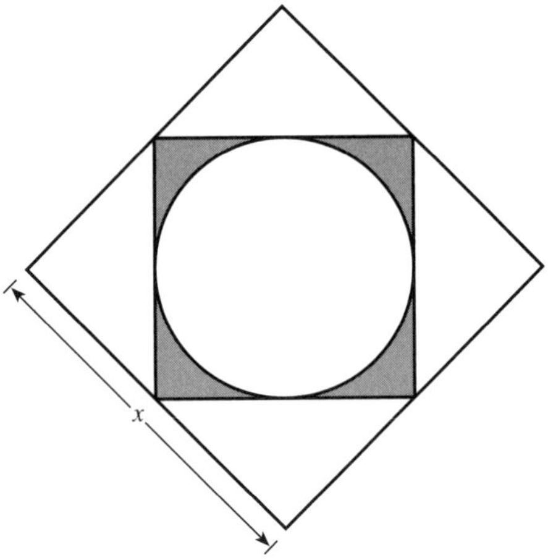

15. In terms of x, what is the area of the shaded region in the figure above, which includes one circle and two squares?
    (A) $\frac{\pi x}{2} - 4$
    (B) $x^2 - 2\pi$
    (C) $\frac{x(2 - \pi x)}{4}$
    (D) $\frac{7x^2}{4}$
    (E) $\frac{x^2(4 - \pi)}{8}$

16. If $a^m = b^n$, what is the value of $a + b + m + n$?

    (1) a, b, m, and n are all non-negative integers less than 10.

    (2) $b^n = 81$

17. M college students agree to rent an apartment for D dollars per month, sharing the rent equally. If the rent is increased by \$100, what amount must each student contribute?

    (A) $\frac{D}{M}$

    (B) $\frac{D}{M} + 100$

    (C) $\frac{D + 100}{M}$

    (D) $\frac{M}{D} + 100$

    (E) $\frac{M + 100}{D}$

18. If n is a positive even integer, and if $n \div 3$ results in a quotient with a remainder of 1, which of the following expressions is NOT divisible by 3?

    (A) $n - 1$
    (B) $n + 5$
    (C) $n + 2$
    (D) $n \cdot 2$
    (E) $n \cdot 3$

19. $\sqrt{\frac{a^2}{b^2} + \frac{a^2}{b^2}} =$

    (A) $\frac{a^2}{b^2}$

    (B) $\frac{2a^2}{2b}$

    (C) $\frac{a^4}{b^4}$

    (D) $\frac{a}{b}\sqrt{\frac{a}{b}}$

    (E) $\frac{a}{b}\sqrt{2}$

20. If $0 < x < 1$, which of the following expressions is smallest in value?

    (A) $\sqrt{x}$

    (B) $\sqrt{\frac{1}{x}}$

    (C) $\sqrt[3]{x^2}$

    (D) x^4

    (E) $\frac{1}{x^2}$

21. A certain purse contains 30 coins; each coin is either a nickel or a quarter. If the total value of all coins in the purse is \$4.70, how many nickels does the purse contain?

    (A) 12
    (B) 14
    (C) 16
    (D) 20
    (E) 22

22. A 30-ounce pitcher is currently filled to exactly half its capacity with a lemonade mixture consisting of equal amounts of two lemonade brands—A and B. If the pitcher is then filled to capacity to conform to a certain recipe, how many ounces of each lemonade brand does the full pitcher contain?

    (1) The recipe calls for a mixture that includes 60 percent brand A.

    (2) When filled to capacity, the pitcher contains 12 ounces of brand B.

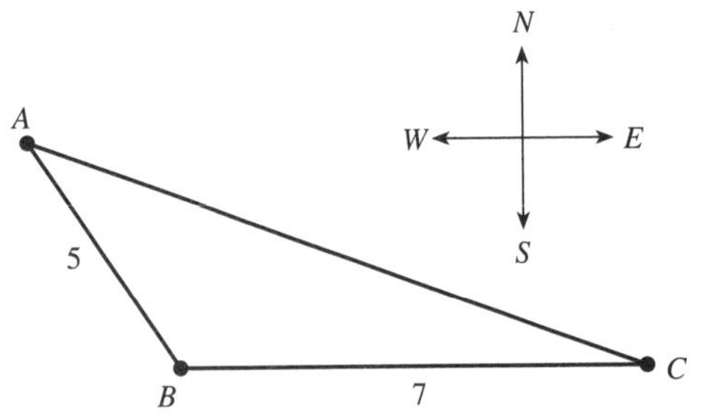

23. Once a month, a crop duster sprays a triangular area defined by three farm houses—*A*, *B*, and *C*—as indicated in the figure above. Farmhouse *B* lies due west of farmhouse *C*. Given the compass directions and distances (in miles) indicated in the figure, what is the total area that the crop duster sprays?

    (1) Farmhouse *C* is located 4 miles further south than farmhouse *A*.

    (2) Farmhouse *C* is located 10 miles further east than farmhouse *A*.

24. Daniel, Carl, and Todd working together can load a moving van in 8 hours. How long would it take Daniel working alone to load the van?

    (1) Working alone, Carl can load the van in 15 hours.

    (2) Carl and Todd working together can load the van in 12 hours.

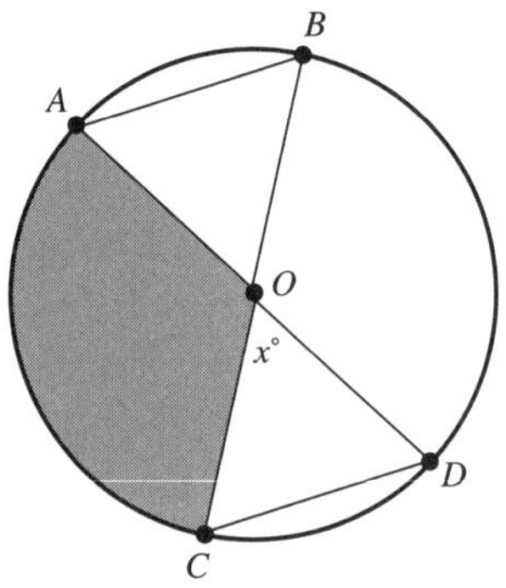

25. In the figure above, is the area of the shaded region less than the combined area of the two triangles?

    (1) $x = 60$

    (2) The length of *AB* equals the circle's radius.

26. If *A* and *B* denote the digits of a three-digit number *BAB*, is *BAB* divisible by 4?

    (1) The product of *A* and *B* is divisible by 4.

    (2) The sum of *B*, *A*, and *B* is divisible by 4.

27. $\frac{7^{77} - 7^{76}}{6} =$

(A) 7
(B) $7^{77/76}$
(C) 49
(D) 7^{75}
(E) 7^{76}

Questions 28 and 29 refer to the following figure.

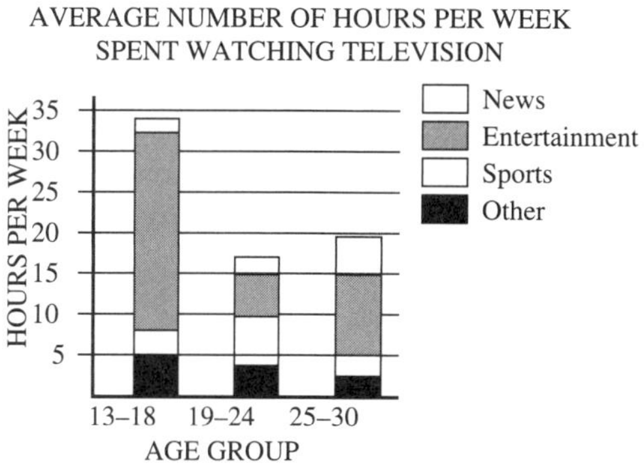

28. According to the graph, the two age groups other than the group that spent the greatest number of hours per week watching sports on television accounted for approximately what percent of the total hours spent watching television among all three age groups?

(A) 27
(B) 36
(C) 55
(D) 75
(E) 80

29. Which of the following is the approximate ratio of the average number of hours per week that the youngest age group spent watching entertainment on television to the average number of hours that the other two groups combined spent watching the same type of programming?

(A) 3:4
(B) 1:1
(C) 4:3
(D) 5:3
(E) 3:2

30. If a portion of \$10,000 is invested at 6% and the remaining portion is invested at 5%, and if x represents the amount invested at 6%, what is the annual income in dollars from the 5% investment?

(A) $5(x - 10{,}000)$
(B) $.05(x + 10{,}000)$
(C) $.05(10{,}000 - x)$
(D) $5(10{,}000 - x)$
(E) $.05(x - 10{,}000)$

31. The denominator of a fraction is twice as large as the numerator. If 4 is added to both the numerator and denominator, the value of the fraction is $\frac{5}{8}$. The denominator of the original fraction is

(A) 6
(B) 10
(C) 12
(D) 14
(E) 16

23

32. What is the maximum number of rectangular boxes, each measuring 2" by 3" by 5", that can be packed into a rectangular packing box measuring 18" by 19" by 35", if all of the smaller boxes are aligned in the same direction?

    (A) 296
    (B) 356
    (C) 378
    (D) 412
    (E) 424

33. If $<u> = u^2 - u$, what is the value of $<\frac{2}{3}> + <-\frac{2}{3}>$?

    (A) $-\frac{2}{3}$
    (B) 0
    (C) $\frac{2}{3}$
    (D) $\frac{4}{9}$
    (E) $\frac{8}{9}$

34. Two buses are 515 miles apart. At 9:30 a.m., they start traveling toward each other at rates of 48 and 55 miles per hour. At what time will they pass each other?

    (A) 1:30 p.m.
    (B) 2:00 p.m.
    (C) 2:30 p.m.
    (D) 3:00 p.m.
    (E) 3:30 p.m.

35. In a boat race between David and Jeff, when Jeff had covered half the 30-mile race distance, David was two miles ahead of Jeff. How long did it take David to travel the entire 30-mile distance?

    (1) David traveled the last 15 miles of the race distance in 40 minutes.

    (2) Jeff traveled the first 15 miles of the race distance in 45 minutes.

36. On the *xy*-plane, two points defined by the (x,y) coordinate pairs $(-1,0)$ and $(3,3)$, respectively, are connected to form a chord of a circle that also lies on the plane. If the area of the circle is $\frac{25\pi}{4}$, what are the coordinates of the center of the circle?

    (A) $\left(\frac{1}{2},\frac{1}{2}\right)$
    (B) $\left(1,\frac{1}{2}\right)$
    (C) $(0,1)$
    (D) $\left(\frac{1}{2},1\right)$
    (E) $\left(-\frac{1}{2},\frac{1}{2}\right)$

37. An investor wants to sell some of the stock that he owns in MicroTron and Dynaco Corporations. He can sell MicroTron stock for $36 per share, and he can sell Dynaco stock for $52 per share. If he sells 300 shares altogether at an average price per share of $40, how many shares of Dynaco stock has he sold?

    (A) 52
    (B) 75
    (C) 92
    (D) 136
    (E) 184

Answer Key

1. B
2. B
3. E
4. E
5. C
6. D
7. E
8. D
9. B
10. B
11. C
12. E
13. E
14. C
15. E
16. C
17. C
18. D
19. E
20. D
21. B
22. D
23. D
24. B
25. D
26. E
27. E
28. D
29. D
30. C
31. C
32. C
33. E
34. C
35. E
36. B
37. B

Hour 24

Sample Test #2 (Verbal Ability)

This hour you'll complete your second sample GMAT CAT by taking a full-length Verbal Ability section, which includes a total of 41 questions. Here are your goals for this hour:

- Take the test under timed conditions
- Check the answer key on page 437
- Assess your performance by checking the score conversion chart on page 474
- Review the explanations (they begin on page 465)

NOTE

The difficulty level of questions here is evenly distributed across various levels. Keep in mind, though, that the GMAT CAT does not necessarily follow this pattern, but instead will determine the difficulty level of each question based on your responses to prior questions.

NOTE

Although the CAT allows you 75 minutes to respond to 41 Verbal questions, you should limit your time on this practice section to 60 minutes. (Working through a computer-based test takes longer than working through a paper-based exam.)

Practice Test

Time—75 Minutes (but see the second note above)

41 Questions

Directions for Sentence Correction Questions

(These directions will appear on your screen before your first Sentence Correction question.)

This question presents a sentence, all or part of which is underlined. Beneath the sentence you will find five ways of phrasing the underlined part. The first of these repeats the original; the other four are different. If you think the original is best, choose the first answer; otherwise choose one of the others.

This question tests correctness and effectiveness of expression. In choosing your answer, follow the requirements of standard written English; that is, pay attention to grammar, choice of words, and sentence construction. Choose the answer that produces the most effective sentence; this answer should be clear and exact, without awkwardness, ambiguity, redundancy, or grammatical error.

Directions for Critical Reasoning Questions

(These directions will appear on your screen before your first Critical Reasoning question.)

For this question, select the best of the answer choices given.

Directions for Reading Comprehension Questions

(These directions will appear on your screen before your first group of Reading Comprehension questions.)

The questions in this group are based on the content of a passage. After reading the passage, choose the best answer to each question. Answer all the questions following the passage on the basis of what is *stated* or *implied* in the passage.

1. Not only smoking cigarettes but also cigar smoking has been banned now from many public places.
   - (A) Not only smoking cigarettes but also cigar smoking has been banned now
   - (B) Cigarette smoking and cigar smoking are both banned now
   - (C) Not only has smoking cigarettes been banned but so has cigar smoking
   - (D) Both smoking cigarettes and cigar smoking is now banned
   - (E) Smoking cigarettes as well as cigars is now banned

2. *The Reluctant Monarch*, which Francis Craig wrote as her third in a series of books about the British Monarchy.
   - (A) *The Reluctant Monarch*, which Francis Craig wrote as her third
   - (B) *The Reluctant Monarch* is the third book written by Francis Craig
   - (C) Written by Francis Craig, *The Reluctant Monarch*, which is her third book
   - (D) Francis Craig wrote *The Reluctant Monarch*, which book is her third
   - (E) *The Reluctant Monarch*, written by Francis Craig, is her third

3. Some varieties of parrots live as long as the age of one hundred years.
   - (A) as long as the age of one hundred years
   - (B) as long as one hundred
   - (C) as long as one hundred years old
   - (D) as long as one hundred years
   - (E) to be one hundred years old in age

4. The earth-moon system, the satellites of Jupiter, and the moons of Saturn are all examples of planetary systems in which a satellite moves in the gravitational field of a much more massive body. In every one of these systems, the satellite moves in an elliptical orbit.

   If the statements above are true, they provide the most support for which one of the following?
   - (A) The more massive a body the more gravitational pull it exerts on another body.
   - (B) Only elliptical orbits can account for the various phases of the moon as seen from earth.
   - (C) Non-elliptical orbits violate the laws of celestial mechanics.
   - (D) The moons of the planet Uranus move in elliptical orbits.
   - (E) All celestial bodies move in elliptical orbits.

5. The nutrient value of animal products is indisputable. Complete protein—the kind with sufficient quantities of the eight amino acids—is found only in animal products. The human body cannot manufacture these eight amino acids, so they must be supplied through proper diet.

   Which of the following is the main point of the argument above?

   (A) Animal products are the main source of the eight amino acids that make up complete protein.
   (B) A proper diet must contain the eight amino acids.
   (C) Animal products must be included in a proper diet.
   (D) Amino acids cannot be manufactured by the human body.
   (E) Animal products are nutritious sources of food.

Questions 6–8 are based on the following passage.

Scientists in the post-1917 Soviet Union occupied an ambiguous position. While the government encouraged and generally supported scientific research, it simultaneously thwarted the scientific community's ideal: freedom from geographic and political boundaries. A strong nationalistic emphasis on science led at times to the dismissal of all non-Russian scientific work as irrelevant to Soviet science. A 1973 article in *Literatunaya Gazeta*, a Soviet publication, insisted: "World science is based upon national schools, so the weakening of one or another national school inevitably leads to stagnation in the development of world science." According to the Soviet regime, socialist science was to be consistent with, and in fact grow out of, the Marxism-Leninism political ideology. Toward this end, some scientific theories or fields, such as relativity and genetics, were abolished. Where scientific work conflicted with political criteria, the work was often disrupted. During the Stalinist purges of the 1930s, many Soviet scientists simply disappeared. In the 1970s, Soviet scientists who were part of the refusenik movement lost their jobs and were barred from access to scientific resources. Nazi Germany during the 1930s and, more recently, Argentina, imposed strikingly similar, though briefer, constraints on scientific research.

6. Which of the following best characterizes the "ambiguous position" (see the first sentence) in which Soviet scientists were placed during the decades that followed the Bolshevik Revolution?

   (A) The Soviet government demanded that their research result in scientific progress, although funding was insufficient to accomplish this goal.
   (B) They were exhorted to strive toward scientific advancements, while at the same time the freedoms necessary to make such advancements were restricted.
   (C) While required to direct their research entirely toward military defense, most advancements in this field were being made by non-Soviet scientists with whom the Soviet scientists were prohibited contact.

(D) They were encouraged to collaborate with Soviet colleagues but were prohibited from any discourse with scientists from other countries.
(E) The Soviet government failed to identify those areas of research that it deemed most worthwhile, but punished those scientists with whose work it was not satisfied.

7. The author quotes an article from *Literatunaya Gazeta* most probably to do which of the following?
   (A) illustrate the general sentiment among members of the international scientific community during the time period
   (B) underscore the point that the Soviet government sanctioned only those notions about science that conformed to the Marxist-Leninist ideal
   (C) show the disparity of views within the Soviet intellectual community regarding the proper role of science
   (D) underscore the Soviet emphasis on the notion of a national science
   (E) support the author's assertion that thc Marxist-Leninist impact on Soviet scientific freedom continued through the decade of the 1970s

8. What is the author's primary purpose in the passage?
   (A) examine the events leading up to the suppression of the Soviet refusenik movement of the 1970s
   (B) define and dispel the notion of a national science as promulgated by the post-revolution Soviet regime
   (C) describe specific attempts by the modern Soviet regime to suppress scientific freedom
   (D) examine the major 20th Century challenges to the normative assumption that science requires freedom and that it is inherently international
   (E) point out the similarities and distinctions between scientific freedom and scientific internationalism in the context of the Soviet Union

9. <u>If speaking too quickly, a court reporter can have trouble producing an accurate transcript based on that witness' testimony.</u>
   (A) If speaking too quickly, a court reporter can have trouble producing an accurate transcript based on that witness' testimony.
   (B) Should he or she speak too quickly, a court reporter can have trouble producing an accurate transcript based on a witness' testimony.
   (C) A court reporter can have trouble if a witness speaks too quickly during testimony, possibly producing an inaccurate transcript.
   (D) An accurate transcript based on a witness' testimony can, if speaking too quickly, produce trouble for a court reporter.
   (E) A court reporter can have trouble producing an accurate transcript based on the testimony of a witness who speaks too quickly.

10. Due to the fact that mean water temperatures in the oceans of the world have not changed significantly over the past century, it is evident that the expected rise in global air temperatures as a result of ozone depletion has not yet begun.

    Which of the following, if true, most substantially weakens the above argument?

    (A) Ocean surface water temperatures fluctuate by as much as 20 degrees yearly.
    (B) Air to water heat transfer is such that a rise of 10 degrees in air temperature will cause a rise of 1 degree of water temperature over a 24 hour period.
    (C) Global ocean water temperatures are controlled mainly by polar ice.
    (D) Global air temperatures have not varied significantly over the past decade.
    (E) The rate of ozone depletion has been shown to be significantly less than as was first reported by scientists.

11. It is commonly held in discussions of capital punishment that there is no evidence that the death penalty deters. This is simply untrue. We have an enormous amount of both informal and formal evidence—from everyday experience and from such "experiments" as increasing the fees for parking violations—that, as a general rule, the greater the punishment, the fewer people will behave in the punished way. Thus, it is perfectly reasonable to expect that the death penalty would have a more dissuasive effect than would life imprisonment.

    Which of the following must be assumed for the above argument to be logically correct?

    (A) Everyday experience shows that the death penalty deters.
    (B) Life imprisonment does not act as a deterrent to murder.
    (C) The death penalty is a greater punishment than life imprisonment.
    (D) Potential murderers consciously weigh the alternatives beforehand and decide that the crime is worth life in prison, but not death.
    (E) The more severe the punishment, the more it acts as a deterrent.

12. Ignorance of the law does not preclude <u>one being arrested for violating it</u>.

    (A) one being arrested for violating it
    (B) arrest for one's violation of it
    (C) one's violation and arrest for it
    (D) one from being arrested for violating that law
    (E) one from an arrest for having violated the law

13. <u>Rationalizing the protracted and bloody war</u> with the Philippines, President McKinley described the process of subjugating the Filipinos as "benign assimilation."

    (A) Rationalizing the protracted and bloody war
    (B) To rationalize the protracted war and bloody war
    (C) The protracted and bloody war was rationalized
    (D) Rationalizing the war, which was protracted as well as bloody
    (E) To rationalize the war, a protracted and bloody one

14. Cambodia remains being a largely underdeveloped country because virtually all educated citizens were slaughtered during the regime of Pon Pen.

    (A) remains being
    (B) is still remaining
    (C) is being
    (D) remains
    (E) remains still

Questions 15–17 are based on the following passage.

A free radical is a highly reactive molecule that contains at least one unpaired electron in its outer orbital shell. Once it is "free" in living tissues, the unbalanced molecule causes cellular damage until it is "neutralized" by a scavenging antioxidant enzyme. Free radicals are extremely detrimental to cellular quality and length of cellular life. When a cell membrane is damaged by a free radical, the cell loses the capacity to transport nutrients, oxygen, water, or waste matter. As a result, cell membranes may rupture, spilling their contents into surrounding tissues, and thereby damage surrounding cells. The worst of these destructive reactions occur in the chromosomes and nucleic acids of the cell. The resulting damage causes changes in the cell replication rate and is the major cause of cancer cell mutations. Moreover, the origin of most cardiovascular disease is closely tied to unrestrained free radical damage to the cell membranes lining the blood vessels. Free radicals are also the implicated "villains" in the cholesterol plaque accumulations that have been linked to the causes of cardiovascular heart disease, advances in the rate of aging, adult onset diabetes, atherosclerosis, and coronary artery disease.

15. It can be inferred from lines 9–15 that cell membranes may rupture as a result of free radical damage because

    (A) the cell membrane is punctured by the free radical
    (B) the contents of the cell exceed the capacity of the cell membrane
    (C) the free radical displaces the contents of the cell
    (D) the cell membrane is dissolved by the free radical
    (E) the cell membrane is torn by the free radical

16. Which of the following best expresses the passage's main idea?

    (A) Free radicals are the major cause of disease.
    (B) Free radicals are the major cause of cell damage.
    (C) Free radicals can be neutralized by antioxidant enzymes.
    (D) Unrestrained free radicals can cause cell damage.
    (E) Free radicals are harmful to cells in living tissue.

17. The author mentions the reactions that occur in the chromosomes and nucleic acids of the cell as a result of free radical damage in order to
    (A) show that unrestrained free radical damage to cells is the origin of most cardiovascular disease
    (B) show how free radical damage to cells causes adult onset diabetes
    (C) show how antioxidant enzymes neutralize free radicals
    (D) describe in detail the damage free radicals cause in the cell membranes that line the blood vessels
    (E) show how damage to cells by free radicals is linked to cancer cell mutations

18. Historians universally agree that all democracies in the past have eventually perished as a result of disputes between competing groups of special interests, coupled with gross inefficiency, waste and corruption in government, and a decline in the moral values of the society at large. Everyday the news reports confirm that all of these maladies are currently present in the United States of America.

    Given that the statements above are true, which of the following conclusions is most strongly supported?
    (A) Communism is a better form of government than democracy.
    (B) Non-democratic societies do not suffer from the same problems as democratic societies.
    (C) If the experience of past democracies is a reliable indicator, democracy in the United States is in decline.
    (D) News reports generally focus only on negative news.
    (E) In the future, the United States will be a dictatorship.

19. Flagrant violations of human rights were cited by the Astonian government as the official reason for ceasing to provide military support to the embattled country of Cretia. But, at the same time, military support continues to be provided to countries with far worse human-rights records than Cretia. Hence, despite the official explanation for this change in policy, this reversal cannot be accounted for solely by the Astonian government's commitment to human rights.

    Which of the following, if true, would most strengthen the conclusion in the above argument?
    (A) Cretia's neighboring countries recently entered into a non-aggression pact with one another.
    (B) Astonia recently entered into long-range trade agreements with Cretia's neighboring countries.
    (C) The newly elected head of the Cretian government is an avowed anti-Astonian.
    (D) Cretia has a longer record of human-rights abuse than other countries to which military support is provided by Astonia.
    (E) The Astonian government's decision to provide military support to a country is made mainly on the basis of the country's capability of defending itself from outside aggression.

20. A study of six patients who all suffer from a rare form of cancer revealed that though they all live in different locations in the county and have quite different medical histories, diet, and personal habits—two smoke cigarettes and three drink alcoholic beverages—they are all employed at a company that manufactures herbicides and pesticides. From this study, it can be concluded that exposure to the chemicals produced by the company is the probable cause of the disease.

The argument proceeds by:

(A) reaching a general conclusion on the basis of insufficient evidence
(B) isolating a common feature through a process of elimination and concluding that this feature is causally related to the event under investigation
(C) reaching a general conclusion on the basis of the experiences of the six patients
(D) providing information that allows the application of a general claim to a specific case
(E) indirectly showing that exposure to the chemicals produced by the company is the likely cause by demonstrating that none of the other alternatives is the cause

21. The average annual salary for executives at World-Wide Travel last year was \$55,000, while the average salary for travel consultants was \$47,000. The average annual salary for all employees was \$38,000.

If the above information is correct, which one of the following conclusions can be properly inferred from it?

(A) There were fewer executives than travel consultants at World-Wide Travel last year.
(B) No travel consultants earned more than an executive last year.
(C) There was at least one employee who earned less than the average for a travel consultant.
(D) Some travel consultants earn more than the lowest paid executives.
(E) All executives earn more than travel consultants.

22. <u>Upon man-made toxins' invading the human body, special enzymes are deployed, rebuilding any damaged DNA strands that result.</u>

(A) Upon man-made toxins invading the human body, special enzymes are deployed, rebuilding any damaged DNA strands that result.
(B) Upon man-made toxins, invasion of the human body, special enzymes are deployed that rebuild any damaged DNA strands resulting from the invasion.
(C) When man-made toxins invade the human body, special enzymes are deployed to rebuild any DNA strands damaged as a result.
(D) Special enzymes are deployed whenever man-made toxins invade the human body; they rebuild any damage that results to DNA strands.
(E) Damage to DNA strands that results when man-made toxins invade the human body are repaired by deployed special enzymes.

23. The fact that the tie between the Manchus and the Chinese was cultural rather than racial helps to account for the homogeneity of the Chinese people.
    (A) cultural rather than racial helps to account for
    (B) not racial but cultural in nature helps explain
    (C) a cultural tie but not racial helps explain
    (D) cultural rather than a racial one helps to explain
    (E) cultural rather than a racial tie helps to account for

24. The atmospheric study reported last month in the *Journal of the Environment* would not have been taken seriously by the scientific community if they were cognizant of the questionable methodology employed.
    (A) have been taken seriously by the scientific community if they were
    (B) be taken seriously by the scientific community in the event that it had become
    (C) have been taken seriously by the scientific community were they
    (D) have been taken seriously by the scientific community when the scientific community became
    (E) have been taken seriously by the scientific community had scientists been

25. Seventeenth-century scientists argued that a void must exist in nature on the grounds that if there were no void, that is if all space were filled with matter, movement would be impossible. Movement would be impossible, they reasoned, because a body could not move unless it displaced another body. But to do this would require that the space occupied by the other body is empty, which it clearly is not because the other occupies it, thus movement is impossible.

    Which of the following, if true, provides the most support for the scientists' conclusion?
    (A) Instantaneous spatial displacement of one body by another is possible.
    (B) Instantaneous spatial displacement of one body by another is impossible.
    (C) Sequential spatial displacement entails that to move one body, all other bodies would have to be moved.
    (D) Sequential spatial displacement of one body by another is possible.
    (E) Sequential spatial displacement of one body by another is impossible.

26. Given that the stated goal of environmentalists is to reduce the amount of carbon dioxide in the atmosphere while at the same time preserving existing plant life on earth, there are two very good reasons for harvesting living trees from old-growth forests. First, doing so would reduce the amount of carbon dioxide in the atmosphere for the simple reason that when old trees die they decompose, thereby releasing their stored carbon dioxide. Second, it would make room for more young trees that absorb carbon dioxide thereby further reducing the amount of carbon dioxide in the atmosphere.

Which one of the following, if true, most seriously weakens the above argument?

(A) Levels of carbon dioxide in the atmosphere have remained relatively constant over the past 100 years.
(B) Reduction in the amount of carbon dioxide in the atmosphere is necessary to reduce the "greenhouse effect."
(C) The amount of carbon dioxide released into the atmosphere through the decomposition of old trees is insignificantly small when compared to the amount released by agricultural waste.
(D) Old-growth forests are the habitat of many species that will not survive if these forests are destroyed.
(E) A reduction in the amount of carbon dioxide in the atmosphere is detrimental to plant life.

27. Too many naive consumers hasty and happily provide credit information to unscrupulous merchants, who provide nothing in exchange but a credit fraud nightmare.

(A) hasty and happily provide
(B) hastily and happily provide
(C) hasty and happy providing
(D) hastily and happily providing
(E) providing hastily and happily

Questions 28–30 are based on the following passage.

The 35-millimeter (mm) format for movie production became a de facto standard around 1913. The mid-1920s through the mid-1930s, however, saw a resurgence of wide-film formats. During this time period, formats used by studios ranged in gauge from 55mm to 70mm. Research and development then slackened until the 1950s, when wide-screen film-making came back in direct response to the erosion of box-office receipts because of the rising popularity of television. This is Cinerama (1952) is generally considered to mark the beginning of the modern era of wide-screen film-making, which saw another flurry of specialized formats, such as Cinemascope. In 1956, Panavision developed Camera 65 for MGM Studios; it was first used during the filming of *Raintree County.* Panavision soon contributed another key technical advance by developing spherical 65mm lenses, which eliminated the "fat faces" syndrome that had plagued earlier CinemaScope films.

Some 40 "roadshow" films were filmed in wide-screen formats during this period. But wide-screen formats floundered due to expense, unwieldy cameras, and slow film stocks and lenses. After the invention of a set of 35mm anamorphic lenses which could be used in conjunction with much more mobile cameras to squeeze a wide-screen image onto theatrical screens, film technology improved to the point where quality 70mm prints could be blown up from 35mm negatives.

28. It can be inferred from the information in the passage that wide-film formats were
    (A) in use before 1913
    (B) not used during the 1940s
    (C) more widely used during the 1920s than during the 1930s
    (D) not used after 1956
    (E) more widely used for some types of movies than for others

29. The passage mentions all the following as factors contributing to the increased use of wide-film formats for moviemaking EXCEPT:
    (A) spherical camera lenses
    (B) Panavision's Camera 65
    (C) television
    (D) anamorphic camera lenses
    (E) movie theater revenues

30. Which of the following statements is most strongly supported by the passage's information?
    (A) If a movie does not suffer from the "fat faces" syndrome, then it was not produced in a wide-film format.
    (B) Prior to the invention of the 35mm anamorphic lens, quality larger prints could not be made from smaller negatives.
    (C) The same factors that contributed to the resurgence of wide-film formats in the 1950s also led to the subsequent decline in their use.
    (D) The most significant developments in 35mm technology occurred after the release of *Raintree County.*
    (E) Movie-theater revenues are not significantly affected by whether the movies shown are in wide-screen format.

31. Analytic propositions provide no information about any matter of fact. This applies to all analytic propositions. In other words, they are entirely devoid of information about the world. It is for this reason that no empirical evidence can refute them.

    Which of the following must be assumed for the above argument's conclusion to be properly drawn?
    (A) The truth or falsity of analytic propositions cannot be determined by empirical evidence.
    (B) Analytic propositions are neither true nor false.
    (C) Analytic propositions are completely uninformative.
    (D) Empirical evidence can only refute propositions that provide information about matters of fact.
    (E) Propositions that are entirely devoid of information about the world are false.

32. An auto mechanic who is too thorough in checking a car is likely to subject the customer to unnecessary expense. On the other hand, one who is not thorough enough is likely to miss some problem that could cause a serious accident. Therefore, it's a good idea not to have your car checked until a recognizable problem develops.

Which of the following, if true, provides the most support for the above argument?

(A) The more complete the mechanical checkup, the more likely a problem, if present, will be discovered.
(B) Some people have enough mechanical knowledge to recognize a problem with their car.
(C) Not all tests performed by mechanics are time consuming and expensive.
(D) Most mechanical problems that are potentially dangerous or expensive to repair cannot be detected by routine checkups no matter how thorough they are.
(E) Many auto mechanics lie to customers about the mechanical condition of their cars.

33. Due to racial discrimination, some of the most gifted and influential jazz musicians were prohibited from dining at the venues they have performed in.

(A) at the venues they have performed in
(B) at the very same venues they have performed in
(C) where they have performed
(D) at the same venues at which they performed
(E) in venues, which were where they performed

34. In asserting that a thing is honorable, a favorable distinction is bestowed upon it.

(A) a favorable distinction is bestowed upon it
(B) we bestow a distinction upon it favorably
(C) we bestow upon it a favorable distinction
(D) a favorable distinction upon it is bestowed
(E) bestowing a favorable distinction upon it

35. Twin-engine aircraft make up the vast majority of airplane accidents—well over ninety percent.

(A) Twin-engine aircraft make up the vast majority of airplane accidents—well over ninety percent.
(B) Accidents involving twin-engine aircraft make up the vast majority—well over ninety percent—of airplane accidents.
(C) Twin-engine aircraft, which make up the vast majority of airplane accidents—well over ninety percent.
(D) The vast majority of airplane accidents—well over ninety percent—are twin-engine aircraft ones.
(E) Well over ninety percent—the vast majority—of airplane accidents are comprised of twin-engine aircraft accidents.

36. People who do not control their cholesterol levels are more likely to have heart disease than those who do. However, even among those who don't control their cholesterol levels, the majority do not have heart disease. Therefore, to avoid heart disease, there is no need to adopt a diet that is low in cholesterol rather than one that is high in cholesterol.

The pattern of flawed reasoning displayed in the above argument most closely resembles the reasoning in which one of the following?

(A) People who swim every day are more likely to develop ear infections than those who jog. However, daily joggers are more likely to develop foot problems than swimmers. Hence, people who want to avoid foot problems and ear infections shouldn't jog or swim on a daily basis.

(B) There is no need to abstain from smoking in order to decrease the likelihood of contracting lung disease because even though smokers are more likely to die of lung disease than non-smokers, most smokers do not die of lung disease.

(C) Overweight people are more likely to die at a young age than persons who are physically fit. However, a surprisingly large number of young, physically fit people die in sports-related accidents each year. Hence, to avoid an early death, it is probably best to be neither overweight nor physically fit.

(D) Crimes of passion are more likely to be committed by young people than by old people. Yet many old people are capable of extremely strong emotional outbursts. Hence, middle-aged people are less likely to commit crimes of passion than either young people or old people.

(E) People who exercise daily are more likely to live longer than people who do not exercise. But "daily exercise" means at least 20 minutes of strenuous aerobic exercise, not just walking around the block or bicycling to the store. For this reason, unless you're willing to really work up a sweat every day, there is little reason to exercise daily.

Questions 37–39 are based on the following passage.

The tension between freedom as the power to participate in public affairs and freedom as a collection of individual rights requiring protection against governmental interference helps define the difference between two political languages that flourished in the Anglo-American world during the eighteenth-century. One, termed by scholars republicanism, celebrated active participation in public life as the essence of liberty. Tracing its lineage back to Renaissance Florence and beyond that to the ancient world, republicanism held that as a social being, man reached his highest fulfillment in setting aside self-interest to pursue the common good. Republican freedom could be expansive and democratic, as when it spoke of the common rights of the entire community. It also had an exclusive, class-based dimension, in its assumption that only property-owning citizens possessed the quality known as "virtue"—understood in the eighteenth century not simply as a personal, moral quality, but as a willingness to subordinate private passions and desires to the public good. "Only a virtuous people are capable of freedom," wrote Benjamin Franklin.

If republican liberty was a civic and social quality, the freedom celebrated by eighteenth-century liberalism was essentially individual and private. According to John Locke, the founding father of eighteenth-century liberalism, government is established to offer security to the "life, liberties, and estates" that are the natural rights of all mankind, and essentially should be limited to this task. For Locke and his eighteenth-century disciples, liberty meant not civic involvement, but personal autonomy—"not to be subject to the inconstant, uncertain, unknown Arbitrary Will of another Man." Protecting freedom required shielding a realm of private life and personal concerns—including family relations, religious preferences, and economic activity—from interference by the state.

37. According to the passage, each of the following is true of eighteenth-century liberalism EXCEPT:

(A) It was a political language.
(B) It defined liberty as a personal, moral quality.
(C) It defined freedom in terms of personal autonomy.
(D) It was founded by John Locke.
(E) It viewed the role of government as limited to protecting the rights of individuals.

38. Which of the following best expresses the passage's main idea?

(A) The defining difference between eighteenth-century liberalism and republicanism is to be found in their views of the proper function of government.
(B) The difference between eighteenth-century liberalism and republicanism is that liberalism can be traced back to the writings of John Locke whereas republicanism can be traced back to the writings of Benjamin Franklin.
(C) The main difference between eighteenth-century liberalism and republicanism is to be found in their definitions of "virtue."
(D) In comparison to eighteenth-century liberalism, eighteenth-century republicanism was concerned with the common good, whereas liberalism was concerned only with the welfare of the individual.
(E) One of the primary differences between eighteenth-century liberalism and republicanism is to be found in their views of the nature of liberty.

39. It can be inferred from the passage that Benjamin Franklin maintained that
    (A) only property-owning citizens are capable of freedom
    (B) only people who pursue the common good are capable of freedom
    (C) only people who are passionate are capable of freedom
    (D) only people who are willing to subordinate themselves to the will of others are capable of freedom
    (E) only eighteenth-century republicans are capable of freedom

40. *Democratic Senator:* The fact that the Republicans have not articulated one good reason in support of their opposition to cuts in social security payments to the elderly shows that they are obviously in favor of them.

    Which of the following best describes the flaw in the senator's reasoning?
    (A) arguing that there are only two possible alternatives to choose from, and since one can be eliminated the other must be true
    (B) arguing that a claim is true because of the lack of evidence that it is false
    (C) arguing that what is true of some members of a group must also be true of all members of the group
    (D) inferring a conclusion from unrepresentative or biased data
    (E) drawing a general conclusion from too small a sample of cases

41. The ancient Greek states boasted that <u>within their domains word and speech were free</u>.
    (A) within their domains word and speech were free
    (B) within its domain word and speech were free
    (C) word and speech were within their domains free
    (D) within their domains both word as well as speech were free
    (E) free word and speech were within their domains

Answer Key

1. B
2. E
3. D
4. D
5. C
6. B
7. D
8. C
9. E
10. C
11. C
12. D
13. A
14. D
15. B
16. E
17. E
18. C
19. E
20. B
21. C
22. C
23. A
24. E
25. B
26. E
27. B
28. A
29. D
30. B
31. D
32. D
33. D
34. C
35. B
36. B
37. B
38. E
39. A
40. B
41. A

Appendix A

Explanatory Answers

Sample Test 1

Analytical Writing Assessment (Hour 19)

Sample Response—Analysis-of-an-Issue

I agree with the statement insofar as both public and private bureaucracies can do more to respond to needs of citizens and consumers. However, the statement unfairly implies that a private business owes as high a duty to its customers as the government owes to its citizens.

First, consider that our government has an inherent duty to serve its citizenry. Yet the government today, chiefly through excessive regulation, often falls short of fulfilling this duty. Our tax system is perhaps the archetypal case. The tax code is beyond understanding to individual taxpayers, and new rules ostensibly designed to simplify matters more often than not create more confusion, even for CPAs and tax attorneys. Recent Congressional probes into IRS audit practices underscore the insensitivity to those whose interests the IRS ultimately serves.

In contrast, private businesses—large and small alike—owe no special obligations to their customers, other than the obligations already imposed by federal regulations and by the laws of torts and contracts. Instead, private corporations must serve their owners' interests—that is, corporations must strive to maximize profits. Moreover, shareholders' interests are not necessarily adverse to those of the customers. By maximizing profits, businesses employ more people, stimulate the economy, and enhance healthy competition—all of which benefit consumers in the long run. Besides, serving customers well gains a company the kind of good reputation that earns repeat business.

Admittedly, examples of insensitivity to customer needs abound today. Delivery systems for legal services reflect a far greater concern by the deliverers for accumulating billable hours than for providing efficient service at a reasonable cost to clients. HMOs force members to either drive great distances to consult preferred providers or settle for substandard care. Insurance carriers often reject claims and coverage in bad faith, and, lacking financial resources to enforce their rights, the customers have little practical recourse. Yet these examples don't prove that big business should do more to satisfy its customers. In time, competition will force unresponsive businesses to change their practices in order to survive.

In sum, examples of insensitivity to the needs of the citizen-consumer abound in both the private and public sectors. But unlike government, big business should improve its responsiveness to customers only to the extent that doing so enhances its own profits.

Sample Response—Analysis-of-an-Argument

On the basis of a two-hour survey conducted at a central location at Grant University, the author concludes that university students in general are apathetic about an upcoming national election. This argument is flawed in two important respects.

To begin with, even though the students questioned for the survey were selected at random, the survey will include only those students who were in one area of the campus at one particular time. For example, students who are in class, or take night classes, or whose classes are located in other parts of the campus, or, for whatever reason, are unlikely to be at the Student Union building during this two-hour period will not be represented in the sample. Common sense tells us that these non-represented students make up a sizable portion of the student body, and for this reason we can conclude that the argument contains a serious sampling error.

Secondly, unless it is assumed that Grant University is representative of all universities in its student makeup, the survey affords scant evidence of university students' attitudes in general toward the upcoming election. For example, if Grant is a rural university composed primarily of undergraduates between the ages of 18 and 22, or a polytechnic university composed of students majoring in engineering, computer science, and other highly technical disciplines, it is somewhat likely that such students will have little interest in politics or national issues. In other words, differences in the average age, or the economic, social, or cultural backgrounds of students could bring about radically different results in the survey.

In the final analysis, the survey provides little evidence of general university student apathy toward the upcoming election. To strengthen the argument, the author would have to show that the students surveyed were representative of the student body at Grant as a whole and that Grant University was representative of universities across the nation.

Quantitative Ability (Hour 20)

1. **(E)** Convert all expressions to decimal form:

(A) $\frac{3}{5} = .6$

(B) $\frac{2/3}{11/19} = \frac{2}{3} \cdot \frac{9}{11} = \frac{2}{1} \cdot \frac{3}{11} = \frac{6}{11} \approx .55$

(C) $\sqrt{.25} = .5$

(D) $.81^2 = (.81)(.81) = .65^+$

(E) $\frac{.2}{.3} = .66^+$

2. **(B)** To solve this problem, set up three equations:

$$A + B = 40$$
$$B + C = 34$$
$$A + C = 42$$

To solve for B, you can first subtract the second equation from the third equation:

$$\begin{array}{r} A + C = 42 \\ \underline{B + C = 34} \\ A - B = 8 \end{array}$$

Then subtract this resulting equation from the first equation:

$$\begin{array}{r} A + B = 40 \\ \underline{A - B = 8} \\ 2B = 32 \text{ (or } B = 16) \end{array}$$

3. **(C)** Neither (1) nor (2) alone provides any information about the second variable or, in turn, about the value of $x + y - 1$. Thus (A), (B), and (D) can easily be eliminated. Next, consider (1) and (2) together. Given a remainder of 2 when x is divided by 3, the value of x must be greater than a multiple of 3 by exactly 2: $x = \{5,8,11,14,\ldots\}$. Given a remainder of 5 when y is divided by 6, the value of y must be greater than a multiple of 6 by exactly 5: $y = \{11,17,23,29,\ldots\}$. Adding together any x-value and any y-value will always result in a sum which exceeds a multiple of 3 by exactly 7 (or by exactly 1). Accordingly, subtracting 1 from that sum will always result in a multiple of 3. Thus, given (1) and (2), $x + y - 1$ is divisible by 3.

4. **(D)** Statement (1) alone suffices to answer the question. Given $AC < BD$, AB (which is smaller than AC) must be smaller than BD. $BD > AB$, and the answer to the question is no. Statement (2) also suffices alone to answer the question. Given $\frac{AD}{2} = CD$, C bisects AD, and $AC = CD$. Thus, AB (which is smaller than AC) must be smaller than CD. Because CD is smaller than BD, $AB < BD$, and the answer to the question is no.

5. **(C)** Neither statement (1) nor (2) suffices alone to determine the values of both x and y. Thus, you can easily eliminate (A), (B), and (D). Next, consider both statements together. The two-digit prime numbers less than 23 include 11, 13, 17, and 19. Their sum is 60, and the average of the four numbers is 15. $x = 15$. Considering statement (2), the positive factors of 60 that are less than 6 include 1, 2, 3, 4, and 5. Their sum is 15. $y = 15$. $x = y$, and the answer to the question, based on statements (1) and (2) together, is no.

6. **(A)** Given statement (1), you can determine the total number of paperbacks sold: $(\$.75)(P) = \$19.50$, or $P = 26$. Given that 55 books were sold altogether, 29 hardback books were sold, and statement (1) alone suffices to answer the question. Statement (2) provides no information about the price of either type of book, and is therefore insufficient alone to answer the question.

7. **(A)** This question involves two steps. First, visually compare the difference in height between Country *X*'s solid bar and the shaded bar for each year. (Be careful to look at County *X*'s bar, *not* Country *Y*'s!) You don't need too determine amounts at this point. A quick inspection reveals that 1987 was the year Country *X*'s exports exceeded its own imports by the greatest amount. Now go to the second step. During 1987, Country *Y*'s imports were approximately \$35 billion and Country *X*'s imports were approximately \$13 billion. The difference is \$22 billion. Answer choice (A) is the only one in the right ballpark.

8. **(B)** The price of two children's tickets together equals the price of one adult ticket. The total admission price is therefore equivalent to the price of three adult tickets.

$$\begin{aligned} 3a &= \$12.60 \\ a &= \$4.20 \\ \text{Price of a child's ticket} &= \left(\frac{1}{2}\right)(\$4.20) \\ &= \$2.10 \end{aligned}$$

9. **(C)** $\frac{5}{9}$ of the legislators voted for the bill. Determine the total number of legislators by setting up and solving the following equation, then subtract 900 from the total:

$$\begin{aligned} 900 &= \frac{5}{9}x \\ 8{,}100 &= 5x \\ 1{,}620 &= x \\ 1{,}620 - 900 &= 720 \end{aligned}$$

10. **(E)** Convert the question into an algebraic equation, and solve for x:

$$M = \frac{P}{100} \cdot x$$
$$100M = Px$$
$$\frac{100M}{P} = x$$

11. **(B)** Each side of the square equals 12 feet. The length of the remaining two sides of the triangle totals 16. The perimeter of the semicircle = $\frac{1}{2}\pi d = \frac{1}{2}\pi(12) = 6\pi$. The length of the two sides of the square included in the overall perimeter totals 24. The total perimeter of the floor = $16 + 6\pi + 24 = 40 + 6\pi$.

12. **(D)** Here are the steps to solve the problem:

$$(4 \blacksquare 3 \blacksquare 5) = 12 - 5 = 7$$
$$(6 \blacksquare 5 \blacksquare 7) = 30 - 7 = 23$$
$$7 + 23 = 30$$

13. **(B)** Competitor 1 must engage in eight matches. Competitor 2 must engage in seven matches not already accounted for (the match between competitors 1 and 2 has already been tabulated). Similarly, competitor 3 must engage in six matches other than those accounted for, and so on. The minimum number of total matches = 8 + 7 + 6 + 5 + 4 + 3 + 2 + 1 = 36.

14. **(A)** Both equations are quadratic. For each one, you can determine the possible values of x by setting the quadratic expression equal to 0 (zero) and factoring that expression. Considering statement (1) alone, solve for x:

$$4x^2 - 4x = -1$$
$$4x^2 - 4x + 1 = 0$$
$$(2x - 1)(2x - 1) = 0$$
$$(2x - 1)^2 = 0$$
$$2x - 1 = 0$$
$$x = \frac{1}{2}$$

Based on the equation given in statement (1), the only possible value of x is $\frac{1}{2}$. Thus, statement (1) alone suffices to answer the question. Considering statement (2) alone, solve for x:

$$2x^2 + 9x = 5$$
$$2x^2 + 9x - 5 = 0$$
$$(x + 5)(2x - 1) = 0$$
$$x + 5 = 0, \ 2x - 1 = 0$$
$$x = -5, \ \frac{1}{2}$$

Based on the equation given in statement (2), there are two possible values of x: –5 and $\frac{1}{2}$. Thus, statement (2) alone is insufficient to answer the question.

15. **(E)** Cross-multiply to solve for y:

$$(9)(y - 1) = (2y)(3)$$
$$9y - 9 = 6y$$
$$3y = 9$$
$$y = 3$$

16. **(C)** Neither statement (1) nor (2) alone suffices to answer the question. You still do not know what portion of the remaining computers are equipped only with modems. However, both statements together establish that 55% (100 – 20 – 25) are equipped only with modems.

17. **(A)** Let x equal the number of nickels:

    $45 - x$ = the number of dimes

    $5x$ = the value of all nickels (in cents)

    $450 - 10x$ = the value of all dimes (in cents)

    Given a total value of 350 cents:

    $$\begin{aligned} 5x + 450 - 10x &= 350 \\ -5x &= -100 \\ x &= 20 \end{aligned}$$

    Lisa has 20 nickels and 25 dimes; thus, she has five more dimes than nickels.

18. **(D)** You can organize this problem's information in a table, as shown in this next figure.

	male	female	
Lange		14%	30%
Sobel	?		70%
	60%	40%	

Because 35% of 40% of the voters (female voters) voted for Lange, 14% (.40 × .35) of all voters were females who voted for Lange. You can now fill in the entire table (the total of all four percentages must be 100%), as shown in this next figure.

	male	female	
Lange	16%	14%	30%
Sobel	44%	26%	70%
	60%	40%	

19. **(E)** The number of days (d) that it takes q workers to paint a house varies inversely with the number of days that it takes $q + 2$ workers to paint a house. You can express the relationship with the following equation: $(q)(d) = (q + 2)(x)$, where x = the number of days that it takes $q + 2$ workers to paint a house. Dividing both sides of the equation by $(q + 2)$ gives you: $x = \frac{qd}{q+2}$.

20. **(C)** In answer choice (C), unequal quantities are subtracted from equal quantities. The differences are unequal, but the inequality is reversed since unequal numbers are being subtracted from rather than added to the equal numbers.

21. **(E)** The total parking fee that ABC pays each month is \$1,920 (\$240 × 8). Of that amount, \$420 is paid for outdoor parking for three cars. The difference (\$1,920 – \$420 = \$1,500) is the total garage parking fee that the company pays for the other five cars.

22. **(A)** Before analyzing the two statements, simplify the fractional expression by canceling b^2 and c from both numerator and denominator. The simplified fraction

is $\frac{a^4bc}{d^2}$. Given statement (1), $a^2 = d$. Substituting a^2 for d in the fraction: $\frac{a^4bc}{d^4} = bc$. Given that b and c are both positive but less than 1, $bc < 1$, and the answer to the question is yes. Statement (1) alone suffices to answer the question. However, statement (2) alone is insufficient to answer the question. Even if d is greater than zero, statement (2) fails to provide sufficient information to determine the relative values of the numerator and denominator. A sufficiently small d-value relative to the values of a, b, and c results in a quotient greater than 1, whereas a sufficiently large relative d-value results in a quotient less than 1.

23. **(C)** Statement (1) alone is insufficient to answer the question because it fails to indicate what percent a 10 cent increase amounts to. Statement (2) alone is insufficient because it fails to provide any information as to the change in sales resulting from an increased price. Together, however, (1) and (2) provide the information needed. You do not need to calculate the percent decrease in sales; you know that the correct answer is (C). Here's how you would perform the calculation, however: A 60-cent increase is 6 increases of 10 cents, so, the decrease in sales that would result is 30% ($6 \times 5\%$).

24. **(D)** Statement (1) establishes a linear equation with one variable: $x + (x + 1) = \frac{1}{2}[(x + 3) + (x + 6)]$. You can determine the second term by solving for x, and statement (1) suffices to answer the question. [The second term is 4.5 ($x = 3.5$); however, you need not determine these values.] Statement (2) also establishes a linear equation with one variable: $(x + 15) + (x + 21) = 43$. The seventh term is $(x + 21)$ because each successive term in the sequence adds to x a number that is one greater than the number that the previous term added to x. Statement (2) alone suffices to answer the question. (Again, $x = 3.5$ and the second term is 4.5, although you need not determine either value.)

25. **(B)** Statement (1) alone allows for more than one possible area, as illustrated below:

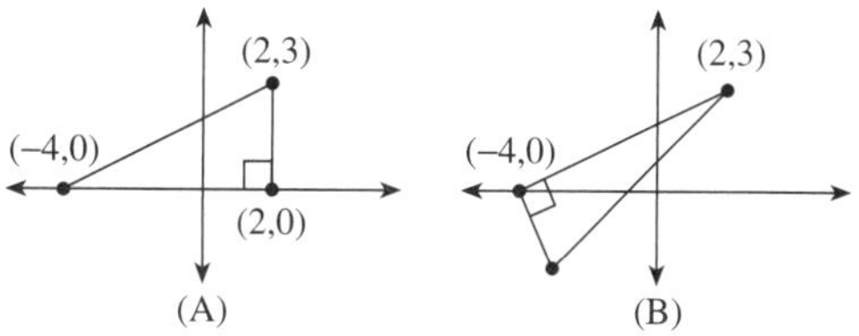

Statement (2) alone, however, allows for only one possible area (and shape and position) of the triangle—diagram (A) above. Thus, statement (2) alone is sufficient to answer the question.

26. **(C)** It is obvious that neither statement (1) nor (2) alone provides sufficient information to determine the angle measure of x. Thus, you can easily eliminate (A), (B), and (D). Next, consider statements (1) and (2) together. Notice that $\angle y$ and $\angle z$ together form a degree measure that exceeds 180° (a straight line) by $x°$. Thus, $y + z - x = 180$. Statements (1) and (2) provide the values of y and z and thus suffice to answer the question ($x = 50$).

27. **(E)** Given $xy < 0$, either x or y (but not both) must be negative. Despite this restriction, statement (1) alone is insufficient to answer the question because it specifies one equation in two variables. Statement (2) alone is also insufficient. Although x must equal either -2 or -1 (x must be a negative integer), y could be any positive integer. Considering statements (1) and (2) together, because there are two possible values of x (-2 and -1) in the equation $x + y = 2$, the difference between x and y could be either 4 or 6. Thus, statements (1) and (2) together are insufficient to answer the question.

28. **(C)** Equate the proportions of the negative with those of the printed picture:

$$\frac{2\frac{1}{2}}{4} = \frac{1\frac{7}{8}}{x}$$
$$\frac{\frac{5}{2}}{4} = \frac{\frac{15}{8}}{x}$$
$$\frac{5}{2}x = \frac{15}{2}$$
$$5x = 15$$
$$x = 3$$

29. **(C)** AC is a diagonal of the square $ABCD$. To find the length of any square's diagonal, multiply the length of any side by $\sqrt{2}$. So first you need to find the length of a side here. Half the length of a side equals the circle's radius, and the circumference of any circle equals $2\pi r$, where r is the radius. Thus, the radius here is 8, and the square's sides are 16 each. Therefore, the diagonal $AC = 16\sqrt{2}$.

30. **(D)** The two greatest two-month percent increases for City X were from 1/1 to 3/1 and from 5/1 to 7/1. Although the temperature increased by a greater amount during the latter of these two periods, the percent increase was greater from 1/1 to 3/1.

    January–February: from 30 degrees to 50 degrees, a 66% increase

    May–June: from 60 degrees to 90 degrees, a 50% increase

    During the period from 1/1 to 3/1, City Y's average daily temperature was midway between its highest and lowest temperatures (between 66 degrees and 62 degrees), or about 64 degrees.

31. **(C)** The only two-month periods in which City Y's temperature was increasing while City X's was decreasing were September–October and November–December. Compare the two midpoints of the line segments for each period:

    September–October: City X's average was 50, City Y's was 46

    November–December: City X's average was 36, City Y's average was 60

    For each city, find the average of the two midpoints:

    City X's average: $\frac{50 + 36}{2} = 43$

    City Y's average: $\frac{46 + 60}{2} = 53$

City *Y*'s average overall was about 10 degrees greater than City *X*'s during these four months.

32. **(D)** In three hours, one ship traveled 72 miles, while the other traveled 30 miles. The ratio of these two distances is 30:72 or 5:12, suggesting a 5:12:13 triangle in which the hypotenuse is the distance between the two ships at 2:30 p.m. That distance is 78 miles.

33. **(D)** You could solve the problem algebraically by using the arithmetic mean formula (x is the seventh number):

$$84 = \frac{86 + 82 + 90 + 92 + 80 + 81 + x}{7}$$

There's a quicker way, however. 86 is 2 above the 84 average, and 82 is two below. These two numbers "cancel" each other. 90 is 6 above and 92 is 8 above the average (a total of 14 above), while 80 is 4 below and 81 is 3 below the average (a total of 7 below). Thus the six terms average out to 7 above the average of 84. Accordingly, the seventh number is 7 below the average of 84, or 77.

34. **(B)** Combine the terms under the radical into one fraction, then factor out "squares" from both numerator and denominator:

$$\sqrt{\frac{y^2}{2} - \frac{y^2}{18}}$$
$$= \sqrt{\frac{9y^2 - y^2}{18}}$$
$$= \sqrt{\frac{8y^2}{18}}$$
$$= \sqrt{\frac{4y^2}{9}}$$
$$= \frac{\sqrt{4y^2}}{\sqrt{9}}$$
$$= \frac{2y}{3}$$

35. **(C)** To answer the question, you must determine the relative volumes of the cylindrical tank and a cube-shaped tank. Statement (1) fails to provide sufficient information to determine these volumes. The volume of the cylindrical tank is $7.5\pi r^2$, and, given statement (1), you can express the cube's volume as r^3. The ratio of the two volumes, then, is $7.5\pi r^2{:}r^3$, or $7.5\pi{:}r$. Accordingly, the relative volumes of the containers vary depending on the value of r. Statement (2) alone is also insufficient to answer the question. Given statement (2), the length of a cube's side is 2.5 feet, and you can determine its volume (s^3). However, you cannot determine the cylindrical tank's volume, because the size of its circular base remains unknown. Statement (1) provides this missing information. Thus, statements (1) and (2) together suffice to answer the ques-

A

tion. (Given statements (1) and (2), the ratio of V [cylinder] to V [cube] is 3π:1, so 10 cube-shaped tanks are required.)

36. **(E)** You can express the amount of sugar after you add water as $.05(60 + x)$, where $60 + x$ represents the total amount of solution after you add the additional water. This amount of sugar is the same as (equal to) the original amount of sugar (20% of 60). Set up an equation, multiply both sides by 100 to remove the decimal point, and solve for x:

$$\begin{aligned} 5(60 + x) &= 1{,}200 \\ 300 + 5x &= 1{,}200 \\ 5x &= 900 \\ x &= 180 \end{aligned}$$

37. **(E)** You can express the distance both in terms of Dan's driving time going home and going back to college. Letting x equal the time (in hours) it took Dan to drive home, you can express the distance between his home and his workplace both as $60x$ and as $50(x + 1)$. Equate the two distances (because distance is constant) and solve for x as follows:

$$\begin{aligned} 60x &= 50(x + 1) \\ 60x &= 50x + 50 \\ 10x &= 50 \\ x &= 5 \end{aligned}$$

It took Dan five hours at 60 miles per hour to drive from college to home, so the distance is 300 miles.

Verbal Ability (Hour 21)

1. **(B)** The original sentence (A) presents an incomplete comparison. Removing the second phrase of the comparison (set off by commas) reveals the omission of *as* (*is as crucial . . . as*). (B) completes the form of the idiomatic phrase by including the word *as*. (C) presents an incomplete form, omitting *crucial* in the second comparison. (D) improperly uses *than* instead of *as* in the first comparison (*as crucial . . . than*). At the same time, the second comparison is incomplete; the comparative clause set off by commas must include *than*. (E) corrects only the first of the two problems with (D), as well as creates a new problem: The word *as* should precede (not follow) the parenthetical comparison.

2. **(E)** The original version creates confusion by separating the two parallel clauses *the greater* . . . and *the less* . . . . Also, *will be* is unnecessary and undermines the parallel structure of the two clauses. (B) improperly omits *between two particles* immediately following *distance,* thereby creating confusion as to what the word *distance* refers. (C) creates a faulty parallel between the two main clauses; *a lesser* should be replaced with *less* to parallel *more* in the preceding clause. In (D), *the less of a* and *the more of a* are both idiomatically improper. (E) remedies both problems with the original sentence. The words *smaller* and *lesser* may be used interchangeably here, because both refer to amount rather than quantity.

3. **(C)** The original sentence improperly uses *who* instead of *whom* to refer to the object of the terrorists' attacks. The original sentence also includes a subject-verb agreement error. The noun clause *who the terrorists are* is the subject of this sentence and is considered singular. (B) fails to correct the subject-verb agreement error. (B) is also awkwardly constructed. The phrase *the terrorists* is not parallel in grammatical construction to *at whom . . . aimed.* (C) corrects both problems with the original version.(D) corrects the subject-verb agreement error by creating a plural subject; but (D) is vague as to whom the pronoun *they* refers. (E) also corrects the subject-verb agreement error by creating a plural subject; but it fails to correct the relative pronoun error.

4. **(C)** The task in this problem is to find an answer that strengthens the argument; that is, one that offers support for the major assumption of the argument or that provides additional evidence for the conclusion. The major assumption of the argument is that there are no reasons other than the one stated (namely, the introduction of more new software products than its competitors) that account for Softec's greater financial success. Response (C) supports this assumption by eliminating other relevant reasons that could account for Softec's greater success.

5. **(D)** The denial of the claim asserted in response (D) is incompatible with the argument; that is, if using plants as a source of drugs and chemicals threatened their survival, then efforts to preserve them would be thwarted. This indicates that the assumption operative in the argument is that using plants for these purposes will not threaten their survival.

6. **(D)** is contradicted by the information in the passages. According to the passage the German states were brought together by the Franco-Prussian war. Since this war occurred after the wars against Denmark and Austria, the inference to be drawn is that the wars against Denmark and Austria were fought by Prussia, not the unified German states. (A) is explicitly mentioned in line 20. (B) is explicitly mentioned in line 7. (C) is explicitly mentioned in line 31. (E) is explicitly mentioned in line 12.

7. **(C)** is unsupported by the passage. There is no indication in the passage that Bismarck personally insulted the people of France. The insult mentioned in line 33 refers to the fact that the German states chose to proclaim the creation of a new German empire on "French soil in the Hall of Mirrors at Versailles." It was this decision and the loss of the territory of Alsace and Lorraine that "was a grievous insult to the people of France."

8. **(B)** The first sentence of the passage signals that the author is most concerned with the role Bismarck played in the creation of the German empire.

9. **(C)** There are two problems with the original version. First, the sentence intends to point out that severe weather can prevent planes *from* departing on time. But the original version omits the crucial word *from*. Also, *some of the time* is wordy. (C) corrects both problems. (B) misuses *sometime*. Also, *their timely departing* is awkward (*their timely departure* would be better). (D) reconstructs the sentence, using the passive voice, not just once, but twice; the result is a very awkward sentence. (E) contains two preposition errors: *for* (*of* is better) and *as a result of* (*by* is better). Moreover, (E) uses the awkward passive voice.

10. **(C)** The task in this problem is to find an answer that weakens the argument; that is, one that undermines the major assumption of the argument, attacks a stated premise, or suggests an alternative conclusion that could be inferred from the premises. The major assumption in the argument is that current dirolin contamination detection methods are inadequate, ineffective, or completely lacking. Response (C) effectively undermines this assumption.

11. **(B)** The information in the passage can be restated as follows:

    Premise: If low blood pressure is the cause of slow recall, then recall time should shorten when blood pressure is raised.

    Premise: Tests show that recall time does not shorten when blood pressure is raised.

    The conclusion that can be inferred from these premises is that low blood pressure is not the cause of slow recall. Response (B) is a paraphrase of this claim.

12. **(D)** In the original version, the position of *alone* improperly suggests that the immigrants are alone. (D) corrects this problem (*more* and *greater* are both acceptable here). (B) is constructed in a confusing and awkward manner; it is unclear as to what *a million* refers. Also, in (C) it is unclear what *a million* refers to. In (E), *such* is redundant and should be omitted; for that matter, the entire phrase *such illegal immigrants* can be omitted without obscuring the meaning of the sentence.

13. **(C)** The original sentence is grammatically correct. But the use of two subordinate clauses is confusing and awkward; and the word *men* set off by itself with commas improperly suggests that *men* is one item in a series of items. (B) misplaces the modifying clause *especially Civil War generals;* this clause should appear closer to its antecedent (*men*). (C) clarifies the sentence's meaning by positioning *generations* immediately before *men*. (D) includes the awkwardly constructed phrase *Civil War generals especially, and men in general*. Not only is the phrase clumsy and unnecessarily wordy, the word *general* carries a different meaning the second time that the sentence uses it, creating further confusion. (E) misplaces the modifier *especially Civil War generals*, suggesting that

Napoleon was a Civil War general, as well as presenting an apparent pronoun disagreement between *generals* and *his*.

14. **(A)** The original version is correct. The phrase *similar to* sets up a comparison between soil composition on Mars and soil composition on Earth. The relative pronoun *that* is proper here to refer to the latter. (B) illogically compares soil composition to a our planet. (C) uses the wrong preposition (*with*); the proper idiom is *similar to*. In (D), *this composition* is awkward; the original version is less awkward and more concise. (E) awkwardly strings together two possessives (*planet's soil's*).

15. **(E)** In lines 9–11 it is explicitly stated that " it is not possible to predict . . . what the outcome on health will be" as a result of the presence of a flawed gene.

16. **(C)** Spinal muscular atrophy is mentioned as a disorder related to flawed genes, not susceptibility genes (line 4). (A), (B), (D), and (E) are mentioned as disorders related to susceptibility genes in lines 21–24.

17. **(A)** In the first paragraph it is explicitly stated that "it is not possible to predict . . . what the outcome on health will be" as a result of the presence of a flawed gene. The last two lines of the second paragraph make a similar point regarding susceptibility genes.

18. **(B)** The pattern of the argument is:

    Los Alamos *has properties X, Y, and Z.*

    Los Brunos *has properties X and Y.*

    Therefore it is likely that _______.

    Based on this comparison of Los Alamos and Los Brunos, the sentence that best completes the argument is: Los Brunos *has property Z,* which in this argument is the property of always electing conservative candidates. Based on this analysis, the unstated conclusion is: Los Brunos residents always elect conservative candidates. (A), (C), (D), and (E) are unsupported by the passage and call for speculation.

19. **(A)** The only causes of yellow fever that are discussed in the passage are mosquito bites and contact with persons who have the disease. Experiments are devised to decide between them, and on the basis of the outcome of the experiments, contact with persons who have the disease is eliminated as the cause.

20. **(B)** From the information stated in the passage, it can be inferred that one-half-inch cubes would require proportionately less cooking time than the twenty minutes required for one-inch cubes. Cooking potatoes for twenty minutes would consequently result in severe overcooking, and this in turn would result in a significant lessening of their food value.

21. **(E)** The task in this problem is to find an answer that strengthens the argument; that is, one that offers support for the major assumption of the argument or that provides additional evidence for the conclusion. The primary reason given in the argument for expecting an increasing number of computer owners to sell their old computers is that increased demand for used computers has exerted an upward pressure on prices of used computers. This suggests that the reason computer owners had not sold their old computers previously is that their old computers did not have sufficient resale value to enable them to purchase newer models. Response (E) explicitly states this reason and thus provides additional evidence for the conclusion.

22. **(E)** One problem with the original sentence is that it makes an illogical comparison, suggesting that a pluralistic democracy is not a system of government—when in fact it is. The solution is to add *other* to the end of the underlined phrase. A second problem with the original sentence is the *in greater degree* is idiomatically improper; *to a greater degree* is the proper idiom. (E) corrects the first error and avoids the second one by replacing *in greater degree* with the concise *more*. (B) results in a sentence fragment (an incomplete sentence). (C) fails to correct the illogical comparison. (D) alters the meaning of the original sentence; *as opposed to* unfairly suggests that no other system of government diffuses power from a center.

23. **(A)** The original version is the best one. The noun clause *whether the universe is bound* is properly considered the subject of the sentence. (B) contains a pronoun reference problem; the intended antecedent of *it* is *question*, but the intervening word *universe* obscures the intended reference. (C) uses the idiom *as to* improperly. Also, *impossibly answered* is nonsensical. (D) includes the nonsensical *impossible answered*. (E) is wordy; *or not* can be omitted, as can the second *a question*.

24. **(D)** The original version contains a subject-verb agreement error: the singular noun *need* is improperly matched with the plural verb *are*. Also, the grammatical element *need for* should not be split. (B) is nonsensical. In (C), the phrase *third world countries' need* is very awkward. (D) corrects both problems in the original version by replacing *are* with *is* and by reconstructing the underlined part. (E) is grammatically correct, but it is wordy and awkward.

25. **(B)** The conclusion of the argument in the passage is based on two specific examples of failed video production businesses. Since no indication is given in the passage that these two cases are representative of the condition of other video production companies or of the industry at large, the general conclusion that all such businesses are in trouble is highly suspect.

26. **(B)** The task in this problem is to find an answer that weakens the argument; that is, one that undermines the major assumption of the argument, attacks a stated premise, or that suggests an alternative conclusion that could be inferred from the premises. The major assumption in the argument is that glass and metal containers are not being disposed of in some way other than the way mentioned in the passage. Response (B) undermines this assumption, thereby calling into question the conclusion of the argument.

27. **(B)** The original sentence lacks proper parallelism; *to* should be omitted. Also, the original sentence is comprised of two main clauses (each of which could stand on its own as a complete sentence) separated only by a comma. This "comma splice" should be corrected by an appropriate connecting word, such as *but*, *yet*, or *although*. (B) corrects both problems with the original version. (C) does not correct the faulty parallel. Also, the connector *and* does not convey the intended meaning effectively (*but* and *yet* are better). (D) does not employ proper parallelism. (E) does not employ proper parallelism (the adverb *decently* should be used instead of the adjective *decent*). Also, (E) does not correct the comma splice problem.

28. **(E)** The author states that a spillover is the "excess of the social rate of return over the private rate of return enjoyed by innovating firms." Since the social rate of return is a measure of the benefits enjoyed by consumers and society at large and the private rate of return is a measure of the economic benefits enjoyed by innovating firms, it can be inferred that a spillover is the excess in the economic value to society over the economic value to private firms that results from their research and development efforts.

29. **(C)** Answer choice (C) is totally unsupported and runs contrary to the passage. The author states that "spillovers occur because knowledge created by one firm is typically not contained within that firm, and thereby creates value for other firms." The clear implication of this statement is that other firms benefit from the knowledge gained by the research and development efforts of innovating firms. (A) is supported by the lines 1–5. (B) is supported by lines 13–15. (D) is supported by lines 30–37. (E) is supported by lines 5–9.

30. **(E)** While the passage indicates that knowledge created by one firm is typically not contained within that firm (lines 26–28), no explanation for this is stated. (A) is answered in the second paragraph where several reasons why spillovers occur are given. (B) is answered in lines 22–37. (C) is answered in line 12 where a "positive externality" is indicated as another term for "spillover." A partial answer to (D) is found in the first paragraph. It can be inferred from lines 13–20 that one reason private firms invest less in research and development than is socially desirable is to avoid spillovers.

A

31. **(B)** The conclusion of the argument is stated in the first sentence of the passage. In the remainder of the passage reasons are offered in support of this sentence. The phrase "the main reason is that" signals that the second sentence states a premise. This premise is elucidated further in the third sentence. The word "also" at the beginning of the fourth sentence indicates an additional premise. Of the answer choices, (B) comes closest to asserting what is asserted in the first sentence, namely, "deterrence is a particularly unconvincing rationale for the death penalty."

32. **(A)** The argument in the passage is essentially that women have the right to earn as much money as men because they have as much right to self-esteem as men. The argument can be represented as follows:

    Premise: Women have as much right to self-esteem as men.

    Conclusion: Women have the right to earn as much money as men.

    The logical gap in this argument that must be filled is the link between a person's self-esteem and the amount of money they earn. The suggestion is that a person's self-esteem is determined by the amount of money they have—the more money they have, the more self-esteem; the less money they have, the less self-esteem. Of the answer choices, response (A) best expresses this assumption.

33. **(D)** The original version misplaces the modifying phrase *when its people obey and revere the law.* As it stands, the pronoun *its* appears to refer to *Lincoln;* but the intended reference is to *democracy.* (D) clarifies the pronoun reference by positioning *its* just after its antecedent *democracy.* (B) fails to remedy the pronoun reference problem; also, the word *they* creates a faulty parallel (between *obey the law* and *they revere the law*). (C) remedies the pronoun reference problem, but it uses the awkward passive voice. In (E), the additional word *who* renders the sentence nonsensical, as well as alters the meaning of the sentence by suggesting that some people might not obey and revere the law.

34. **(A)** The original sentence (A) is the best choice; it contains no errors in grammar, diction, or usage. (B) improperly uses *which* instead of *that.* Also, *but rather* is idiomatically preferable to *but instead* in this sentence. Finally, this sentence's overall construction, especially considering the final clause, is somewhat awkward. (C) includes the awkward phrase *most instilling.* Placing the phrase *in the populace* between the verb *instilling* and the direct object *a sense* . . . confuses the sentence's meaning. (D) is awkwardly constructed. The modifying phrase *a suit of gold and greed* should appear immediately after the subject to which it refers—the California gold rush. (E) uses the awkward passive construction (*was instilled by*) instead of the preferred active construction (*gold rush instilled*).

35. **(E)** The original sentence makes an illogical comparison between *speech* and *region*. (B) and (D) fail to correct the illogical comparison between *speech* and *region*. Also, (B) incorrectly uses the singular verb *distinguishes* instead of the plural form. (C) corrects the illogical comparison. However, (C) incorrectly uses the singular verb *distinguishes*. The verb must agree with its plural subject *utterances*. (C) also incorrectly uses *those* instead of the correct relative pronoun *that* (to refer to the singular *speech*). (E) corrects the problem in the original version by adding *that of*.

36. **(B)** The argument in the passage can be restated as follows:

    Premise: Lies are morally justified only if they are told to save a person's life.

    Premise: Most lies are not told to save a person's life.

    Conclusion: Most lies are morally unjustified.

    (B) is the best response. The argument in response (B) can be restated as follows:

    Premise: Capital punishment is justified only if the convicted offender is guilty.

    Premise: Many convicted offenders are not guilty.

    Conclusion: Many instances of capital punishment are unjustified.

    A comparison of this argument with the passage argument outlined above reveals a close similarity between the premises and conclusions of these arguments. In each, the first premise is constructed by connecting two independent clauses with the phrase "only if"; the second premise states the denial of the clause following "only if;" the conclusion states the denial of the clause preceding "only if."

37. **(E)** The main focus of the passage is to argue for the claim expressed in (E). In the third sentence of the first paragraph a paraphrase of (E) is asserted. The remainder of the passage is devoted to offering reasons in support of this claim.

38. **(A)** The author is careful to distinguish between quotas and "goals and timetables." In the first paragraph, (lines 13–15) the author states that "quotas were used to keep out qualified members." It can be inferred from this that the author maintains that quotas are a means of discriminating against those who are otherwise qualified for vacant positions.

39. **(B)** Answer choice (B) confuses information in the passage. Among the examples of preferential treatment in lines 43–45 the author includes "employers hiring the sons and daughters of their economic and social equals," but no mention of employers giving preference to their *own* sons or daughters is made.

40. **(A)** The following information is stated in the passage: (1) Every philosopher of science of the twentieth century who was either a realist or an empiricist was influenced by the logical positivists. (2) No one who was influenced by the logical positivists maintains that scientific theories can be proven to be true. From (1) it necessarily follows that every philosopher of science of the twentieth century who was a realist was influenced by the logical positivists. Moreover, given this and the information stated in (2), it necessarily follows that no twentieth century philosophers of science who are realists maintain that scientific theories can be proven to be true.

41. **(B)** The original sentence awkwardly mixes the active voice (first clause) and the passive voice (second clause). It also includes the unnecessarily wordy *by way of*. (B) corrects both problems with a concise second clause in the active voice. (C) alters the meaning of the original sentence. The use of *so* (which means "therefore") suggests a logical premise and conclusion; but the original sentence makes no such suggestion. (C) also suggests nonsensically that the only protection provided by domestic laws is for hybrid species (the key is the improper placement of *only*). (D) is poorly worded; *domestic protection* is confusing, and *so protect* is very awkward. (E) alters the meaning of the original sentence, which does not suggest that hybrid species *require* any legal protection. Through the use of the relative pronoun *which*, (E) also shifts the balance (and emphasis) of the sentence toward the first clause, thereby altering the intended meaning of the original sentence, at least to some extent. (By using *but*, the original sentence intends to place equal emphasis on the two clauses.)

Sample Test 2

Analytical Writing Assessment (Hour 22)

Sample Response—Analysis-of-an-Issue

I agree that high art enriches the society; that it elevates the collective spirit of its members and strengthens the society's social fabric is palpable. For several compelling reasons, however, I believe the government should play no discretionary role in supporting any form of art.

First, subsidizing the arts is neither a proper nor necessary job for government. Although public health is generally viewed as critical to a society's very survival and therefore an appropriate concern of government, this concern should not extend tenuously to our cultural "health" or well-being. A lack of private funding might justify an exception; in my observation, however, philanthropy is alive and well today, especially among the new technology and media moguls.

Secondly, government cannot possibly play an evenhanded role as arts patron. Inadequate resources call for restrictions, priorities, and choices. It is unconscionable to relegate normative decisions as to which art benefits the society and which harms the society to a few legislators and jurists, who may be unenlightened in their notions about art. Also, legislators are all too likely to make choices in favor of the cultural agendas of those lobbyists with the most money and influence.

Thirdly, government favoritism of some art forms over others is a de facto restriction on artistic expression, which smacks of encroachment on the constitutional right of free expression. In any case, governmental favoritism may chill creativity, thereby quashing the collective spirit which high art is intended to foster in society and its members.

In the final analysis, government cannot philosophically or economically justify its involvement in the arts, either by subsidy or sanction. Responsibility lies with individuals to determine what art nurtures the society and what art harms the society.

Sample Response—Analysis-of-an-Argument

The implicit conclusion of this argument is that caffeine causes birth defects in humans. The basis for this conclusion is a presumed similarity in the effects of caffeine on pregnant rats and pregnant humans. This argument is unacceptable for several reasons.

In the first place, we are given too few details about the study to properly assess the validity of the central claim that caffeine causes birth defects in rats. For example, lacking information about the number of rats involved in the study, the percentage of those who gave birth to deformed offspring, and the conditions under which the experiment was performed, the truth of this claim is open to question.

Secondly, the only grounds we are given for accepting the claim that caffeine causes birth defects in rats is that the study was conducted at a "major university." If it turns out, however, that the university in question is a liberal arts school with minimal research facilities and poorly trained science faculty, this fact would seriously undermine the acceptability of this finding.

Moreover, even if we accept the claim that caffeine causes birth defects in rats, the crucial issue is whether rats are relevantly similar to humans in their response to caffeine. For this to be the case, it would have to be shown that female rats and humans are sufficiently similar physiologically to insure that the effects of caffeine on pregnant women would be similar to the effects on pregnant rats. No evidence for this crucial assumption is presented in the argument.

A final reason for questioning the implicit conclusion of this argument is that the amount of caffeine likely to be consumed by pregnant women is vastly lower (as a fraction of body weight) than the amount reportedly consumed by the rats in the study. At best, the study shows only that "massive" doses of caffeine ingested over a short period of time can cause birth defects; it does not show that caffeine, in the moderate amounts normally consumed by humans, can cause birth defects.

In conclusion, the argument on which the warning is based is rather weak. To strengthen the argument, the author would have to provide additional details about the study and the competence of the research faculty who performed the experiment. To better assess the argument, we would also need evidence for the underlying assumption that female rats and female humans are relevantly similar in their response to caffeine.

Quantitative Ability (Hour 23)

1. **(B)** All variables except a and e cancel out:

$$\frac{a}{\cancel{b}} \cdot \frac{\cancel{b}}{\cancel{e}} \cdot \frac{\cancel{e}}{\cancel{d}} \cdot \frac{\cancel{d}}{e} \cdot x = 1$$

To isolate x on one side of the equation, multiply both sides by $\frac{e}{a}$:

$$\frac{e}{a} \cdot \frac{a}{e} x = 1 \cdot \frac{e}{a}$$

$$x = \frac{e}{a}$$

2. (B) Four distinct sets of three women are possible: *ABC, ABD, ACD,* and *BCD.* Three distinct sets of two men are possible: *XY, XZ,* and *YZ.* The probability that *B, C,* and *D* (but not *A*) along with *Y* and *Z* (but not *X*) will be selected is 1 in 12 (4×3).

3. **(E)** The question asks you to compare rates, or speeds. To determine a speed you need to know time and distance. Statement (1) alone provides only Maria's time, not Lupe's, so it is insufficient alone to answer the question. Statement (2) compares their driving distances, but provides no information about Lupe's driving time. Because Lupe's driving time is a critical fact missing from both statements, the correct answer is (E).

4. **(E)** Statement (1) alone provides no information about how many students a bus can carry, so it is insufficient to answer the question. Statement (2) provides only an average. Some buses might have a much greater capacity.

5. **(C)** Statement (1) alone provides no information about b and is therefore insufficient to answer the questions. Statement (2) alone is also insufficient because a and b could be either positive or negative. Either $a - b = 1$ or $a - b = -1$. Given both statements together, try substituting 3 and –3 for a into statement (2)'s two equations, and you get these possible values for b: 2, –4, 4, or –2. Because you now know all possible values for a and b, you can determine the minimum value of $|a + b|$. (The answer to the question is 1.)

6. **(D)** Statements (1) and (2) provide two different forms of the same equation. You can use either one to find the value of x. (The equation in (2) is the factored form of the equation in (1). The factored form (in statement (2)) makes clear that x has two roots: 3 and –2. Given that $x < 0$, the value of x must be –2.

7. **(E)** A median is the number that ranks exactly in the middle of the set. To know the median here, you would need to know what the six specific values are, not just their range and/or their average.

8. **(D)** Extend BE to F (as in the diagram below). $\angle EFD = \angle ABE = 40^\circ$. $\angle FED$ must equal 110° because there are 180° in a triangle. Since $\angle BED$ and $\angle FED$ are supplementary, $\angle BED = 70^\circ$ ($x = 70$).

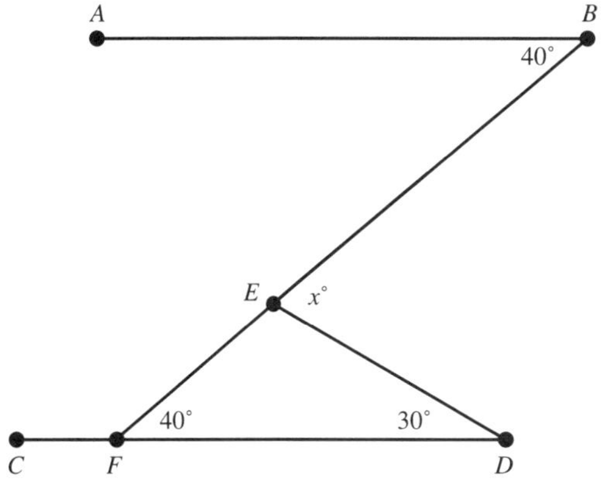

9. **(B)** \$54 is 90% of what he collected. Express this as an equation:

$$54 = .90x$$
$$540 = 9x$$
$$x = \$60$$

If each paper sells for 40 cents, the number of paper he sold is $\frac{60.00}{.40}$, or 150.

10. **(B)** You can solve the problem algebraically as follows:

$$23 - x = 2(15 - x)$$
$$23 - x = 30 - 2x$$
$$x = 7$$

An alternative method is to subtract the number in each answer choice from both Lyle's age and Melanie's age.

11. **(C)** Add the two equations:

$$\begin{aligned} x + y &= a \\ x - y &= b \\ \hline 2x &= a + b \\ x &= \frac{1}{2}(a + b) \end{aligned}$$

12. **(E)** The shelter houses $d + c$ animals altogether. Of these animals, d are dogs. That portion can be expressed as the fraction $\frac{d}{d + c}$.

13. **(E)** Since the figure has 5 sides, it contains 540 degrees:

$$180(5-2) = 540$$

The sum of the five angles is 540, so solve for x:

$$540 = x + 110 + (x - 90) + 120 + 100$$
$$540 = 2x + 240$$
$$150 = x$$

14. **(C)** Statement (1) establishes the total contributions of Willot and Tilson counties relative to those of Stanton and Osher counties, but the statement provides no additional information about Stanton County's specific percentage contribution. Statement (1) alone is therefore insufficient to answer the question. Based on statement (2) alone, Tilson County's non-subsidized farms must have accounted for 6% of all revenues (18–12%). Accordingly, Stanton County's non-subsidized farms must have accounted for 9% of all revenues (the percentages in the leftmost column must total 30). However, this information is insufficient to determine Stanton County's subsidized farm contribution. With both statements (1) and (2) together, Osher County's revenues must total 36% (because statement (2) stipulates that Osher county contributed twice the revenues of Tilson county, which you now know contributed 18% of all revenues). At this point, you have partially completed the table as shown in the following figure:

	non-subsidized farms	subsidized farms	
Willot County	7%		
Tilson County	(6%)	12%	(18%)
Stanton County	(9%)		
Osher County	8%	(28%)	(36%)
(Total Percentages)	30%	(70%)	

It is now evident that Stanton County's subsidized farms contributed 6% of the total revenues (Stanton and Osher county revenues must account for 50% of the total). Thus, statements (1) and (2) together suffice to answer the question.

15. **(E)** To determine the area of the shaded region, subtract the area of the circle from the area of the smaller of the two squares. First, determine the area of the smaller square. Each of the four outside triangles is a $1:1:\sqrt{2}$ right triangle, with a side of the smaller square as the hypotenuse. Each leg of these triangles is $\frac{x}{2}$ in length; thus, each side of the smaller square is $\frac{x\sqrt{2}}{2}$ in length. Accordingly, the area of the smaller square is $\left(\frac{x\sqrt{2}}{2}\right)^2$, or $\frac{x^2}{2}$. Next, determine the area of the circle. Its diameter is $\frac{x\sqrt{2}}{2}$ (the length of each side of the smaller square). Thus, its radius is half that amount, or $\frac{x\sqrt{2}}{4}$. The circle's area is:

$$\pi\left(\frac{x\sqrt{2}}{4}\right)^2 = \pi\frac{x^2 \times 2}{16} = \frac{\pi x^2}{8}$$

Subtract this area from the square's area:

$$\frac{x^2}{2} - \frac{\pi x^2}{8} = \frac{4x^2 - \pi x^2}{8} = \frac{x^2(4 - \pi)}{8}$$

16. **(C)** Statement (1) alone is insufficient because you can make several possible equations using the integers 0 through 9. Statement (2) alone is insufficient for the same reason. Adding (1) to (2) leaves you with only two possibilities for *bn*: 3^4 or 9^2. Given that $am = bn$, you can now answer the question. The sum of the four integers is 3 + 4 + 9 + 2, or 18.

17. **(C)** The total rent is $D + 100$, which must be divided by the number of students.

18. **(D)** Start with 2, then 4, then 6, and so forth (positive even integers), as the value of *n*. Test each value in turn. You'll find that only the numbers in the following sequence leave a remainder of 1 when divided by 3: {4, 10, 16, . . .}. Notice that the numbers increase by 6 in sequence. Next, try a few of these numbers as the value of *n* in each of the five expressions. You'll find that all but $(n \cdot 2)$ are divisible by 3.

19. **(E)** First, combine the two terms inside the radical, using the common denominator b^2. Then remove squares from the radical:

$$\sqrt{\frac{a^2}{b^2} + \frac{a^2}{b^2}} = \sqrt{\frac{a^2 + a^2}{b^2}} = \sqrt{\frac{2a^2}{b^2}} = \frac{a}{b}\sqrt{2}$$

20. **(D)** From largest to smallest, the order is: (e), (b), (a), (c), (d). Let $x = \frac{1}{2}$. Using this value in each of the five expressions:

(A) $\sqrt{\frac{1}{2}} \approx .71$

(B) $\sqrt{\frac{1}{\frac{1}{2}}} = \sqrt{2} \approx 1.4$

(C) $\sqrt[3]{\left(\frac{1}{2}\right)^2} = \sqrt[3]{\frac{1}{4}} \approx \frac{1}{1.6}$, or .625

(D) $\left(\frac{1}{2}\right)^4 = \frac{1}{16}$

(E) $\sqrt{\frac{1}{(\frac{1}{2})^2}} = \frac{1}{\frac{1}{4}} = 4$

21. **(B)** Let x = the number of nickels. $30 - x$ = the number of quarters. Convert both expressions to cents:

$5x$ = the value of nickels in cents

$750 - 25x$ = value of quarters in cents

The total of these two expressions is 470. Set up the equation, then solve for x:

$$\begin{aligned} 5x + (750 - 25x) &= 470 \\ -20x &= -280 \\ x &= 14 \end{aligned}$$

22. **(D)** The question itself provides that the pitcher currently contains $7\frac{1}{2}$ ounces of each brand. Given statement (1), 60 percent of the 30 quart mixture, or 18 ounces, must be brand A. We've answered the question with statement (1) alone. Given statement (2) alone, subtract $7\frac{1}{2}$ from 12 to find the remaining amount of brand B needed ($10\frac{1}{2}$ ounces). Then subtract 12 from 30 to find the amount of brand A (18). Finally, subtract

A

$7\frac{1}{2}$ from 18 to find the remaining amount of brand A needed ($10\frac{1}{2}$ ounces). You've answered the question with statement (2) alone.

23. **(D)** The area of any triangle equals $\frac{1}{2} \cdot$ *base* $\cdot$ *height*. Using 7 miles as the base of the triangle in this problem, the triangle's height is the north-south (vertical) distance from *A* to an imaginary line extending westerly from *B*. Statement (1) explicitly provides the triangle's height. Statement (2) also provides sufficient information to determine this height.

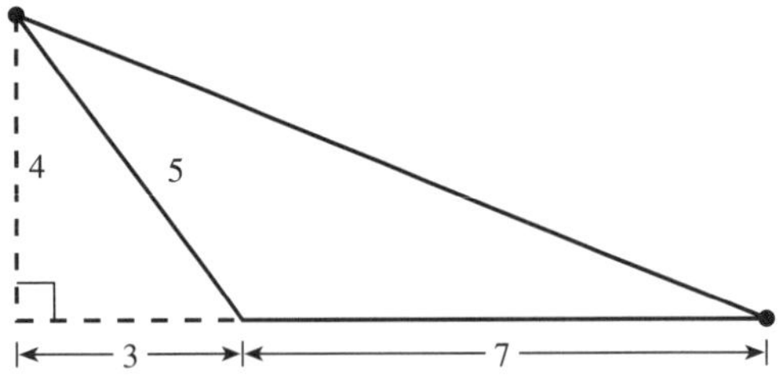

As indicated in the figure above, the triangle's height is 4 miles (32 + 42 = 52, per the Pythagorean Theorem). Accordingly, either statement alone suffices to determine the triangle's area. [The area = $(\frac{1}{2})(7)(4) = 14$.]

24. **(B)** To answer the question, you need to compare Daniel's rate of work with that of Carl and Todd working together. Statement (1) provides Carl's rate, but not Todd's; so statement (1) alone is insufficient to answer the question. Statement (2) provides Carl's and Todd's combined rate. By comparing this combined rate with the rate of all three working together, you can determine Daniel's rate. Statement (2) alone suffices to answer the question. Although you don't have to do the math, here's how you would answer the question. All three workers can load $\frac{1}{8}$ of the van in one hour. Similarly, Carl and Todd can load $\frac{1}{12}$ of the van in one hour. Subtract $\frac{1}{12}$ from $\frac{1}{8}$ to obtain Daniel's rate:

$$\frac{1}{8} - \frac{1}{12} = \frac{1}{24}$$

Daniel can do $\frac{1}{24}$ of the job (loading the van) in one hour, so it would take Daniel 24 hours to load the van.

25. **(D)** Statement (1) alone suffices to answer the question. Given that $x = 60$, the area of each of the two triangles must be less than $\frac{1}{6}$ $(\frac{60}{360})$ of the area of the circle (the difference is the region between each triangle and the circle's circumference). So the combined area of the two triangles is less than $\frac{1}{3}$ the area of the circle. Given that $x = 60$, $\angle AOC = 120$, and the area of the shaded region is exactly $\frac{1}{3}$ $(\frac{120}{360})$ that of the circle. Statement (2) alone also suffices to answer the question. Given that *AB* equals the radius, each of the two triangles is equilateral, and all angles are 60°. You can now apply the same reasoning as with statement (1) to answer the question.

26. **(E)** This question requires a bit of trial and error. Even considered together, (1) and (2) are insufficient to answer the question. For example, the number 242 satisfies both (1) and (2) but is not divisible by 4, whereas 444 satisfies both (1) and (2) and is divisible by 4.

27. **(E)** The expression involves subtraction, so neither the base numbers nor the exponents can be combined. Only (E) is equivalent to the original expression. To confirm this without a calculator, factor 7^{76} from both terms:

$$\frac{7^{77} - 7^{76}}{6} = \frac{7^{76}(7^1 - 1)}{6} = 7^{76}$$

28. **(D)** The age group that spent the most time per week watching sports on television was the 19–24 year-old group, which spent an average of approximately 6 hours per week watching sports programming. At this point, look at the height of the first and third bars combined, and compare it to the total combined height of all three bars. What's your guess as to the percent of one to the other? At least 70%, right? Eliminate (A), (B), and (C). Compute the total hours watching television for all three groups (it's okay to approximate here to save time): 33 + 17 + 20 = 70. Of this total, the two groups other than the 19–24 age group accounted for 53 hours, or $\frac{53}{70}$, or about 75%, of the total hours for all three age groups.

29. **(D)** Your task here is to compare the size of the entertainment portion of the left-hand bar to the combined sizes of the same portion of the other two bars. Size up the ratio visually. The portion on the first chart is just a bit larger than the other two combined, isn't it? So you're looking for a ratio that's greater than 1:1. You can rule out answer choices (A) and (B).

Approximate the height of each three portions:

13–18 age group: 25 hours

19–24 age group: 5 hours

25–30 age group: 10 hours

The ratio in question is 25:15, or 5:3.

30. **(C)** The amount invested at 5% is $10{,}000 - x$ dollars. Thus, the income from that amount is $.05(10{,}000 - x)$ dollars.

31. **(C)** Represent the original fraction by $\frac{x}{2x}$:

$$\frac{x + 4}{2x + 4} = \frac{5}{8}$$

Cross multiply, and solve for x:

$$8x + 32 = 10x + 20$$
$$12 = 2x$$
$$x = 6$$

The original denominator is $2x$, or 12.

32. **(C)** This question requires a bit of intuition. The objective is to minimize the unused space in the packing box by turning the smaller boxes on their appropriate sides. Align the 2" edge of each box along the 18" edge of the packing box (9 boxes make up a row). Align the 5" side of each box along the 35" edge of the packing box (7 boxes make up a row). Arranged in this manner with the 18" by 35" face of the packing box as the base, one "layer" of small boxes 3" high includes 63 boxes (9 × 7). Given that the packing box's third dimension is 19", 6 layers of boxes, each 3" high, will fit into

A

the packing box, for a total of 378 boxes. An unused layer 1" high remains at the top of the box. (You could reverse the alignment of the 2" and 3" sides and arrive at the same result.)

33. **(E)** Substitute $\frac{2}{3}$ and $-\frac{2}{3}$ individually for u in the defined operation $\langle u \rangle = u^2 - u$. Then subtract:

$$\left\langle \frac{2}{3} \right\rangle = \frac{4}{9} - \frac{2}{3} = \frac{4}{9} - \frac{6}{9} = -\frac{2}{9}$$

$$\left\langle -\frac{2}{3} \right\rangle = \frac{4}{9} + \frac{2}{3} = \frac{4}{9} + \frac{6}{9} = \frac{10}{9}$$

$$-\frac{2}{9} + \frac{10}{9} = \frac{8}{9}$$

34. **(C)** The total distance is equal to the distance that one bus traveled plus the distance that the other bus traveled (to the point where they pass each other). Letting x equal the number of hours traveled, you can express the distances that the two buses travel in that time as $48x$ and $55x$. Equate the sum of these distances with the total distance and solve for x:

$$48x + 55x = 515$$

$$103x = 515$$

$$x = 5$$

The buses will pass each other five hours after 9:30 a.m.—at 2:30 p.m.

35. **(E)** Statement (1) alone provides no information about how long it took David to travel the first 15 miles, and is therefore insufficient by itself to answer the question. Statement (2) alone provides even less information about how long it took David to travel the entire distance. Although you can determine from statement (2) that David traveled the first 17 miles in 45 minutes, you cannot determine how long it took David to travel the remaining 13 miles. Statements (1) and (2) together establish that David traveled 32 miles (17 + 15) in 85 minutes (45 + 40). However, 2 of the 32 miles are accounted for twice. Without knowing either the time that it took David to travel the 16th and 17th miles of the race or his average speed over those two miles, you cannot determine David's total time for the 30 mile race. Thus, statements (1) and (2) together are insufficient to answer the question.

36. **(B)** Given that the area of the circle is $\frac{25}{4}\pi$, you can determine the circle's radius and diameter:

$$A = \pi r^2$$

$$\frac{25}{4}\pi = \pi r^2$$

$$\frac{25}{4} = r^2$$

$$r = \frac{5}{2}$$

$$d = 5$$

On the coordinate plane, the distance between the points whose coordinates are (−1,0) and (3,3) is 5 (the chord forms the hypotenuse of a 3:4:5 right triangle, as illustrated in the figure below). Let P and Q represent the two points, respectively. Since the distance between P and Q is 5, chord PQ must be the circle's diameter. The circle's center lies on chord PQ midway between P and Q. The x-coordinate of the center is midway between the x-coordinates of P and Q (−1 and 3), whereas the y-coordinate is midway between the y-coordinates of P and Q (0 and 3). Accordingly, the center of the circle lies the point $(1,1\frac{1}{2})$.

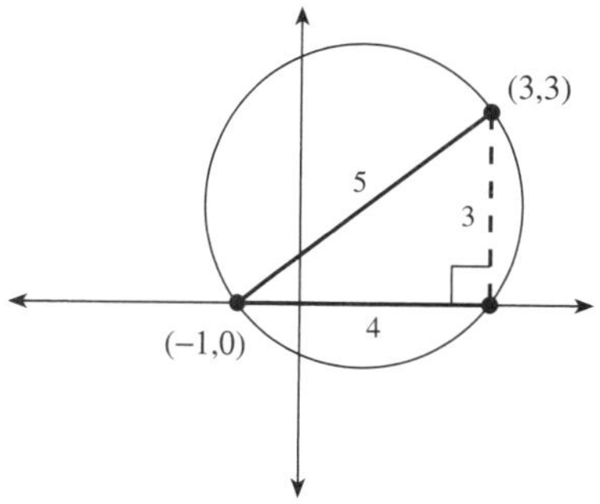

37. **(B)** The value of Dynaco shares sold plus the value of MicroTron shares sold must be equal to the value of all shares sold (that is, the "mixture"). Letting x represent the number of shares of Dynaco sold, you can represent the number of shares of MicroTron sold by $300 - x$. Set up an equation in which the value of Dynaco shares sold plus the value of MicroTron shares sold equals the total value of all shares sold, then solve for x:

$$\begin{aligned} \$52(x) + \$36(300 - x) &= \$40(300) \\ 52x + 10{,}800 - 36x &= 12{,}000 \\ 16x &= 1{,}200 \\ x &= 75 \end{aligned}$$

The investor has sold 75 shares of Dynaco stock. Checking your work:

$$\begin{aligned} \$52(75) + \$36(300 - 75) &= \$12{,}000 \\ \$3{,}900 + \$36(225) &= \$12{,}000 \\ \$3{,}900 + \$8{,}100 &= \$12{,}000 \end{aligned}$$

A

Verbal Ability (Hour 24)

1. **(B)** In the original version, the terms following each part of the correlative *not only . . . but also* are not parallel. The sentence is also awkward. (B) reconstructs the sentence in a clear and concise manner. (C) is awkward and confusing, especially in its inappropriate use of the correlative *not only has . . . but so has*. In (D), *smoking cigarettes* and *cigar smoking* are not grammatically parallel; also, the singular verb *is* does not agree with the compound subject (which is considered plural). (E) distorts the meaning of the original sentence by suggesting that what is banned is smoking both cigarettes and cigars *at the same time.*

2. **(E)** The original sentence (A) is a long sentence fragment with no predicate. (B) is unclear as to whether Francis Craig wrote all the books in the series or just the first three books. (C), like (A), is a long sentence fragment. (D) uses the awkward *which book is;* the phrase

should exclude the word *book*. (E) completes the sentence by reconstructing it.

3. **(D)** The original version contains superfluous words; either *the age of* or *years* should be omitted. (B) is incomplete; *years* should be added to the end of (B). (C) is redundant; *old* should be omitted. (D) corrects the original version by omitting *the age of*. (E) is redundant; either *old* or *in age* should be omitted.

4. **(D)** From the information given in the passage we can reasonably assume that Uranus and its moons constitute a planetary system. From this assumption and the claim that in all of the planetary systems mentioned the satellite moves in an elliptical orbit, we can infer that the moons of the planet Uranus move in elliptical orbits. This is exactly what response (D) asserts.

5. **(C)** The main point or final conclusion of this argument is not overtly stated. The intermediate conclusion is stated in the last line—"so they must be supplied through proper diet." The pronoun "they" in this line refers back to the eight amino acids, which, we were told earlier, are found in sufficient quantities only in animal products. Since these eight amino acids can only be found in animal products and they are necessary for a proper diet, it can be concluded that animal products must be included in a proper diet. This is the main point of the argument and this is exactly what response (C) asserts.

6. **(B)** According to the passage, the ambiguous position of Soviet scientists was that the Soviet government encouraged and generally supported scientific research, while at the same time, it imposed significant restrictions on its scientists. Statement (B) restates this idea.

7. **(D)** This part of the passage is concerned exclusively with pointing out evidence of the Soviet emphasis on a national science; given the content of the excerpt from *Literatunaya Gazeta*, you can reasonably infer that the author is quoting this article as one such piece of evidence.

8. **(C)** The passage as a whole is indeed concerned with describing Soviet attempts to suppress scientific freedom.

9. **(E)** In the original sentence, the modifier *If speaking too quickly* is misplaced. As it stands, this phrase appears to refer to the court reporter. However, the sentence clearly intends that this phrase refer to the witness. The sentence must be reconstructed to position this modifier closer to the phrase that it modifies. (B), (C), and (D) each include a misplaced modifier. (E) is the only choice that corrects the modifier problem in the original sentence without creating a new one. (E) reconstructs the original sentence so that *speaking too quickly* clearly refers to the witness.

10. **(C)** The task in this problem is to find an answer that weakens the argument; that is, one that undermines the major assumption of the argument, attacks a stated premise, or that suggests an alternative conclusion that could be inferred from the premises. The major assumption of the argument is that water temperatures in the oceans of the world are controlled by global air temperatures. Response (C) directly contradicts this assumption, and consequently, if true, substantially weakens the argument.

11. **(C)** The argument stated in the passage is basically as follows:

    Premise: The greater the punishment, the fewer people will behave in the punished way.

    Conclusion: The death penalty will have a more dissuasive effect than would life imprisonment.

    The assumption required to fill the gap in the above argument is that the death penalty is a greater punishment than life imprisonment. This is exactly what response (C) asserts.

12. **(D)** In the original version, *one being arrested* should be replaced either with *one from being arrested*, with *one's arrest*, or with the noun clause *one's being arrested.* (Noun clauses take the possessive verb form.) Also, *it* would more clearly refer to its antecedent *the law* if it were positioned closer to the antecedent or replaced with the antecedent. (D) corrects both problems with the original version. An even better version would include *one's arrest* instead of *one from being arrested;* nevertheless, (D) is the best of the five choice. (B) is vague as to who is being arrested. Also, *violation of it* is awkward, and *it* does not refer clearly to its antecedent. (C) creates a nonsensical sentence that suggests that ignorance . . . does not preclude *violation . . . for it.* (E) is unclear as to who is being arrested. Also, *having violated the law* is less clear and concise than *violating that law.*

13. **(A)** The original version is correct; the first clause modifies *President McKinley,* and the two elements are appropriately juxtaposed to form a clear expression of the intended idea. (B) seems to refer to two distinct wars—a protracted one and a bloody one. (B) would be clearer if the first *war* were omitted. (C) is nonsensical, and it is awkward in its use of the passive voice. (D) and (E) are similarly awkward and confusing. (D) is also wordy.

14. **(D)** The original version uses the awkward (and improper) *remains being*. Either *is still* or simply *remains* should be used instead. (D) corrects the problem. (B) and (E) each combine the two acceptable idioms to form redundant phrases. (C) is no better than the original version.

15. **(B)** The author states, "When a cell membrane is damaged by a free radical, the cell loses the capacity to transport nutrients, oxygen, water, or waste matter. As a result, cell membranes may rupture, spilling their contents into surrounding

tissues, and thereby damage surrounding cells." The clear implication of this information is that the cell membrane ruptures because it can no longer contain the various materials. In other words, the contents of the cell exceed the capacity of the cell membrane.

16. **(E)** The passage deals mainly with the various ways in which free radicals harm cells. The line of the passage indicates that the damage occurs in "living tissues."

17. **(E)** In lines 16–21 the passage states that damage resulting from the "destructive reactions" in the chromosomes and nucleic acids of the cell causes "changes in the cell replication rate and is the major cause of cancer cell mutations."

18. **(C)** The task in this problem is to find the answer choice that is most likely to be true on the basis of the information stated in the passage. Basically, what the stated information boils down to is that the United States suffers from all of the problems that led to the demise of other democracies in the past. Given this, the inference that the United States will likewise perish as a result of these problems is highly probable. Of the answer choices, (C) come closest to asserting this claim. It should be noted that while answer choice (C) requires that we assume that the United States of America is a democracy, this assumption is not, by commonsense standards, an implausible, superfluous, or incompatible assumption.

19. **(E)** The task in this problem is to find an answer that strengthens the argument; that is, one that offers support for the major assumption of the argument or that provides additional evidence for the conclusion. Of the answer choices, response (E) is the best choice because it does the latter; that is, it provides a convincing rationale for the seemingly inconsistent action on the part of the Astonian government.

20. **(B)** The argument in the passage presents a textbook example of eliminative causal reasoning—reasoning in which a common causal factor is discovered through a process of elimination of possible factors. This is exactly the method described in answer choice (B).

21. **(C)** The task in this problem is to find the answer choice that must be true or that is most likely to be true given the information stated in the passage. If executives and travel consultants were the only employees, the combined average for all employees would be $51,000. Since the passage states that combined average for all employees was $38,000, it can be inferred that there must have been other employees besides executives and travel consultants. Furthermore, it can be inferred that the average salary of these other employees was $12,000. Moreover, while the number of other employees is indeterminable, since their average salary was $12,000 it can be inferred that at least one of them must have earned less than $47,000, so it follows that at least

one employee must have earned less than the average for a travel consultant. This is exactly what answer choice (C) states.

22. **(C)** In the original sentence, the antecedent of *that result* is unclear. Is it DNA strands or damage to those strands that result from the deployment of enzymes? Also, the use of the noun clause *man-made toxins' invading* in a prepositional phrase here is somewhat awkward, albeit grammatically correct. (B) improperly uses *that* instead of *which*. Also, it is unclear what "resulting" refers to here—DNA strands or damage to the DNA strands. (C) improves on the awkward use of a noun clause in the first part of the original sentence. The infinitive *to rebuild* and the phrase *as a result* clarify the meaning of the second part of the sentence. In spite of its use of the passive voice (*enzymes are deployed*), (C) is the best response. (D) uses the plural verb form *result* in reference to the singular noun *damage*. (D) also separates the pronoun *they* from its intended antecedent *enzymes*. (E) improperly uses the plural *are repaired* and *result* in reference to the singular *damage*. Also, the phrase *deployed special enzymes* awkwardly strings together a verb (used as an adjective) and another adjective.

23. **(A)** The original version is correct. By omitting *rather*, (B) obscures the meaning of the sentence; the original version is clearer. (C) sets up a faulty parallel—between *cultural tie* and *racial*. (D) also sets up a faulty parallel—between *cultural* and *a racial one*. (E) also sets up a faulty parallel—between *cultural* and *a racial tie*.

24. **(E)** The original sentence (A) confuses the subjunctive verb form (which deals with possibilities rather than facts) and past-perfect tense. (A) also contains a pronoun-antecedent agreement problem; *scientific community* is singular, calling for the singular pronoun *it* rather than *they*. (B) mixes verb tenses. The progressive verb *would not be* is a present-perfect form, whereas the verb *had . . . become* is a past-perfect form. Moreover, in the context of the sentence as a whole, neither tense is appropriate; the subjunctive form should be used instead. (C) properly uses the subjunctive form (*were*) but fails to remedy the pronoun-antecedent agreement problem. (D) improperly uses the past tense (*when the scientific community became*) rather than in the appropriate subjunctive verb form. (E) remedies both problems in the original sentence. It uses the subjunctive form consistently—at both the beginning and end of the phrase. It also replaces the incorrect plural pronoun *they* with *scientists*.

25. **(B)** The task in this problem is to find an answer that strengthens the argument; that is, one that offers support for the major assumption of the argument or that provides additional evidence for the conclusion. The major assumption of the scientists' argument is that no two bodies can occupy the same space at the same time. Response (B) provides support for the major assumption by ruling out the

possibility of instantaneous spatial displacement of one body by another.

26. **(E)** The task in this problem is to find the answer that weakens the argument; that is, one that undermines the major assumption of the argument, attacks a stated premise, or that suggests an alternative conclusion that could be inferred from the premises. The major assumption of the argument is that the two elements of the stated goal of environmentalists are compatible with one another; that is, that preserving existing plant life and at the same time reducing the amount of carbon dioxide in the atmosphere are not conflicting aims. Response (E) directly contradicts this assumption, and as a result weakens the argument.

27. **(B)** The original sentence (A) improperly uses the adjective *hasty* instead of the adverb *hastily* to modify the verb *provide.* (B) remedies the problem in the original sentence. (C) fails to correct the error in the original sentence and commits a similar error in its use of *happy* instead of *happily.* (C) also creates two successive modifying phrases, but no predicate; the result is a long sentence fragment. (D) also creates a long but incomplete sentence. (E) creates confusion by separating the verb *providing* from its object *credit information.* Also, like (C) and (D), (E) establishes a long but incomplete sentence.

28. **(A)** The passage refers to the establishment of a de facto 35mm standard around 1913, followed by a "resurgence" of wide-film formats (in the mid-1920s to the mid-1930s). This resurgence suggests that wide-film formats were not new because they had been used before the 35mm standard was established—that is, before 1913.

29. **(D)** According to the passage's last sentence, anamorphic lenses, used with more mobile cameras, made it possible to create quality 70mm prints from 35mm negatives. In this respect, the invention of the anamorphic camera lens contributed to the demise (not the increased use) of wide-film moviemaking.

30. **(B)** The passage's final sentence states that after the invention of the 35mm anamorphic lens, quality 70mm (larger) prints could be made from 35mm (smaller) negatives. It is reasonable to assume that larger prints could not be made from smaller negatives prior to that invention.

31. **(D)** The argument in the passage can be restated as follows:

    Premise: Analytic propositions do not provide information about any matter of fact.

    Conclusion: Empirical evidence cannot refute analytic propositions.

    In this restatement it is fairly obvious that the assumption that is required for the conclusion to be properly drawn is one that will link empirical evidence with propositions that provide information about matters of fact. Response (D) provides this link, thus closing the gap in the stated argument. This closure is clearly demonstrated in the following reconstruction of the argument.

> *Premise:* Analytic propositions do not provide information about any matter of fact.
>
> *Assumption:* Empirical evidence can only refute propositions that provide information about matters of fact.
>
> *Conclusion:* Empirical evidence cannot refute analytic propositions.

32. **(D)** The task in this problem is to find an answer that strengthens the argument; that is, one that offers support for the major assumption of the argument or that provides additional evidence for the conclusion. Response (D) offers additional evidence for the conclusion. The claim that the thoroughness of routine check-ups is inconsequential in detecting dangerous or costly mechanical problems provides an additional reason for waiting to have your car checked until a recognizable problem develops.

33. **(D)** The original version incorrectly mixes the past tense (*were prohibited*) with the present perfect tense (*have performed*), resulting in confusion as to the proper time frame. Also, ending the sentence with a preposition (*in*), although not grammatically incorrect, is somewhat awkward and should be avoided if possible. (B) helps clarify the meaning of the original sentence by adding *very same;* however, (B) fails to correct either problem with the original version. (C) incorrectly mixes tenses in the same way as the original version. (D) corrects both problems with the original version, as well as clarifying the meaning of the sentence by adding the word *same*. (E) is awkward, and it distorts the meaning of the original sentence by suggesting that these musicians were prohibited from dining at any "venue" and that "venues" were the only places they performed.

34. **(C)** The original version includes a dangling modifier. The sentence fails to refer to whoever is doing the asserting. The original version also uses the awkward passive voice. (C) corrects both problems. The first clause now refers clearly to *we*, and the underlined clause has been reconstructed using the active voice. (D) fails to correct the dangling modifier problem; it also uses the awkward passive voice. (E) fails to correct the dangling modifier problem. Also, (E) renders the sentence a fragment (an incomplete sentence).

35. **(B)** The original sentence makes an illogical comparison between *aircraft* and *accidents*. (The grammatical construction suggests that twin-engine aircraft are accidents.) Also, the phrase *well over ninety percent* is intended to modify *vast majority,* so the two elements should be positioned nearer to each other. (B) corrects both problems. (C) is a sentence fragment. (C) also fails to correct either problem with the original version. (D)

corrects both problems with the original version. However, the antecedent of the pronoun *ones* is too vague; the pronoun should be positioned closer to its intended antecedent *accidents*. (E) is awkwardly constructed and poorly worded.

36. **(B)** The argument in the passage can be restated as follows:

> *Premise:* People who do not control their cholesterol levels are more likely to have heart disease than people who do.
>
> *Premise:* Most people who do not control their cholesterol levels do not have heart disease.
>
> *Conclusion:* There is no need to control one's cholesterol level in order to avoid heart disease.

(B) is the best response. The argument in response (B) can be restated as follows:

> *Premise:* Smokers are more likely to die of lung disease than non-smokers.
>
> *Premise:* Most smokers do not die of lung disease.
>
> *Conclusion:* There is no need to abstain from smoking in order to decrease the likelihood of contracting lung disease.

A comparison of this argument with the argument in the passage as outlined above reveals a striking similarity in the structure of the premises and the conclusions of these arguments.

37. **(B)** Answer choice (B) confuses information in the passage. In line 26, virtue is defined as a "personal, moral quality," and is associated with eighteenth-century republicanism, not liberalism.

38. **(E)** The first sentence of the passage states that the two views of the nature of freedom (i.e., liberty) "helps define the difference between two political languages (i.e., republicanism and liberalism). The remainder of the passage discusses their differing views of liberty in detail.

39. **(A)** Lines 22–24 state that only property-owning citizens possess virtue. Lines 28–29 (attributed to Franklin) states that only virtuous people are capable of freedom. From these two statements it can be inferred that Franklin maintained that only property-owning citizens are capable of freedom.

40. **(B)** In the stated argument, the Republicans' failure to articulate good reasons in support of their opposition to cuts in social security is taken as evidence that they are in favor of cuts in social security. Of the answer choices, response (B) best describes this reasoning error.

41. **(A)** The original version is correct. (B) incorrectly uses the singular form *its*; the verb should agree in number with its plural subject *states*. (C) awkwardly splits the grammatical element *were free*. (D) uses the redundant and improper correlative *both . . . as well as . . . .* (E) confuses the meaning of the sentence; the construction unfairly suggests that free word and speech could be found *only* in the Greek states.

Appendix B

Score Conversion Tables for Sample Tests

Determine Your Analytical Writing Assessment (AWA) Scores

To evaluate your performance on the essay sections (Hours 19 and 22), score each of the two essays in a test on a scale of 0 to 6, based on the scorecard in Hour 17. Your final AWA score is simply the average of these two individual scores, rounded up to the nearest one-half point.

Determine Your Verbal, Quantitative, and Total Scaled Scores

To determine your scaled score for any Quantitative or Verbal section, follow these steps:

1. Determine your total number of *correct* responses for the section, based on the answer key. This is your *raw score.*
2. Subtract one-quarter point from that total for each *incorrect* response; round off this number to the nearest integer. The result is your *corrected raw score.* (This is how the paper-based GMAT penalizes test-takers for incorrect responses. Recall, however, that the computer-adaptive GMAT penalizes you for an incorrect response by posing easier subsequent questions, for which correct responses add fewer points to your score than do correct responses for more difficult questions.)
3. Refer to the appropriate column in the conversion table below to compute your *scaled score* (0–60).

Corrected Raw Score	*Verbal*	*Quantitative*	*Corrected Raw Score*	*Verbal*	*Quantitative*
41	52	—	20	28	32
40	51	—	19	27	31
39	50	—	18	25	30
38	48	—	17	24	28
37	47	53	16	23	27
36	46	52	15	22	25
35	45	51	14	21	24
34	44	50	13	20	23
33	43	49	12	19	22
32	42	48	11	18	21
31	41	47	10	17	20
30	39	45	9	16	18
29	38	44	8	15	17
28	37	43	7	14	16
27	36	41	6	13	14
26	35	40	5	12	13
25	33	38	4	11	12
24	32	37	3	10	11
23	31	36	2	9	10
22	30	34	1	8	9
21	29	33	0	7	8

4. To determine your total scaled score, add your two corrected raw scores together and convert the total corrected raw score to a scaled score (200–800) using the conversion table below.

Corrected Raw Score	*Total Scaled Score*	*Corrected Raw Score*	*Total Scaled Score*	*Corrected Raw Score*	*Total Scaled Score*
63 and up	800	41	580	19	370
62	790	40	570	18	360
61	780	39	560	17	350
60	770	38	550	16	340
59	760	37	540	15	330
58	750	36	530	14	330
57	740	35	530	13	320
56	730	34	520	12	310
55	720	33	510	11	300
54	710	32	500	10	290
53	700	31	490	9	280
52	690	30	480	8	270
51	680	29	470	7	260
50	670	28	460	6	250
49	660	27	450	5	240
48	650	26	440	4	230
47	640	25	430	3	220
46	630	24	420	2	210
45	620	23	410	0–1	200
44	610	22	400		
43	600	21	390		

Interpret Your Scaled Scores

The GMAT score report you receive will indicate not only your scaled scores but also your *percentile ranking* (0 to 99%) based on your Verbal, Quantitative, and total scaled scores. These three percentile rankings indicate how you performed relative to all others taking the GMAT over a recent multi-year period. A percentile ranking of 60%, for example, indicates that you scored higher than 60% of all other test-takers (and lower than 40% of all other test-takers).

NOTE

The testing service reports only the scaled scores, not percentile rankings, to the business schools.

Refer to the percentile ranking conversion chart below to determine your rankings for the two sample tests.

Total Scaled Score	*Precentage Below*
740	99
720	99
700	98
680	97
660	95
640	93
620	89
600	85
580	80
560	74
540	68
520	61
500	53
480	46
460	39
440	32
420	26
400	20
380	15
360	11
340	8
320	6
300	4
280	2
260	1
240	1
220	0

Verbal and Quantitative Scores		
	Percentages Below	
Scales Scores	*Verbal*	*Quantitative*
50	99	99
48	99	99
46	99	97
44	98	95
42	95	91
40	92	87
38	87	82
36	82	75
34	75	68
32	67	60
30	59	52
28	50	43
26	42	34
24	34	27
22	26	20
20	20	14
18	15	9
16	10	5
14	7	3
12	4	1
10	2	0
8	1	0
6	0	0

Appendix C

How to Obtain the Official GMAT Essay Questions

The 230 official GMAT essay questions are available at the official GMAC Web site (*www.gmat.org*). You can obtain the list of questions free of charge. To get the most out of the AWA materials in this book (Hours 17 and 18), crank up your PC, go online, and follow the 8 steps below.

> **NOTE**
>
> ETS publishes the questions in printed form as well, but not in the official (and free) *GMAT Bulletin*. Instead, the questions are printed in an ETS publication entitled *The Official Guide for GMAT Review.* (You'll have to fork over about $20.00 for the book.)

Step 1: Go directly to the AWA download page.

You can access the GMAT essay questions via our Web site; point your Web browser to:

http://www.west.net/~stewart/awa

You can also access the essay questions directly from the GMAC Web site, at the following URL:

http://www.gmat.org/mba_store/store_complist.html

TIP

In case the GMAC changes the location of this page, you can always find the link by going to the GMAC home page (www.gmat.org) and checking the site map or index.

Step 2: Download the file that contains the essay questions.

The file is only about 153 kilobytes in size, so it shouldn't take long to download. (*Note:* you may also have to use the "Save Next Link As . . ." or "Save to Disk" function of your Web browser.) Unless you are using a client-server system, the file will download onto your PC's hard drive—in the directory you've specified in your Web browser as your download directory.

Step 3: Download Adobe Acrobat Reader onto your computer (the software is free).

The file you just downloaded is in Adobe Acrobat format. (Acrobat files are denoted by a .pdf extension at the end of the file name.) You'll need special software called Acrobat Reader to view and print the material. You can download the software via our Web site (*http://www.west.net/~stewart/awa*). Or you can go directly to Adobe's site to download the appropriate version for your system (e.g., Windows 95 or Windows 3.1):

http://www.adobe.com

Step 4: Install Adobe *Acrobat Reader*.

Once you've downloaded Acrobat Reader, you'll need to install it on your computer. Your computer system may be enabled with a utility that does it automatically. If not, quit your Web browser, double-click the newly downloaded file (the filename should look something like either "ar32e301.exe" or "ar16e301.exe"), and follow the instructions on your screen.

Step 5: View the AWA questions on your computer screen.

When you install Acrobat Reader on your computer's hard drive, a program icon will be added to your desktop. You can open the Acrobat Reader program just as you would open any other application. Once you've opened Acrobat Reader, open the AWA file that you downloaded, just as you would open a file in any other application. In Acrobat Reader you can view an entire page, part of a page, or multiple pages. The 115 Issue questions run 12 pages in length altogether. The 115 Argument questions run 18 pages in length altogether.

Step 6: Print the AWA questions.

In Acrobat Reader, you can generate a printout of all 230 AWA questions. Your printout will include the same number of pages—30 altogether—and look the same as the version appearing on your computer screen.

NOTE

> You can also copy and paste the material into a word-processing program (such as Word or WordPerfect), then format and print from that program.

Step 7: On your printout, number all 115 Issue questions and all 115 Argument questions.

On your printed copy of the Issue questions, take a pencil and number all questions in each list, sequentially from 1 to 115. Why? Because we refer to these essays by number in Hour 17 of this book and in our sample essays at our Web site.

Step 8: Congratulate yourself for successfully completing Steps 1–7!

Notes

Notes

Notes

Notes

Notes

Notes

Notes

Notes

Notes